Never Surpassed: Ensign Leeke and the 52nd Light Infantry

WILLIAM LEEKE AGED 17.

Never Surpassed: Ensign Leeke and the 52nd Light Infantry

The Peninsular War and Personal Experiences of the Waterloo Campaign, 1808-18

ILLUSTRATED

William Leeke

Edited by John H. Lewis

Never Surpassed: Ensign Leeke and the 52nd Light Infantry
The Peninsular War and Personal Experiences of the Waterloo Campaign, 1808-18
by William Leeke
Edited by John H. Lewis

ILLUSTRATED

FIRST EDITION

Leonaur is an imprint of Oakpast Ltd
Copyright in this form © 2021 Oakpast Ltd

ISBN: 978-1-915234-34-6 (hardcover)
ISBN: 978-1-915234-35-3 (softcover)

http://www.leonaur.com

Publisher's Notes

The views expressed in this book are not necessarily those of the publisher.

Contents

An Introduction by the Editor	7
1755—1803: Some Account of the 52nd Light Infantry from Its Formation	19
1808, 1809: The 52nd in the Peninsula, Corunna	32
1809-1811: The 52nd in the Peninsula	50
1812: The 52nd at the Siege and Assault of Ciudad Rodrigo, and also of Badajos	68
1813, 1814: The 52nd at the Close of the Peninsular War	84
1815: 52nd Light Infantry at Waterloo 1	112
1815: 52nd Light Infantry at Waterloo 2	133
Defeat of the Imperial Guard by the 52nd Light Infantry	149
1815: 52nd Attack and Defeat the Imperial Grenadiers	165
1815: Defeat of the French Imperial Guard by the 52nd Alone	187
1815: Siborne's, Alison's, and Shaw Kennedy's Mistakes Refuted	237
1815: March to Paris	266
1815: Paris, the 52nd Encamped in the Champs Elysées	280
1815, 1816: The 52nd quartered at Versailles, St. Germain, and Clermont	297
1816: Cantonments in the North of France	300

1816: Amusements in Cantonments	305
1816: Amusements and Incidents in the North of France	310
1816, 1817, 1818: Leave to England and Paris. Return of the Army to England	324
Sundry Matters Connected with Waterloo, and with the 52nd at Waterloo	334
The Appendices	350
1815: List of 52nd Waterloo Officers and Their Services	356

An Introduction by the Editor

Our team has been producing Leonaur imprint titles for over a decade and a half (at the time of writing) and so we can declare that during that time no day has passed that we have not given some consideration to our books and how potential readers might wish to see them presented for publication.

We have discovered that this is a complex and subjective matter and in consequence (as the saying goes) 'every day has been a school day'. The book you are holding is a prime example of how an original work has been substantially restructured by us with a contemporary readership in mind and so it is probably worthwhile to outline why the Leonaur team believed—in this case—that was necessary.

Many students of the Napoleonic Wars (and the activities of the British Army during the Peninsular War and at Waterloo in particular) will have heard about or read William Leeke's two volume work which was published in 1866, titled, 'The History of Lord Seaton's regiment, the 52nd Light Infantry at the Battle of Waterloo'. As a matter of fact, (and as implausible as it might seem) that fifteen word title—counting the numerals as one—is actually the short version of what appears on the title pages of Leeke's books. One may imagine, however, that it is unambiguous as an indication of their content.

Anyone now reading this introduction who has actually accessed Leeke's original volumes would be able to confirm that assumption is, unfortunately, quite far from the case. For those who have not read Leeke's works but who may be drawn to their potential content by the promise of their title—it is important to note that although this book is not 'those books', nothing that the author wrote on the subject of the Battle of Waterloo which was published within them has been omitted from these pages.

Whilst taking nothing from the value of much of Leeke's original offering as an insight into early 19th century life from the perspective of an English cleric—we assume that most readers who have purchased this book under the Leonaur imprint justifiably expect it to contain information concerning the war with Napoleonic France as it was fought by a famous light infantry regiment under the talented leadership of John Colborne (later Lord Seaton). It does and, more significantly, this applies to the exclusion of practically any other subject.

It was regularly the case that 19th century authors of memoirs, having embarked upon writing a book concerning a momentous period of their lives then, possibly enthused by the prospect of realising their endeavours in published form, continued writing for some distance beyond their initially declared topic. Repeated experience of this phenomenon has taught us that the manner in which this occurs within books of this era is often quite similar in content.

The reader may discover that having, in good faith, embarked upon a campaign and battlefield account it has become a dissertation or polemic on the subject of religion, a description of the author's own experiences whilst travelling, an extended insight into the author's (often not very engaging) later military and civilian career, regimental detail not germane to the authors own experiences or anecdotes concerning personages of social standing at the time with whom the author became acquainted. All these are worthy topics without doubt, but not necessarily perhaps what the reader of military history is looking for.

One or more of these topics may appear within a single book. Sometimes, however, all of them feature and Leeke's two volume work is (more or less) a classic example. Should the disappointment of a such a development be insufficient for the modern reader it is also the case that the chapters of Leeke's book do not run chronologically. All of these considerations formed the foundation for this Leonaur edition and we hope—by this point—the reader has understood our motives.

The book you are holding is transparently, at 364 pages in this edition, considerably shorter than the 951 pages of both original volumes combined, notwithstanding that this Leonaur edition contains maps and illustrations which were not present in the original. Readers should also note that differing page sizes, typeface point sizes and leading also contribute to these kinds of disparities even when texts are identical. Any relevant illustrations and maps which did appear originally are, of course, also included. It may be (and only the reader can decide) that the text content we have elected to excise from this single volume edition would be of interest and so following we will give a brief outline of what that comprised and what has been retained.

Volume one commences promisingly as Leeke describes the march to Waterloo from his own perspective as a young officer of the 52nd. The battle itself is quite concisely described until the final attack and defeat of the French Imperial Guard. The following four chapters describe the action of the 52nd at that time with considerable attention given to the contentious issue of which regiments should (or should not) have been acknowledged as worthy of the principal share of the credit for that action. Need it be said that Leeke's view on the subject is entirely partisan as one might expect—though as a 17 year old ensign of the 52nd present on the field during these events, his is an essential perspective by any standards of authenticity.

The following six original chapters describe the march to Paris following Napoleon's defeat and the activities of the 52nd as part of the army of occupation from the author's perspective as a participant until its return to England in 1818. This relevant content appears within this book.

Leeke then describes his experiences from 1819 to 1821 in Italy, Ireland, at Sandhurst and in Canada in Newfoundland and New Brunswick in the following chapters to the end of volume one and that material is not included in this Leonaur edition.

Volume two commences in in the year, 1824 and continues the author's recollections. Leeke returned from North America and resigned from the army having transferred to the 42nd regiment and the Ceylon Regiment. In 1825 he became a student at Queen's College, Cambridge and developed an interest in becoming a cleric. Domestic, travel, religious and church issues and pastoral recollections take the reader through almost 300 of the initial pages of this volume. In 1828 he was married, in 1829 ordained deacon and the following year ordained into the priesthood. His views and recollections continue to the year 1863 and, since they do not concern military matters, have been excised from this edition. Thereafter the autobiography of his later life was paused as Leeke once again turned his attention retrospectively to the services of his former regiment.

All of that material of military interest appears in this Leonaur edition. The origins of the 52nd are briefly described followed by an interesting recounting of the regiment's campaigning throughout the Napoleonic period. What makes this particularly interesting is that although Leeke did not join his regiment until 1815—firstly as a 'gentleman volunteer' and shortly thereafter as a gazetted ensign—he has been able to draw on the experiences of his brother officers who had served during the campaigns in Spain and the South of France. This material appears in this book in its chronological place and in this edition serves as an introduction to Leeke's own first—hand perspectives.

After the Peninsular War history Leeke turned his attention to the Indian Mutiny of 1857 describing the services of the 52nd within a single chapter. This chapter concerns events which took place decades after Leeke had resigned from the army and so has been excluded in this edition as are several other concluding chapters on various subjects not connected to military matters.

Today Leeke's writings can be viewed from two perspectives. Firstly, he has provided valuable insights into the 52nd during the Peninsular War and a first-hand account of the Battle of Waterloo by a regimental officer. More than that he was in a position to witness the final act of that great drama as Napoleon's Imperial Guard came to ruin. We are fortunate indeed to have these kinds of accounts left to us because each one adds to the body of source material and is unique in its own way.

The second perspective is consideration of his evidence surrounding the attack and defeat of the Imperial Guard at Waterloo. There is no doubt that the flanking action of the 52nd contributed, to a large degree in that part of the field, a significant reverse upon attacking French infantry. No one could expect Leeke's view of that achievement to be any other than a justified reflection of his loyalty and pride in the regiment whose colour he carried that day. Irrespective of Leeke's inevitable partiality, any aspect of history—perhaps especially contentious ones—has abiding academic interest.

The overarching context of this matter is nevertheless, that by that point in the engagement, as Blücher's Prussian Army streamed onto the battlefield, there was no longer any doubt that the battle was coming to its conclusion, would result in an Allied victory and so bring about the total destruction of both Napoleon's army and his personal aspirations. We may speculate, that the French column, elevated in renown because the soldiers were Napoleon's elite, would have fared no better than others of its kind in the past against the fire of the British line waiting to receive them. Had the matter come to steel against unyielding steel they would have been, once again, at no advantage. Had their remnants then, nevertheless, then broken through the British line at that point in the battle, how many would remain, what would they then do and where would they go without soon after being brought to account?

Waterloo was more than a battle won—it was the end of an epoch. The repulse of the Imperial Guard was an episode within the battle elevated in renown because the soldiers labouring up that slope to the Allied position were Napoleon's elite rather than any other less evocatively titled body of French troops. Students of wider military history may bring to mind that during the Battle of Gettysburg, 1863, the 20th Maine instituted a similar flanking manoeuvre in the defence of Little Round Top. The repulsed Confederate infantry were principally the brave men of the 15th and 47th Alabama regiments who are infrequently acknowledged.

Acts of prodigious courage and sacrifice had been numerous during the Campaign of 1815. The Guards on the ridge and within and about Hougoumont—which was pivotal to everything that occurred at that end of the line—had lived and died in a manner equal to their standing and reputation. The 'swinging door' manoeuvre was bold, timely and inspirational, but to be effective the 'hinges' of such a door must be supported by a 'rock-solid wall' and we may speculate that it was fortunate that the 'wall' was in part comprised of the Guards rather than some other potential components of Wellington's army. The same may be said of the support provided by the other regiments of Adams' brigade.

Leeke's obsession with the issuing of credit where he felt it was properly due was one of principles concerning the intangibles of honour and ideals of justice from his own invested perspective. Those considerations would only ever be, pragmatically, as significant as those— other than Leeke and his confederates—needed them to be. None of that detracts from what Leeke remembered or saw at Waterloo, though the same can be said of other eye-witnesses. Certainly, no one was in a position to clearly see everything, especially regarding the activities of the largest British battalion on the battlefield.

One of those eye-witnesses was Captain H. W. Powell of the First Guards who wrote in his journal:

> Immediately the brigade sprang forward. *La Garde* turned and gave us little opportunity of trying the steel. We charged down the hill till we had passed the end of the orchard of Hougoumont, when our right flank became exposed to another heavy

column who were advancing in support of the former column, This circumstance, besides that our charge was isolated, obliged the brigade to retire towards its original position.

Opportunely, Sir F. Adam's Light Brigade had in the meantime come round the knoll between the position and Hougoumont, when we had been ordered to take ground to our left, and were advancing under the hedge and blind line along the northern side of the orchard at Hougoumont. As soon as we had uncovered their front, we halted and fronted. The two brigades now returned to the charge which the *chasseurs* did not wait for, and we continued our forward movement till we got to the bottom of the valley between the positions.

The following is part of a letter written by Lord Saltoun of the 3rd battalion, First Guards to William Siborne:—

> Your next point is the attack (as you call it) of the First Brigade of Guards against a body of infantry previous to the attack of the Imperial Guard, etc. You seem to have mistaken the advance not of that brigade, but of one battalion of them, *viz.*, the Third Battalion Grenadier Guards, and have concluded that this was an attack against a regular body of infantry, but that was not the case. The circumstances were as follows:—
>
> During the cavalry attacks on the centre, a great number of the enemy's sharpshooters had crept up the slope of the hill, and galled the Third Battalion, who were in square, very severely. At that time the Second Battalion Grenadier Guards (the other battalion of the brigade) was likewise formed in square, about 100 yards in rear of the Third Battalion. The Third Battalion, who suffered severely from this fire, wheeled up into line, and drove them down the hill, and advanced to a point I have marked E. and there, re-formed square. A small body of Rifles were at a point I have marked with a X, and the 52nd Regiment in line at F G G.
>
> In this position we received the first attack of cavalry I saw that day, who, refusing us, passed between us and the *inward rear angle of the orchard*, and receiving our fire, did not pass between us and the left of the 52nd, where the Rifles were, but rode along the front of the 52nd, with a view of turning their right flank, and were completely destroyed by the fire of that regiment. After this, we, the Third Battalion, retired to our original position

in square, as I conclude the 52nd did also, as the next I saw of them was their attack, with the rest of General Adam's Brigade, on the second column of the Imperial Guards. As to any attack made about that time by the outward angle of the orchard of Hougomont, I could not from my position see or know anything about it.

Your next point is with respect to what took place towards the close of the action, and during the momentary confusion that took place in the First Brigade from the cry of "form square."

It will not do, in an account such as yours, to put down any order that was not given, however scientific it might be, still less to make me give an order to retire, when that was the last thought that came into my head at that moment. The word of command passed was—"Halt! Front, form up;" and it was the only thing that could be done—any other formation was impossible; and as soon as this order was understood by the men it was obeyed, and everything was right again. To prove this, I must take you a little into the drill-book. The original information of this brigade at the commencement of the action was in contiguous column of battalions, at quarter-distance, right in front. From that they formed squares on their respective leading companies.

When they were ordered towards the end of the day to form line of four deep, instead of being deployed into line to either flank, they were wheeled up into line from square (in order that they might get the quicker back into square should that formation be required again). It followed from this that when in line the Grenadier Company and No. 1 formed the centre of each battalion, and the right sections of each company formed the right wing, and the left sections formed the left, thus completely separating the companies, and rendering any formation upon our principles of drill utterly impracticable, except the one before mentioned of wheeling back into square.

From this you will at once, I should think, see that any such account as you suggest would, to any soldier acquainted with the circumstances of the formation of that brigade, prove its own inaccuracy, and do your account more harm than good. For such person would at once know that no fresh formation was practicable with those battalions, until one of two things had been done.

Either they must have been re-formed into square, from that to column, and then deployed in the regular way; or they must have been ordered to fall out, and formed again as at the beginning of a parade to their respective covering sergeants, when all the process of a fresh telling off would become necessary. You had better therefore, I think, have it as I have given it to you, *viz.*, that as soon as the men were made to understand they were not to form square, but to *Halt, front, and form up*, they did it; the left shoulders were then brought forward, and we advanced against the second column of the Imperial Guards, but which body was defeated by General Adam's Brigade before we reached it, although we got near enough to fire if we had been ordered so to do; and, as far as I can recollect at this distance of time, we did fire into that column.

—*The March to Hougoumont: Lord Saltoun & the First Guards from Sicily, Walcheren and the Peninsular War to Waterloo, 1805-15. (Leonaur 2020.)*

Historians can only piece together most likely scenarios from (hopefully) objectively evaluated source material. Though as Flaubert aptly noted, 'There is no truth. There is only perception'. Were that not perennially the case there would be far fewer actual battles.

Every personal recollection of the Napoleonic age adds to our repository of knowledge in the only way now possible. However, they often also contain material that is less than completely reliable. The 'truth' can be embroidered and honest memories become distorted by passing time between an event and when it is recalled in writing. That is why it is difficult to correlate different versions of events that absolutely concur. However, when recollection gives way to opinion the modern student should proceed with especial caution.

In this book, for example, Leeke recorded the Guards who fought in and around Hougoumont by omitting the role of the light companies of the First Guards. This was, by this editor, initially attributed to a not uncommon oversight in research and so on balance unworthy of note. However, Leeke's writing tone becomes increasingly vitriolic. At one point he indignantly wrote, 'Did the 1st Guards on that occasion, *or on any other on that day*, do anything beyond receiving and defeating various charges made by French cavalry, and driving off, by an advance of their left battalion in line, the mass of skirmishers of the French Guard. etc.'

Leeke's ire was particularly directed at the First Guards which was demonstrably not responsible for anything which would deserve his enmity. That regiment was engaged during the most demanding phases of the battle, repelling, *sans* differentiation, whichever elements of the enemy army that came before it.

As demonstrated by the passages quoted here, the officers of the First Guards claimed for themselves no credit for the achievements of others. The regiment was not, presumably, able to unilaterally award itself encomiums or distinctions. Whilst taking absolutely nothing away from the well documented performance and actions of the 52nd at Waterloo, by the time Leeke implied that the advance of the Prussian Army was foundering, but for the intercession of the 52nd (page 100 of this edition) the sobriety of his opinions had become in measure questionable.

Leeke's substantial body of correspondence is included in this edition. Whether this might be considered repetitive and eventually tedious is for the reader to determine, though it does include input from a number of soldiers who were present at Waterloo. We have those opinions, of course, through the author's filter and intercessions. One may almost see the 17 year old uncharitable dogmatist in Leeke's ranting rather than the elderly churchman who was actually the author.

Two hundred years after the event with no discarnate luggage attached to matters of regimental honour, common sense dictates that the 52nd, despite its large effective numbers, could not be evaluated—as Leeke essentially requires us to do—in complete isolation, ignoring the context of everything else that had happened and was happening to bodies of troops on either side of the conflict in that time and place in the Battle of Waterloo.

That this British battalion of over a thousand bayonets performed its flanking manoeuvres and attack when its time came, equal to its outstanding Light Division' *esprit de corps* and Peninsular War experience under the command of Colborne (an officer said to possess, 'a singular talent for war'), with complete success is, pragmatically perhaps, less remarkable than if it had failed.

It is equally unsurprising that a triumph of the magnitude of Waterloo would be memorialised by the victors in several ways. We may speculate that the Prince Regent and influential others would be receptive to the proposal that the premier infantry regiment of the royal household—hitherto simply the 'First'—would carry a distinction in a title. Precedent existed since the second regiment of Guards was principally known by its name, the 'Coldstream'. Most of the defeated battalions of the Imperial Guard's last assault were *chasseurs*—a word which would never be appended to a Guards regimental title. 'Grenadier' is a suitably English sounding word (derived for apparent reasons from 'pomegranate'—the seeded apple) and in use in the army by contrast. If the link between that title and the detail of the action from which it derived was tenuous and it pleased His Royal Highness—then who would be prepared to split hairs over the matter? After all, the name of the battle itself, no less, had received a similar treatment.

The answer to that question was, of course, those inclined to pursue the matter to the letter of a definition of their own manufacture, championed by William Leeke. Did Leeke then proffer valid points? Certainly, and if by his obsessions he was able to shine a scintilla of light on actual events, posterity thanks him as it does all chroniclers of their times. A pity then, perhaps, that he did not make those points cogently, academically concise and devoid of bile, because in the longer term they would probably have been more influential.

If, however, as seems likely, his principal motive was to rescind decisions and bring about exceptional acknowledgements and awards for the 52nd to the exclusion of the First Guards, he was 'shouting into the wind' and should have known better. In fact, he was aware that was the case, because he records others telling him so. Notwithstanding those words of caution, readers will note that Leeke went on to pen a polemic regarding the status of Guards regiments and their officers.

So Leeke's crusade to convince anyone who mattered or cared about his issue was almost certainly a doomed one, because disputes very rarely bring about conversions in points of view in their own time, especially among those who, pursuing one agenda or another, had their own interests in the outcomes.

Finally, on a far more prosaic level, we hope most readers will approve of our efforts and agree that this book finally presents Leeke's indispensable military writings in a cohesive form.

It is probably worth mentioning that Professor Charles Oman produced a very interesting article in two parts concerning the strengths and casualties of the French Army at Waterloo including the Imperial Guard. Oman states that this information—drawn from impeccable French sources—had never been previously published and his own work—naturally—postdates Leeke by decades, though not necessarily as regards accuracy, of course, that of more modern commentators.

This editor makes no claims of definitive expertise himself, but for those interested, that work was incorporated into a Leonaur book, 'The Great Contest', which is a compilation of some of Oman's writings on the Napoleonic age.

John H. Lewis, 2021

CHAPTER 1

1755—1803: Some Account of the 52nd Light Infantry from Its Formation

The 52nd *Record*, from which I shall extract much which will help to form the contents of this and some of the following chapters, was published in 1860, under the direction of the following committee of officers who had served in the regiment, and was edited by Captain W. S. Moorsom:—

His Grace the Duke of Richmond, K.G., Chairman,
Lieut.-General Sir J. Frederick Love, K.C.B., Dep. Chairman,
Lieut.-General Sir John Bell, K.C.B.,
Lieut.-General Sir William G. Moore, K.C.B.,
Major-General Eaton Monius,
Colonel Edward A. Angelo, K.H.,
Colonel George Gawler, K.H.,
Colonel George Napier, C.B.,
Colonel George Campbell, C.B.,
Lieut.-Colonel Sir John Tylden, Kt.,
Lieut.-Colonel Lord Charles J. F. Russell,
Captain W. S. Moorsom, Hon. Secretary,
Captain H. M. Brownrigg,
Captain J. J. Bourchier.

The origin of the 52nd Regiment dates from the eve of the commencement of the contest known in history as the 'Seven Years' War.' In December, 1755, eleven regiments of infantry were raised, and were numbered from the 50th to the 60th inclusive. The present 52nd was first numbered the 54th, but on the disbandment, in 1757, of the 50th and 51st, which had only been raised for service in North America, it became the 52nd.

The regiment proceeded to Ireland in 1758, and remained there till 1765. On the 6th of June in that year it embarked at Cork for North America, and reached Quebec in the August following. It remained in Canada till about the middle of 1774, when it proceeded by sea to Boston, to reinforce the army assembled there. In April the flank companies of the 52nd, and of several other corps, were engaged in destroying the military stores collected at Concord, and in the affair at Lexington, at which the 52nd lost three rank and file killed, two wounded, and one sergeant missing.

On the 17th of June, 1775, just forty years before Waterloo, the regiment took part in the severe action of Bunker's Hill, when it particularly distinguished itself. It suffered, however, severely; the whole of the grenadier company, with the exception of eight men, were either killed or wounded.

> This seems to have been the first occasion on record in which the 52nd acted in unison with the 43rd, afterwards so honourably linked as their brothers-in-arms on many a field of the Peninsula.

In the beginning of July, 1776, the American Congress issued their Declaration of Independence, and in the next month the 52nd were engaged at Brooklyn, the result of which compelled the Americans to evacuate New York.

They continued in America till the end of October, 1778, when, having been much reduced in numbers, in various actions in which they had been engaged, and many of those remaining having volunteered into other corps, they embarked for England, and arrived there before the close of the year.

> A letter dated 31st August, 1782, conveyed to the regiment His Majesty's pleasure that county titles should be conferred on the infantry, and the 52nd in consequence received the designation of the Oxfordshire Regiment, in order that a connexion between the regiment and that county should be cultivated, which it was considered might be useful in promoting the success of the recruiting system.

The 52nd embarked for India in 1783, and after having been engaged in various services in that country, during a period of fifteen years, they returned to England in August, 1798.

Prior to their embarkation at Madras, the following complimentary General Orders were issued by the commander-in-chief:—

Headquarters, Chaultre Plain, 8th February, 1798.

His Majesty's 52nd Regiment, being under orders of embarkation for Europe, the commander-in-chief, while he feels sincere regret at losing so valuable a corps from under his command, embraces the opportunity to assure Major Monson, the officers, and men, that he shall ever retain a strong impression of the discipline and gallantry of that corps during a period of fifteen years' service in India,

(Signed) James Robinson, Dep. Adj.-Gen.

Fort St. George, February 18th, 1798.

Upon this occasion the Right Honourable the President in Council feels it incumbent upon him to convey to Major Monson, the officers, and men, of the 52nd Regiment, the thanks of this government for the share they have had in supporting its authority during a period of fifteen years, and in extending the conquests of the nation in the late glorious war against the Tippoo Sultaun.

By order of the President in Council,

(Signed) T. Webb, Secretary.

The 52nd remained in England about two years, during which period a second battalion was added to it, and it received upwards of two thousand volunteers from the militia in the course of twelve months.

On the 25th of June, 1800, the first battalion of the 52nd embarked at Southampton, having been ordered to form part of a force which was being collected for a secret service. The second battalion embarked also at Southampton on the 2nd of July, but returned to that place on the 14th of the same month. Early in August it again embarked at Southampton, having been selected to form part of the expedition under Lieut.-General Sir James Pulteney, Bart.

The armament of which the first battalion formed a portion, reached the bay of Quiberon on the 8th of July; and the 23rd, 31st, first battalion of the 52nd, and 63rd Regiments landed on the Isle de Honat, where they remained encamped under the command of Brigadier-General the Honourable Thomas Maitland until the 19th of August, when they again embarked and joined the expedition under Lieut.-General Sir James Pulteney, destined for the coast of Spain. The strength of the two battalions amounted to nearly 1,800 men. Both battalions landed near Ferrol on the 25th of August, and on the morning of the 26th attacked the enemy, and gained possession of the heights above the town. In the action near Ferrol the first battalion of the 52nd had eight rank and file killed. Captain Samuel Torrens was wounded, and died in consequence. One sergeant, one drummer, and thirty-eight rank and file were wounded. The second battalion had two rank and file killed, and three wounded.

Lieut.-General Sir James Pulteney, in his official despatch, dated, at sea, 27th August, stated:—

> At daybreak the following morning a considerable body of the enemy was driven back by Major-General the Earl of Cavan's brigade, supported by some other troops, so that we remained in complete possession of the heights which overlook the town and harbour of Ferrol; but from the nature of the ground, which was steep and rocky, unfortunately this service could not be performed without some loss. The first battalion, 52nd Regiment, had the principal share in this action. The enemy lost about one hundred men killed and wounded, and thirty or forty prisoners.

The regiment re-embarked on the 27th, and proceeded to the Bay of Cadiz, where the whole army was ordered into the flat boats, with three days' provisions in their haversacks, for the purpose of attacking the town of Cadiz; but the design was abandoned, and the fleet sailed for Gibraltar, where a force was selected to accompany General Sir Ralph Abercromby to Egypt; but the two battalions of the 52nd Regiment, being enlisted for service in Europe only, could not form a part of it, although they immediately volunteered to extend their services to any part of the world; this, however, Sir Ralph did not feel himself authorised to accept, and the regiment returned to Lisbon, where it landed on the 25th November.

In January, 1803, the regiment was made light infantry, which event may be considered to form a new era in its history. The following is a copy of the General Orders relative to the formation of the 52nd Light Infantry:—

Horse Guards, 10th January, 1803.

It being His Majesty's pleasure that from the 25th *ultimo* the second battalion of the 52nd Regiment should be numbered the 96th Regiment of Foot.

I am commanded by the commander-in-chief to signify the same to you, and to desire that in consequence of this arrangement you will be pleased to give the necessary orders for posting a due proportion of the officers of the present battalion of the 52nd Regiment to the 96th Regiment.

In carrying this into effect, His Royal Highness desires that the two senior lieut.-colonels may be posted to the 52nd Regiment, and that the same rule may be observed with regard to the senior majors, captains, subalterns, and staff officers, as far as the establishment will allow.

But although the commander-in-chief points out this mode of posting the officers, yet should any of the seniors of the respective ranks prefer being removed to the 96th Regiment, in preference to remaining in the 52nd Regiment, His Royal Highness will not object to their being posted in the 96th Regiment, excepting in the case of the two senior lieut.-colonels, both of which are to remain in the 52nd Regiment.

H. Calvert, Adj.-General.

Major-General Moore has, in consequence of the instructions contained in the letter of which the above is an extract, directed a list of the officers of the two battalions to be made out, placing the senior of each rank to the 52nd Regiment, and the juniors to the 96th Regiment, that the officers may directly see their respective situations, and be better able to make the option which is given to them by His Royal Highness the Commander-in-Chief.

    Memorandum—

Such of the officers in the list of the 52nd Regiment who prefer being removed to the 96th, will give their names to the Major-General tomorrow morning.

    (Signed)   John Moore, Colonel.

Horse Guards, 18th January, 1803.

Sir,

I have received the commander-in-chief's directions to inform you that on the separation of the two battalions of the 52nd Regiment, for the purpose of nominating the second battalion the 96th Regiment, it is His Majesty's gracious pleasure that the first battalion, which will then become the entire 52nd Regiment, shall be formed into a corps of light infantry, retaining, however, its present number and distinction of Oxfordshire Regiment of Foot, and in every respect its rank in the service. You will, therefore, be pleased immediately to select such men from the second battalion as you may judge best adapted for the light infantry, and replace them from the first battalion by men less calculated for such service.

I shall, hereafter, have the honour to communicate to you His Majesty's pleasure respecting the clothing, arms, and accoutrements and other appointments of the 52nd Regiment.

I have, &c,

H. Calvert, Adj. -General.

Major-General Moore,
Colonel 52nd Regiment.

In consequence of the above communication, the men who were considered unfit for light infantry were transferred to the second battalion, which was about to become the 96th Regiment, and were replaced by an equal number of eligible soldiers from that battalion. Lieut.-Colonel Henry Conran, being the senior officer present with the regiment, carried the above arrangement into effect, and afforded every facility in selecting the men for the 52nd Light Infantry. All the necessary arrangements having been completed, the final separation of the battalions took place on the 23rd of February, 1803, when the first division of the 96th Regiment marched from Chatham to Gillingham to embark, and proceeded to Ireland.

On the 18th of May the 52nd Light Infantry marched from Chatham, and arrived at Canterbury on the 20th, where the regiment halted about a fortnight, and then proceeded to Riding Street barracks.

The following regiments were formed into a brigade, under the command of Major-General Moore, and encamped at Shorncliffe, on the 9th of July, 1803:—

4th Foot,
52nd Light Infantry,
59th Foot,
70th Foot,
95th (Rifle) Regiment.

The most active drill being now about to commence, Major-General Moore explained to the commanding officers of the regiments the system he wished them to adopt. He permitted each commanding officer to fix upon the most convenient hours for drill, but required to be informed at what time the different corps were to be on parade, and he seldom failed to attend, by which means he became acquainted with the systems of the different regiments; and corrected any errors that existed.

In consequence of Lieut.-Colonel Vesey being at this time on the staff in America, Lieut.-Colonel McKenzie had the command of the 52nd Light Infantry, and was indefatigable in superintending the training of it on an entirely new system—to give the soldier a free, unconstrained attitude, and to march with the utmost ease and steadiness, was the primary object.

The country about Shorncliffe was well adapted for the subsequent part of the light infantry drill. And this period of the threatened invasion was peculiarly favourable to the formation of a light corps, as every individual was kept in the same constant state of activity and vigilance as if absolutely in the presence of an enemy; and the careful superintendence of Major-General Moore infused a soul and spirit throughout every rank, which made them perform their various duties with a zeal and alacrity seldom attained in other corps; and in what degree the 52nd Light Infantry profited by those advantages, will be hereafter shown by a communication from the Horse Guards, after His Royal Highness had made a minute personal inspection of the battalion in the month of August, 1804. On the 21st of July, 1803, the light companies of the 4th and 70th Regiments were attached to the 52nd for the purpose of being instructed in light infantry drill.

Notwithstanding the unremitting attention that was paid to drill, every pain was taken to have the brigade in the most efficient state to march against the enemy in the event of an invasion. The heavy baggage was put into store at Gravesend, and the officers were only permitted to retain in camp a small portmanteau each and their beds. One bat-horse per company was provided for the officers' baggage, and tents were to be carried with the brigade in the proportion of one for thirty men. The regiment was accustomed to parade in light service order, and Major-General Moore detailed very minutely what portion of necessaries each soldier was to carry.

From the systematic arrangements which were adopted, the brigade was expected to be formed in column, (with baggage packed and tents struck,) and the whole ready to move off in one hour after receiving the preparatory order for march. At this period the alarm post for troops for the county of Kent was between Dover and Romney Marsh.

On the 1st of August, 1803, His Royal Highness the Commander-in-Chief reviewed the 52nd Light Infantry, formed in brigade with the 4th, 59th, 70th, and 95th Regiments.

In consequence of a light infantry corps requiring a greater proportion of officers and non-commissioned officers than a battalion of the line, His Majesty was pleased to order that an augmentation of one lieutenant, one sergeant, and one corporal, per company, should be made to the establishment of the 52nd from the 25th of October, 1803.

Towards the end of November, the encampment broke up, and the regiment went into winter cantonments. On the 26th of this month, the 52nd marched from the camp to Hythe barracks, and during the time the regiment remained there it was not permitted to relax in the slightest degree from its former alertness. Arrangements were made to enable the battalion to assemble at the shortest notice, either by day or night; and in order to accustom the soldiers to carry their knapsacks, the regiment marched a few miles into the country twice a week.

1804.

The 4th and 52nd Regiments encamped at Shorncliffe on the 8th of June, and the 43rd arrived on the 15th. His Royal Highness the Commander-in-Chief reviewed the brigade on Shorncliffe on the 23rd of August, and on the following day the 52nd Regiment manoeuvred singly in the presence of His Royal Highness, who was pleased to express his entire satisfaction at its very high state of discipline, &c, and the following communication was received from the Horse Guards a short time afterwards.

Horse Guards, 29th August, 1804.

My dear General,

I have the honour of your letter of the 25th *ult*, and am commanded to communicate to you, that in consequence of the superior state of the 52nd Regiment on the Commander-in-Chiefs late personal inspection of it, His Royal Highness has been pleased to recommend to the king, that the promotion should be more extensive in that corps than has been usually granted, and His Royal Highness trusts that this distinguished proof of His Majesty's approbation will be a strong inducement to the officers to persevere in the same course of industry, zeal, and intelligence.

I have, &c, J. W. Gordon.

Major-General Moore, Colonel 52nd Regiment.

Upon the receipt of this gratifying communication the following Regimental Orders were issued:—

REGIMENTAL ORDERS.

Major-General Moore directs the above letter may be inserted in the orderly book of the regiment, as an honourable record at once of the superior discipline of the corps, of His Royal Highness's approbation, and of the reward which follows.

The promotion given to the regiment on this occasion exceeds perhaps whatever, at any one period, has been accorded. to a regiment.

The officers owe it to their own good conduct, and to the attention they have paid to their duty, but above all to the zeal with which they have followed the instructions of Lieut.-Colonel McKenzie, to whose talents and to whose example the regiment is indebted for its discipline and the character it has so justly acquired.

(Signed)   John Moore, Colonel.

★★★★★★

The *Royal Military Calendar* of 1820 states:—"Lieut.-Colonel McKenzie commenced with the 52nd a plan of movement and exercise in which Sir John Moore at first acquiesced with reluctance, the style of drill, march, and platoon "exercise being entirely new; but when he saw the effect of the whole in a more advanced stage, he was not only highly pleased, but became its warmest supporter.

"The other light corps were ordered to be formed on the same plan, and the 43rd and 95th Regiments were removed to Shorncliffe camp to be with the 52nd.

Letters from Sir John Moore are now extant which corroborate the assertion that the improved system of marching, platoon exercise, and drill, were entirely Lieut.-Colonel (afterwards Major-General) McKenzie's."

★★★★★★

Towards the close of 1804 a second battalion was added to the 52nd.

Major-General Moore ever had the most paternal regard for his regiment, which did not fail to produce a reciprocal feeling of esteem on the part of both officers and men; and in the year 1805, when Sir John Moore was created a Knight of the Bath, the officers availed themselves of this favourable opportunity to testify their gratitude and respect by presenting him with a diamond star (value 350 guineas).

The following is a copy of the correspondence which took place on the occasion:—

Sandgate, 8th April, 1805.

My dear Stewart,

Notwithstanding what passed yesterday, I cannot help, in this manner, again requesting that you will express my best thanks to the officers of the regiment for the present they have made me, and that you will assure them, as I feel towards them the most cordial attachment and the warmest interest in their welfare and honour, so nothing can be more grateful to me than any mark which leads me to hope that I possess their friendship and good opinion. I accept the star as a token of their regard, and shall wear it with pleasure for their sakes, and in remembrance of a corps of officers already distinguished by their conduct, the knowledge of their duty, and by the manner in which they discharge it, and who will, I am persuaded, distinguish themselves still more when the opportunity offers, by proving to the enemies of their country that, when discipline is added to the natural bravery of British soldiers, no troops on earth can resist them.

Ever, my dear Stewart,
    Faithfully and sincerely yours,

John Moore.

Lieut.-Colonel Stewart,
Commanding 52nd Regiment.

Shorncliffe, 9th April, 1805.

Dear Sir,

I am directed by the officers of the regiment to say that the very flattering manner in which you have accepted their acknowledgment of regard and gratitude, leaves them nothing to desire but an opportunity to realise the favourable hopes you have formed of their conduct in the held.

In this wish I must cordially acquiesce, and have only to regret that the indisposition of an officer, to whom we all look up with confidence and esteem, should, in these times, have deprived us of the benefit of his experience, and himself the happiness of making known to you the feelings I have endeavoured to express.

I am, my dear Sir,
etc., etc., etc.,

John Stewart,
Lieut.-Col. Commanding 52nd.

Major-General Sir John Moore, KB.

The following letter from Sir John Moore is preserved in the *Record* of the 92nd Highlanders, and is interesting to the 52nd as showing the pride their colonel took in the formation of the "first Light Infantry Regiment," and also as recording the debt they owe to their gallant comrades of the 92nd:—

Richmond, November 17th, 1804.

My dear Napier,

As a Knight of the Bath, I am entitled to supporters. I have chosen a Light Infantry soldier for one, being Colonel of the First Light Infantry Regiment, and a Highland soldier for the other, in gratitude to, and in commemoration of, two soldiers of the 92nd, who, in the action of the 2nd of October, raised me from the ground when I was lying on my face, wounded and stunned, (they must have thought me dead,) and helped me out of the field. As my senses were returning, I heard one of them say, 'Here is the general, let us take him away;' upon which they stooped and raised me by the arm. I never could discover who they were, and therefore concluded they must have been killed.

******

Note:—1799, at Egmont-op-Zee, where the 92nd fiercely charged a French brigade, and a *mêlée* ensued, with victorious result to the Highlanders. Sir John Moore offered £20 for the discovery of the private soldiers who had thus aided him, but in vain.

******

I hope the 92nd will not have any objection (as I have commanded them, and as they rendered me such a service,) to my taking one of the corps as a supporter.

Believe me, my dear Napier, sincerely, etc.,
(Signed) John Moore.

To Lieut.-Colonel Napier, of Blackstone.

Sir John Colborne, when created Lord Seaton in 1839, took for his supporters—on the dexter side, a soldier of Her Majesty's 52nd (or

Oxfordshire) Regiment of Foot, habited and accoutred, in the exterior hand a musket, all ppr.; and on the sinister side a Canadian Red Indian, holding in his dexter hand a tomahawk, and in the exterior a spear, all ppr.

Sir Harry Smith chose two soldiers—the one of the Rifle Brigade, the other of the 52nd—as the supporters to his arms.

On the 10th of June, the 43rd and 1st battalion 52nd Light Infantry encamped at Shorncliffe. The 2nd battalion occupied a part of Hythe barracks, and, owing to the unremitting attention which Major Robert Barclay paid to its drill and formation, it was, on the 15th of August, placed on the same footing as the 1st battalion in regard to the several allowances and equipments to be issued to regiments fit for service.

His Royal Highness, the Commander-in-Chief, reviewed the 43rd and 1st battalion 52nd Light Infantry at Shorncliffe, on the 26th of August, and those regiments received orders, on the 4th of September following, to hold themselves in readiness for immediate embarkation. In the course of a few days, however, the intention of sending them abroad was given up, and they remained in camp until the 26th of October, when the 1st battalion 52nd Light Infantry marched to Hythe, and the 43rd moved into Shorncliffe barracks.

Towards the end of 1806, the 1st battalion of the 52nd proceeded to Sicily, and in 1807 the 2nd battalion formed part of the expedition to Copenhagen, and returned to England in the month of November. The first battalion landed at Portsmouth from Sicily in January, 1808, and proceeded to Canterbury.

An OFFICER & PRIVATE of the 52ⁿᵈ REGᵗ of Lᵗ INFANTRY.

OFFICIER
52 Régiment d'Infanterie.

CHAPTER 2

1808, 1809: The 52nd in the Peninsula, Corunna

In August, 1808, both battalions of the 52nd landed in Portugal; the 2nd battalion, under Lieutenant-Colonel John Ross, landed on the 19th, just in time to take part in defeating the French, under Junot, at Vimiero, on the 21st. Sir Arthur Wellesley states in his despatch that, "On the right of the position the enemy were repulsed by the bayonets of the 97th Regiment, which corps was successfully supported by the 2nd battalion of the 52nd Regiment, which, by an advance in column, took the enemy in flank."

After the convention of Cintra, both battalions of the 52nd formed part of Sir John Moore's army, designed for separate service in Spain. The army began to leave Lisbon at the end of October, 1808, and the 1st battalion of the 52nd reached Ciudad Rodrigo on the 16th of November, and Salamanca on the 21st; the 2nd battalion was in Major-General Beresford's brigade, and proceeded to Salamanca by Coimbra and Almeida. Sir David Baird's corps joined Sir John Moore at Mayorga on the 20th of December.

I give the whole account of the retreat from Sahagun to Corunna, and of the death of Sir John Moore, from the 52nd *Record*:—

"On the 23rd the British Army, consisting of 25,000 men, was collected between Sahagun, Grahal del Campo, and Vallada, and all the arrangements were completed for attacking Soult's corps, amounting to 18,000 men, very strongly posted behind the River Carrion.

"The different general officers had received their instructions, and about half-past five o'clock in the evening of the 23rd of December, the reserve commenced its march from Grahal del Campo upon the town of Carrion, where the enemy had a strong post of about 5000 men.

"It was expected that this post would be carried early next morning, and that the troops would be able to continue their march the same night upon Saldana, where the principal part of Marshal Soult's force was already concentrated.

"The snow was very deep upon the roads, which impeded the march of the artillery so much that the reserve had made but little progress at midnight, when Captain George Thomas Napier, of the 52nd, arrived from Sahagun with an order for the reserve to return to its former station.

"The column immediately countermarched, and the regiments were in the occupation of their former quarters at daylight in the morning.

"This sudden change was occasioned by the arrival of a courier at Sahagun with intelligence that Bonaparte was in full march on Benavente with the whole of the disposable force he could collect at Madrid. Fortunately, this information was received by Sir John Moore at Sahagun two hours previously to the time appointed for the march of the troops from that place. On the 24th those divisions commenced their retreat on Astorga; the reserve followed on the 25th, and arrived at Mayorga late that night.

"The 1st battalion of the 52nd Regiment was chartered in a convent in the town; it rained so heavily that the men could not cook out-of-doors, and they incautiously lighted fires for that purpose in the gallery of the building; at about ten o'clock next morning, when the regiment was falling in to march to Valderas, it was discovered that the hot tiles had set fire to the joists of the floor, but by the exertions of the soldiers it was soon extinguished with very little injury to the convent.

"On the 26th the regiment marched from Valderas to Castro Gonzalo, and early next morning passed the Esla and went into quarters in the town of Benavente.

"At Castro Gonzalo the French cavalry had closed upon the reserve, and there being a very thick fog at the time, it was deemed necessary in that open country for the regiments to march in column of companies at quarter-distance, with flank parties of skirmishers a little distance from the columns; however, no attack was made upon the division during this march, but in the evening a few French dragoons, under cover of the fog, charged a picket of the 43rd without effect, and retired after having cut down a sentry.

"On the 28th, the enemy appeared on the opposite bank of the Esla, and the different regiments repaired to their alarm-posts; but as soon as the enemy had completed the reconnoissance he retired, and the British troops returned to their quarters in the convent.

"The main body of the army marched from Benavente on the 28th, and at about nine o'clock on the morning of the 29th the reserve commenced its march on La Beneza; the cavalry were to follow in the course of the day.

"Shortly after the reserve had quitted the town, five or six hundred cavalry of the French Imperial Guard, under the command of General Le Fèbre Desnouettes, forded the Esla, the bridge having been blown up a few hours before. Lieut.-General Lord Paget, and Brigadier-General the Hon. Charles Stewart, with the cavalry, quickly defeated this force, and in the course of an hour after, the celebrated French cavalry general passed the column of reserve a captive.

"The 2nd battalion of the 52nd Regiment now composed a part of Brigadier-General Catlin Craufurd's light corps which quitted the great route at La Beneza and marched upon Vigo. One hundred picked men from each of those battalions were pushed on by forced marches to secure the bridge of Orense.

"The reserve marched on the 30th from La Beneza to Astorga, and in the afternoon of the 31st moved to Camberos, and waited there the arrival of the cavalry; marched again at midnight, and reached Benbibre next morning, just as the preceding divisions of the army had left it.

"The scene that the reserve witnessed here was the most disgraceful that can be imagined; on entering the town they found the streets and houses full of drunken stragglers from the preceding divisions; parties were immediately employed to collect them all together, and the church being the most convenient building in the town, it was quickly filled with those drunken wretches.

1809.

"On the morning of the 2nd of January, 1809, the reserve marched from Benbibre to Calcabellos, and as the army was now entering into a mountainous country, almost the whole of the cavalry were sent forward to Villafranca on this day, and the arduous task of covering the retreat devolved upon the reserve.

"The recollection of the horrid scene at Benbibre determined everyone to check instantly the slightest disposition to plunder or drunkenness; an opportunity was not long wanting, for a short time after the regiments were in their quarters at Calcabellos, three men were found plundering a deserted house in the town. One was a straggler from the Artillery, another from the Guards, and the third was a man of the name of Lewis, of the 1st battalion of the 52nd Regiment.

"Considering this a fit opportunity to make an impression on the minds of the soldiers, next morning, the 3rd of January, Major-General the Hon. Edward Paget assembled the reserve in square, about a mile in front of Calcabellos, and the delinquents were brought out for execution. The ropes were already round their necks, and the unfortunate men were held up in the arms of those who were to perform the execution. The major-general was pointing out the necessity of enforcing the strictest discipline, when, at this instant, a cavalry officer galloped into the square, and reported the enemy's advance.

"The general immediately communicated this to the division, and at the same time declared that if the French cavalry were absolutely ready to charge the square, he should not be deterred from executing the punishment; but that if the reserve would now promise faithfully that similar acts should not occur, he would spare the lives of those unhappy men: and (to give the greatest solemnity to this engagement) he ended by saying, 'If you mean to fulfil your promise, you will all repeat distinctly three times, Yes, yes, yes.' The words resounded from all parts of the square, and the men were taken down. But little time was left for reflection, for at the same instant a second cavalry officer reported that the pickets had been some time engaged, and were then hard pressed, and commanding-officers were ordered to march their regiments to the alarm posts which had been previously assigned to them in the town.

"The man Lewis, of the 52nd, who although a sad plunderer was a gallant soldier, was afterwards killed at Orthes, by the side of the present Duke of Richmond, who was in command of a company of the regiment on that day. He generally contrived to have an attack of rheumatism soon after getting into action, and thus got out of sight of his officers for the purpose of filling his haversack.

"Sir John Moore arrived soon after this episode, and withdrew the reserve to a small range of hills, about half a mile behind the town of Calcabellos, leaving five companies of the 95th Rifle corps to dispute its possession with the enemy; at about three o'clock p.m. a heavy column of cavalry was observed winding down the road leading into

Calcabellos; the French *chasseurs* dismounted as they approached (securing their horses by throwing the bridle-rein of one over the neck of the other) and then attacked in light-infantry order.

"The 95th fell back gradually, and although the skirmishing was very hot in the vineyards behind the town, little loss was sustained, with the exception of a few riflemen who were posted in the houses at the entrance of the village, and who neglected to provide for their own safety in case of retreat. Two British guns which were posted on the high-road leading to Villafranca, on the slope of the hill, played upon the French column as it advanced; amongst others, the French General Colbert fell, by the well-directed fire of those guns. He was an officer of great promise, and the French bulletin emphatically announced his loss in the following words:—'His hour was come, he died nobly.'

"The skirmishing ceased with the daylight, and the reserve retired upon Villafranca, but without halting there marched to Hererias, where they arrived very much fatigued about four o'clock in the morning of the 4th of January. The men rested until about ten o'clock, when the march was again resumed. This day two companies of the 52nd (Captains Charles Rowan's and Hunt's) formed the rear-guard of the division.

"A great many waggons, loaded with Spanish clothing and other stores for the Marquis of Romana's army, were found unprotected on the ascent of a hill close to Hererias. The stores were destroyed, and the shelving nature of the road at this place afforded a good opportunity of obstructing the enemy's passage. The rear-guard collected the empty waggons and placed them in rows across the road, filling up the intervals with straw, empty casks, and all combustible matter that could be found in the adjoining houses; as soon as the barrier was completed the whole was set on fire, and the rear-guard followed the division, and had the satisfaction afterwards to know that the enemy's march was retarded several hours by this immense fire.

"The reserve reached Nogales on the evening of the 4th, and at ten o'clock next morning the regiments were formed in column in the streets ready to move off.

"It was found impossible to move the whole of the stores which had collected at this place, and several casks of salt provisions were destroyed.

"The reserve having already suffered many privations, both men and officers now filled their haversacks with salt beef and pork, which fatigue compelled them to throw away a few hours afterwards, and the want of bread was very severely felt at this time.

"The skirmishing with the pickets announced the near approach of the enemy, and as a small part of the military chest was still left without the means of transport, a message was sent to commanding-officers to say that their officers might receive money on account of *bât* and forage. Colonel Barclay considered the inconvenience (under the existing circumstances) of suffering all the officers to leave the battalion, and judiciously permitted none but the captains of companies to go. Three hundred dollars were issued to each of them on this account, and having no other means of carrying the money, they were compelled to distribute it among their companies, by entrusting a few dollars to the care of each soldier.

"A few miles in rear of Nogales, the road to Lugo leads over a steep mountain; here the weary oxen were unable to drag along the heavy-laden carts, and as the enemy was pressing upon the rear-guard, it was found impossible to save the military chest. Casks containing dollars to the amount of £25,000 were thrown over the precipice on the right-hand side of the road, and rolled from one declivity to another until they at last settled in the bottom of a narrow, rugged ravine, quite out of reach of the column.

"The rear-regiments of the reserve only were present when the money was cast away, and certainly not a man of those left their ranks in the hope of obtaining a portion. This discipline, however, did not extend to the 'followers,' who, as soon as they arrived at the spot where the dollars were rolling over the mountain-side, at once began a scramble, in which the wife of the regimental master-tailor, Malony, (who was a merry one, and often beguiled a weary march to the men with her tales,) was so successful that her fortune was apparently made. The poor woman went through all the subsequent perils and hardships of the retreat, but on stepping from the boat to the ship's side on embarking at Corunna, her foot slipped and down she went, like a shot, and owing to the weight of dollars secured about her person, she never rose again.

"The enemy's advance-guard, in a few minutes after, passed over the very spot on the road where this occurrence took place, and was then entirely ignorant that the treasure was abandoned.

"The fatiguing effects of the retreat now became very apparent; the men had been living for several days on salt provisions, without either bread or vegetables, and the rain fell in such torrents that they seldom had a dry shirt; consequently, great numbers were suffering from dysentery, and the very bad state of the roads left many without shoes.

"The present Major-General Diggle, quoting this time of distress, writes:—

> Well do I remember the kind act of a worthy woman, Sally Macan, the wife of a gallant soldier of my company, who, observing me to be falling to the rear from illness and fatigue, whipped off her garters, and secured the soles of my boots, which were separating from the upper-leathers, and set me on my feet again; even then, decorated as I was with the garters, I should have fallen into the hands of the French, had not Colonel Barclay sent his horse to the rear for me, being unable from weakness to fetch up my lee-way. A year or so after this I had the opportunity of requiting the kindness of poor Sally Macan, by giving her a lift on my horse the morning after she had given birth to a child in the bivouac.

"The skirmishing continued almost the whole of this day, (the 5th,) and Sir John Moore never quitted the rear-guard for a moment; whenever the country presented a favourable situation for checking the enemy, a stand was made to give time to the weakly men to get forward.

"The reserve arrived close to the village of Constantino at about four o'clock in the evening. This village is situated on a small elevation, forming a gentle slope down to a stream within musket-range; beyond this rivulet the road crosses a small valley and ascends the opposite hill in a straight line. On the summit of this hill the rear-guard, with two pieces of artillery, kept the enemy in check, while Major-General the Hon. Edward Paget, with the other regiments of the division, descended into the valley, crossed the bridge, and took up a position with his left resting on Constantino. The enemy followed the rear-guard quickly down the hill, and commenced an attack upon the position, but after a few discharges of artillery the firing died away, and the men began to cook; it rained excessively at the time.

"As soon as this hasty meal was finished, an order was sent round for the men to fall in quietly behind their fires; at eleven o'clock the division marched off in column of companies at quarter-distance with fixed bayonets; a short time afterwards the pickets were withdrawn from the bridge, the men silently retiring by two or three at a time. Sir

John Moore himself rode round the outposts, and directed where fires should be made to deceive the enemy, and the positions were so well chosen, and the arrangements for keeping the fires alight were so well executed, that it was nearly daylight before the enemy discovered that the division had marched.

"The reserve suffered more from the want of sleep on this night-march than on any other during the retreat; the columns moved on, but in what could scarcely be called a state of wakefulness: every instant someone or other unconsciously stalked off the road and fell into the ditches.

"The officers encouraged the men, purposely mentioning in their hearing that they had only a league or two further to march, and at length daylight appeared, but still the march was continued until the reserve passed Lugo a Spanish league; it was then about one o'clock, (the 7th,) rations were issued as expeditiously as possible, and just as the men were beginning to cook, intelligence was received that the divisions which had halted at Lugo were attacked; the reserve got under arms immediately and marched back there, drenched with rain; in this state the troops were crowded into a convent.

"The officers of the 20th regiment, 52nd, and Rifle corps, occupied a room with only one window, and scarcely space enough for the whole of them to lie down, and having shut the door and window, and lighted a charcoal pan to procure some warmth, the adjutant of the 52nd, who was the first to lie down, was seized with convulsions. Being immediately carried out, he recovered, and the rest of the party were thus made aware of the danger which they had escaped—of suffocation from the fumes of the charcoal. Next morning, (the 8th,) an hour before daylight, the British Army marched to a position about a mile and a half in front of Lugo, and remained there the whole of the day, offering battle to the enemy's superior force. But Marshal Soult did not think proper to accept the challenge, and soon after dark the British Army began to retire from this position and fall back on Betanzos.

"The duty of the rear-guard now became very laborious; it had not only to defend the rear of the army, but the good of the service and other feelings required it also to protect as far as possible those who were unable to keep up with the columns: the stragglers from the preceding divisions being very numerous, some from weakness, others from a manifest apathy or a desire to plunder. Every house contiguous to the road was crowded with these men, cooking flour and apparent-

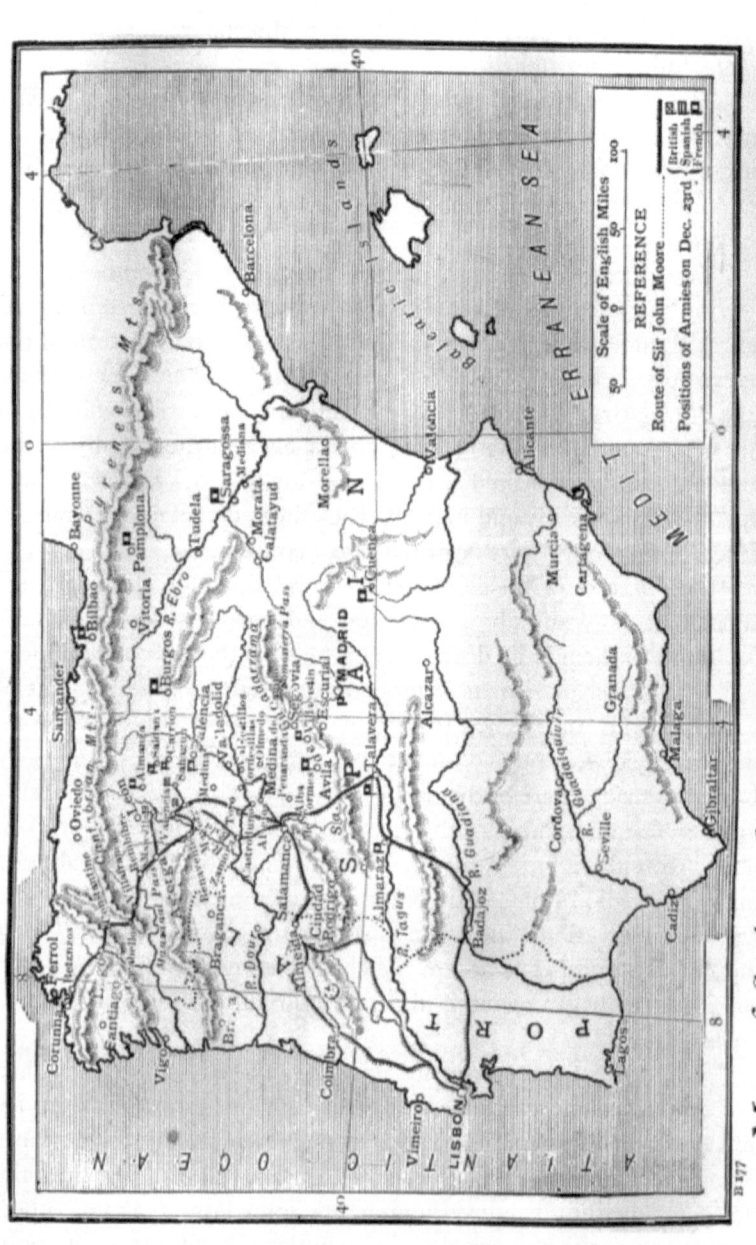

Map of Spain and Portugal to illustrate Moore's Campaign

ly enjoying the greatest security. As the reserve came up, they detached small parties to search the houses for stragglers and to warn them of their danger, but the persuasions and entreaties of the officers were heard with cold indifference. In the former part of the retreat there was a mingled feeling of indignation and pity for the loiterers, but now all commiseration was at an end; the rearguard had only one object in view, to keep the army as effective as possible, and the soldiers of the reserve were so disgusted with the conduct of those worthless fellows, that they beat and kicked them forwards on the road.

"At daylight next morning (the 9th) the reserve halted upon an extensive table-land behind the River Ladro, and in order to give the stragglers every chance of rejoining the army, the destruction of the bridge was deferred until the enemy were close up to it: all the weakly men were selected from the regiments of this division and sent forward to Corunna under charge of an officer from each battalion; in the evening the reserve began to fall back slowly upon Betanzos, and in the forenoon of the following day took up a position in front of that town to cover the main body of the army, which went into quarters there.

"Lieut.-Colonel Cadell, in his *Narrative of the Campaigns of the 28th Regiment*, (reprinted as *The Slashers*; Leonaur 2008), writes:—

> On the afternoon of the 9th a considerable force of French cavalry came upon some of the stragglers. A sergeant of the 52nd, who happened to be behind, looking after some of his men, collected a considerable number, and gallantly repulsed the cavalry, by which means he saved many who would otherwise have fallen into the enemy's hands.

(The name of this sergeant has not been preserved.)

"On the 11th the army marched from Betanzos to Corunna, and Major-General the Hon. Edward Paget followed with the reserve to the village of El Burgo and its adjacents.

"On the 13th the divisions which occupied Corunna marched out, and the whole army was placed in position about two miles in front of the town, the reserve occupying the small village of Monelos, in rear of the centre of the position on the Betanzos road.

"On the 14th the enemy cannonaded the left of the British line, and on the 15th his whole army made a forward movement, and took up a strong position in front of the British; this evening an affair took place in which Colonel Mackenzie, of the 5th Regiment, fell in endeavouring to take two of the enemy's guns.

"The transports having arrived at Corunna on the evening of the 14th, the embarkation of the sick, the artillery, cavalry, and baggage, was nearly completed on the morning of the 16th, and the reserve had received orders to be in readiness to embark at four o'clock that evening.

"The enemy's line was observed to be getting under arms at a little before two, and shortly afterwards the light troops of both armies were engaged, and the action soon became general.

"Major-General Paget advanced with the reserve to support Lieut.-General Lord William Bentinck's brigade, which the enemy was endeavouring to turn.

"The 52nd Regiment and five companies of the Rifle corps, being part of the reserve, were brought to the front in order to oppose a movement of the French left, which threatened to outflank the right of the British line. The French attack in front on the village of Elvina, held by the British, was repulsed by the divisions of Baird and Hope, while the reserve, after moving to the right of the British line, not only succeeded in repelling the attack of the French, but absolutely established themselves firmly on a part of the enemy's position.

"Near Elvina fell that noble general under whose immediate and personal instruction his regiment, the 52nd, acquired that admirable discipline and that system of light-infantry drill which contributed so largely to the honour of the British Army throughout the war of the Peninsula and the campaign of Waterloo, and which have been transmitted through the successors, whose discipline has been conspicuous down to the present times.

"The historian of the Peninsular war writes:—

> Sir John Moore, while earnestly watching the result of the fight about the village of Elvina, was struck on the left breast by a cannon-shot. The shock threw him from his horse with violence, but he rose again in a sitting posture, his countenance unchanged and his steadfast eye still fixed upon the regiments engaged in his front, no sign betraying a sensation of pain. In a few moments, when he was satisfied that the troops were gaining ground, his countenance brightened, and he suffered himself to be taken to the rear. Being placed in a blanket for removal, an entanglement of the belt caused the hilt of his sword to enter the wound, and Captain Hardinge (the late General

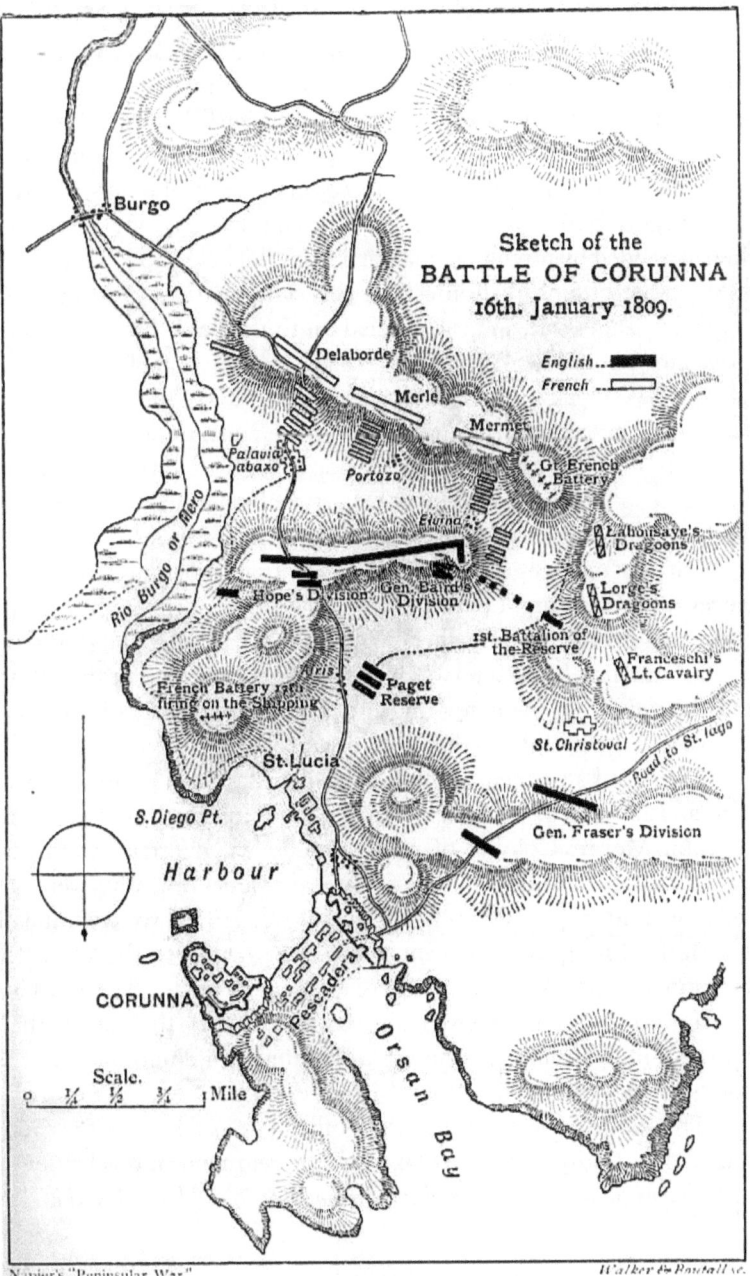

Viscount Hardinge, Commanding-in-Chief), attempted to take it away altogether, but with martial pride the stricken man forbade the alleviation—he *would not part with his sword in the field*.

"The body of Sir John Moore, wrapped in a military cloak, was interred by the officers of his staff in the citadel of Corunna. The guns of the enemy paid his funeral honours, and Marshal Soult, with a noble feeling of respect for his valour, raised a monument to his memory.

"The French Army having been thus checked at all points, fell back to its original position a little before dark, and the 52nd, after collecting their wounded by torchlight, marched from the field about ten o'clock to the place of embarkation at St. Lucia. The men got into the boats as quickly as possible, and each pulled on to the nearest transports, but owing to the darkness of the night, and the unfavourable tide, it was nearly two o'clock in the morning before the last of the regiment got on board. The company commanded by Lieutenant Diggle had made prisoners a French captain of light troops, Goguet by name, and fourteen of his men, and Lieutenant Diggle succeeded in bringing all of them off as prisoners on board one of the British frigates.

"On the morning of the 17th, the enemy brought down some pieces of artillery, and opened a cannonade upon the shipping; some of the masters of transports precipitately cut their cables and stood out to sea, but a few hours afterwards the fleet got collected in the offing, and the signal was made for England. The first battalion of the 52nd arrived at Portsmouth on the 25th of January.

"The 52nd sustained the following casualties at Corunna:—Five rank and file killed, and ninety rank and file missing. Lieut.-General Sir John Moore, Colonel of the regiment, was mortally wounded. Captain Robert Campbell and Lieutenant James Ormsby were severely wounded. One sergeant and thirty rank and file were wounded.

"Both Houses of Parliament voted their thanks to the army 'for its distinguished discipline, firmness, and valour in the Battle of Corunna,' and the 52nd received the Royal authority to bear on their colours and appointments the word 'Corunna,' in common with the troops employed under Sir John Moore.

"The following extracts from the official despatch and from General Orders, testify to the part taken by the regiment in this battle:—

"*Extract from Lieut.-General the Honourable John Hope's Official Despatch.*

The enemy, finding himself foiled in every attempt to force

the right of the position, endeavoured by numbers to turn it. A judicious and well-timed movement, which was made by Major-General Paget with the reserve, (20th, 28th, 52nd, 91st, and 95th Regiments,) which corps had moved out of its cantonments to support the right of the army, by a vigorous attack defeated this intention. The major-general having pushed forward the 95th (Rifle corps) and 1st battalion 52nd Regiments, drove the enemy before him, and in his rapid and judicious advance threatened the left of the enemy's position.

"*Extract from the General Orders issued by Lieut.-General the Honourable John Hope, who succeeded to the command on Lieut.-General Sir David Baird being wounded.*

"To Major-General the Honourable E. Paget, who, by a 'judicious movement of the reserve, effectually contributed to check the progress of the enemy on the height, and to the 1st battalion 52nd and 95th Regiments, which were thereby engaged, the greatest praise is justly due.'

"The 2nd battalion, which had embarked at Vigo on the 13th of January, landed at Ramsgate towards the end of the same month and marched to Deal barracks.

"The 1st battalion remained on board their transports at Portsmouth about ten days, waiting for a fair wind to carry them to the Downs.

"The regiment disembarked at Ramsgate on the 14th of February, and marched to Deal barracks on the following day, to recover from the effects of the campaign.

"The advantage of a very superior state of discipline cannot be better illustrated than by noticing that although the 1st battalion 52nd was one of those regiments which covered the retreat of the army from the neighbourhood of Sahagun to Corunna, its loss upon the whole of that harassing march amounted only to one bugler and ninety-two rank and file; and as a proof of the men's perseverance and patience under fatigue, it may be stated, that a short time after the return of the regiment to England, the return of deaths notified from the different hospitals happened to make on one day an aggregate amount of thirty men.

✶✶✶✶✶✶

Note:—The following duty-state shows how much the regiment suffered from the effects of the retreat to Corunna. In

November, 1808, the 1st battalion marched into Spain; effective, 54 sergeants, 18 buglers, 828 rank and file.

State of the 1st Battalion 52nd Regiment, 1st March, 1809.

	Sergeants.	Buglers	R & F.
Present fit for duty	26	8	269
With Officers on the Staff	0	0	3
Sick left in Portugal	1	0	4
" in Hospital	22	8	440
" at Ramsgate	3	0	21
" at Portsmouth	2	0	4
On furlough	0	0	1
Missing before 16th January	0	1	92
Missing since 16th January	0	0	11
	54	18	845

The 2nd battalion also suffered severely.

******

"The following General Orders were issued to the army by order of His Royal Highness the Commander-in-Chief, eulogising the life and conduct of the late Lieut.-General Sir John Moore, Colonel of the 52nd Light Infantry.

GENERAL ORDERS.

Horse Guards, February 1st, 1809.

The benefits derived to an army from the example of a distinguished commander do not terminate at his death; his virtues live in the recollection of his associates, and his fame remains the strongest incentive to great and glorious actions.

In this view, the commander-in-chief, amidst the deep and universal regret which the death of Lieut.-General Sir John Moore has occasioned, recalls to the troops the military career of that illustrious officer for their instruction and imitation.

Sir John Moore from his youth embraced the profession with the feelings and sentiments of a soldier; he felt that a perfect knowledge and an exact performance of the humble but important duties of a subaltern officer are the best foundations for subsequent military fame; and his ardent mind, while it looked forward to those brilliant achievements for which it was formed, applied itself with energy and exemplary assiduity to the duties of that station.

In the school of regimental duty, he obtained that correct knowledge of his profession so essential to the proper direction of the gallant spirit of the soldier, and he was enabled to establish a characteristic order and regularity of conduct, because the troops found in their leader a striking example of the discipline which he enforced in others.

Having risen to command, he signalised his name in the West Indies, in Holland, and in Egypt. The unremitting attention with which he devoted himself to the duties of every branch of his profession, obtained him the confidence of Sir Ralph Abercromby, and he became the companion in arms of that illustrious officer, who fell at the head of his victorious troops in an action which maintained our national superiority over the arms of France.

Thus, Sir John Moore, at an early period, obtained with general approbation that conspicuous station in which he gloriously terminated his useful and honourable life.

In a military character, obtained amidst the danger of climate, the privations incident to service, and the sufferings of repeated wounds, it is difficult to select any one point as a preferable subject for praise; it exhibits, however, one feature so particularly characteristic of the man, and so important to the best interests of the service, that the commander-in-chief is pleased to mark it with his peculiar approbation.

The life of Sir John Moore was spent amongst the troops.
During the season of repose his time was devoted to the care and instruction of the officer and soldier; in war, he courted service in every quarter of the globe. Regardless of personal considerations, he esteemed that to which his country called him the post of honour, and by his undaunted spirit and unconquerable perseverance he pointed the way to victory.

His country, the object of his latest solicitude, will rear a monument to his lamented memory, and the commander-in-chief feels he is paying the best tribute to his fame by thus holding him forth as an example to the army.

By order of his Royal Highness the Commander-in-Chief,
Harry Calvert, Adjutant-General.

"Lieut.-Colonel Barclay assembled every man who was capable of leaving the hospital, and read the above General Orders to the regiment formed in square in the barrack-yard at Deal; there were many soldiers who could not suppress those honest feelings, so creditable to human nature, when they reflected that they had lost a father and a friend, as well as a gallant brother-soldier.

"The officers of the regiment subscribed 150 guineas to obtain a portrait of their lamented colonel."

SIR JOHN MOORE

BRIGADIER-GENERAL ROBERT CRAUFURD

CHAPTER 3

1809-1811: The 52nd in the Peninsula

On the 25th of May, just four months after its arrival from Corunna, the first battalion of the 52nd embarked at Dover and proceeded again to the Peninsula, in company with the first battalions of the 43rd Light Infantry, and the 95th Rifles. They landed at Lisbon on the 5th of July, and proceeded, under the command of Brigadier-General Robert Craufurd, to join Sir Arthur Wellesley's army, which was then moving on Talavera. Having marched by Santarem, Abrantes and Oropesa:

> They arrived at Oropesa on the forenoon of the 28th, having that morning performed a tiresome march of twenty-four miles. Here some of the Spanish fugitives, from the first day's fighting at Talavera, spread an alarm of the defeat of their own party, and Craufurd, fearing that the British Army might be pressed, resolved to push vigorously forward. The regiments had just bivouacked, when they were ordered to prepare to march again. As soon as the men had cooked and eaten their dinners the march was resumed, and these regiments arrived in the vicinity of Talavera before daylight on the morning of the 29th, having performed a forced march of forty-eight miles, in excessively hot weather, in addition to the twenty-four miles of the preceding day: in all, sixty-two miles in twenty-four hours, each man carrying his arms, ammunition and accoutrements, weighing between fifty and sixty pounds. This march, one of the most extraordinary on record, is said to have been performed with the loss of only seventeen stragglers from the three regiments, 43rd, 52nd and 95th Rifles.
>
> The enemy having retired from Talavera during the night of the

28th, General Craufurd's brigade marched over a part of the field of battle towards the Alberche and took up an advanced line of posts near the bridge leading to St. Oballa.

In February 1810, the following General Order was issued by Lord Wellington:—

> The 1st and 2nd battalions of Portuguese *Chasseurs* are attached to the brigade of Brigadier-General Craufurd, which is to be called the *Light Division*.

It was not till the beginning of June that the two regiments of *Caçadores* joined Craufurd's Brigade and the famous Light Division was formed.

On the 10th of July Massena took Ciudad Rodrigo, and the Light Division, which had been acting as a corps of observation during the short siege of that place, soon afterwards fell back on Almeida and came in for its first regular fight as a division, near that place, on the 24th of July. It has been called the Battle of Almeida, and also the fight at the Coa. It is described as follows in the 52nd *Record*:—

> Soon after the fall of Ciudad Rodrigo, Massena put his army in movement towards the line of the Upper Mondego, and Ney's corps advanced upon Almeida, about 20,000 strong in infantry, with between 3,000 and 4,000 cavalry, and 30 guns. Craufurd's division, still acting under orders only as a corps of observation, consisted of the 43rd, 52nd, and 95th Rifles, the 1st and 3rd Regiments of Portuguese Caçadores, in all about 3,200 infantry, with eight squadrons of British and German cavalry, and six guns, and was disposed on a semicircle in front of Almeida, towards the Ciudad Rodrigo road, its right resting on the ravines of the Coa, about three miles above Almeida, and its left reaching to the same river about three miles below that fortress.
>
> On the morning of the 24th of July, Ney drove in the pickets of the division stationed on the Rodrigo road at Val de Mula, four miles east of Almeida, and then showing a front of fifteen squadrons, with artillery in their front, and about 7,000 infantry on the right of his advance, while the other troops were seen advancing on his left towards the ravines of the Coa, Craufurd became aware that retreat must be inevitable.
>
> He seems to have viewed himself as bound to prevent the investment of Almeida if possible, and therefore to have clung to a false position longer than sound military judgment would have dictated if unfettered by such view. Be this as it may, the Light Division was

concentrated, on the hour of Ney's attack, between Almeida and the Coa, on a front of barely a mile and a half, with ravines running transversely from the left front to the right rear which to some extent protected the right flank, but which must also be crossed in the face of an overwhelming force, in order to reach the only point then passable over the Coa, *viz.* the, bridge on the road to Valverde which was about half a mile from the right, and upwards of a mile from the left of the division thus posted. The 52nd were posted in the rugged spurs on the right, except half a company, which was detached under Lieutenant Henry Dawson, in an old stone windmill tower, on which the left flank rested, and at which were also posted two guns of Captain Ross's troop of horse artillery.

A Spanish garrison gun was in this tower, and at the first discharge it broke through the floor of the mill, and was afterwards useless. Next to this tower was the 43rd, then the 95th Rifles, and then the 1st and 3rd Caçadores closed the front with the 52nd on the right. Ney's attack was made with an impetuosity which outstripped the orders of Craufurd to retire in echelon of battalions from the left, while he sent his cavalry and artillery first over the bridge.

A horse artillery ammunition-waggon was overturned in the road, the 43rd and some of the 95th were thrown rapidly across a knoll which in some degree commanded the road near the bridge, although overlooked by the heights which Ney's troops and artillery had gained; these checked the advance; the 52nd defended each rugged steep, retiring by companies as the ground admitted, and a charge of a company of the 52nd recovered the ammunition-waggon, which Lieutenant M'Donald of the artillery brought off, while the other companies of the regiment, having crossed the bridge, instantly arranged themselves on the left bank among the broken steeps; the artillery went to the higher ranges of the mountain, wherever Captain Ross could find a place for his guns, and the safety of the division was ensured.

No French column crossed that bridge through the death-storm of bullets which swept over it: gallant were the efforts made by Frenchmen to force that pass, and twice repeated with equal gallantry; a few fine fellows succeeded in crossing, but they were obliged to skulk behind the rocks, and Ney became aware that in face of such troops, now properly posted, the attempt to force the bridge *en masse* was vain; torrents of rain caused a cessation of fire about four in the afternoon, and during the night the division was withdrawn.

The half company under Lieutenant Dawson, being unable to re-

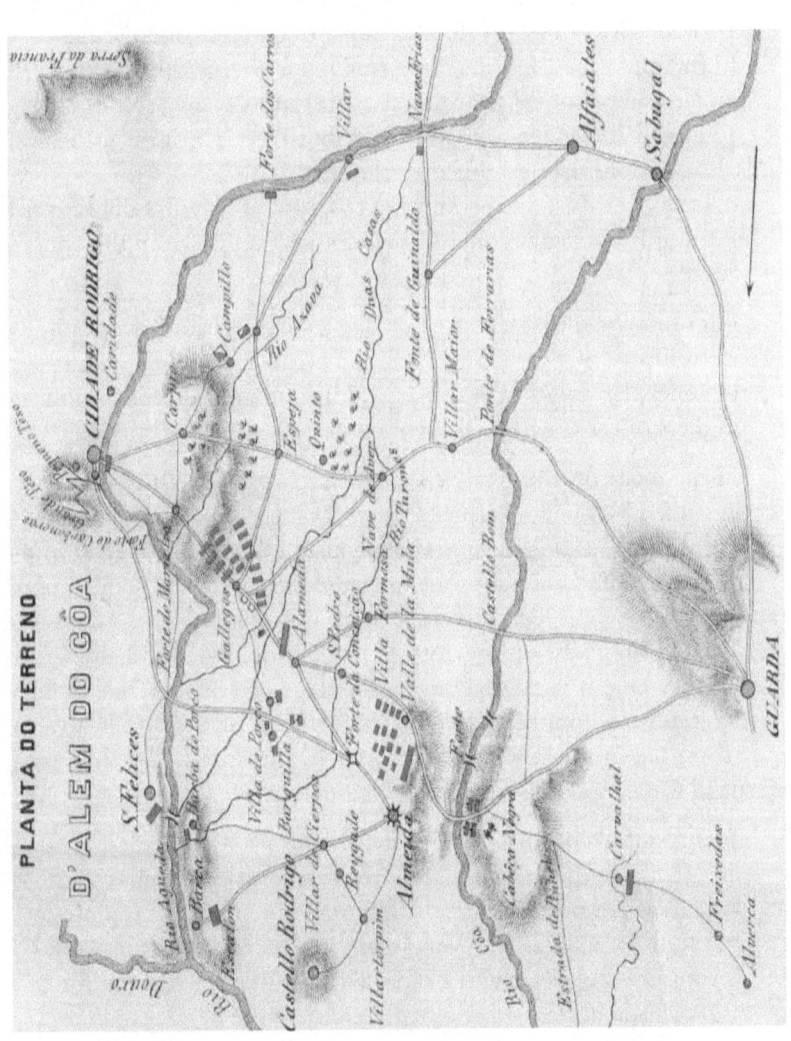

treat at speed with the horse artillery guns, had been cut off in the tower by the rapid advance of Ney's right; finding his post passed by the enemy and not attacked, Dawson remained quiet till nightfall and then drew off his men under the glacis of Almeida and along the right bank of the Coa, and, without being observed by the enemy, rejoined his regiment by Pinhel,—a fine example of coolness and daring.

In this affair the Light Division suffered a loss of 30 killed and 270 wounded and prisoners. Marshal Massena states his own loss as having been 'nearly 300 killed and wounded,' but there is reason to believe that it was more than double that number.

A little after dark, in the night of the 24th of July, the division fell back towards Freixadas without further interruption from the enemy.

Viscount Wellington stated in his despatch:—

> I am informed that throughout this trying day the commanding officers of the 43rd, 52nd, and 95th Regiments, Lieut.-Colonels Beckwith, Barclay, and Hull, and all the officers and soldiers of these excellent regiments distinguished themselves.

In the affair on the River Coa, on the 24th of July, the regiment, commanded by Lieut.-Colonel Robert Barclay, sustained the following casualties:—Major Henry Ridewood and Captain Robert Campbell were severely wounded; one rank and file killed, and sixteen rank and file were wounded; three men were missing. The Light Division fell back to Freixadas on the 26th of July, and on the 30th halted near Celerico, where it remained during the siege of Almeida. The French broke ground before that place on the 15th of August, and it surrendered on the 26th. At Celerico, on the 4th of August, the following General Order was issued by Lord Wellington:—

> The Light Division is to be divided into two brigades, *viz.*, the 43rd Regiment, 3rd Caçadores, and four Companies 95th Regiment, in one brigade; the 52nd Regiment, 1st Caçadores, and four companies 95th Regiment in the other brigade.
> Lieut.-Colonel Beckwith of the 95th is to command the former brigade, and Lieut.-Colonel Barclay of the 52nd is to command the latter brigade.

****

On the 27th of September following the 52nd was engaged in the general action of Busaco, and with the other regiments of the Light Division greatly distinguished itself. The following is an extract from

Lord Wellington's despatch on the occasion:—

> On the left the enemy attacked with three divisions of Infantry of the 6th corps that part of the Sierra occupied by the Light Division commanded by Brigadier-General Robert Craufurd and by the brigade of Portuguese Infantry commanded by Brigadier-General Pack. One division of infantry only made any progress towards the top of the hill, and they were immediately charged with the bayonet by Brigadier-General Craufurd with the 43rd, 52nd, and 95th Regiments and 3rd Caçadores, and driven down with immense loss.
> In this attack, Brigadier-General Craufurd and Lieutenant-Colonels Beckwith of the 95th, and Barclay of the 52nd, and the commanding officers of the regiments engaged distinguished themselves. The loss sustained by the enemy in his attacks on the 27th has been enormous. I understand that the General of Division Meste and General Maucune are wounded, and General Simon was taken prisoner by the 52nd Regiment, and 3 colonels, 33 officers and 250 men.

Private James Hopkins of Captain Robert Campbell's company, to whom General Simon surrendered, was awarded a pension of £20 *per annum* as the reward of his bravery, and private Harris, who shared in the capture, some years after also received a pension on the representation of his captain, the late Sir Frederick Love.

The following amusing anecdote connected with that period is related in the regimental *Record*:—

A man of the 52nd, named Tobin, in the company commanded by Lieutenant J. Frederick Love, was found to be absent, and was about to be reported as a deserter. Lieutenant Love, who knew the man well, and was therefore convinced he was not a deserter, but must have been killed or taken prisoner, had him reported as missing. A few days afterwards, when the division was on the march, this man rejoined his company, and when asked where he had been, replied, with a brogue, that he had been 'on a visit to the French giniral.' Lieutenant Love, not satisfied with this, ascertained from him that between the French and English out-pickets there was a wine-house and still at which the patrols used to meet and take their grog; but one night, drinking more than he ought, he fell asleep, and was taken by a patrol not acquainted with the arrangement, and the better to enable him to make his escape, he said he was a deserter.

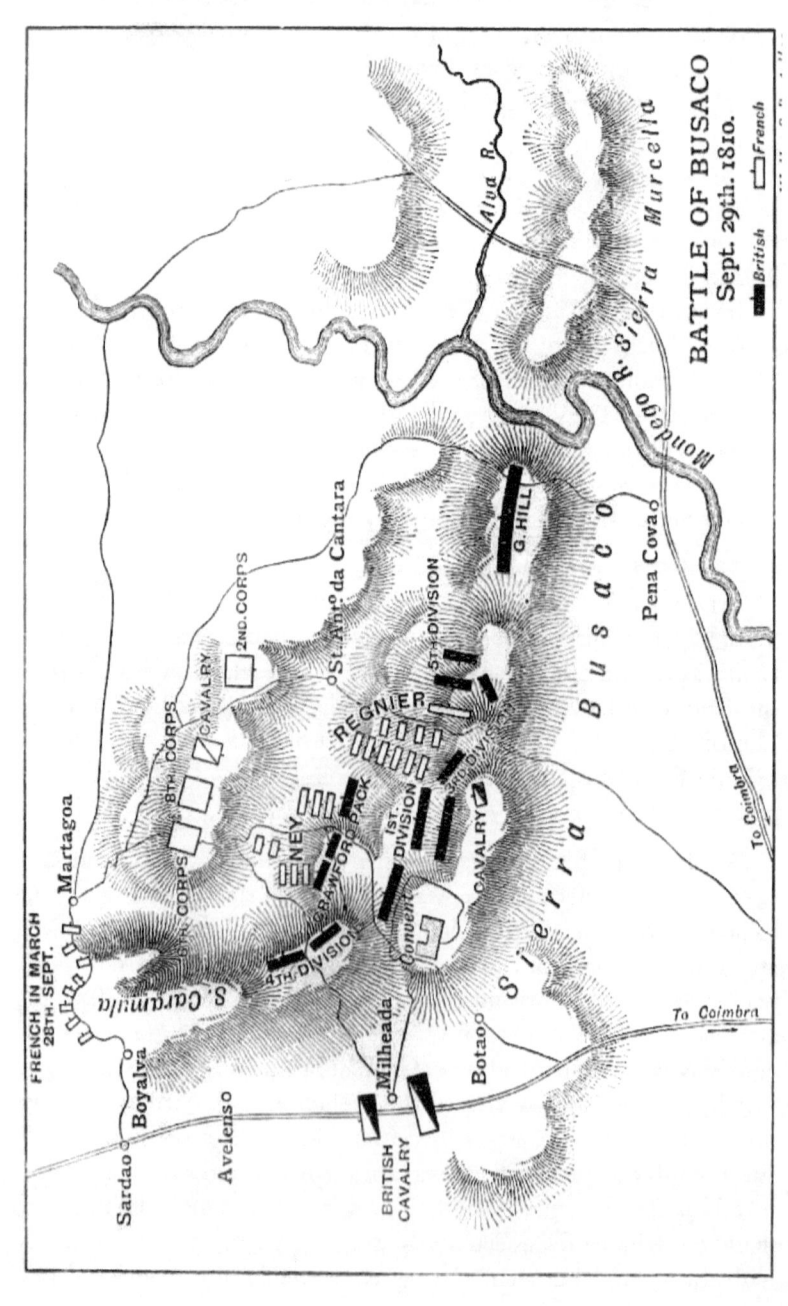

Some time afterwards, previous to the Battle of Fuentes d'Onor, an officer in the French service, an Irishman, and *aide-de-camp* to Marshal Massena, came to the advanced picket with a flag of truce and some letters for the general, and seeing the 52nd on their breastplates, asked Lieutenant Love, who was then commanding the picket, if there was a man in the corps of the name of Tobin. The captain replied that he was in his company, and called Tobin out. The *aide-de-camp* recognised him, as having been taken prisoner, and gave him a dollar, observing that Marshal Massena had declared, with 20,000 such men he would beat any army double that number.

The *aide-de-camp* then related that Tobin had been brought before the marshal as a deserter, which from his manner he (the *aide-de-camp*) saw was not the case, but that he had been taken prisoner, and as he wished to serve a countryman, he affected to treat him as a deserter, and offered to act as interpreter to the marshal. The soldier answered with clearness the questions put to him, until asked the strength of the Light Division. Here the poor fellow was at fault, and not wishing that his division should be poorly thought of, he replied in an off-hand, Irish way, 'Tin Thousand.' Upon which the marshal, irritated, exclaimed, 'Take him away— the lying rascal.'

Tobin seeing that the marshal was angry, said with a *naiveté* of manner, 'What's the matter with the ginniral?'—I replied, 'He says you are telling lies; he knows the Light Division was very little above four thousand when it advanced, and as it has been engaged above four times since that, it must have lost at least four or five hundred men.'—'Och, thin, the ginniral don't belave me!' said Tobin; 'till him thin to attack thim the next time he meets thim with tin thousand men, and see if they don't give him a good licking.'—'When,' said the *aide-de-camp*, 'I explained this to the marshal, he offered to make Tobin a sergeant if he would take service. Tobin asked a day to consider, and having made friends with the cook, filled his haversack, and took leave of us in the night.'

In 1811, the Light Division, of which the first battalion of the 52nd formed part, marched from Pombal early on the morning of the 12th of March, and found the enemy's light troops occupying the entrance of the defile and the woods about two miles in front of the village of Redinha, having his main body drawn up on the plain. The corps of General Ney thus formed the rear-guard of Marshal Massena's army.

The Rifle corps and 52nd advanced through the wood to the left of the road, and succeeded in dislodging the enemy. Having cleared the defile and gained the opposite side of the wood, Captain Mein's company advanced into the plain, and in a few minutes had to sustain the fire of a French battalion in line, being charged nearly at the same moment by a squadron of dragoons, but Captain Mein, with great promptness, rallied the company round him and effectually resisted the charge. However, his loss from musketry was very considerable, having two subalterns and eighteen rank and file killed and wounded. The strength of the ground, and the able disposition of his troops upon it made by General Ney, induced the belief that a stronger force might be in the position than was the case, and Lord Wellington therefore checked the advance of the Light Division on the left, and of the third division, which had been pushed forward on the right to turn the French left, until the rear divisions could come up.

As soon as this was done the army deployed into two lines, and advanced against the enemy, who fell back under cover of a heavy fire of artillery as the assailants advanced, and withdrew rapidly to the difficult ground on the right bank of the Redinha River, leaving the village itself in flames between them and the pursuers.

On the 13th the Light Division, under the command of Major-General Sir Wm. Erskine, encamped about a league beyond Condeixa, and next morning, closely following the French rearguard, directed its march on Miranda do Corvo. Shortly after the division had moved off, it fell in with the enemy near Cazal Novo. Captain William Jones's and Captain George Thomas Napier's companies were the first sent out to force back the enemy's light troops, which were posted behind some stone enclosures, and the heavy fog which prevailed at the time rendered it very difficult to ascertain the exact position which the enemy occupied, but these companies were reinforced by Captain William Mein's, and as the bugles repeated the sound to advance, the companies pressed forward, although engaged against vastly superior forces, and the enemy gave way; but in gaining this first ridge Captains Jones, Napier, and Mein, were wounded, and Lieutenant Theophilus Gilford killed.

The fog cleared off, and the French line was discovered again formed on a retired range of hills. Colonel Beckwith's brigade attacked it in front, whilst the 52nd made a movement which brought it full on the enemy's right flank. A vigorous attack at this point forced back a strong body of the enemy, on the road by which his line had to retire, and Captain John Graham Douglas's and Captain James Henry Reynett's companies continued to pour a destructive fire on the fugitives as they passed along their front. Thus, ended this affair of the 14th of March, and the division halted for the night close to Miranda do Corvo.

The division marched from Miranda do Corvo at about eleven o'clock on the morning of the 15th, and in the evening arrived on the left bank of the Ceira, a short distance from Foz de Aronce. The men had lighted fires, and were making preparations for bivouacking for the night, when the division was suddenly ordered to fall in, and instantly commenced a vigorous attack upon Marshal Ney's corps, which still remained on the left bank of the river.

The enemy were forced back rapidly upon the bridge, and Captain Joseph Dobbs's and William Madden's companies pressed upon them so closely that their rear was seized with a panic, and in their impatience to escape, great numbers were drowned and trampled upon, but the confusion was completed by the French divisions formed on the opposite bank, who, having in the dark mistaken their own fugitives for the advance of the British, commenced a heavy fire upon them, and it was a considerable time before order could be restored. The bridge was blown up by the enemy during the night.

The 52nd, commanded by Lieutenant-Colonel John Ross, sustained the following casualties on the 12th, 14th, and 15th March:— Lieutenant Theophilus Gifford and twelve rank and file killed; Captains George Thomas Napier, William Mein, and William Jones, (all severely,) Lieutenants John Cross, (slightly,) John Winterbottom, Adjutant, (severely,) and Ensign Richard Lifford, (severely,) five sergeants and seventy rank and file wounded. Ensign Lifford afterwards died of his wounds.

In these affairs the 52nd gained great praise from Viscount Wellington, who stated in his despatch that—

> Major-General Sir William Erskine particularly mentioned the conduct of the 52nd Regiment and Colonel Elder's Caçadores on the 12th, in the attack of the wood near Redinha, and I must add that I have never seen the French infantry driven out from a wood in more gallant style.

In relating the occurrences of the 14th, Lord Wellington says:—

> In the operations of this day, the 43rd, 52nd, 95th Regiments, and 3rd Caçadores, under the command of Colonels Drummond and Beckwith and Major Patrickson, Lieut.-Colonel Ross, and Majors Gilmour and Stuart, particularly distinguished themselves.

GENERAL ORDERS.

March 16th, 1811.

No. 1.—The Commander of the Forces returns his thanks to the general and staff-officers and troops for their excellent conduct in the operations of the last ten days against the enemy.

He requests the commanding officers of the 43rd, 52nd, and 95th Regiments to name a sergeant of each regiment to be recommended for promotion to an ensigncy, as a testimony of the particular approbation of the Commander of the Forces of these three regiments.

In consequence of the above Order, Sergeant-Major Mitchell of the 52nd was promoted to an ensigncy in the 88th Regiment, of which he was appointed Adjutant.

The Light Division halted on the 16th, and the rear-divisions of the army closed up.

On the 17th the Light Division forded the Ceira about a mile above the bridge, and marched to San Miguel de Poyaries; on the 18th, after a cannonade, it passed the Alva, and bivouacked near Route de Murcella.

On the six succeeding days the division marched by Morta, Golizes, St Jago, Pinhancos, and St. Payo to Navazienis, where it arrived on the 24th and halted there on the 25th. On this day the second battalion 52nd joined the Light Division, having embarked at Portsmouth on the 26th of January, and landed at Lisbon on the 6th of March. The division marched to Celerico on the 26th, halted there on the 27th, and next day marched upon Sabugal.

On the morning of the 3rd of April, the Light Division crossed the Coa at a ford about two miles above the town of Sabugal, with the intention of getting round the enemy's left flank, whilst two British divisions were to attack him in front; but in consequence of the very hazy state of the atmosphere the movement of the Light Division, then under the command of Major-General Sir William Erskine, was not sufficiently extended, and instead of getting in rear of the enemy's flank, it came in full contact with it, before the other two divisions had arrived at their points of attack.

Colonel Beckwith's brigade (the 43rd and the 95th Rifles) led the march of the Light Division, and having passed the ford too much to its left became first engaged with the enemy's left, in his front instead of in flank. They were thus opposed to a very superior force, and a vigorous charge of cavalry on his right, and the fire of numerous infantry in his front, compelled Colonel Beckwith to fall back behind some stone enclosures, which enabled him to resist the efforts of the enemy until the arrival of the 2nd brigade, consisting of the two battalions of the 52nd and a battalion of Caçadores.

The impetuosity of Colonel Beckwith's attack had been such that the 43rd Regiment, in two most daring charges, had driven back the French infantry and captured a howitzer; but when the 1st brigade was compelled to fall back to the enclosures they were forced to relinquish this piece, and the enemy again surrounded it, and turned its fire on the British brigades.

The 2nd brigade, however, which had marched somewhat more to the right, and had gained nearly the crest of the ridge without fighting, now formed on the right of the 43rd, and the 52nd advancing at the charge, drove back the enemy's columns which had repulsed the 1st brigade. These columns were supported by cavalry which made a spirited charge upon the 52nd while they were still disordered by their rapid advance; the cavalry however was repulsed, the 43rd howitzer was recaptured by a company of the 52nd, commanded by Lieutenant J. Frederick Love, and remained in possession of the regiment until it was handed over to the artillery,—not however before Lieutenant Robert O'Hara of the 52nd, who well knew the comfortable practices of the artillery, had relieved the limber of a couple of fine hams and a keg of concentrated *eau de vie*, which were most acceptable as a finish to the action.

Viscount Wellington thus described this action in his despatch:—

> Four companies of the 95th and three of Colonel Elder's Caçadores drove in the enemy's pickets, and were supported by the 43rd Regiment.
> They were however again attacked with a fresh column with cavalry, and retired again to their post, when they were joined by the other brigade of the Light Division, consisting of the first and second battalions of the 52nd and 1st Caçadores.
> These troops repulsed the enemy, and Colonel Beckwith's brigade and the first battalion 52nd Regiment again advanced upon them. They were attacked again by a fresh column supported by cavalry, which charged the right, and they took post in an enclosure upon the top of the height from whence they could protect the howitzer which the 43rd had taken, and they

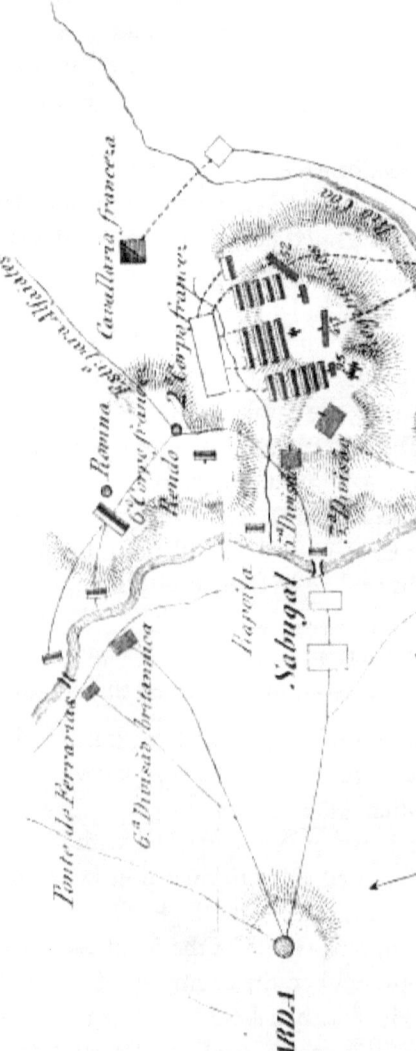

drove back the enemy.

I consider the action that was fought by the Light Division, by Colonel Beckwith's brigade principally, with the whole of the 2nd corps, to be *one of the most glorious that British troops were ever engaged in.*

After the action at Sabugal, the French Army hastened across the Agueda, and the regiment marched from Sabugal to Quadracies on the 4th, to Forcalhos on the 5th, to Albergaria on the 6th, and went into cantonments at Gallegos on the 9th of April.

On the morning of the 23rd of April, the enemy pushed forward a reconnaissance to the right bank of the Azava. Captain Robert Campbell's company commanded by Lieutenant Henry Dawson, and a sub-division of the Rifle corps under the command of Lieutenant Eeles, were posted on picket at the bridge of Marialva, and Captain Dobbs's company was stationed at the ford of Malenos de Flores.

At about seven o'clock a.m. the enemy commenced an attack upon the Marialva picket, and Captain Dobbs, knowing that heavy rain had fallen during the night, suspected that the ford which he was appointed to guard must have become no longer fordable. He soon ascertained that this was the fact, and leaving a corporal and three men to watch the ford, at once dashed off with the remainder of his company to the bridge; at which he arrived most opportunely, the enemy having forced the passage. Seeing the state of affairs whilst he was coming over the height above the bridge, Captain Dobbs without hesitation charged down on the enemy, who, supposing that his was only the advance of a much larger force, gave way, and recrossed the bridge.

On this the companies of the 52nd and the small party of the 95th placed themselves among the rocks on one side of the bridge, and kept up such a fire upon it that the French were unable to force the passage a second time. The manner of the French in advancing was rather singular. A drummer always led, beating what we used to nickname 'Old trousers,' and as long as 'Old trousers' encouraged them they continued to advance, but as soon as the poor drummer fell, they immediately turned tail and ran back, till their officers stopped them and began the same process over again. This continued till the two battalions of the 52nd came up, and effectually secured the passage, when the French force retired. In this affair Ensign Pritchard, one sergeant, and fourteen rank and file were wounded. Captain Dobbs received four shots through various parts of his clothing.

Napier says the attacking force on this occasion consisted of 2,000 infantry and a squadron of cavalry. If they had succeeded much mischief might have ensued, as our horse-artillery were all out foraging, and their cavalry would have got into our quarters at Gallegos.

On the following day the enemy made another attack upon the Marialva picket, and were again repulsed by Captain Reynett's company under the command of Lieutenant James Frederick Love.

The following casualties occurred in the 52nd:—On the 23rd of April, Ensign Samuel Dilman Pritchard, one sergeant, and fourteen rank and file were wounded; and on the 24th of April, two sergeants and eight rank and file were wounded.

Extract from Lord Wellington's Despatch.

The enemy had on the 23rd attacked our pickets on the Azava, but were repulsed. Captains Dobbs and R. Campbell, of the 52nd Regiment, and Lieutenant Eeles of the 95th Regiment, distinguished themselves on this occasion, on which the allied troops defended their posts against very superior numbers of the enemy.

The enemy repeated their attack upon our pickets on the Azava on the 24th, and were again repulsed.

Very early on the 5th of May the Light Division moved to its right, and was posted in support of the 7th (Houston's) division, near Poço Velho, with the British cavalry, scarcely more than 1,000 sabres, on the plain above. Massena's attack was led by two corps,—one directed upon the village of Fuentes, the other upon Poço Velho, while large bodies of his troops were seen threatening to turn the British right. The 7th division was pressed step by step out of Poço Velho, and the French cavalry turned the right flank, and drove back the advanced squadrons of the British, and were debouching in force upon the plain.

Lord Wellington upon this instantly corrected his front, which it was evident was too much extended. The Light Division, thrown into squares in echelon of battalions, and supported as well as might be by the cavalry, was ordered to cover the retreat of its own horse-artillery and of the 7th division towards Villa Formosa, while the 7th division itself crossed the Turones, and retired by the strong ground on its left bank towards the same point.

The cross-ridge of rocky hill which runs down to the Dos Casas at Fuentes also runs down to the Turones near Villa Formosa, and on this a new front was to be opposed to the advancing masses of the French left. Never perhaps in modern war was a more beautiful movement made, nor at a more critical moment, than by the Light Division on this occasion. The cavalry of Montbrun, numbering 5,000 sabres, and flushed with their advantage, pressed round the battalion squares without daring to storm them; the French artillery plunged into their close ranks wherever a clear range could be got; and for nearly three miles these veterans held in their conduct the fate of the British Army. But in one hour the rocky points which bounded the plain were reached, a British battery was in position to answer the French guns, and the Light Division, closely connected with the 1st division on its left and with the 7th division on its right,—and now under the command of its old chief, Craufurd, who had rejoined from sick leave,—swept the plain with a fire before which the troops of Massena quailed and withdrew out of range.

Meantime the French attack on the village of Fuentes had succeeded so far as to give them possession of all but the upper part of the village. Here, however, they could not succeed against the obstinate bravery of the regiments of the 3rd division, which maintained the church and the upper houses, and towards evening a brigade of the Light Division, in which was the 52nd, was sent to relieve them. More accustomed to desultory fighting, these troops soon pushed back the French to the banks of the river, and then, as evening closed in, by that common compact so well known to old friends on opposite sides, the British sentries were posted on the left and the French on the right bank of the Dos Casas without further mutual molestation.

The French field-officer, on placing his pickets along the right bank, to a captain of the 52nd, across the stream said:

I am glad to see you here, we shall now understand each other. When you want water, and our sentries challenge, call out *aqua*, and you shall have it. Will you give your boys (*à vos enfants*) similar orders?'

Of course, this was done.

Soon after dusk a French sergeant, a fine, handsome soldier, was brought in prisoner to the captain (J. F. Love) of the 52nd picket. The report made was that he had come over the line of sentries to take leave of a Spanish girl in the village, and was captured in the act. 'Eh bien! capitaine,' said the sergeant to Captain Love '*c'est l'amour qui m'a fait votre prisonnier.*'—'Eh bien donc!' was the reply, '*pour cette fois-ci nous ne serons pas trop exigeants: retournez chez votre capitaine, et dites-lui que si l'amour vous a joué un mauvais tour, l'amour vous a dédommagé. Je m'appelle Love; vous ne l'oublierez pas de sitôt.*'

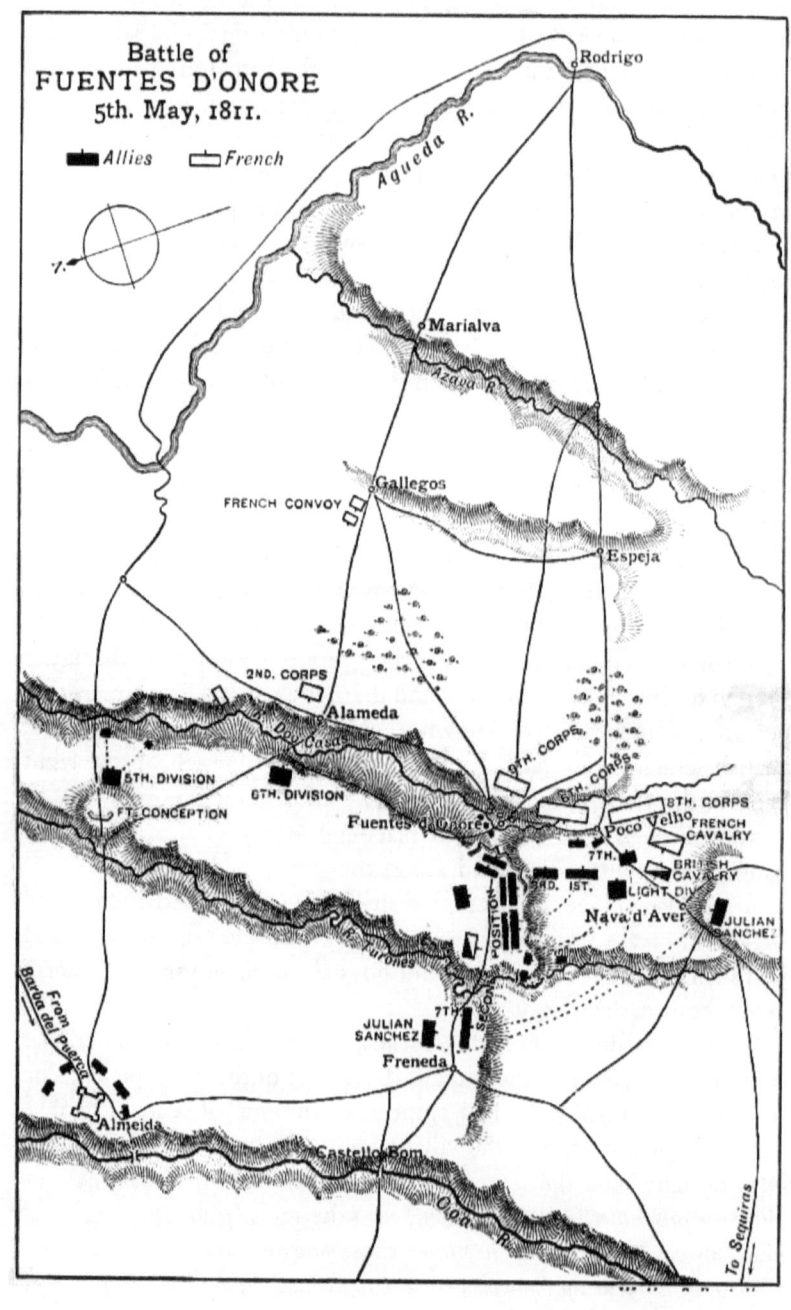

******

Note:—'Ah, Sir, Love has made me your prisoner.'—'Well, then,' was the reply, 'we will not be hard upon you for once; go back to your captain, and tell him if Love got you into this scrape, Love gets you out again. My name is Love, and you will not forget it.'

******

These amenities were the small jewels which in that day disguised the bloodstained robes of the God of War.

During the night of the 5th of May, breastworks were thrown up between the Dos Casas and Turones, which rendered the new front of the British Army, in the opinion of Massena, unassailable with any prospect of success; for after hovering about the ground, and idly parading his prisoners, who were chiefly made in Fuentes on the forenoon of the 5th, he gave up the hope of relieving Almeida and retreated.

In relieving their sentries on this occasion, the French placed a straw figure, with a French cap on its top and a pole by its side, to resemble the barrel of a musket, and the *ruse* was generally successful, so far as to give time to withdraw the rear-guards from their positions.

CHAPTER 4

1812: The 52nd at the Siege and Assault of Ciudad Rodrigo, and also of Badajos

On the 8th of January, 1812, the Light Division, commanded by Major-General Robert Craufurd, marched from El Bodon, crossed the Agueda, and took up its ground beyond the ridge of hill called the great Teson, on the north side of Ciudad Rodrigo. It was about mid-day, and as the place was not regularly invested, the French garrison in the Francisco redoubt imagined the affair was one of observation rather than in earnest, and amused themselves with saluting and bowing to their English friends. However, at nightfall a party for the purpose of storming the redoubt was formed from each regiment of the Light Division, under the command of Lieut.-Colonel John Colborne, (later General Lord Seaton, G. C. B.), of the 52nd Regiment, who himself arranged the plan of attack and the details, and saw them effectually carried out.

The party was composed of companies commanded by the senior captains of each battalion: two from the 43rd, four from the 52nd, two from the 95th, and one from each of the Caçadore (Portuguese) battalions. Four companies were selected for the advanced guard, to occupy the crest of the glacis and open fire, while the party with the ladders, in charge of Lieutenant Alexander Thomson, of the Royal Engineers, in the rear of those companies, could be brought up and be assisted in placing the ladders for the assault: in the rear of these followed the companies destined for the actual escalade. In this order the whole started and advanced, after a caution had been given by Colonel Colborne with respect to *silence,* and each captain had been instructed precisely where he was to post his company, and how he was to proceed on arriving near the redoubt.

An officer of the 95th and two sergeants had been stationed before dark on the brow of the hill, to mark the angle of the redoubt covering the steeple of a church in Ciudad Rodrigo, and this gave an accurate direction to the party in the dusk of the evening. When the party reached the point marked by the officer, Colonel Colborne dismounted, and again called out the four captains of the advanced guard, and ordered the front company to occupy the front face, and the second company the right, and so on. Captain Mulcaster, of the Engineers, then suggested that it would be better to wait for the light ladders which were coming up; Colonel Colborne however thought that no time should now be lost, and proceeded with the very heavy ladders which had been made during the day.

When about fifty yards from the redoubt, Colonel Colborne gave the word double quick. This movement, and the rattling of the canteens, alarmed the garrison, but the defenders had only time to fire one round from their guns before each company had taken its post on the crest of the glacis, and opened fire. All this was effected without the least confusion, and not a man was seen on the redoubt after the fire had commenced. The party with the ladders soon arrived, and placed them in the ditch against the palisades, so that they were ready when Captain Mein of the 52nd came up with the escalading companies. They got into the ditch by descending the ladders, and then placing them against the fraises. The only fire from which the assailants suffered was from shells and grenades thrown over from the ramparts.

During these proceedings Lieutenant Gurwood, of the 52nd, came from the rear of the redoubt, and mentioned that a company could get in by the gorge of the redoubt with ladders, on which Colonel Colborne at once desired him to take any ladders he could find. The company at the gorge, however, had forced open the gate, or it had been opened by some of the defenders endeavouring to escape.

★★★★★

Note:—It afterwards appeared that a sergeant of the French artillery, in the act of throwing a live shell upon the storming party in the ditch, was shot dead: the lighted shell fell within the parapet of the redoubt, and was kicked by some one of its defenders out of their neighbourhood towards the gorge, where, stopped by the bottom of the gate, it exploded and blew the gate open.

★★★★★★

The redoubt was entered simultaneously by means of the ladders

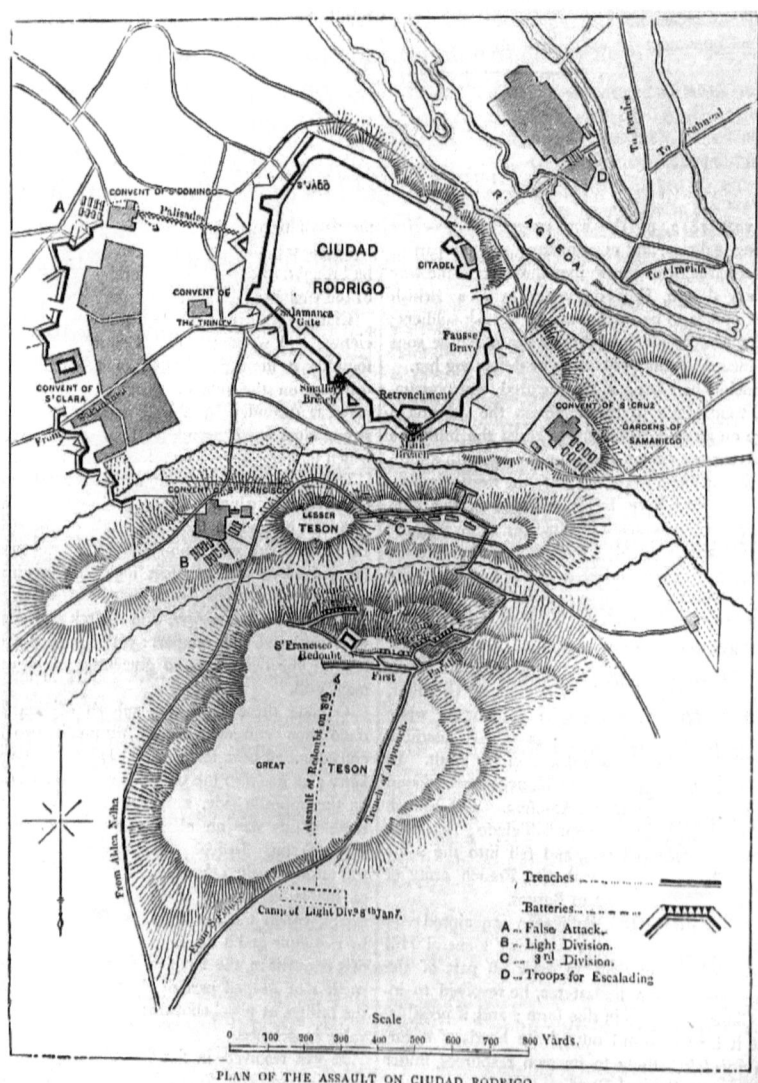

PLAN OF THE ASSAULT ON CIUDAD RODRIGO.

at the faces, and no further resistance was made; Captain Mein was wounded, as was believed, by an accidental shot from one of our own companies as he was mounting on the rampart. Most of the defenders had fled to the guard-house, and not a man of them was killed after the redoubt was entered by the assailants.

The garrison of Ciudad Rodrigo opened a heavy fire on the redoubt the moment it was known to be in possession of the assailants, and the attacking party was then collected outside, and marched by Colonel Colborne down to the rivulet near the foot of the glacis of the place, where it was then disposed so as to cover the working parties opening the first parallel, until moonlight. Such good use was made of the night, that by daylight the redoubt had been converted into an efficient lodgement under cover, with a communication to the rear, and the first parallel was thrown up for a length of 600 yards. Had the redoubt not been thus taken, five days would have been required to attack it regularly; the governor of the town had been in it about half an hour before the attack, and it was fortunate for His Excellency that his stay there was so short.

The remarkable success of this assault was probably due to the following points:—the clear conception and explanation of the plan of attack, so that each individual in charge knew what he had to do; the high discipline and order in which the plan was carried out, under the eye of the officer commanding the party; and the care taken to cover the redoubt with a sheet of fire while the escalade was being made, rather than trusting to the rush of a few bayonets against many defenders.

Another instance of similar care in the plan and guidance by its chief, accompanied by success, may be found in the assault of the Picurina outwork at Badajos, on the evening of the 25th of March, 1812; while the failure in the assault of Fort Christobal, at the first siege of Badajos, on the 6th of June, 1811, seems to have been caused by an irregular rush of fine soldiers without a well-concerted plan, and without sufficient protection from the means of defence exerted against them during the necessarily disadvantageous position of assault.

Viscount Wellington thus referred in his despatches to the storming of the advanced redoubt of Ciudad Rodrigo:—

> Accordingly, Major-General Craufurd directed a detachment of the Light Division, under Lieut.-Colonel Colborne of the 52nd Regiment, to attack the work shortly after dark; the at-

tack was very ably conducted by Lieut.-Colonel Colborne, and the work was taken by storm in a short time; 2 captains and 47 men were made prisoners, and the remainder put to the sword.

******

Note:—This statement in Lord Wellington's despatch is contrary to that of the 52nd *Record*, that "not a man of them was killed after the assailants entered the redoubt." See above. W. Leeke.

******

We took three pieces of cannon.

I cannot sufficiently applaud the conduct of Lieut.-Colonel Colborne, and of the detachment under his command.

The 1st, 3rd, and 4th divisions as well as the Light Division were employed in the siege by turns, while the remaining divisions of the army were in observation against the approach of Marshal Marmont for the relief of the place. The Light Division thus took its turn in the trenches every fourth day, being stationed in El Bodon when off trench-duty. The march to and from the trenches was not agreeable, as the Agueda was half frozen, and had to be forded to arrive at the ground, so that a pair of iced breeches were usually the accompaniments of each man, on twenty-four hours' sharp duty. The riflemen of the 95th did good service in keeping down the fire of the garrison, and the saps were pushed forward vigorously, but the approach of Marmont determined Viscount Wellington to make the assault at the earliest moment that should present a probability of success; and the counter and enfilading batteries accordingly had to perform the office of breaching.

On the 19th of January two breaches were reported practicable, and at nine o'clock at night the Light Division was formed behind the convent of St. Francisco in a double column of sections, and shortly afterwards advanced to the attack of the lesser breach, which was very gallantly carried.

The forlorn hope was led by Lieutenant Gurwood, of the 52nd, with twenty-five volunteers. The storming-party followed, consisting of 100 volunteers from each regiment; those of the 52nd under Captain Joseph Dobbs, those of the 95th under Captain Samuel Mitchell and Lieutenants William Johnston and John Kincaid, while Captain James Fergusson and Lieutenants John O'Connell, Alexander Steele, and John Bramwell, headed those of the 43rd; the whole under command of Major George T. Napier of the 52nd. These troops entered the ditch opposite a ravelin, which some mistook for the point of attack, and the forlorn-hope diverged to their left along the face of the ravelin, both parties reunited at the flank, and with an impetuous rush the top of the breach was won and the defenders beaten back.

Captain Ellicombe, Royal Engineers, was in orders to guide the troops to the descent of the ditch, and Lieutenant Alexander Thompson, Royal Engineers, guided the stormers and was wounded at the breach. Lieutenant Theodore Elliott, of the Royal Engineers, at the edge of the ditch finding a party of the stormers were mistaking their directions, most opportunely pointed out to them the true breach and saved the waste of some valuable lives.

As the supporting regiments mounted the lesser breach, the sections of the 43rd and 52nd wheeled outwards—the 52nd to the left, and the 43rd to the right—towards the great breach, and cleared the ramparts both to the right and left. This advance caused the enemy to abandon the retrenchment behind the great breach, which they had to that moment successfully defended, and in a few minutes afterwards the town was in the possession of the British.

The following casualties were sustained by the 52nd Regiment, in the attack on Ciudad Rodrigo, on the 19th of January:—The first battalion, commanded by Lieut.-Colonel Colborne, had Captain Joseph Dobbs, and eight rank and file killed. Lieut.-Colonel John Colborne, (severely,) Major George Thomas Napier, (severely, right arm amputated,) Captain William Mein, Lieutenant John Woodgate, one sergeant, and thirty-three rank and file wounded. The second battalion, commanded by Major Edward Gibbs, had one sergeant and three rank and file killed; Lieutenant John Gurwood and five rank and file wounded.

Lieutenant Gurwood of the 52nd, who led the forlorn-hope, afterwards took the French Governor, General Barrie, prisoner in the citadel. Lord Wellington presented Lieutenant Gurwood with the sword of General Barrie, on the breach by which Gurwood had entered,—a fitting and proud compliment to a young soldier of fortune!

******

Note:—I have mentioned in my account of Waterloo, that Gurwood had left the 52nd, and had got a troop in the 10th Hussars. The following anecdote respecting him was current in the 52nd in my time, and I remember the particulars very distinctly, as I have often related them since. Sometime after the Battle of Waterloo Gurwood was stationed at Brighton with his regiment, and frequently dined, as all the officers did, at the Pavilion. One day he was the first person to arrive, and the prince got into conversation with him, and made him give him the whole history of his leading the forlorn-hope at Rodrigo, of his taking the governor prisoner, and of Lord Wellington's giving him back the governor's sword on the breach. When Gurwood had finished his account, the prince patted him on the back and called him a fine fellow.

Shortly afterwards some of his friends advised him to solicit the prince to obtain a brevet majority for him. This Gurwood took an opportunity of doing, and the very next time he dined at the Pavilion, on one of the invitations sent to the officers of the 10th, the prince took no notice of him. This continued to be his conduct towards him on two or three occasions afterwards; at last, one day he came up to him and said, at the same time placing his hand in a friendly manner behind his shoulder "Well! my fine fellow, I have settled your business at last, but I have had hard work to manage it." It was supposed that the Duke of York, for some reason or other, made a great difficulty about giving this brevet step to Gurwood; and that if the prince regent had found it expedient to give way in the matter, he would not have mentioned the subject again, and would have taken no further notice of Gurwood.

See anecdote of the gallant conduct at Rodrigo of the Earl of March, the Prince of Orange, and Lord Fitzroy Somerset, later in chapter 13.

******

In Viscount Wellington's despatch, dated 20th of January, of which the following are extracts, the conduct of the officers and men of the 52nd Regiment was thus noticed:—

> The 4th column, consisting of the 43rd, 52nd, and part of the 95th Regiment, being a portion of the Light Division under Major-General Crauford, attacked the breaches on the left, in front of the suburb of St. Francisco.
>
> Major-General Craufurd and Major-General Vandeleur, and the troops of the Light Division on the left were likewise very forward on that side, and in less than half an hour from the time the attack commenced our troops were in possession of and formed on the ramparts of the place.

I have to add to this list, Lieut.-Colonel Colborne of the 52nd Regiment, and Major George Napier, who led the storming party of the Light Division, and was wounded at the top of the breach. I have already reported my sense of the conduct of Major-General Craufurd and of Lieut.-Colonel Colborne, and of the troops of the Light Division, in the storming of the redoubts of St. Francisco on the evening of the 8th instant. The conduct of these troops was equally distinguished throughout the siege, and in the storm nothing could withstand the gallantry with which these brave officers and troops advanced and accomplished the difficult operation allotted to them, notwithstanding all their leaders had fallen.

I particularly request Your Lordship's attention to Major-Generals Craufurd and Vandeleur, Lieut.-Colonel Barnard, 95th, Lieut.-Colonel Colborne, Majors Gibbs and Napier, 52nd, and Lieut.-Colonel M'Leod, 43rd Regiment; the conduct of Captain Duffy of the 43rd, and of Lieutenant Gurwood of the 52nd Regiment has also been reported to me.

The following officers of the regiment were promoted:—

Major Edward Gibbs, to be Lieut.-Colonel in the army, 6th February, 1812.

Major George Thomas Napier, *ditto, ditto.*

Captain William Mein, to be Major in the army, 6th February, 1812.

Lieutenant John Gurwood, to be Captain of a Company in the Royal African Corps, 6th February, 1812.

Lieutenant John Woodgate, to be Captain of a Company in the Bourbon Regiment, 20th February, 1812.

The following are the names of the officers who volunteered for the storming party:—

Major George Thomas Napier commanded the storming party of the division.

Captain William Jones (afterwards killed at Badajos).

Lieutenant John Gurwood led the forlorn-hope.

Captain William Jones ('Jack Jones' of Busaco celebrity) made himself remarkable immediately after the assault of Ciudad Rodrigo. A French officer having surrendered to Jones, Jack made use of him somewhat as Valentine is represented to have used Orson,—to show quarters for his men,—and having placed some of them in a large store, the French officer led the way into the church, in front of which Lord Wellington and some of the staff were collected. Some fire had been lighted already (supposed by Portuguese soldiers) on the pavement, and the Frenchman entering, and seeing the fire, instantly started back, exclaiming, '*Sacré bleu!*' and ran out with looks of the utmost horror.

Jones, not understanding French, did not catch the idea: '*Sacré bleu*' puzzled him, until going further in, he saw powder about the floor and powder-barrels near the fire. '*Sacré bleu*' became at once identified with *powder*, and he immediately got the help of two or three of his men (whose names are not known,) and carried with his own hands the powder-barrels out of the way of immediate danger. This deed passed unrequited at the time: let the memory of it now receive our admiration!

Orders having been received to draft the second battalion of the 52nd Regiment into the first, the Earl of Wellington (to which dignity he was raised for the capture of Ciudad Rodrigo) notified that arrangement to the army in the following terms:—

> *Extract from General Orders, 23rd February, 1812.*
> No, 3.—The Commander of the Forces having received orders to draft the second battalion 52nd Regiment into the first, the following arrangement is to be made for that purpose.
> No. 8.—The Commander of the Forces begs the second battalion 52nd Regiment will accept his thanks for their very distinguished services. Since they have been in the Peninsula they have had various opportunities of displaying their gallantry and good conduct, and the Commander of the Forces has had reason on every occasion to be satisfied with their behaviour.

Ten sergeants, 7 buglers, and 487 rank and file were in consequence transferred from the second to the first battalion; and 10 sergeants, 5 buglers, and 85 rank and file, being unserviceable, were transferred to the second battalion.

On the 25th of February the skeleton of the second battalion marched for Lisbon on its way to England.

Ciudad Rodrigo having been placed under the command of a Spanish governor, the British commander determined to take Badajos, if possible, before Marshals Marmont and Soult could unite their forces for its defence.

On the 26th of February the first battalion, commanded by Brevet Lieut.-Colonel John Philip Hunt, marched from Guinaldo upon Badajos by the following route;—Aldea de Ponte, Sortelha, Escarigo, Alpadrinha, Alcairo, Castel Branco, Niza, Castello de Vide, Portalegre, Monches, and Elvas, where the regiment arrived on the 16th of March.

Early on the morning of the 27th the Light Division formed on the glacis of Elvas, and started for the siege of Badajos to the enlivening tune, struck up by every corps of buglers, of 'St. Patrick's Day in the Morning.' It crossed the Guadiana by the bridge of boats about four miles from Elvas, and marching onwards for about ten miles, took up its position as the extreme left of the investing army, just beyond long shell-range from the walls. The left brigade was nearly due south of fort Pardeleras, a little in rear of the Sierra del Viento, à *cheval* (astride) on the road to Torquemada. The space between its left and the Guadiana was unprotected, except by a night picket on the Olivenza road.

Soon after dusk a detachment of the 52nd, marching to its right by a circuitous route parallel to the works of the town, joined near the heights of San Miguel the covering and working parties of 3,800 men, which, in a storm of wind and rain, broke ground about one hundred and sixty yards from Fort Picurina.

To the Light Division, and especially to its left brigade, this long route to the trenches across the upper branches of the Calamon and Rivellas, in a cold and very rainy season, formed one of the greatest hardships of the siege. In going to the trenches all of course proceeded in order by the appointed route, but in returning in the evening numerous were the attempts at short cuts homeward, notwithstanding the dashes of the French cavalry and round shot from the town. The Earl of Wellington kindly humoured these irregularities by placing a picket in a covered hollow, to keep the French cavalry at bay.

On the evening of the 25th the parties going off duty from the trenches, under the command of Major-General Kempt, were ordered to storm Fort Picurina, before their relief and departure to camp. The Picurina was a very strong ravelin with flanks, on a mamelon four hundred yards from the covered way of the place, with which it was connected by a covered way of communication.

One hundred men of the 52nd, under the command of Captain Ewart, headed the attacking parties, with ladders, grassbags, crowbars, and axes. The ditch was so deep, and the escarp so strongly fraised, that the first assault was made on the triple line of thick and high palisades with which the gorge was enclosed. The struggle was very fierce and prolonged, and Ewart fell wounded. At length the support was directed against the salient angle above the fraises, and made good its footing, while Nixon, Ewart's subaltern, with his axemen broke through the gate of the palisades in rear, Nixon falling severely wounded within it. Another struggle in the narrow interior, and this most important fort, which was calculated to have held out for five days longer, was carried. Captain John Ewart and Ensign William Nixon were wounded, and thirty-four rank and file out of the 52nd hundred were killed or wounded.

The capture of Picurina placed in the power of the besiegers sites for breaching batteries against the bastions of Trinidad and Santa Maria. The whole front however of the trenches towards these bastions was inundated by means of a dam in a bridge over the Rivellas, close in the rear of the Ravelin of St. Roque. About ten in the evening of the 2nd of April, Lieutenant Blackwood of the 52nd, with three sappers carrying bags of powder, silently left the advanced trench, and creeping behind the ravelin, lodged the powder with a lighted match upon the dam. (Robert Temple Blackwood, killed at Waterloo as Captain 69th Regiment, uncle to the present—1866—Lord Dufferin.) They regained the trench in safety, with a harmless shot in the dark from the French sentinel, and the bags exploded—unhappily for some hundreds of valuable lives in the subsequent storming—without sufficient effect.

Although not armed with the rifle, the shooting of the 52nd was sometimes called into play with considerable effect. One of the first counter-batteries was so overpowered by the enemy's fire, that Lieutenant John Dobbs, who was covering the battery in a trench in front of it, was called on to keep down the enemy's guns. He accordingly gave the opposite embrasures in charge of his men, and in twenty minutes the gunners were unable to stand to their guns, and the embrasures were blocked with gabions by the enemy to escape the fire.

On the 6th of April three breaches were reported to be practicable so long as the fire of the allied batteries prevented the fixing of impediments upon them. These batteries, however, were more than four hundred yards off, with the inundation of the Rivellas intervening, in consequence of which the covered way could not be approached by a direct march, and the counterscarp seventeen feet deep, with an irregular rocky bottom, remained intact. The ditch, also, for nearly one-half of the front attacked, was filled with water from a branch of the inundation of the Rivellas, which Lieutenant Blackwood and the sappers had so gallantly and ineffectually endeavoured to drain.

At 9 p.m., on the 6th of April, the Light Division, commanded by Colonel Barnard, and the 4th division by Major-General the Honourable Charles Colville, assembled near the small bridge over the Calamon, a brook tributary to the Rivellas, about a thousand yards from the breaches. The Light Division moved off in columns of sections, the ladder parties, to which were attached engineer officers, (Captain Nicholas and Lieutenant de Salaberry,) leading; then the grassbag, axe, and crowbar men; next one hundred volunteers from each regiment as storming parties, and then the divisions themselves.

The night was very dark, but as the swollen Rivellas was all the way close on the right hand there was no difficulty in tracking the route. The besiegers' batteries, after firing heavily, suddenly ceased; in this, however, there was nothing unusual. The advance silently neared the covered way. All was very still. The town-clock tolled the hour of ten, and the sentries along the walls successively gave their usual cry of '*Sentinelle, garde à vous*,' translated by our men into 'All's well in Badahoo.' Suddenly a fireball rising high in air from the bastion of Santa Maria fell near the axe and crowbar parties, but a shovelful of earth at once extinguished it, and all was dark and still again.

The ladder-party of the 52nd crept quietly through the broken palisades of the covered way, and planted against the counterscarp its six ladders, just in front of the salient part of the proper right face of the unfinished ravelin. The officer of it, Ensign Gawler, the engineer officer leading, Lieutenant de Salaberry, and about twelve or fifteen men were in the ditch, when, with a blinding blaze of light and a regular chorus of explosions of all kinds, the enemy's fire opened. The leading assailants pushed up the unfinished ravelin, in the hope of tracing a practicable passage to the centre breach; but the summit, in the very focus of the fire, was rendered still more untraversable by a field-piece in the flank of Santa Maria, which poured incessant charges of grape across the ravelin, and on to the covered way of the Trinidad, in which now appeared the head of the 4th division endeavouring to plant its ladders.

The deceitful inundation below carried away all that were led down, so that excepting some reckless fellows (among whom was Lieut.-Colonel Hunt of the 52nd) who jumped down the counterscarp, and were almost shaken to death, and a few active fellows who scrambled down the remains of one or two narrow ramps which the enemy had cut away, the whole of those who got into the ditch descended by the six

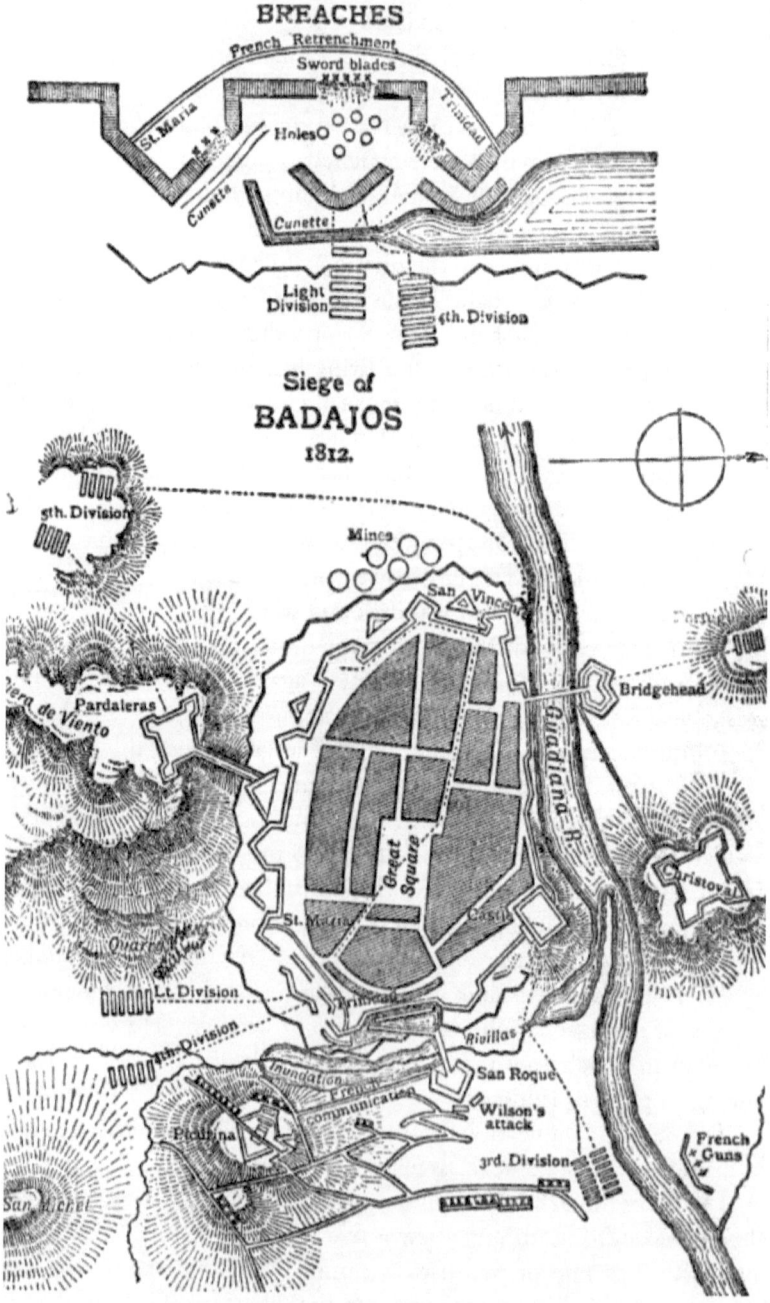

ladders planted before the fire opened; of which also the one nearest the salient angle, having slipped into a rocky hole, was too short.

It then became evident, that the highest discipline and the most devoted courage should not be calculated upon to counterbalance the neglect of those precautions, which long engineering experience has inscribed as essential. Of these the blowing-in of the counterscarp when it exceeds the height of about eight feet, is one.

The two massive columns were first checked almost hopelessly on the crest of the glacis, under the fire within sixty yards of veteran soldiers well covered, with several firelocks each, and adding to their bullets wooden cylinders set with slugs. Then officers and men, British, Germans, and Portuguese, of various regiments, became practically undisciplined mobs at the foot of the ladders. Then there were desperate rushes, in which the confused mass divided into three parties, according to each man's fancy for a particular breach.

Then came the lighted fire-balls and tar-barrels, the explosions of heavy shells, powder-barrels, and fougasses, and the crashes of logs of wood rolled incessantly from above. Then, halfway up the breach, were barrows turned the wrong side upwards, and planks studded with pointed nails. On the summit was a close row of *chevaux-de-frise* of sharp sword-blades well chained together, and from these projected the muzzles of the muskets of grenadiers with their recollections fresh of two previous successful defences.

The most desperate and persevering gallantry distinguished the assailants; some fell even under the *chevaux-de-frise*. It is not however difficult to conceive that at no one time was any body of men launched against the breach, in sufficient numbers, organisation, and unanimity of effort, to overcome the immense combination of obstacles. Captain Currie of the 52nd, a most cool and gallant soldier, seeing the impossibility of success without powerful concert, examined the counterscarp beyond the Santa Maria breach, and having found a narrow ramp imperfectly destroyed, ascended it and sought out the Earl of Wellington, who with a few of his staff was a short distance off. 'Can they not get in?' was the earl's anxious and emphatic question.

On Currie's reply, that those in confusion in the ditch could not, but that a fresh battalion might succeed by the descent he had discovered, one from the reserve was committed to his guidance. From the difficulties of the broken ramp, these men as they got in became mixed up with the confused parties rushing at or retiring from the breaches, and this last hope vanished.

The buglers of the reserve were then sent to the crest of the glacis to sound the retreat; the troops in the ditch, grown desperate, at first would not believe it genuine, and struck the buglers in the ditch who attempted to sound; but at length sullenly reascended the counterscarp as they could, saved only from complete destruction by the smoke of the expiring combustibles of the defenders, and the foul and worn-out condition of their flintlocks.

Cool generosity did not forsake the British soldier to the last—one of them made a wounded officer of the 52nd take hold of his accoutrements that he might drag him up a ladder, or,' said he, 'the enemy will come out and bayonet you.' The fine fellow was just stepping on to the covered way, when a thrill was felt by the hand which grasped his belts, and the shot which stretched him lifeless threw his body backward into the ditch again, while the officer whom he had thus rescued crawled out upon the glacis. (This man's name is unknown, even to the officer thus saved—the present Colonel Gawler, K.H.).

As the last stragglers crossed the glacis the town-clock was heard again, heavily tolling twelve; but Picton was in the castle to the right, and Leith in the bastion of St. Vincente to the left, and no French sentinel from that day to this has cried again '*Garde à vous*' from the ramparts of Badajos.

****

The following is the return of the casualties of the 52nd during the

	Killed.				Wounded.					
	Captains.	Lieutenants.	Serjeants.	Rank and File.	Lieut.-Colonel.	Captains.	Lieutenants.	Ensigns.	Serjeant-Major.	Serjeants.	Buglers	Rank and File.
From the 19th of March to the 21st	...	...	...	1	...	...	...	1	...	1	...	2
„ 23rd to 24th	...	...	1	1	...	...	...	...	...	...	...	3
„ 25th	...	...	...	8	...	1	...	1	...	3	...	34
April 5th	...	...	...	...	...	...	...	...	...	...	1	4
„ 6th	3	2	3	50	1	3	9	1	1	18	1	261
General total, 415												
Total	3	2	4	60	1	4	9	3	1	23	1	304

Officers Killed.
Captain William Jones.

" William Madden.
" Clement Poole.
Lieutenant Charles Booth.
" Job Watson Uoyle.
Officers who volunteered for the Storming Party.
Captain William Jones.
Lieutenant James M'Nair.
" Charles Booth.
Ensign George Gawler.

******

I have heard M'Nair, in after days, (*i e.*, four or five years after Badajos, where he was one of the stormers,) speak of the difficulties of the breach and of the impossibility of breaking down the *chevaux-de-frise* made of sword-blades. He went three times to the top of the breach, and whilst attempting, on the third occasion, to break the sword-blades was severely wounded all along the top of his head, but whether it was by a musket-shot, or by the thrust of a bayonet or by a sword-cut over *the chevaux-de-frise*, he could never tell. I think his regimental cap could not be found the next morning; but there were several 52nd officers' caps to be procured, whose former owners had been killed.

******

Officers Wounded.
Major and Brevet Lieut.-Colonel Edward Gibbs, severely, lost an eye.
Brevet Major William Mein, severely.
Captain Robert Campbell, *ditto.*
" Augustus Merry, *ditto*, died.
" John F. Ewart, *ditto.*
Lieutenant James M'Nair, *ditto.*
" Charles Kinlock, slightly.
" Charles York, ditto.
" Robert Blackwood, severely.
" Francis John Davies, slightly.
" William Royds, *ditto.*
" George Ulrick Barlow, severely.
Ensign William Nixon, *ditto.*
" George Hall, *ditto.*
" George Gawler, slightly.

CHAPTER 5

1813, 1814: The 52nd at the Close of the Peninsular War

At the Battle of Salamanca, which was fought on the 22nd of July, 1812, the Light Division formed the extreme left of the British line, and was held in reserve as a check upon the right divisions of Marmont's army. After this they had a great deal of outpost duty—some of it very severe—until, on the 25th of November, they went into cantonments at Rodrigo and Guinaldo.

The campaign of 1813, opened about the 20th of May, and the decisive Battle of Vittoria, in which the French Army was utterly routed, was fought on the 21st of June. They lost all but two out of 153 pieces of artillery, 415 caissons, a large quantity of ammunition, their military chest, and all their baggage and papers. The Light Division took up the pursuit, which they continued for several miles, and the rout was most complete. (Captain Currie, of the 52nd, was killed, and Lieutenant Northey was wounded in the head by a cannon-shot, at Vittoria.) The Light Division reached Vera on the 15th of July, and fell back to Lesaca on the 20th, where Lieut.-Colonel Colborne, having recovered from his wound received at Ciudad Rodrigo, resumed the command of the 52nd:—

Napoleon was at Dresden during the armistice which, on the 4th of June, 1813, terminated the campaign of Lützen and Bautzen, when the intelligence of Lord Wellington's having passed the Ebro reached him, and by an order dated the 1st of July, he directed Marshal Soult immediately to proceed to take the command of what he still called the armies of Spain.

The marshal arrived at his headquarters on the 13th, and presently

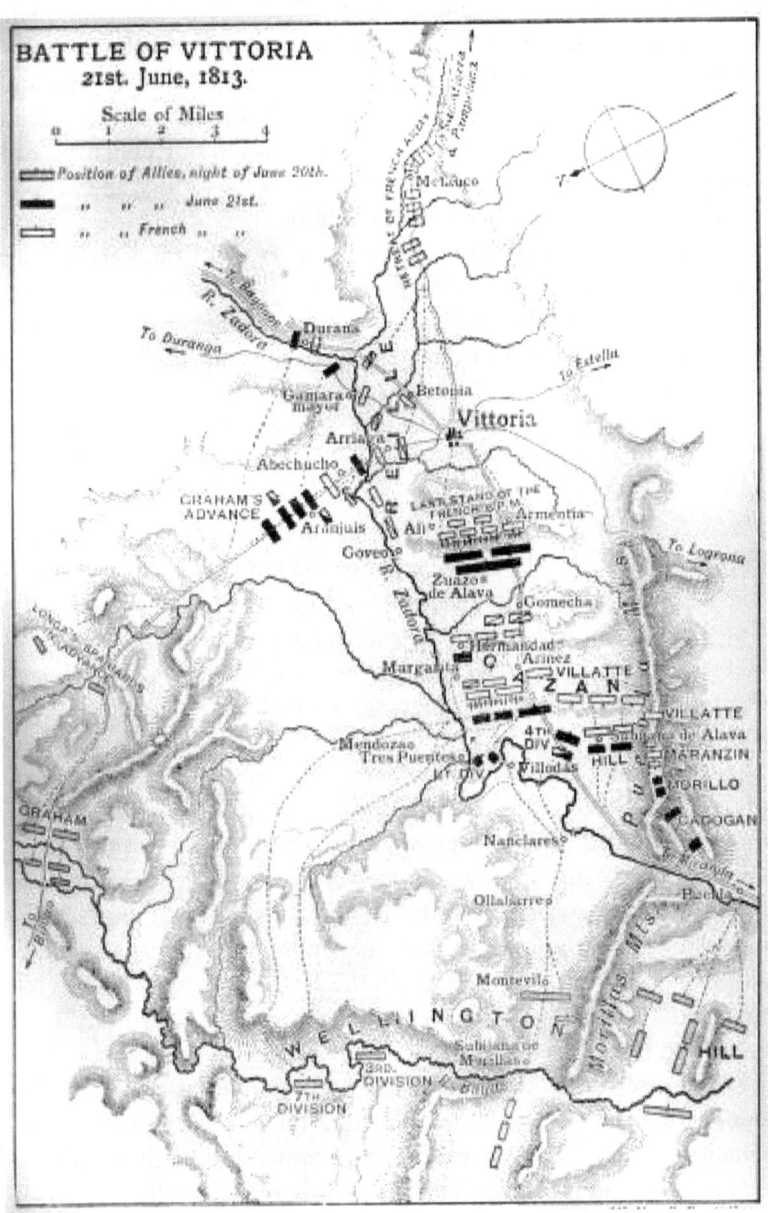

commenced his operations for a great offensive movement.

By the 24th he had collected nearly forty thousand men at St. Jean Pied de Port, with which he designed to penetrate by Ronçesvalles; and three divisions more, amounting to about twenty thousand men, under Count d'Erlon, were destined for the attack of the passes of Maya, his object being first to raise the blockade of Pamplona and then to operate to his right, so as to enable the reserve from Irun to join him and relieve St. Sebastian. For this ulterior design he had prepared by bringing with him a large body of cavalry and a great number of guns, neither of which could be used to any great extent in the difficult country between the Pyrenees and Pamplona, and his confidence was expressed in the proclamation issued to his troops setting forth his intentions, and saying, 'Let the account of our success be dated from Vittoria, and let the birthday of the emperor be celebrated in that city.'

Against him was posted, in the front line guarding the pass of Ronçesvalles, Major-General Byng's brigade (not more than 1600 men) of the 2nd division, with 4,000 Spaniards; and Byng's nearest support was the 4th division, 6,000 strong, under Sir Lowry Cole, three leagues in their rear, the whole distance to Pamplona being only eight and a half leagues, or about thirty-four miles. For the defence of the Col de Maya, Sir R. Hill and the remainder of the 2nd division, about 10,000 men, of which two brigades were in advance guarding its passes, and another brigade (Portuguese) about half way between Maya and Ronçesvalles.

Soult made his onset on the morning of the 25th of July, the day of the unsuccessful assault of St. Sebastian by Sir Thomas Graham; and though, as stated in Lord Wellington's despatch of the 1st of August, the position of the allies was very defective, inasmuch as the communication between the 'several divisions was tedious and difficult, and in case of attack those in the front line could not support each other, and would look for support only in the rear;' yet, in spite of his great superiority of numbers, Soult encountered a most determined resistance, and his progress was not at all equal to his anticipations.

After a series of attacks made on the scattered brigades and divisions of the allies in the rugged passes of the Pyrenees, Soult's combinations were foiled, partly by foggy weather and partly by want of due concert and vigour among his generals, while, on the other hand, the British divisions obstinately resisted, each on its own ground, and gradually retired until a sufficient concentration of force was effected to resume the offensive. Thus, Soult found himself eventually beaten back with the loss of about 15,000 men, and on the 2nd of August his army was cantoned behind the general line of the Bidassoa.

The enemy's project for relieving Pamplona having thus failed, the Light Division countermarched, and again arrived at Sumbella on the 1st of August, and re-occupied Vera on the 2nd.

At daybreak on the 30th of August, a considerable French force was assembled on the position above Vera, with a view of drawing off the garrison of St. Sebastian by forcing through the covering army of Spaniards, which were posted on the heights of St. Marcial; the columns soon began to descend the hill, and the Light Division pickets having been driven out of the town, the enemy passed the Bidassoa at a ford a little lower down, where the river forms a kind of elbow, its course at the bridge leading to Lesaca being nearly at a right angle with the ford which the enemy passed. The uncertain result of the operations rendered it inexpedient to destroy the Lesaca bridge; but to secure the brigade from sudden attack during the night, this bridge was partially blocked up with large casks filled with stones, leaving only a narrow passage for one man.

The attack upon the Spaniards on the heights of St. Marcial on the 31st having failed, the enemy returned the same night to regain their former positions above Vera, but the heavy fall of rain had rendered the ford which the enemy passed on the 30th impracticable, and his only resource was to force the Lesaca bridge. Favoured by the dark, tempestuous night, he succeeded in disposing of the double sentry of the 95th Rifle corps which was posted on it, and the column commenced passing over as rapidly as the circumstances would permit, his passage being greatly impeded by the 95th picket posted in a house near the bridge. As soon as the enemy's object was ascertained, some companies of the 52nd joined the Rifle corps in a heavy fire upon the fugitives, and at daylight three hundred dead bodies were found near the bridge, and many more of the enemy were drowned in endeavouring to swim across the river.

Meantime the siege of St. Sebastian had been committed to the 5th division and some Portuguese brigades, and was pushed on as well as the arrival of tardy supplies from England would admit. It was the 19th of August before the Marquis of Wellington received from England the battering train which he had long before demanded, and even then, the train arrived without its ammunition. However, a breach having been made in the rampart and wall on both sides of the tower of Mésquitas, and also in the long curtain between the tower of Los Hornos and the demi-bastion of St. Elmo, it was arranged that the assault should take place on the 31st of August, a little before noon.

It was supposed that the troops engaged in the siege were discouraged by its tedious length and by a former unsuccessful assault, and therefore, besides the 5th division, it was ordered that the storming party should consist of 750 volunteers from the Light and some other divisions,—'men,' in the words of the Marquis of Wellington, 'who could show other troops how to mount a breach.' Of these volunteers 150 were from the Light Division, under the command of Lieut.-Colonel John P. Hunt, and the quota of the 52nd was—one captain, Robert Campbell; one subaltern, Lieut. Augustus Harvest; three sergeants, and thirty-five rank and file. As soon as the order was communicated to the regiment, entire companies volunteered, and the captains had a difficult task in selecting the men most fit for such an undertaking without hurting the feelings of the others; in many cases lots were resorted to to settle the claims of those gallant fellows who contended for the honour of upholding the fame of their regiment.

In the private journal of F. S. Larpent, Esq., Judge Advocate-General of the British Forces in the Peninsula, published in 1853, it is related, on the 19th of August, 1813:—

> There was nothing but confusion in the two divisions here last night (the Light and 4th), from the eagerness of the officers to volunteer, and the difficulty of determining who were to be refused and allowed to go and run their heads into a hole in the wall, full of fire and danger! Major Napier was here quite in misery, because, though he had volunteered first, Lieut.-Colonel Hunt, of the 52nd, his superior officer, insisted on his right to go. The latter said that Napier had been in the breach at Badajos, and he had a fair claim to go now. So, it is among the subalterns—ten have volunteered where two are to be accepted. Hunt, being lieut.-colonel, has nothing but honour to look to; as to promotion, he is past that. The men say they do not know what they are to do, but they are ready to go anywhere.

The manner in which this detachment had been called from other divisions not engaged in the siege, created such indignation in the 5th division, that it was said at the time they would bayonet the men of the detachment if they got into the town before them; and Major-General Leith, who commanded the 5th division, and who had the entire arrangements on the day of assault, in consideration of a feeling in which he in some degree participated, would not suffer the volunteers from the other divisions to lead the assault, but disposed them along the trenches to keep down the fire of the hornwork, which was expected to be severe on the advance to the breach, while the stormers were selected from the 5th division.

At 11 o'clock a.m., on the 31st of August, the storming party filed out of the trenches. Almost at the same moment a mine was exploded at the left angle of the counterscarp just as the forlorn-hope had passed, destroying a few men at the head of the column, which continued to advance, and covered the exterior face of the breach. Here they found no access to the town—as entrenchments had been formed behind the breach—except by climbing the broken extremity of the rampart. The enemy had cleared away the rubbish within the breach so as to render the direct descent perpendicular, while the opposite houses were loopholed, and the crest of the breach was exposed to the fire of shells and grape from the batteries of the castle. The orders had been to form a lodgement inside the breach, but as the rubbish had been cleared away, and no materials for the purpose had been brought up with the assaulting party, it was impossible to do this, and the whole of the surface of the breach was soon completely covered with killed and wounded, while all those who attempted to climb up the rampart were instantly bayoneted by the French and thrown back on the crest.

Seeing that no progress was made, Sir Thomas Graham directed the batteries on the other side of the Urumea to fire over the heads of the British on the breach upon the French on the ramparts above. This was continued for half an hour, and it was evident that the defence was thus greatly weakened. Fresh troops were then filed out of the trenches to continue the assault, and the detachment of volunteers from the Light Division advanced, together with the 2nd brigade of the 5th division, and after some desperate fighting the former effected a lodgement in some buildings on the right of the great breach; but fortune did more for them than foresight, for soon after an explosion took place behind the rampart of the curtain, (the combustibles gathered there by the French to pour upon the heads of the assailants had accidentally caught fire,) and destroyed many of the defenders.

The French were evidently much discouraged by it; the men could with difficulty be kept to the defence, and the officers were seen beating them forwards with their swords. At length the efforts of the British were successful in forcing a way over the ramparts; and, driving the discouraged defenders before them, they succeeded in obtaining possession of the town at about three o'clock p.m., the remains of the French garrison having succeeded with much skill and courage in retiring into the castle.

While the main attack was being made on the greater breach, Major Kenneth Snodgrass of the 52nd, who then commanded the 13th Portuguese Regiment, had been conducting an assault on the lesser breach. He had gone down the night before at half-past ten o'clock, and ascertained (as he had previously suspected) that the River Urumea was fordable opposite to the lesser breach, the water reaching somewhat above his waist. Not content with having ascertained this, he clambered up the face of the breach at midnight, gained its summit, and looked down upon the town, contriving marvellously to elude the vigilance of the French sentinels. He applied for leave to lead an attack on the lesser breach, and was permitted to make the attempt with 300 men of his regiment, who volunteered for the service, and with whom he effected an entrance there, nearly at the same time that the principal assault proved successful.

A detachment, consisting of four sergeants, one bugler, and sixty-nine rank and file, under the command of Captain John Sneddon, arrived from England, and joined the first battalion at Vera on the 1st of September, 1813.

During the seven or eight weeks that the French occupied the heights above Vera, they were actively employed in constructing redoubts on the projecting points in advance of their line, and the position became very formidable.

On the evening of the 6th of October the plan of attack was communicated to the officers commanding companies; the redoubts were to be carried by repeated charges of the 52nd in close column, while the other two regiments of the brigade (the Rifle corps and the Portuguese Caçadores) were to act as *tirailleurs*; the irregularity of the hill where the charging column might find shelter to breathe between its attacks was distinctly pointed out to the officers. The men took a highly creditable interest in the success of the operations, and requested permission to leave their knapsacks behind them in the bivouac, and received orders accordingly.

At eight o'clock on the morning of the 7th of October the two brigades made a simultaneous attack; the right brigade, commanded by Major-General James Kempt, advanced by the Puerto to the right of the town of Vera; the left brigade, commanded by Lieut.-Colonel John Colborne, skirted the left: a deep rugged ravine which ran down between the ridges of the main range of mountains prevented all communication between the brigades, and each had to fight its way independently to the summit of the enemy's position. There were five redoubts surmounting each other on the part of the hill which the left brigade was to attack. The Rifle corps and *Caçadores* spread themselves across the brow of the hill to protect the formation of the 52nd column previous to its attack on the first redoubt. The difficult ascent compelled the men to scramble up singly, and whilst the column was forming up in this manner the enemy rushed out of the redoubt to charge it; five companies of the regiment had just completed their formation, and the sixth was in progress. The shock was parried without hesitation by a countercharge of these five companies, led by Lieut.-Colonel Colborne; the enemy gave way, and the redoubt was carried.

The assailants having now established a footing at the bottom of the range of hills, a few minutes were allowed for the men to breathe, after which the attack was prosecuted according to the original plan, and each redoubt was captured in succession. On arriving at the last, which formed the enemy's centre, an ineffectual resistance was made by the line of French troops there posted, which, however, soon fled, leaving three small pieces of artillery in the hands of the brigade; but not content with this extraordinary success, the pursuit was continued down the reverse of the hill, and twenty-two officers and nearly four hundred men surrendered themselves prisoners to a part of the regiment led on by Lieut.-Colonel Colborne. Thus, ended the most brilliant achievement that perhaps was ever performed by a regiment. The 52nd, in this action, was commanded by Brevet-Major Wm. Mein, who was severely wounded: he was promoted to the brevet rank of lieut.-colonel in the army on the 7th of October, 1813.

The affair of Vera may serve to show how much mutually depends upon good leaders and good troops. Colonel Colborne, during the short time that the camp of his brigade was in this neighbourhood, was constantly on horseback from morning till night, reconnoitring the country over which his brigade might have to act. Thus, when he led the troops into action, he knew the ground, and was enabled to take advantage of every inequality for cover from the enemy's fire, and of any other accidental irregularity that favoured his movement at the moment. He thus inspired the highest confidence in the mind of every officer and soldier whom he led, that whatever they might have to do would be done in the best manner and with the least possible exposure to loss.

On the evening before the attack on Vera, being desirous to examine a point within the enemy's lines which could not be seen from the English side of the valley, he took the adventurous step of going in with a flag of truce, and thus accomplished his object. The capture of a large number of prisoners of the *Neuvième Légère* (Napoleon's favourite regiment at Marengo), was due in great measure to Colonel Colborne's quick perception of the advantages of ground, as well as to his personal coolness and intrepidity; for Major-General Cole, commanding the 4th division in support of the attack, had sent word that he would not support the advance of the left brigade beyond the crest of the ridge; yet Colonel Colborne, seeing his advantage, kept the 52nd on the high spurs commanding the dips into which the French had run, and summoned them to surrender, where the headmost companies of the regiment, though a few yards behind, had in fact intercepted the retreat of the French, and Lieut. J. S. Cargill of the 52nd received on the spot the swords of fourteen of the French officers.

A writer in the *United Service Journal* remarks on the affair of Vera:—

> The attack was greatly facilitated by numerous skirmishers (95th Rifle corps and *Caçadores*) detached from the columns. These having gained the flanks and rear of the enemy, rendered by their fire the defence of the entrenchments difficult, as these were chiefly open to the rear, and so in proportion they aided the attack of the columns. The conduct of the Light Division, particularly Colonel Colborne's brigade, most obstinately resisted, was very praiseworthy. It ascended in the finest order in columns, and by deployment, as the nature of the ground would admit, it gained the formidable heights, carrying the entrenchments defended by the splendid division of Taupin, capturing three pieces of cannon, and causing a loss of nearly 900 chosen soldiers, including the officers in command of the 9th and 31st Light Infantry, and the 26th of the line, its own loss being not quite 400; a number, considering the strength of the position, almost incredible, and only to be accounted for by the skilful employment of numerous skirmishers; the nature of the ground, particularly on our right, favouring very much this system of movement.

The casualties of the 52nd in the capture of the heights of Vera on the 7th of October, were one sergeant and eleven rank and file killed.

The wounded were Brevet-Major William Mein, (severely,) Captains Patrick Campbell, (slightly,) John Graham Douglas, (severely,) John Sneddon, (slightly,) Lieutenant William Hunter, (severely,) Ensign Alexander John Frazer, (died on 19th October,) two sergeants, two buglers, and sixty-two rank and file.

The Marquis of Wellington, in his despatch, stated that:—

> Colonel Colborne of the 52nd Regiment, who commanded Major-General Skerrett's brigade in the absence of the major-general on account of his health, attacked the enemy's right in a camp which they had strongly entrenched; and the 52nd, under the command of Major Mein, charged in a most gallant style, and carried the entrenchment with the bayonet. The 1st and 3rd Caçadores and the second battalion 95th Regiment, as well as the 52nd, distinguished themselves in this attack.
>
> Major-General Kempt's brigade attacked by the Puerto, where the opposition was not so severe, and Major-General Charles Alten has reported his sense of the judgment displayed both by the major-general and by Colonel Colborne in these attacks; and I am particularly indebted to Major-General Charles Alten for the manner in which he executed this service. The Light Division took 22 officers and 400 men prisoners, and three pieces of cannon.
>
> These troops carried everything before them in a most gallant style till they arrived at the foot of the rock on which the hermitage stands, and they made repeated attempts to take even that part by storm; but it was impossible to get up, and the enemy remained during the night in possession of the hermitage.

On the 9th of October the regiments of the Light Division encamped to the right of the road leading through the pass of Vera, and in a few days afterwards the 52nd Regiment moved up to the heights of La Rhune, but nothing particular occurred until the 10th of November.

On the night of the 9th of November, the regiment, commanded by Brevet-Major Patrick Campbell, moved from its camp on La Rhune, and silently approached within 300 yards of the advanced point of the enemy's fortified heights of La Petite Rhune. The brigade was commanded by Lieutenant-Colonel Colborne.

A narrow ravine ran parallel to the head of the column, forming nearly a right angle with the enemy's line of defence on the left side of the hill.

The signal of attack was made at daybreak on the morning of the 10th, and two companies of the 52nd moved with great rapidity along the enemy's front without firing a shot, until they arrived at the redoubts on the right of this line; in the meantime, the right brigade having moved round the right of the hill, the enemy abandoned his redoubts after a slight resistance, and the Light Division formed on the summit of La Petite Rhune, waiting the appointed time to take its share in the future operations of the day. As soon as the enemy was driven out of the village of Sarre the whole army moved forward to attack his entrenched line.

The 2nd brigade of the Light Division advanced against a strongly fortified part of the enemy's position; the flanks of it were covered with impracticable ravines, and the position could be only approached in front over a very narrow low neck, exposed to the fire of two redoubts, and of trenches cut in the hill half-way down the slope. Seeing, however, that shelter could be obtained under a bank on the opposite side, the 52nd, headed by Lieut.-Colonel Colborne, crossed the ridge in single file, regardless of the fire from the defences. When collected under the bank the bugles sounded the advance; and the men ran up the slope with cheers, which had the effect of inducing the enemy to abandon his lines, and the redoubt which supported them.

In following up this success, the regiment advanced against a very strong irregular star fort, and under a heavy fire from its garrison formed columns of wings, and instantly charged up to the ditch; but the enemy's fire was too powerful, and a trifling inequality on the slope of the glacis afforded the men sufficient protection to keep up a fire against the garrison, and in a few minutes afterwards a second effort was made.

Upon a preconcerted signal, both wings cheered and rushed forward; some men of the leading companies leaped into the ditch, but their efforts were unavailing. The scarp being twelve feet high it was impossible to ascend it without ladders, and the regiment was withdrawn a short distance out of the enemy's fire, by the companies falling back in regular succession, commencing with the rear. The success of Marshal Sir William Beresford's operations, however, of whose corps the 3rd division was now pressing on successfully towards the bridge of Amotz, left no hope for the garrison to escape, and 560 men surrendered themselves prisoners, laying down their arms on the glacis. The details of this day's operations are thus related by an eyewitness,

(Lieutenant, later Colonel, G. Gawler of the 52nd):—

'The morning of the 9th November, 1813, found the different regiments of the Light Division in their usual positions at and in front of the pass of Vera; holding La Rhune to their right front with a strong detachment, and having their pickets at the very base of the ridge, in the plains of France, towards St. Jean de Luz and the country to the eastward of it.

'In the dusk of the evening the columns fell in, and moved by wild passes across the lower slopes of La Rhune to within two and a half miles of La Petite Rhune. Pickets were thrown out, (Captain William Rowan's company for the 52nd,) and the men laid themselves down in their blankets.

'A full hour before daybreak the 2nd brigade fell in, and advancing, formed a line of contiguous quarter-distance columns, just behind the summit of the last lateral ridge of the Great Rhune. Between it and the French fieldworks on La Petite Rhune there was only the enormous ravine, which, commencing at the little isthmus that connects the two Rhunes, runs for five or six hundred yards nearly perpendicular to the face of the Great Rhune, and then rounds off towards the north, and towards that part of the French position near Ascain.

'The sky was almost cloudlessly clear; the twilight rapidly brightened, and the mighty outlines of the mountains had become distinctly marked, when the flash and echoing report of a mountain three-pounder on the extreme point of La Rhune gave the signal to advance. The columns sprang from their concealment, and a few small French pickets, on the face of their mountain, commenced a dropping fire.

'The right brigade went directly at the French works by the isthmus and its western slopes. The second battalion of the 95th kept up the communication between it and the 52nd. The latter regiment hastened straight down the slope in its front, but as soon as it had crossed the rocky watercourse at the bottom, brought up its right shoulders, and pushed rapidly on, in a line nearly parallel to the watercourse on its left, and to the French works, about 500 yards off, on its right.

'The enemy, either in the darkness of the mountain shadows did not see, or perceiving, had not the presence of mind to attempt to check this bold flank movement of Colonel Colborne's own devising. The 52nd gained the line of the extreme flank of the French works, brought up its left shoulders, scrambled up the rocky slope, and stood in rear of the enemy's right, on the plateau of the Petite Rhune.

'At this point a scene of extraordinary magnificence burst upon the view. The sun was just springing in full glory above the horizon, and lighting up the boundless plains of the south of France. The Pyrenees stretched away to the eastward in an abrupt series of enormous sloping walls, and the long lines of white wreathing smoke near their bases, showed the simultaneous advance of the whole Allied Army.

'In the foreground, to the right, the 1st brigade of the Light Division had done its work, and was rapidly pouring over the entrenchments. The French defenders of the last of their Pyrenean summits were rushing into the huge, rough punch-bowl which is bounded by the eastern and western spurs of La Petite Rhune. A large portion of the Light Division, in pack-of-hounds order, followed down the slope for twelve hundred yards in pursuit, but our men were so thoroughly winded, and the fugitives, on their part, so fresh, that the results were insignificant. An officer and forty or fifty men who garrisoned their extreme right redoubt, actually crossed close along the front of the leading company of the 52nd (Captain William Rowan's) without any loss of consequence, so thorough was the exhaustion from the tough struggle up the very rugged mountain's side.

'The 52nd collected on the right rear of the now abandoned French redoubts of La Petite Rhune. The line of the French main position, commencing upon a comparatively low range of hills, was in front of the regiment, with an intervening rocky watercourse, which, it would seem, was deemed impassable by our enemies.

'The 52nd moved by threes to the small open ravine and wood in their front, under a smart fire of artillery from the ridge which was next to be assailed. In front of this wood the watercourse was crossed by a small and narrow stone bridge, on the opposite side of which was a road running close and parallel to the watercourse, with a sheltered bank towards the enemy.

'The officers and men of the 52nd crept by twos and threes to the edge of the wood, and then dashing over a hundred yards of open ground, passed the bridge, and formed behind the bank, which was not more than eighty yards from the enemy's entrenchments. The signal was then given, the rough line sprang up the bank, and the enemy gave way with so much precipitation as to abandon, almost without firing a shot, the works on the right of the advanced ridge, under, no doubt, the apprehension that their retreat would be cut off if they remained to defend them.

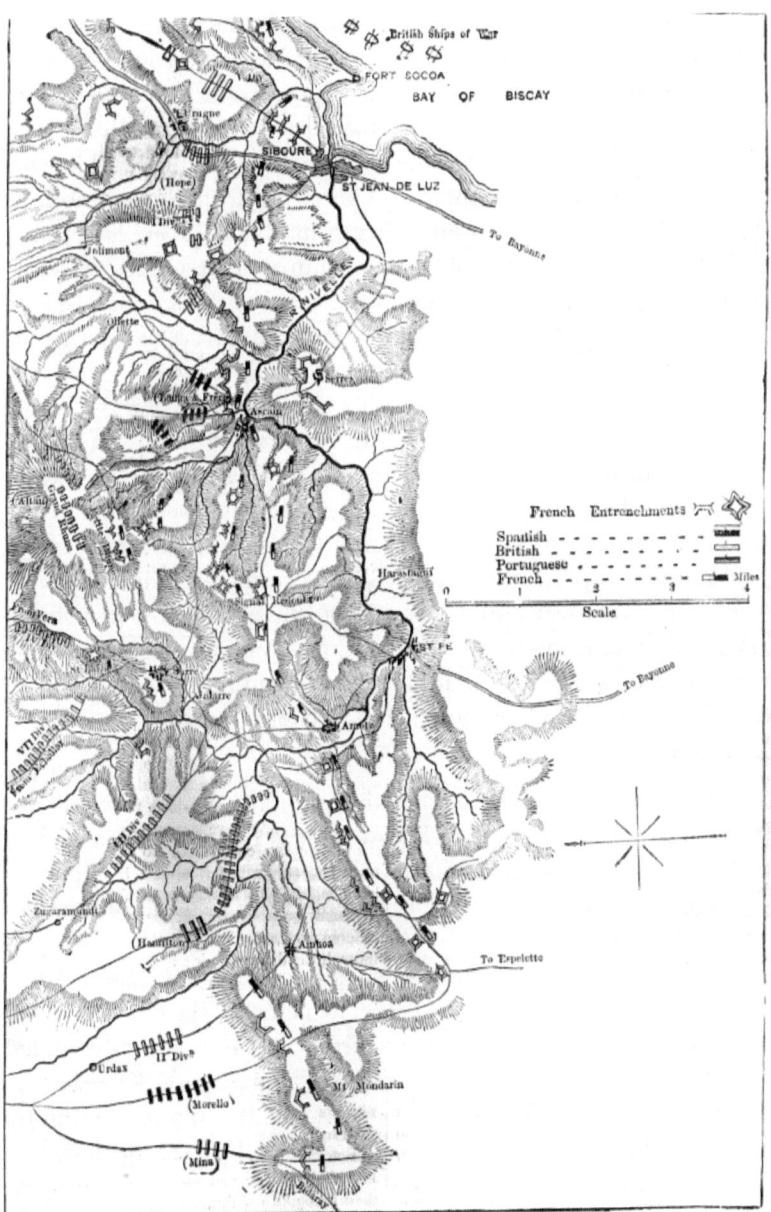

PLAN OF THE BATTLES OF THE NIVELLE.

'The 52nd soon paid dearly for this (with the exception of the passing of the bridge) easy victory.

'Full eight hundred yards beyond this advanced ridge was the main ridge of the enemy's position, and on its most prominent summit was a large and strong redoubt, garrisoned by a battalion of the French 88th Regiment, under its old and veteran *chef*. No supports appeared near it, and it was determined that the 52nd, single-handed, (which it had been from the time of leaving the position on La Petite Plume,) should make the assault. (This is said to have been done in consequence of a mistaken order. See Napier's *Battles and Sieges in the Peninsula*.) Moving off therefore in column at quarter-distance, left in front, the right wing took a long spur that led to the redoubt, and the left wing the next to it, which was so far to the left as to menace the enemy's rear.

'The calculation probably was, that the garrison, like those which had been attacked before, would retire rather than risk the occupation of its line of retreat. The veteran *chef-de-bataillon*, however, remained firm to his charge, and his men to their ramparts. The 52nd, moving up the long-exposed slopes in massive formations, suffered fearfully. The great strength of this main redoubt became evident, and that it was impossible to surmount its nine or ten feet walls if its defenders stood firm. Happily, for the honour of the old corps, there was between the two wings the head of a rounded ravine; into this they obliquely moved, and lay down within twenty yards of the edge of the ditch.'

"After taking breath for a little while, Colonel Colborne could not refrain from another attempt. The word was passed to stand up and move on, the leading ranks sprang into the ditch, but no mere human courage and activity could get further, and the mass steadily *stepped back* to its cover.

"At this moment an interesting episode occurred. Baron Alten, seeing from the lower ridge the desperate nature of the effort, endeavoured to send an order to prevent further attempts. It was confided to the Brigade-Major, Harry Smith. (The present—1866—Lieut.-General Sir H. G. W. Smith, Bart, and G.C.B.) Trusting to the shifting character of the mark of a horseman in motion, he tried the desperate venture; but it was impossible: no single living creature could reach the 52nd under the concentrated fire from the forts. The horse was soon brought down, and Captain Smith had to limit his triumph to the carrying off of his good and precious English Saddle, which he performed with his accustomed coolness, to the amusement of observing friends and enemies.

"The hairbreadth escape of another fine fellow deserves to be recorded. Sergeant Mayne, who had volunteered into the 52nd regiment from the Antrim militia, was among the foremost to spring into the ditch of the redoubt. Unable to climb the ramparts, when his comrades fell back, he threw himself on his face. A Frenchman rising on the parapet, reversed his musket and fired. Mayne had stuck the bill-hook of his section at the back of his knapsack. The tough iron flattened the ball, and, unhurt by the blow, he lived for many years to tell the remarkable tale.

"The precarious position of the 52nd was not of long duration. Colonel Colborne's coolness and ingenuity had not forsaken him. Making a bugler sound a parley, he hoisted his white pocket-handkerchief, and, rising, walked round to the gate of the redoubt. To his summons to surrender, the old chief replied indignantly, 'What! I, with my battalion, surrender to you with yours!'—'Very well,' said Colonel Colborne, in French, 'the artillery will be up immediately, you cannot hold out, and you will then be given over to the Spaniards' (some of whom were appearing in the distance). The word 'Spaniards' was all-powerful. Officers and men pressed round their commander till he gave his reluctant assent. In a few seconds the 52nd stood formed in a double line at the gate of the redoubt, to give to the fine old fellow his required satisfaction of marching out with the honours of war. A detachment of the 52nd, under Captain William Rowan, took them down the hill towards Sarre, and gave them over to the British cavalry.'

"After a little manoeuvring in advance of the captured redoubt, the 2nd brigade of the Light Division took up its bivouac for the night about a mile and a half to the left front, or rather to the original rear of this redoubt, 'where,' says the historian of the Peninsular war, 'there fell two hundred soldiers of a regiment never surpassed in arms since arms were first borne by men.'

"On the 10th of November the regiment had two sergeants and thirty rank and file killed. The wounded were, Captain William Rentall, (severely,) Lieutenants Charles Yorke, (slightly,) George Ulrick Barlow, (severely,) Matthew Anderson, (severely,) Charles Kenny and Matthew Agnew, (both slightly;) seven sergeants, three buglers, and one hundred and ninety-two rank and file.

"The Marquis of Wellington again bore testimony to the gallantry of the Light Division, in the following terms:—

> I have also omitted to draw Your Lordship's attention in the manner it deserved, to the conduct of the Light Division, under the command of Major-General Charles Baron Alten.

> "*These troops distinguished themselves in this as they have upon every occasion in which they have been engaged.*

> Major-General Kempt was wounded at the head of his brigade, at the beginning, in the attack of the enemy's work on La Petite Rhune, but continued in the field, and I had every reason to be satisfied with his conduct as well as with that of Colonel Colborne of the 52nd Regiment, who commanded Major-General Skerrett's brigade in his absence.

> "Another distinction was gained by the regiment, the word 'Nivelle' being conferred on the corps for its distinguished conduct on this occasion.

> "After the action of the 10th of November, the regiment halted for the night near St. Pé, and next day encamped near Arbonne, and on the 19th went into quarters in the village. The enemy made a reconnaissance on the 20th, and in this affair of pickets the 52nd had three rank and file wounded.

> "Brevet Lieut.-Colonel John Philip Hunt was promoted to Lieut.-Colonel in the 60th Regiment on the 11th of November, 1813, and on the same day Brevet Lieut.-Colonel William Mein was appointed Major in the 52nd Regiment.

> "A defensive line of posts being appointed for the different divisions of the army stretching from the sea to Arcangues, the Light Division changed its quarters on the 24th, and the 52nd occupied the *château* of Castleneur and some farmhouses in the neighbourhood of Arcangues.

> "On the 9th of December, Lieut.-General the Hon. Sir John Hope's corps reconnoitred Bayonne closely, and the Light Division drove in the enemy's outposts in front of Arcangues, in order to make a diversion in favour of Lieut.-General Sir Rowland Hill's corps, which passed the Nive at Cambo on this day, and took up a position with its right upon the Adour and its left at Ville Franche.

> "Early on the morning of the 10th of December, the Light Division pickets at Arcangues were very vigorously attacked, and the enemy's columns pressed on so rapidly on the flanks that the pickets

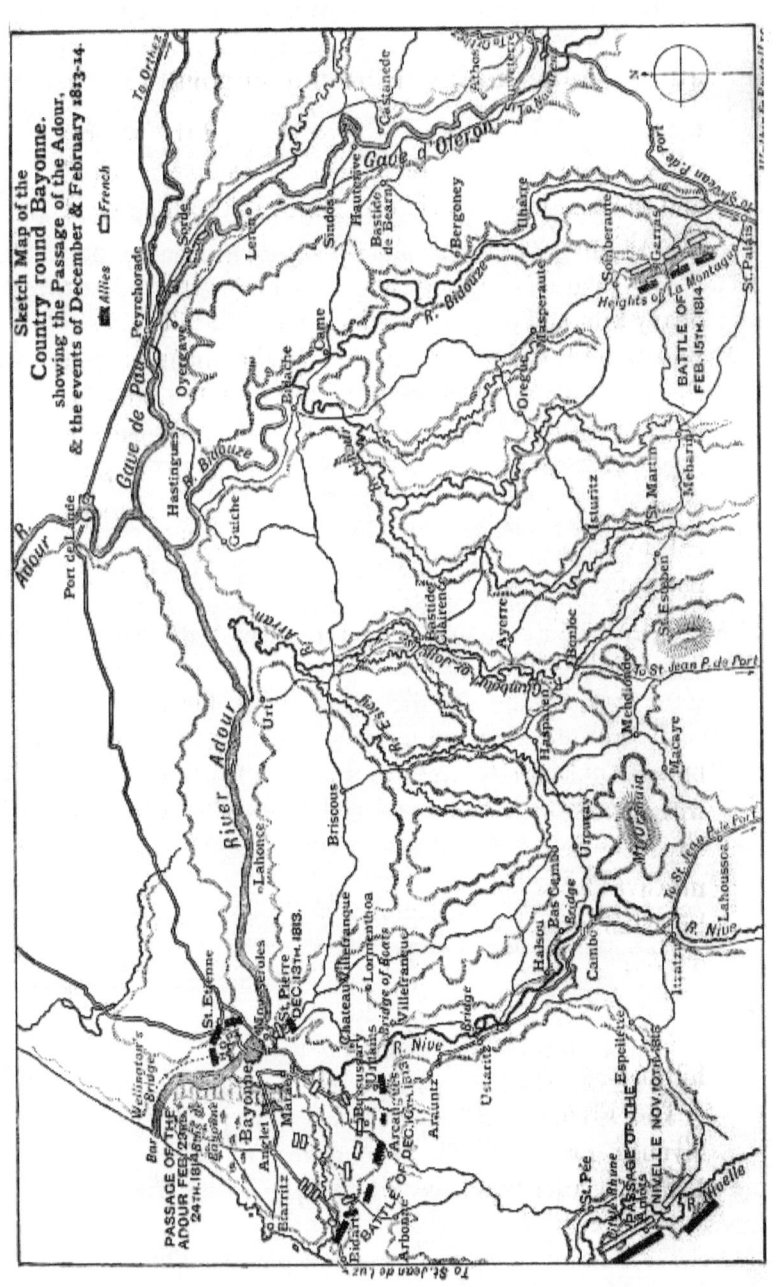

had no opportunity of making a serious stand until they arrived at the Abattis near the *château* of Castleneur, behind which Captain John Graham Douglas formed up his company and made a very gallant resistance against the enemy's overwhelming force. Unfortunately, he received a musket-shot in the head, of which he died a few days afterwards, much regretted by the regiment; his subaltern, Ensign Frederick Radford, and Major Mein (who was field officer of the pickets) were also wounded in this affair.

"As soon as the pickets were driven back, the enemy occupied the range of hills at Castleneur, and the Light Division was posted on a parallel ridge in their front, having converted a farm-house, which stood in the centre of the position, into a post of defence. Skirmishing was continued throughout the day, and in the evening the enemy's columns got under arms and made a demonstration of attack, which was not pressed beyond the picket-houses, in the small valley which separated the positions of the two armies.

"On both the 10th and 11th the efforts of the enemy were directed against Lieut.-General the Hon. Sir John Hope's corps, which formed the left of the British line on the road to St. Jean de Luz; and having failed in his attempts against this part of the position, on the 13th he attacked Sir Rowland Hill on the right of the Nive, with no better success.

"At the passage of the Nive the brigade was commanded by Lieut.-Colonel Colborne, and the regiment was commanded by Brevet-Major Patrick Campbell, who received the gold medal for this occasion. The casualties were four rank and file killed, six officers, two sergeants, one bugler, and twelve rank and file wounded; and four men missing.

"The officers wounded were:—

"Major and Brevet Lieut.-Colonel William Mein, severely.

"Captain John Graham Douglas, *ditto*, died.

"Brevet-Major Kenneth Snodgrass, (attached to Portuguese service,) slightly.

"Captain William Henry Temple, slightly.

"Lieutenant Lord Charles Spencer, (on the staff,) severely.

"Ensign Frederick Radford, severely.

"On the night of the 12th two battalions of Nassau troops came over to the allies, and were received by the pickets of the Light Division.

"The enemy having retired towards Bayonne, on the morning of the 13th, the Light Division went into cantonments on the 14th, and the 52nd returned to nearly the same quarters that it occupied previous to the attack on the 10th of December.

"On the 4th of January the 1st battalion marched to Anainz, on the 5th to Ustaritz, and went into cantonments at Sala on the 8th of that month.

"The 1st battalion broke up from its cantonments at Sala on the 16th of February, and marched by Mobzao, La Bastide, St. Martin, St. Palais, and Etcharry, arriving near Orion on the 24th.

"On the 25th of February, the Light Division arrived close to Orthes, and halted upon the heights above the bridge. As soon as a close examination of the loop-holed houses which defended its passage was effected, the division retired into the low ground and encamped for the night. On the 26th the division moved to its right, with the intention of passing the river at a ford above the town, but in the course of the evening the column countermarched, and halted for the night near the village of Berenx. Early on the morning of the 27th the regiment, commanded by Lieut.-Colonel Colborne, moved from its bivouac to the left, in order to strengthen the British left with the Light Division, and crossed the Gave de Pau by a pontoon bridge, which was laid over the river a little below the village.

"The left of the French position rested upon Orthes, and from thence the line was continued along a range of hills in the direction of Dax; the right terminated on a commanding height behind the village of St. Boes.

"In the early morning the French left was threatened by Hill's corps, which subsequently crossed the river above Orthes, and advanced sufficiently to endanger the retreat of the French being cut off in the afterpart of the day, when the British left had eventually succeeded in driving the French from their formidable positions on the ridges of St. Boes.

"The 4th and 7th divisions attacked the enemy's right, the 3rd and 6th divisions attacked the centre of the French position, and the left brigade of the Light Division (in which was the 52nd) was in reserve, on a spur of the main ridge of St. Boes, partially covered by the old Roman camp. The right brigade, comprising the 1st battalion of the 95th Rifles and the 43rd Regiment, were some miles in the rear, near St. Jean de Luz, receiving their clothing.

"In consequence of the difficult approach to the enemy's right, and the narrowness of the ridge on which alone the leading brigade could deploy, the attack did not succeed at that point, and Cole's lead-

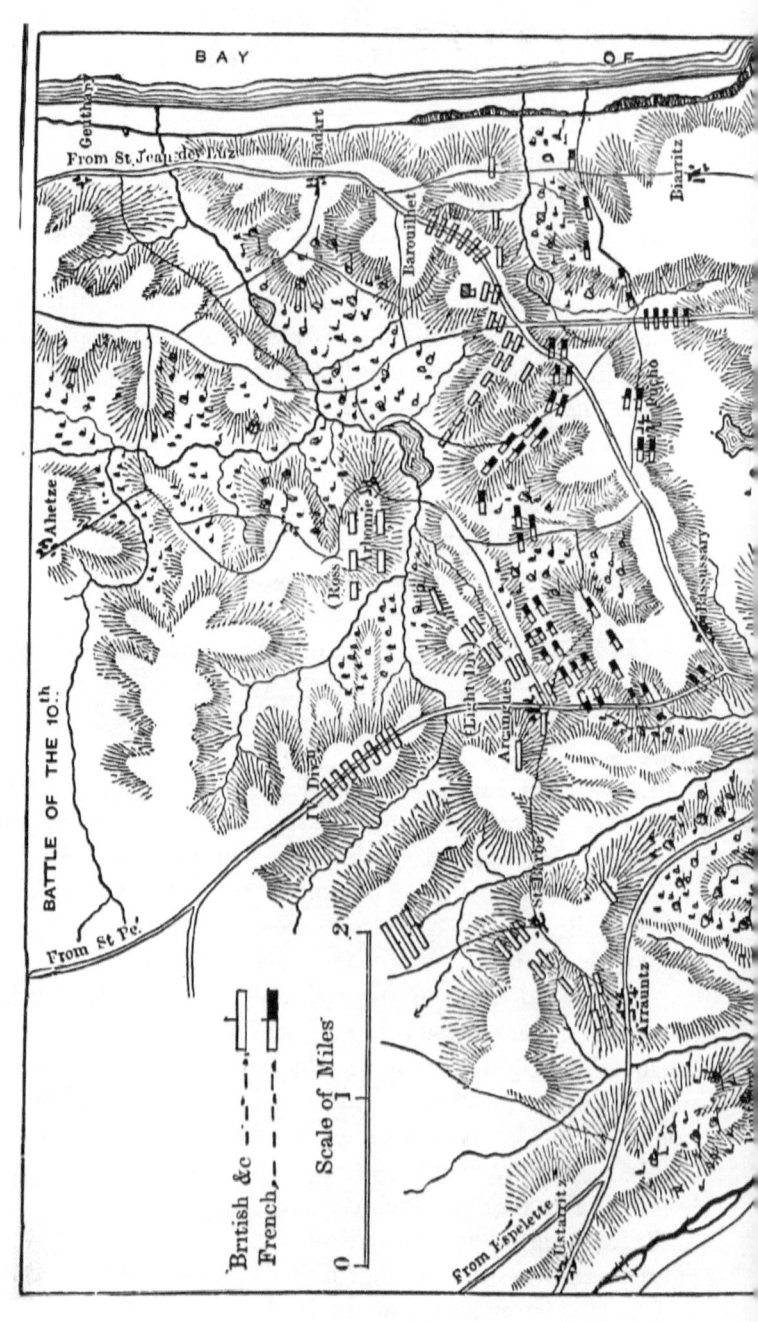

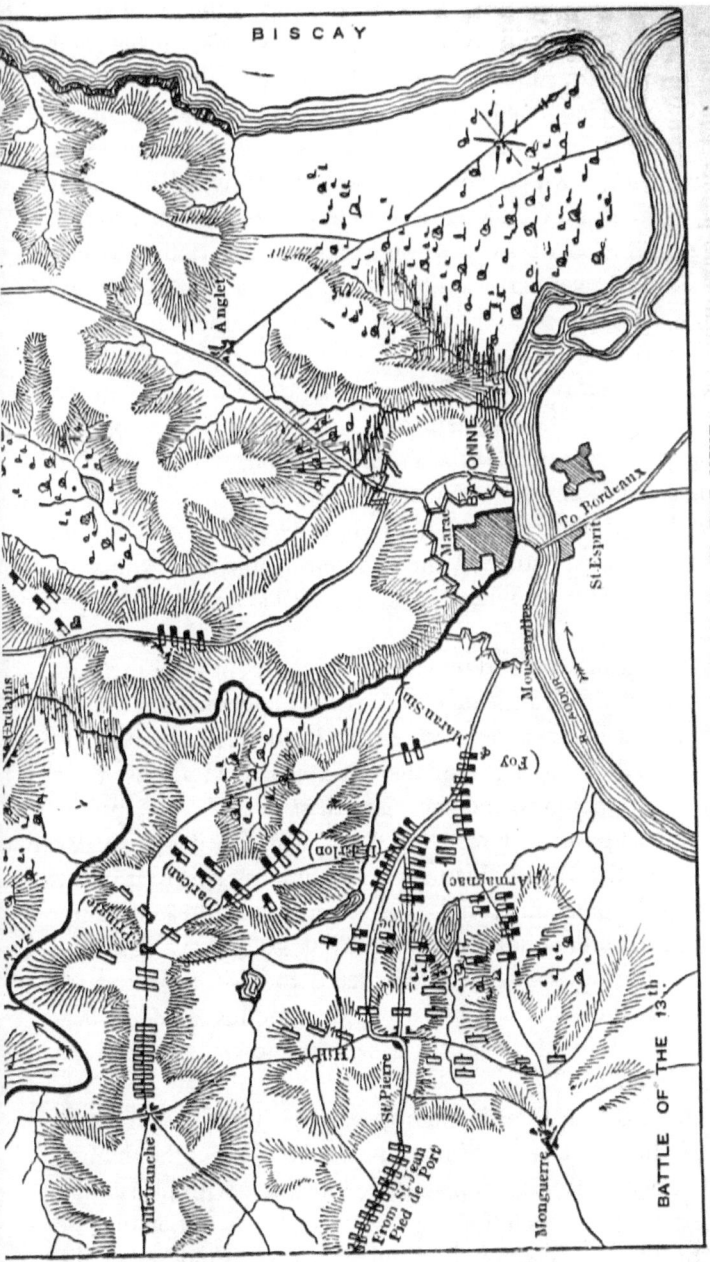

PLAN OF THE BATTLES ON THE NIVE.

ing regiments, after partially gaining the village of St. Boes, were again driven back and cut up by French artillery on their left flank. Neither was the centre making any progress, and a portion of the 3rd division had been repulsed down the hill, when the left brigade of the Light Division was ordered to attack the left flank of the heights which the enemy's right occupied. The Rifle corps (2nd battalion and part of the 3rd battalion) remained on the knoll in support; the Portuguese Caçadores had been thrown out to the left and were driven back, when the 52nd Regiment moved along in column of threes to the front.

"The retrogression of the divisions, both on the right and left, placed the 52nd in a very critical situation, and the importance of the movement was known to every individual. The regiment moved up the road to St. Boes from the Roman camp till it arrived close to the ridge on which Major-General Cole was anxiously looking out for support. At this point the regiment deployed to the right across the low and marshy ground under the French position, and advanced in line, wading steadily through the marsh, and accelerating the pace as it approached the hill occupied by the right of General Foy's division. As soon as the crest was attained, the regiment halted and opened its fire on the force opposite, which at once gave way and retired with all its guns.

"Lord Wellington, who had directed the movement from the Roman camp, instantly sent a message to Colonel Colborne, not on any account to advance further, and to remain in line, and quickly the divisions on the left and right of the 52nd advanced against their now disordered opponents, and the 52nd then occupied the prominent part of the position which had been abandoned by Foy. By these movements five British divisions were united against four of the French. Hill, at the same time, on the British right, was threatening the left and rear of the French, and Marshal Soult skilfully showing a front on each ridge of ground that favoured a stand, to cover the retreat of his now disordered divisions, eventually made good his retreat by Sallespice, across the River Luy de Bearn, with the loss of six guns and four thousand men.

"This retreat of the French might have been more disastrous to them had not the Marquis of Wellington received a ball in the thigh at the latter part of the day, which materially interfered with his riding.

"To illustrate how much 'fortune' has to do with war, it may be remarked, that the marsh which the 52nd crossed was supposed by the French to be impassable for troops. The peasants said there were rarely

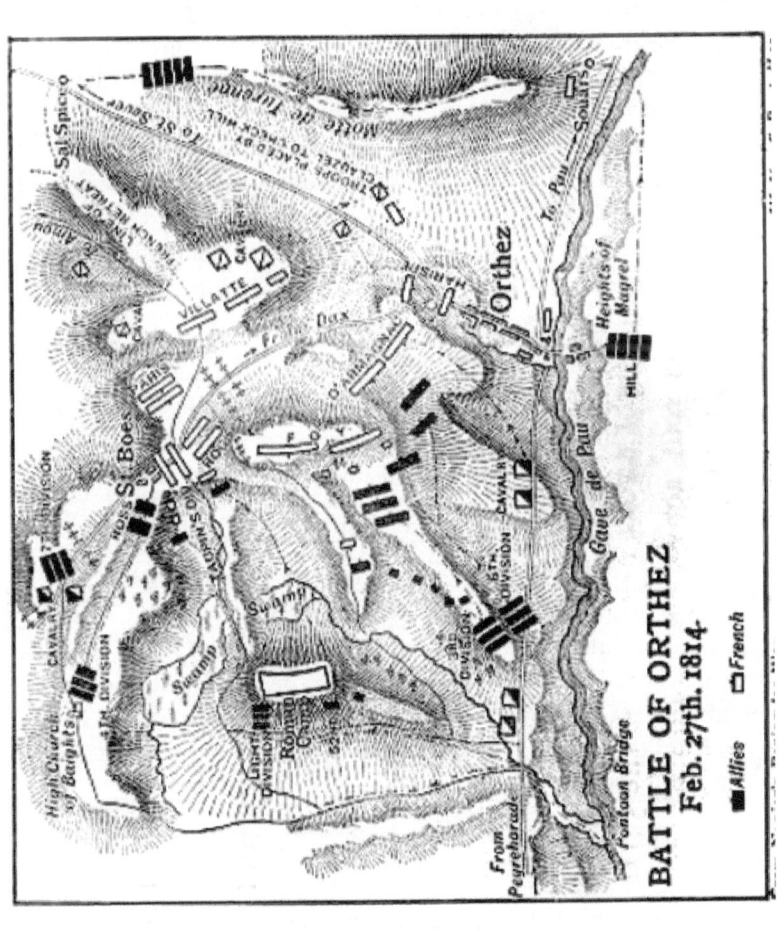

twenty days in the year in which it could be crossed by individuals. The mounted officers of the battalion were obliged to ride round by the flanks, and Lord Fitzroy Somerset, who brought orders to the regiment, on trying to force his way through it was bogged, and thrown from his horse.

"The Earl of March, (the late Duke of Richmond, K.G.), who was on the headquarter staff, had been promoted to a company in the 2nd battalion of the 52nd, then at home. He requested to be allowed to join the 1st battalion, and was in command of the leading company in the advance from the Roman fort, and on reaching the crest of the hill, was struck in the chest by a musket-ball, which was never extracted.

"The following passage from the Marquis of Wellington's despatch bears the highest testimony to the 52nd having mainly contributed to the success of the day.

St. Sever, 1st March, 1814.

Major-General Baron Charles Alten, with the Light Division kept the communication and was in reserve between these two attacks. (*i.e.* of the 4th and 7th divisions on the left, and the 3rd and 6th divisions on the right of the reserve.)] I moved forward Colonel Barnard's brigade of the Light Division to attack the left of the heights on which the enemy's right stood. This attack, led by the 52nd Regiment under Lieut.-Colonel Colborne, and supported on the right by Major-General Brisbane's and Colonel Keane's brigade of the 3rd division, and by simultaneous attacks on the left by Major-General Anson's brigade of the 4th division, dislodged the enemy from the height and gave us the victory.

"Captain Brialmont, of the Belgian Army, in his *Life of Wellington*, says:—

The Battle of Orthes appeared lost, when Wellington changed his plan of attack and directed Picton's two divisions and a brigade of the Light Division against the left of the height which was held by Reille's Rifle corps. This vigorous effort produced an unexpected result, and was particularly creditable to the 52nd Regiment, which received orders to take in flank and rear the troops which were pushing back the column from St. Boes. That gallant regiment crossed a marsh, under the fire of the enemy, and threw itself with such violence upon Foy's and

Taupie's divisions that it compelled them to retire.

"In this battle the 52nd had seven rank and file killed, and seven officers, two sergeants, one bugler, and seventy-six rank and file wounded. The names of the officers were:—

Brevet-Major Patrick Campbell, slightly.
Brevet-Major Kenneth Snodgrass, (attached to Portuguese service,) severely.
Captain Charles Earl of March, severely.
Captain Charles York, severely.
Lieutenant James Price Halford, slightly.
Lieutenant William Richmond Nixon, severely.
Lieutenant John Leaf, severely.

"The regiment halted at Bonnegarde, after the Battle of Orthes, on the 27th of February, and marched next day to near Montant. On the 1st of March the regiment arrived at Mont de Marson, and marched the following day in the direction of St. Maurice, where it arrived on the 3rd, and went into cantonments at Barcelone on the 9th of the same month.

"The regiment marched to Plaisance on the 19th, to Haget on the 20th, and on that day attacked the enemy near Tarbes. In this affair Lieutenants Charles Kenny and G. H. Love were wounded. Two rank and file were wounded.

"During the night of the 21st, the French Army retired upon Toulouse, and on the 22nd the regiment marched to Lannemezan, pursuing its route by Ganon, Agacen, Sieverer, Plaisance, Cregneaux, and arrived at St. Simon and Portel on the 29th. The division moved to Selle on the 4th of April.

"On the morning of the 10th of April, the Light Division crossed the Garonne by a pontoon bridge near the village of Ausonne, and the whole army moved forward to the attack. The Light Division approached Toulouse by the Montauban road, and subserviently moved to its left to the support of Lieut.-General Don Manuel Freyere's Spanish corps, which were destined to attack the heights of La Pugade.

"The Spaniards, having failed in their attack, fell back in the greatest disorder, abandoning the bridge of Croix d'Aurade, but by a forward movement of the 2nd brigade of the Light Division, under Colonel Barnard, the French were checked in their pursuit, and the communication over the River Ers was preserved.

"In the course of the afternoon the divisions of Lieut.-Generals

Sir Lowry Cole and Sir Henry Clinton attacked the redoubts of La Pugade, on the Calvinet side, whilst the 52nd and 95th advanced on the opposite side; after a very determined resistance, the enemy abandoned all his works about five o'clock in the evening, and the allied army formed upon the heights overlooking the town.

"The French Army retired from Toulouse during the night of the 12th, and the 52nd pickets entered the suburbs of the town at daylight on the morning of the 13th of April; in the course of this day couriers arrived at Toulouse, announcing the decree of the French Senate of the 2nd of April, and on the 18th a convention was agreed upon for the suspension of hostilities between the Marquis of Wellington and Marshal Soult.

"The line of demarcation having been arranged, the 52nd went into cantonments at Castel Sarrasin on the 22nd, and remained there until arrangements were made for evacuating the south of France. On the 3rd of June the regiment marched from Castel Sarrasin and proceeded to Bordeaux. Whilst on the route thither, the two regiments of Portuguese Caçadores (1st and 3rd) which had formed a part of the Light Division for nearly four years, took their departure at Bargas to recross the Pyrenees, and return to their native country.

"The regiment arrived at Bordeaux on the 14th of June, and was reviewed by Field-Marshal the Duke of Wellington on taking leave of the army previous to its return to England. On the 17th of June, the 52nd embarked at Panillac on board His Majesty's ship *Dublin*, and landed at Plymouth on the 28th. Thus terminated the Peninsular war service of the 52nd, during which, as Napier relates:—

> The army containing those veterans had won nineteen pitched battles and innumerable combats; had made or sustained ten sieges, and taken four great fortresses; had twice expelled the French from Portugal, and once from Spain; had penetrated France, and killed, wounded, or captured two hundred thousand enemies, leaving of their own number forty thousand, whose bones whiten the plains and mountains of the Peninsula.

"But we may add, whose memory is revered by all in Britain who love to hear or to read of noble deeds, and whose example has left in their regiments an emulation and a spirit to strive after that which is noble as well as daring, which will never be extinguished in the 52nd.

"It was not till the year 1821, that the following letter was received by the regiment."—

Horse Guards, 1st of March, 1821.

Sir,

I have the honour to acquaint you, by direction of the Commander-in-Chief, that His Majesty has been pleased to approve of the 52nd Regiment being permitted to bear on its colours and appointments, in addition to any other badges or devices which may have hitherto been granted to the regiment, the words—

Hindoostan.	Nive.	Ciudad Rodrigo.
Corunna.	Toulouse.	Salamanca.
Fuentes d'Onor.	Vimiera.	Nivelle.
Badajos.	Busaco.	Orthes.
Vittoria.		

In commemoration of the distinguished services of the regiment in the several actions in which it was engaged in India, from September 1790 to September 1793; and in the Battle of Vimiera, on the 21st of August, 1808; at Corunna, 16th of January, 1809; at Busaco, on the 27th of September, 1810; at Fuentes d'Onor, on the 5th of May, 1811; at Ciudad Rodrigo, in the month of January, 1812; at the siege of Badajos, on the 16th of March, 1812; at the Battle of Salamanca, on the 22nd of July, 1812; at Vittoria, on the 21st of June, 1813; in the passage of the Nivelle, on the 10th of November, 1813; in the passage of the Nive, on the 9th, 10th, and 13th of December, 1813; at Orthes, on the 27th of February, 1814; and in the attack of the position covering Toulouse, on the 10th of April, 1814

    I have the honour,

    etc., etc., etc.,

    (Signed)   Henry Torrens, A.-General.

Officer commanding 52nd Regiment.

The words Pyrenees, Peninsula, Waterloo, and Delhi, are also borne on the colours and appointments of the 52nd.

CHAPTER 6

1815: 52nd Light Infantry at Waterloo 1

It was intended that I should have been a sailor, in which profession my two elder brothers were, but my eldest brother having been killed in action in 1810, (see Appendix No. 1) my mother no longer thought of that career for me, and it was never mentioned to me; she then intended me for the church, but to this arrangement I had a great repugnance, as I considered myself altogether unfit to be a clergyman; then the law was very seriously thought of, and I turned my attention to it for some months after leaving school at the age of sixteen; but all intentions in that direction were completely upset by my meeting at a ball a young officer of the 51st Light Infantry, who had just returned from Spain, and to whose account of his adventures I listened with the greatest avidity for two or three hours, and then immediately determined that I would go into the army.

Our friend and relative, Sir John Colborne, afterwards Lord Seaton, then in command of the 52nd, was written to; but before any course could be recommended, the Peninsular War came to an end. He, sometime after, advised that I should go to a military institution, at which Captain Malortie de Martemont received a few young men who were preparing for the army. Captain Malortie was a French royalist, and professor of fortification at the Woolwich Academy. I was there for several months, and made some little progress in fortification and military plan drawing, &c.

In the early part of 1815, Sir Theophilus and Lady Pritzler and their family were staying with my mother, preparatory to their embarking for India; they were relatives of ours, and he commanded the 22nd Light Dragoons. On hearing of my plans, they proposed that I should purchase a vacant cornetcy in the 22nd, and follow them to India. Arrangements were made accordingly at the Horse Guards, and

SIR JOHN COLBORNE

LATER AS FIELD-MARSHAL LORD SEATON, G.C.B.

I was written to, and a little time was allowed for my decision. It had, however, been before arranged with Sir John Colborne that, if the American war continued, I should proceed with the 52nd to America.

Just at the time that the cornetcy in the 22nd Dragoons was mentioned to me, we were daily expecting to receive the account of the ratification of peace with America, so that, although I was much pleased with the arrangement about India, I felt that I had better not take the decided step about going there, until there was an end of all hope of seeing active service on the other side of the Atlantic. In a short time, the news of the ratification of peace with America appeared in a second edition of the papers; and, in the very same papers, was a third edition, announcing the landing of Bonaparte in the south of France from Elba, on the 1st of March.

If the intelligence of Bonaparte's return to France had reached me four-and-twenty hours later, all my steps forgetting my cornetcy and for proceeding to India would have been taken, and probably mine would have been an Indian life for many years. As it was, I determined on doing nothing until I saw what success Bonaparte's enterprise met with. I knew that, if it succeeded, the 1st battalion of the 52nd, already embarked at Cork, would most probably be ordered with other troops to reinforce the 10,000 men we already had in Flanders under the Prince of Orange.

When we heard of Bonaparte's arrival at Paris on the 20th of March, I immediately wrote to Sir John Colborne, who was military secretary to the Prince of Orange, to beg of him to let me know what I had better do under the circumstances. Several weeks passed away, and I received no reply to my letter, and I hardly knew what to think of Sir John Colborne's silence, when, towards the end of April, a letter arrived from him, but it was directed to my mother, who opened it with considerable anxiety, and then produced the one which had been sent in answer to my first letter some weeks before.

My poor mother had felt justified, considering my youth, (I was rather more than seventeen,) in opening and keeping back from me my own letter, until she should again communicate with Sir John Colborne on the subject. His reply was, that he could not give any other advice than that which he had already given in his letter to me. The advice he had given, which so alarmed my mother, and which he still gave, was that I should at once lodge my money for an ensigncy in the 52nd, and come out immediately and join the 1st battalion as a volunteer.

The day after the arrival of Sir John Colborne's letter, on Friday, the 28th of April, I left home for London. I am writing this more than fifty years after that first step in my military career, and so rapidly has the time passed away, that it seems to be only a few years since my dear mother, when the carriage was at the door, to convey me to the place where I should meet the coach for London, pressed me to her, and begged me with many tears not to go, saying, it was not necessary that I should run into such danger, or that I should go into any profession whatever.

I felt this parting very much, but of course it was impossible for me to yield to her wish, dearly as I loved her. The kind relatives, at whose house I was during the few days that I remained in London, had secured for me the assistance of a colonel in the Guards, who kindly devoted to me many hours on the day after my arrival, and went with me to the several tradesmen to order my outfit. During my short stay in town I saw Mrs. and Miss Moore, the mother and sister of General Sir John Moore, who fell at Corunna, and who had been so much respected and beloved by the 52nd. At the house of my aunt, I met with the widow of my cousin, Captain Bogue, who had fallen at the Battle of Leipsic about eighteen months before, in command of the British Rocket Brigade (see Appendix No. 2.) I recollect she regarded me and my enthusiasm about the 52nd, and my commencing career, with much kind and melancholy interest.

On Tuesday, May 2nd, I left London for Dover by the evening coach, with all my outfit, as a 52nd officer, complete. I was to embark for Ostend on the evening of the 3rd, and did not know very well what to do with myself during the day. The 2nd battalion of the 52nd was stationed at Dover, and, under my circumstances, I was not anxious to fall in with any of the officers, having some undefinable fear that something might turn up to prevent my getting out at once to the 1st battalion. However, I only came across one solitary bugler of the regiment the whole day. I was in a military great coat, with 52nd cap and sword.

After seeing what there was to be seen, I strolled into a billiard room, where I found several officers of the old 95th, (now the Rifle Brigade); they were very civil and kind, and I played with them for some hours. I was rather a good player at billiards, and consequently won almost every game we played; and, although we played for small sums, I was ashamed to find, when it was nearly time for me to embark, that I was a winner of between four and five pounds.

I had hardly time for another game, but still I arranged to play one, and contrived, by offering odds, to have quite as much at stake as I had won altogether, with the full intention of losing the game. When I had got about half way through it, and was rather behind-hand in my score, I told them I feared I should be too late for the packet, and that, as I was sure to lose the game, I would pay my losses and not play it out. My 95th friends, however, I think rather suspecting what I was aiming at, begged me to finish it, which I did to save appearances, and to prevent them from refusing to take the money I had won from them. I soon managed, by making two or three bad hits, to lose the game, and, putting down my money, I hastened off, and was just in time not to lose my passage.

I left Dover for Ostend on the evening of the 3rd of May. I recollect little more of the voyage than that I was dreadfully seasick—so much so, that it was a great trouble to me to think that I could not reach England again without passing through the same fearful ordeal. We had rather a head wind and a short chopping sea; and the first time we tacked and were in stays, when I was half asleep in my berth in the middle of the night, I, who had never been at sea before, fancied, for a few seconds, that the ship had met with some disaster and was settling down and sinking. I well remember that the first thought was. Oh, then, I shall get rid of this horrid sea-sickness!

I arrived at Ostend in the forenoon of Thursday, the 4th of May, which, as I afterwards found, was the date of my commission as ensign in the 52nd. As I landed on the quay, they were unloading cannon-balls from an arsenal transport, pitching them up as bricklayers do bricks; I thought it looked very warlike. At Ostend I found Lieutenant Cottingham, and four men just come out of hospital, who were going up in four days from that, to join the regiment at Lessines; I arranged to wait and go with them. The only thing I recollect doing at Ostend was the buying a baggage-horse; I took a fancy to him from his very superior powers in leaping over the very broad gutters across the street, which were filled with water by the pouring rain.

I went part of the way to Ghent in the canal-boat; my only fellow-passenger was Major-General Sir James Kempt, who was going up to the army to take the command of a brigade in Picton's division. He was very kind to me: when, after some hours' abstinence, we began to feel hungry I volunteered to go and see what was the state of the larder, and came back with the report that there was literally nothing to eat on board, the general produced two gingerbread nuts from a paper, and gave me one of them. Even little kindnesses of that sort are often remembered for years afterwards.

The having fallen in with Cottingham made my march up from Ghent very agreeable, and also took off from the awkwardness attending my first introduction to the officers of the regiment. We reached Lessines on the 11th of May, exactly five weeks and three days before the Battle of Waterloo. When we arrived, the regiment had marched out some miles, and we only found a Sergeant's guard at the entrance of the town. Soon, however, we heard the martial notes of the bugles, and I had the great delight of seeing a regiment of upwards of 1,000 men, whom I looked upon as the finest soldiers in the world, come winding down the road amongst the corn, marching to the sound of one of those stirring tunes, which one always connected with feats of arms and deeds of daring.

When the regiment was dismissed, many of the officers gathered round Cottingham and me, and he talked away with them for three or four minutes, quite forgetting that he was leaving me in a somewhat awkward position, as I was unknown to any of them, till at last one of them said, "Cottingham, will you not introduce your friend to us?" when, they of course, received me very kindly. That afternoon I was put in orders, as Volunteer Leeke, and attached to Captain McNair's company.

During the Peninsular War, and how long before I know not, it was very occasionally permitted to young men, who had difficulty in getting a commission, with the consent of the commanding officer, to join some regiment on service before the enemy. In action the volunteer acted as a private soldier, carrying his musket and wearing his cross belts like any other man. After a campaign or two, or after having distinguished himself at the storming of some fort or fortress, he would probably obtain a commission. He messed with the officers of the company to which he was attached. His dress was the same as that of an officer, except that, instead of wings or epaulettes, he wore shoulder straps of silver or gold, to confine the cross belts.

My case was somewhat different; my money was lodged for the purchase of my commission, and it was known that only a short time would elapse before I was gazetted, and that I had come out as a volunteer to avoid being sent to the 2nd battalion in England, with which I should have had to remain for at least six mouths. In fact, the notification of my having been gazetted as an ensign in the regiment appeared in orders about ten days after I joined. Under the circumstances Colonel Charles Rowan desired me not to have the wings removed from my jacket. I was an anomalous sort of personage; and I recollect at first some of the men saluted me, and others did not, when they passed me in the streets.

Two or three days after I arrived, Sir John Colborne joined from Brussels, and took the command of the regiment. I had only seen him once before, and stood in considerable awe of him, though I was thoroughly convinced that he had the kindest feeling towards me. He was a sort of nephew of my mother's, her brother having married his mother. He told me, I remember, that he thought, from Sir James Kempt's description of the person he had met in the canal-boat, that I had arrived out. He recommended me to purchase a riding-horse in addition to the one I had for my baggage; I told him I had been intending to try and do without a horse, until after the first action, in which, no doubt, many officers would be killed, and then a horse would be purchased at a cheap rate; he smiled, I suppose at my warlike and sanguinary ideas, and merely said, "You had better get a horse at once." This I did, and purchased a black horse with a long tail, very much like those used by the Life Guards and Blues; he was consequently called in the regiment "the Life Guardsman."

Sir John Colborne always strongly advocated the importance of infantry officers, when on active service, having riding-horses, and used to say, that if, from insufficiency of income, they found it difficult to manage this, still they should stint themselves in wine, and in everything else, in order to keep a horse if possible. As mounted officers they were more useful, under very many circumstances; they were less tired at the end of a day's march, and more ready for any duty which might be required of them; they could be more effective in bringing up stragglers on a long and weary march; some of them might be usefully employed when extra staff officers were required. I think, on the long march of upwards of fifty miles, which we had from Quevres-au-camps to Waterloo, all but two of the officers of the 52nd were mounted.

During the five weeks between my joining at Lessines and our start for Waterloo, I went through some portion of my drill, which, soon after our arrival at Paris, was completed in the Champs Elysées.

At Lessines, on one occasion when the regiment was at ball-practice not far from the bank of the Dender, and were firing volleys by companies at targets set close to a very thick wood, we were all astonished and horrified, and our firing put a stop to, by the appearance, round the side of the wood, of a man and woman with uplifted arms and horror-stricken countenances, No one had the least idea that there was any habitation in the wood; but it turned out that these poor people occupied a cottage somewhere within it. No wonder that they were alarmed, for, before they could get round the skirts of the wood, several volleys had been fired into it by the ten companies, each consisting of about one hundred men.

There were fully sixty officers with the regiment at that time. We messed at the same hotel, in two separate rooms; after mess, each day, between thirty and forty horses were usually paraded, and we used to have some excellent steeple-chasing or rather brook-leaping in the meadows adjoining the town. I recollect particularly Whichcote, now General Whichcote, as the most determined rider on those occasions; it was really a very pleasant and happy time.

About 150 of the 52nd had volunteered from the South Hants Militia, and I selected a servant from amongst them, that I might have one who came from the same part of the country that I did. I recollect well the being laughed at by my brother officers, when first I joined, for talking of the right or left "side" of the company instead of the "flank," and of being "behind" instead of being "in the rear" of it. In our company's mess, they voted me a very good messmate, for not liking eggs, or strong tea, or brandy.

When furnishing a canteen which I purchased in London, I was wise enough, although I was going to the continent, to desire the two large bottles, containing about three pints each, to be filled with the best brandy which the canteen maker could procure. Before I lost my canteen, which I did with the rest of my baggage at Waterloo, I found that, although I did not drink brandy myself, some of my friends had no objection to it, for without being particularly invited to do so, they had emptied my bottles of brandy in no very long space of time. One of their jokes with me was that, if I was a lucky fellow, I should get made "a field officer" before Lille, by which they meant that I should perhaps be killed and buried under the sod before Lille.

Whilst we were at Lessines there was a grand review of the greater portion of the splendid cavalry and horse-artillery of Great Britain and of the King's German Legion. This took place near Grammont, about eight or nine miles from Lessines. There were about 7,000 men present. There were no particular incidents; but we were exposed to a most drenching rain for some time. The Prince of Orange and his brother, who were on a break with some young Englishmen, were placed by them, well wrapped up in great coats and tolerably well exposed to the storm, on the box of the break, the seat of honour, whilst their young friends got a much better berth themselves under the body of the vehicle.

When I had been four weeks at Lessines, I one day asked Sir John Colborne if he had any objection to my going for a day to Brussels, which was about twenty miles off, as possibly I might not again have so good an opportunity of seeing it. He told me he thought I had better be getting on with my drill; he however kindly added, "but you can go if you like." As I saw he had some reason for thinking I had better not go there at that time, I gave it up; and it was well that I was not there on the 16th of June, for two of the 52nd captains, who were at Brussels on leave at that time, had the misfortune not to be able to find their regiment.

They probably, misled by various reports, rode about in vain on the roads between Brussels, Lessines, Ath, Enghien, and Quatre Bras. One of them never reached the regiment at all, until after the action at Waterloo; the other only reached it in the evening, just at the moment it was advancing to charge the French Imperial Guard, and thereby, to the regret of his brother officers, lost his brevet-lieutenant-colonelcy, which fell to the lot of a junior brevet-major.

Towards the latter end of May, Sir Henry Clinton's division, of which Adam's light brigade, in which the 52nd was, formed a part, proceeded to occupy the country beyond Ath towards the French fortress of Condé, and they assembled for division drill in a large domain, surrounded by extensive plantations, in the neighbourhood of Quevres-au-camps. Here they practised the formation of an encampment by means of blanket tents, which appeared to be a most troublesome affair, and did not meet with much favour on the part of officers or men.

We remained there only a few days, and then returned to our former cantonments. About the 12th of June, the 52nd finally left Lessines, and the 2nd division of the British Army made another demonstration towards Condé.

It was known that the Emperor Napoleon was likely soon to make his attack either on the Prussian or the English Army, and great watchfulness was exercised along the front of both armies, which extended over a length of upwards of 100 miles. Regular information also reached the Duke of Wellington of the movements of various bodies of the French troops; but still all was uncertainty as to the point at which Bonaparte would strike his first blow.

Sir Henry Clinton's division had been some days near Quevres-au-camps, occupying the villages near that place in the direction of Ath, and were preparing for a division field day, on the morning of the 16th of June. The 52nd were at Elleguies St. Ann, and were assembling on the various company parades at ten o'clock. I was on the parade of No. 9, Captain McNair's company, with one man and one bugler only besides myself, when the general's *aide-de-camp* came cantering down the village, and delivered the following order to me, "Your company. Sir, is to be a mile on the Ath road in twenty minutes from this time."

He then rode forward, the bugler sounded the assembly, and the men who were close at hand, came pouring in immediately, and the company was at the rendezvous on the Ath road at the time appointed. Everyone was on the *qui vive*, and various reports of the advance of the enemy were afloat. After halting a short time, that the baggage might come up, we were ordered to move on Ath and Enghien; we reached the latter place a little after two o'clock. There we halted for two or three hours, and the men cooked their ration beef.

During this time we distinctly heard the cannonade of Quatre Bras, although it was twenty-two miles from us. Yet strange to say, two days afterwards, the troops at Hal, under Sir Charles Colville, though they were only eight miles distant, never heard the firing or anything about the action at Waterloo, till the morning of the 19th. When we first heard the cannonade at Quatre Bras, one of the old soldiers exclaimed, "there they go shaking their blankets again." The sound of a distant cannonade is not unlike that arising from the shaking of a carpet or a blanket.

From Enghien we marched a considerable distance on the Hal road, passing the road leading back towards Mons. After proceeding several miles towards Hal, we countermarched, and I think retraced our steps till, about two miles before reaching Enghien again, we struck into the above-mentioned road leading to Mons, and afterwards, leaving that road, we must have got, by some cross road to the left, to Braine-le-comte, without going through Soignies, which place I have no recollection of. I remember one good halt after leaving Enghien, which we made from about eight till half-past nine.

There was also another halt on the 16th, which took place in a large open wood. As we moved off again, the band struck up a march, the horse in a sutler's light covered cart, frightened by the band, dashed off amongst the trees, and the last I saw of the occurrence was that the body of the cart separated from the wheels and axletree and shafts, with which the horse ran off, leaving the poor woman inside the body of the cart. I think she could not have been much hurt; but it would probably be some considerable time before she and her husband, if she had one, would be able to join the division again.

We reached Braine-le-comte at midnight, on the 16th, and remained there till a little after two on the morning of the 17th, in the midst of torrents of rain. It was with some difficulty that I got my horse under cover. I found there were some persons in a large barn, and, on making some attempt to open the large door, was told in a strong Scotch accent, "There's no room here, we are all full here;" however by kicking up a great row and insisting on having the door opened, I at last succeeded, and found within only two men of the 71st Highlanders. The lower room of an adjacent *auberge* I found crowded with men of the brigade waiting for their turn to purchase something to eat; I was directed to a room upstairs, where I found some bread and cheese on the table, and two 71st officers lying their full length on two beds fast asleep.

After eating some bread and cheese, I took the liberty of lying down by the side of one of them, although they were perfect strangers to me, judging that, according to the laws of war, the one half of the bed fairly belonged to me. I could not sleep, so, after lying there about an hour and getting a good rest, I left my friends of the 71st not at all aware of the honour I had conferred upon them.

We reached Nivelles about seven o'clock; the narrow streets were full of cavalry horses tied to the doors and windows of the houses. The morning had become fine, and the 52nd got into a large orchard. Here we got our breakfast, and here about thirty of the officers of the 52nd, I being amongst the number, saw their baggage for the last time. There was much confusion on the road between Waterloo and Brussels on the 18th, and thus the baggage of nearly half the officers of the army was plundered, either by foreign allies running away from the action or by the Belgian peasantry.

In the middle of the day on the 17th we moved off from Nivelles along the direct road from that place to Hougomont, Waterloo, and Brussels; this road joins the road from Charleroi, Quatre Bras, and Genappe, on which the French were advancing, near the farm of Mont St. Jean. Shortly after leaving Nivelles, we found ourselves marching in a parallel line with British artillery and cavalry, we being on the road and they moving for some distance along the fields on either side. At the same time a Dutch Belgian battalion was trying to cross our line of march in the direction of Genappe. We moved very slowly, the men being wearied with their long march, and by the heavy load which each had to carry; this consisted of the knapsack, containing the kit and blanket, (the great coats had been sent to England,) the musket, and bayonet, and 120 rounds of ball-cartridge, sixty rounds of the latter being in the knapsack; this was a wise precaution adopted by the commanding officer.

Had the Germans, posted in the farmhouse of La Haye Sainte on the 18th, been thus provided with the reserve of ammunition in their knapsacks, it is very probable that the French would never have taken that important post; and had the brigade of the 1st British Guards been similarly provided, the 52nd would probably not have been left without support in their singlehanded attack on the columns of the French Imperial Guard. Sir John Byng, who succeeded to the command of the two brigades of Guards when General Cooke was wounded, gave this to Sir John Colborne as his reason for not advancing Maitland's brigade to his support.

Colonel Hall tells me:—

Near Nivelles we overtook Barlow, captain in the 69th. He had been promoted from the 52nd about a year before. Through the fault of the Prince of Orange, the 69th, in the act of changing position, had been charged by French dragoons. Barlow, and many others, lay down and escaped hurt, except from the trampling of the horses. He was limping along, very sore and lame, and feelingly declaimed against the common notion, that a horse will not tread on a man lying on the ground. His jacket was blackened with the marks of horse shoes. I suppose in such a case the horse has no choice and cannot pick its way.

About midway between Nivelles and Hougomont, the 52nd halted for rather more than two hours, 200 yards to the left of the road. I heard Sir John Colborne (for the future I think I shall call him Lord Seaton,) asking if any of the officers could lend him the cape of a boat-cloak, as he wished to lie down for a couple of hours, and try and get some sleep; I had a very large boat-cloak with a cape and hood to it, I unhooked the cape and hood and handed them to him. He wore them over his uniform during the whole of the Battle of Waterloo.

Whilst we were halted on this occasion, several waggons, with those wounded at Quatre Bras, passed along the main road towards

Waterloo and Brussels.

After our halt we came on to the road again just ahead of a regiment of Dutch Belgians, and formed open column of companies from subdivisions as each company reached it, so that our allies had to halt till we were all on the road. Each side of the road was now *lined* with soldiers of different regiments, and with some women and drummer boys, who had fallen out from fatigue. From this time until sometime after we had reached the entrance to Hougomont, no less than five mounted officers were sent, one after the other, to bring up stragglers belonging to the 52nd.

About a mile and a half before we reached Hougomont, we saw something of the French troops on our right, marching on the Charleroi road, towards Maison du Roi and Rosomme. This was the first we had seen of them. Shortly after this we halted, still in open column of companies, and loaded. Two French staff officers rode down to within 200 yards of us to reconnoitre, and one of them I saw writing down what he observed. On our arriving at the avenue leading to the Château of Hougomont, the head of the column turned to the right, and had advanced some distance down the avenue, when it was halted and countermarched, from which it was supposed that the original intention was that our brigade should occupy Hougomont for the night.

About this time, half-past seven, the British and French armies were taking up their positions on the Field of Waterloo. The French, at first, appeared not quite to understand that the English had arrived at their position, and had to be restrained by Picton, from behind La Haye Sainte, opening a cannonade from two brigades of artillery upon a mass of French infantry, which had advanced along the Charleroi road to some little distance in front of La Belle Alliance. In other parts of the field, between the two positions, there were some spirited little affairs of cavalry at intervals, in which our troops, forming part of the rear-guard under the Earl of Uxbridge, very much distinguished themselves.

When we were on the slope, to the rear of Hougomont, looking towards La Belle Alliance, we had close to us a British light dragoon regiment with white facings, who appeared to have just come up the slope after one of these encounters. As they faced about and re-formed on our position there was some cheering amongst them. As we were marching at ease across the slope just about this time, and appeared to be not far from the French, I heard one of our men say we were likely to be engaged at once, when another replied, "There will be no battle tonight, but tomorrow; all the Duke of Wellington's great battles have been fought on a Sunday."

Whilst we were halted near Hougomont, a heavy clap of thunder from the direction of Mont Plaisir startled us all; my first idea was that the French artillery in that direction were opening upon us. Siborne speaks of there having been much thunder and lightning during the evening and night of the 17th of June, but that was the only clap of thunder I heard; there was much rain during the night. (*Vide Siborne's 1815 Campaign*:Volumes 1, 2 & 3 by William Siborne; Leonaur, 2015.)

Just after this, when it was decided to what part of the ground we should move, Lord Seaton directed me to ride and see if the regiment could get through a hedge about two hundred yards off, in the direction of the village of Merbe Braine; it was a stiff hedge cut down to stakes nearly five feet high, with gaps here and there through which a single file might pass, and I was somewhat afraid if I reported that the regiment might pass through it, I might get into a scrape, if the column should be brought up by it. I reported it passable, and we marched through it without any great difficulty, and took up our position in a ploughed field, just in advance of Merbe Braine, looking towards Hougomont, and at about two miles to the eastward of the town of Braine-la-leud.

I was ordered with a fatigue party to go into the village to bring straw for the company. As we passed along the street we saw lying in the middle of the road, opposite to one of the cottages, the dead body of one of the 95th Rifles; I supposed he had been plundering and had been killed by one of the inhabitants. I proceeded with my fatigue party to the principal farm, where I found our general of brigade, Adam, who had taken up his quarters there. We could find no straw in the barn, and so, as "*necessitas non habet leges*," we took the straw from the roof of the barn itself, which had been recently thatched. A German soldier was walking off with a fine calf about a month old, when the mistress of the house appealed to us for assistance, and the general's *aide-de-camp*, Campbell, coming out at the moment, gave the fellow a good kicking, and took the calf from him.

On my return to the bivouac, our servants made a bed of straw on the wet ploughed field, and all four of us, McNair, Hall, Yonge, and I, lay down and, being covered with our boat cloaks, tried to go to sleep; it was very hot and there was heavy rain, and the straw conducted the rain into the inside of my stock, so that I was soon glad to get up. I think it was a little after ten o'clock when we were ordered to fall in again, as we were going to move, and each man was to take his straw with him. I don't know where the others were, but I found myself to be for a short time the only officer with the company. We moved in file, left in front, and I was very proud of my command, when Colonel Charles Rowan rode up to me, as 'No. 9 formed up into line on the left of No. 10, and said to me, "Leeke, dress your company in a line with that distant fire."

Our line then faced the French position, and was about 400 yards in rear of the crest of the British position, and about 500 yards from Merbe Braine. Here, having formed open column of companies, we piled arms and remained for the night. My friend Yonge shared my boat-cloak and straw with me, and we consequently both of us got very wet. The horses were picketed near us, and very soon some half-dozen of them got loose and galloped away towards Hougomont and the French position, and then came back again at speed towards the horses they had left, nearly passing over us, and only being prevented from doing so by our jumping up; they galloped about in this way the whole night, and thus made this wretched night still more wretched. I fell asleep several times, then dreamt we were advancing and closing with the enemy, then started up again, then thought of home and all my beloved ones there; again I dozed off, then came our horses like a furious charge of cavalry, and we had to start up and scare them off; and this kind of thing went on till the night had passed, and the morning of the 18th broke upon us.

As the morning of this eventful day advanced, the heavy rain of the preceding night passed off and was succeeded by fine weather. The men of the regiment were soon to be seen in every direction in their shirt sleeves, drawing the charges from their muskets and cleaning and drying their arms, and thus preparing for the coming conflict. The French line of battle was about three-quarters of a mile from that of the English. The great road from Charleroi to Brussels ran through the centres of each line, dividing the right wing of each army from the left.

On the right of the British Army were the *château* and farm and grounds of Hougomont, the whole in a square each side of which was a quarter of a mile in length. The northern side of the enclosure towards Brussels was nearly a quarter of a mile from the British position; the southern side of the enclosure was about the same distance from the position occupied by General Foy's 9th division of the French Army, and the western side was a quarter of a mile from Prince Jerome's division.

In the centre of the British position, 300 yards down the slope and close to the right of the Charleroi road, was the farm house of La Haye Sainte; its yard and orchard extended nearly a quarter of a mile along the right of the road, and the enclosure, in its whole length, was about eighty yards in width; the left of the British position extended about a mile and a half from the centre above La Haye Sainte, and was composed of Picton's division (in which were Kempt's and Pack's British, and Von Vincke's Hanoverian brigades) containing upwards of 7,000 men; and of Lambert's and Best's brigades of Cole's division, containing upwards of 5,000 men, and, further to the left, of Vandeleur's and Vivian's brigades of light cavalry, containing 2,500 men.

Along the front of the left wing, and extending down to the farm of Papelotte and the village of Smohain, were Perponcher's Dutch Belgian division, in which were Bylandt's and Prince Bernhard of Saxe Weimar's brigades, containing 7,500 men; a quarter of a mile in rear of Kempt's infantry brigade was Sir William Ponsonby's Union Brigade, containing the Scots Greys, the Enniskillens, and 1st Royal Dragoons, about 1,200 heavy cavalry; 300 yards to the rear of these, to the left of the farm of Mont St. Jean, were a reserve of upwards of 1,000 Belgian horse under General Ghigny; so that from the left of La Haye Sainte and of the Charleroi road to the extreme left of the British position there were stationed about 24,000 men, who formed the left wing of the army.

The right wing of the army extended away, from the centre to the right, for about the same distance of a mile and a half. Colonel Von Ompteda's brigade of four battalions of the King's German Legion, had its left resting on the Charleroi road. To the right of Ompteda's brigade stood Count Kielmansegge's brigade of six battalions of Hanoverian *landwehr* or militia; and further to the right was Sir Colin Halkett's British brigade of four battalions. These three brigades formed Count Alten's division, and occupied about 800 yards of the British position, from the centre towards the right; they contained about 8,000 men. In rear of Alten's division were General Von Kruse's Nassau contingent of 3,000 infantry, Lord Edward Somerset's brigade of the Life Guards, Blues, and 1st Dragoon Guards, Trip's and Van Merlen's brigades of Dutch Belgian cavalry, and Arentschildt's light cavalry brigade.

On the right of Alten's division were Cooke's 1st division of the British Army, composed of Maitland's and Byng's brigades of Guards. Maitland's brigade consisted of the 2nd and 3rd battalions of the 1st regiment of Guards, and Byng's consisted of the 2nd battalion of the 2nd or Coldstream Guards, and of the 2nd battalion of the 3rd Guards. The division was nearly 4,000 strong; Byng's brigade was posted on the higher ground above Hougomont; the light companies of all the four battalions of the division occupied the farm house and buildings, and the garden of Hougomont; there were also in the enclosure of Hougomont a battalion of the Nassau troops and two companies of Hanoverians. To the right of the Guards and to the rear and northwest of the grounds and enclosure of Hougomont, Mitchell's brigade, of Sir Charles Colville's division was posted; it consisted of the 51st Light Infantry, and of a battalion of the 14th regiment and another of the 23rd Fusiliers, and was about 1,800 strong.

Between these last mentioned troops and the village of Merbe Braine, on the reverse slope of the British position, there was a most imposing force, which formed a very strong reserve; and which, if the French had attempted to advance upon Brussels to their left of Hougomont and by Hal, as the Duke of Wellington expected, would most completely have intercepted them and defeated their intention. These troops were composed of the three brigades of Sir Henry Clinton's division, namely, General Adam's brigade, consisting of the 52nd Light Infantry, the 71st Highland Light Infantry, six companies of the 2nd battalion of the old 95th Rifles (now the Rifle Brigade), and of two companies of the 3rd battalion of the 95th Rifles; these fine regiments contained 2,600 men.

The other two brigades of Clinton's division, amounting together to 4,000 men, were Colonel Du Plat's 1st brigade of the King's German Legion, and Colonel Halket's Hanoverian brigade. To the left of Merbe Braine and between it and the road from Nivelles to Brussels, were the Brunswickers, infantry, cavalry, and artillery, making up 6,000 or 7,000 men; in rear of the guard, also, were Grant's, and Dornberg's, and other brigades of cavalry. The British and Allied artillery, amounting to 196 guns and upwards of 8,000 men, were attached to their several divisions or brigades.

The above is a rough but tolerably accurate account of the positions occupied by the British and Allied troops on the morning of the 18th of June; but whilst some of the troops occupied the same ground the whole day, others, and more especially our own brigade, passed over a large portion both of the British and French positions.

Here I beg leave to state, that I do not profess to give any detailed account of any other regiment than my own. I may have occasion to mention some of those other glorious regiments, but I have scarcely any details which I could give, if I wished to do so, excepting such as relate to the 52nd; and those statements which I may make respecting the 52nd at the battle of Waterloo will be almost all such as I witnessed myself.

Early on the 18th, Captain Diggle's company. No. 1 of the 52nd, was sent with two or three companies of the 95th into the enclosures of the village of Merbe Braine, facing Braine-la-leud; they were withdrawn sometime before the action commenced. Some little time after we were all stirring, I wandered off a short distance to a fire belonging to the 71st, at which one or two officers were standing; I was very glad to get the opportunity of warming and drying myself. I found a plank, of about my own length, near the fire; where it came from I have no idea, but I took the liberty, as no one was using it, of laying myself at full length on it before the fire; I very soon fell asleep and must have slept three hours, which much refreshed me, when my servant came to tell me some breakfast was going on amongst the officers of Captain McNair's company, the company to which I belonged.

Our breakfast consisted of a biscuit each and some soup, which was in one of the servants' mess tins; I was, unintentionally on his part, done out of my drink of broth by one of the officers exclaiming, just as I put my lips to the tin, "Come, Master Leeke, I think you have had your share of that." This half-mouthful of broth and a biscuit were all I tasted that day until after nine o'clock, when I got a lump of bread about as big as my fist from a French loaf. About ten o'clock, Lord Hill, with his staff, came galloping along, about fifty yards in the rear of the 52nd, through the high corn; he was riding towards the extreme right of our position; as he passed me, I recollect he gave me one of his pleasant smiles.

Shortly after this we got under arms, and Nettles and I were warned by Winterbottom, the adjutant, that we were to carry the colours; on our taking them over from the sergeants, we both agreed that it was not our turn to carry the colours, and wondered why we had been told off to them. I recollect observing, that it would suit me very well, that I had not been long enough in the regiment (I had only joined five weeks before) to be of any other use, but that I could carry a colour.

Major William Chalmers rode up to us and said, "The regiment is going to act in separate wings; I am going to command the right wing, and one of you gentlemen will go to my wing," and addressing me, he added, "You, sir, will go to the right wing."

Now I was anxious, as I did not know so much of the other officers as I did of those belonging to my own company, No. 9, to be in the left wing with them, which I knew was the proper wing for the regimental colour, carried by me as the junior ensign of the two. I therefore ventured to tell Major Chalmers that mine was the regimental colour which should be with the left wing, but he did not choose to rectify the immaterial mistake, which nobody else, probably, discovered at the time, for our colours, which had been with the regiment and the light division all through the Peninsular War, were little more than bare poles. Immediately afterwards, poor Nettles and I separated, not to meet again; he was killed by a cannon-shot, about seven o'clock in the evening. There were two brevet-majors by the name of William Chalmers in the 52nd; the one at Waterloo, being a dark man, was always called "Black Will," the other, "White Will."

The following extracts, from a letter I have lately received from Captain the Hon. William Ogilvie, relates to circumstances which occurred before the action commenced, and should find insertion here, and will be read with interest:—

> I was in Robert Campbell's company, commanded by Captain Cross, afterwards Lieut.-Colonel of the 68th. I was the senior subaltern, poor Nettles also belonged to the company, I am not sure if we had any other officer at this time. I happen to have preserved the parade state of the company on the 16th of June, on which morning I dare say you will remember we turned out for one of Sir H. Clinton's field days. Cross, not being very well, did not come out, and, by the time I had inspected the company, a cavalry man was seen on a jaded horse coming up the road, and, it was soon known that he brought an order for the division to march on Enghien, &c.
>
> In the agreeable excitement at the news, Winterbottom did not collect the states. The state is interesting from shewing the splendid condition of the corps then. The company, 87 rank and file, under arms, five tailors left at Lessines employed on the soldiers' clothing, and only one man sick; officers' servants, batmen, band, &c. making a total of 104 rank and file. I have no doubt the other companies were equally strong. What a noble battalion it was!

★★★★★★

Note—:The men at Lessines, amounting to between forty and fifty, probably joined us at Enghien or Nivelles. Siborne states, that the 52nd had 1,038 men at Waterloo, which amount would agree with this company's parade state.

※※※※※※

One additional circumstance, which I have not seen anywhere mentioned, occurred shortly before the action. An order came for a working party from the brigade with entrenching tools; it was accordingly paraded; William Rowan, now General Sir William Rowan, commanded it, and it chanced to be my turn for that duty also. When ready, I heard the brigade-major direct Rowan to march on a single tree, far to our left, where he would receive further orders. The party, however, had proceeded but a very short way, when the French attack on Hougomont commenced, and we were immediately recalled. I have since had very little doubt that the purpose was to have used the working party to strengthen the post of La Haye Sainte, had time allowed, and it was unfortunate it was not thought of a few hours sooner.

About eleven o'clock the 52nd moved from the ground on which it had bivouacked, about 300 yards more to the rear. The right wing of the regiment was in column of subdivisions, about twenty yards in front of the steep bank between it and Merbe Braine; the left wing was in line to the left of the front subdivision of the right wing, with an interval of a few paces between the wings. Captain Siborne, in his first plan of the field of Waterloo, places the 52nd, when in reserve, 200 yards more in advance, and 100 yards more to the eastward than they were.

The whole line will advance

CHAPTER 7

1815: 52nd Light Infantry at Waterloo 2

Exactly at twelve o'clock, by Chalmers's watch, the battle was begun by a cannon shot fired from the French position at the Duke of Wellington, who, with a numerous assemblage of general and other staff officers, had taken post about a third of a mile in our front on the high ground in rear of the north-eastern corner of the enclosure of Hougomont, from whence he could see the greater part of the French position. Such an assemblage was sure to attract the attention of the enemy, and unnecessarily to bring on itself the opening cannonade. It was said the duke told some of the generals they were "rather too thick upon the ground."

Whilst we were in reserve above the village of Merbe Braine, the regiment suffered several casualties from the shot and shell which passed over the British position in our front. I think the first occurred to Major Chalmers. The regiment was lying down; I was forced to remain with the colour in rear of the centre subdivision of the right wing, but several of the officers were standing in a group round Chalmers's horse when a ricochet shot came lobbing in amongst them, but fortunately did no other injury than that of breaking the horse's leg; Chalmers drew a pistol from his holster and put the animal out of his misery.

Most of our casualties at this time were occasioned by shell bursting over us, but we saw many cannon-shot ploughing up the ground near us: I had been already regarding several of them with great respect, when my colour-sergeant, Rhodes, who took great care of me and shewed me much kindness all the day, said, pointing to a shot passing through the standing corn, on the right of the column, "There, Mr. Leeke, is a cannon-shot, if you never saw one before. Sir!" Sergeant Houseley, (see Appendix No. 4), whilst standing in rear of the column, narrowly escaped having a round shot through him, by stooping just as he saw it in a line with him at some little distance; this was quite allowable when his comrades were lying down at their ease.

One of my narrow escapes occurred whilst we were lying here in reserve; I had my head against my colour-sergeant's knapsack, and was trying, but in vain, to get some sleep, when all at once there was a great rattle against the mess-tins, which, fitting one within the other, were strapped to the back of every man's knapsack; a piece of shell about the size and about as thick as the half of the palm of one's hand, had struck, and lodged in the inner tin; we both sat up, and he extracted the inner tin and the piece of shell, saying, as he pitched them both away, "If that had hit either you or me on the head. Sir, I think it would have settled our business for us."

On our leaving this ground I looked back and saw we had left two poor fellows in 52nd uniform lying dead under a tree, and could scarcely refrain from shedding tears at the melancholy sight; one of them was the assistant sergeant-major, a man greatly respected in the regiment. We lost, whilst in reserve, these two men killed, and I think about ten or twelve men wounded, who were taken to Merbe Braine.

Colonel Hall, speaking of the casualties which occurred at this time in the 52nd, says:—

> A young lad, (Kearns) of our company was struck by a cannon-shot, and was borne off motionless and white as a sheet. Those about me and myself concluded he was dying. Two or three days afterwards I could scarcely believe my eyes, when I saw him walk into the bivouac. The shot had carried away his pouch so cleanly, that he suffered no injury beyond the temporary shock and fright.

The 52nd remained about three hours in reserve just above Merbe Braine, and during that time three of the principal attacks of the French took place on our position. The first of these was made on the post of Hougomont, by large bodies of skirmishers and their supports detached from Prince Jerome Bonaparte's and General Foy's divisions. Hougomont was defended by the light companies of the two brigades of the British Guards, by the Hanoverian riflemen, and by the Nassau battalion. The French and English skirmishers advanced on and gave way before each other with alternate success.

At one time the French, superior in numbers, had almost got into the farmyard of Hougomont, but were repulsed by the light company of the Coldstream Guards; the French did actually pass round to the northern side of the enclosures near to the British position. Some of the masses sent forward by Foy and Prince Jerome, were forced to retire by the fire opened on them from the British and German guns and howitzers. Some companies from the Coldstream and 3rd Guards, having reinforced the gallant defenders of Hougomont, the enemy were driven off from the *château* to the lower enclosures of the place.

The attack on Hougomont was preparatory to, and appears also to have been, in a great measure, a feint to draw off attention from, a grand attack which the emperor caused to be made about half-past one or two on La Haye Sainte and the centre of the Allied position, by the whole of Count d'Erlon's corps, which formed the right wing of the French Army, supported by a division of cavalry from the left wing and by the fire of no less than seventy-four pieces of cannon, intended, whilst the troops were forming for the attack in advance of La Belle Alliance, and whilst they crossed the lower ground and the first rise of the British position, to draw off the fire of the British artillery from them. In the latter part of the action, the most of these pieces and many others were abandoned by the French, in consequence of the rapid advance of the 52nd to the British left of La Belle Alliance between eight and nine o'clock in the evening, after they had defeated the columns of the French Imperial Guard.

This attack of the centre and left wing of the Allied position was made by about 17,500 infantry supported by cavalry. The left division of this force under General Donzelôt tried in its advance to gain possession of the farm of La Haye Sainte, but were successfully resisted at that time by Major Baring and his Hanoverians. The French attack embraced the whole of the left wing, so that the Nassau troops under Prince Bernhard, of Saxe Weimar, were driven by the French skirmishers from the farm of Papelotte, which, however, they speedily retook.

The first and chief brunt of the attack appears to have fallen on Kempt's brigade of Picton's division, composed of the battalions of those fine regiments, the 28th, 32nd, 79th Highlanders, and (those old friends of the 52nd in the light division in Spain) the 95th Rifles. The French sent forward as usual a mass of skirmishers. Bylandt's Dutch Belgian brigade was in advance of the interval between Kempt's and Pack's brigades, and shamefully fled past the British brigades, notwithstanding the efforts of their officers to restrain them, directly they felt the fire of the advancing skirmishers; Picton ordered Kempt's brigade to advance on the enemy, which they did, and fired on them and charged them as they were reaching the crest of the position and completely routed them. In this *mêlée* the gallant Sir Thomas Picton was killed.

******

Note:—After his death it was discovered that his hip had been very severely contused by a spent cannon shot at the action of Quatre Bras, two days before; this wound he had concealed, that he might not be absent from the grand battle, which was fought at Waterloo. In the United Service Museum, (at time of writing), on the wall just above Captain Siborne's model of the Battle of Waterloo, hangs the map of Belgium which poor Picton carried in the breast of his coat when he was killed. It is stained in several places with his blood.

******

The 1st light battalion of the King's German Legion, belonging to Colonel Von Ompteda's brigade, crossed to their left of the Charleroi road, and joined Kempt's brigade in this charge. The French advancing in front of Pack's brigade were repulsed with equal gallantry by that brigade, consisting of the 1st Royals, the 42nd, and 92nd Highlanders, and the 44th regiment.

Some of the French supporting cavalry advanced to their left of La Haye Sainte and inflicted severe loss on one of Kielmansegge's Hanoverian regiments, which had been sent by the duke to reinforce the troops holding La Haye Sainte. Whilst this was taking place, and during the advance of Kempt's and Pack's brigades, Lord Uxbridge ordered forward the Household Brigade of cavalry under Lord Edward Somerset, consisting of the Life Guards, Blues, and the 1st Dragoon Guards; and also, Sir William Ponsonby's brigade, consisting of the Enniskillen Dragoons, the Scots Greys, and 1st or Royal Dragoons. Ponsonby's brigade charged to the left of Kempt's brigade and was somewhat mixed up with Pack's. They took two eagles, and with Somerset's brigade, which advanced more to the right, greatly contributed to consummate the rout of this large French force, which Picton's division had initiated. The French fled in in all directions, leaving two eagles and 3,000 prisoners in our hands, and having many pieces of cannon disabled.

The English had two generals. Sir Thomas Picton and Sir William Ponsonby, killed on this occasion. The Union Brigade, as Ponsonby's was called, from its consisting of an English, an Irish, and a Scotch regiment, and also a portion of the Household Brigade, after the rout of the French, did not know when to pull up, but followed them on to the French position, and thereby, after causing much confusion, suffered most severely, when attacked in their scattered state and cut off by the formed cavalry of the enemy.

Sir Colin Campbell, who was on the Duke of Wellington's staff, told me that he saw what I have attempted briefly to state, respecting the attack and defeat of the French on this occasion, including the splendid charge of the two brigades of cavalry, and that he saw the white horses of the Scots Greys carrying confusion into the French ranks, as far as the eye could reach; he saw also the enemy detaching troops in various directions to cut them off in detail.

The supporting regiment of the Union Brigade in charging got mixed up with those in advance, and Vandeleur consequently moved down two of the regiments of his brigade, the 12th and 16th Light Dragoons, in support, and by charging and routing the French lancers, secured the retreat of some of the scattered remnants of Ponsonby's brigade. In the charge of the 12th Light Dragoons, Colonel the Hon. Frederick Ponsonby was disabled in both arms, and his horse carried him on to the French position where he was struck to the ground by a sabre cut. (See Appendix No. 5.)

About three o'clock, the emperor ordered Marshal Ney to make a grand attack with 6,000 cavalry on the right wing of the British; it extended from La Haye Sainte in the centre to Hougomont on the right of the position; as these troops advanced they could only see the British artillery standing to their guns on the crest of the position; the infantry was in battalion squares on the reverse incline of the position. The duke had moved up the Brunswickers from their place in reserve, and also Colonel Du Plat's brigade of the King's German Legion. After firing round shot and grape into the advancing cavalry of the enemy till they could no longer stand to their guns, the British and German artillerymen took refuge in the squares nearest to them.

The French, on reaching the summit of the position, found the whole line of guns deserted, and found themselves in presence of the British, German, and Brunswick squares, which they charged and which opened fire upon them. The French cavalry did not attempt to charge home on any one of the squares, but inclined to the right and left and rode between them, receiving the fire of the four faces of almost every square. They were thrown into much confusion, which the Allied cavalry taking advantage of, charged and drove them from the position. Directly this occurred, the artillerymen ran to their guns and

52ND CHARGE AT WATERLOO

opened a most destructive fire on the retiring squadrons. The French soon rallied, and supported by 7,000 fresh cavalry, again attacked the guns and the squares with the same result, suffering very severe loss in killed and wounded and being thrown into very great and irretrievable confusion by the mixing up of various divisions, and various brigades, and regiments.

On one of these occasions. Sir Colin Campbell told me, that he, having lost his horse, got under an ammunition waggon near the centre of the position, to avoid the charge of the French cavalry. Directly the French cavalry had fled, the French artillery again opened a tremendous fire on our position, under cover of which the enemy sent forward a large force of infantry and cavalry, which maintained itself in the hollow to the Allied right of La Haye Sainte until nearly the close of the action.

During the occurrence of nearly all the stirring events briefly recorded in the foregoing portion of the chapter, the 52nd were lying down in reserve in front of Merbe Braine. About three o'clock or a little after, the whole regiment formed open column of companies to the left, and proceeded about a quarter of a mile along the right of the road from Braine-la-leud, in an eastern direction, nearly to the angle formed by the junction of that road with that running from Nivelles to Brussels, and formed square on No. 10 company. We there saw the grand charge of the French cavalry, before described, all along the British position, a quarter of a mile in our front, and numbers of our guns deserted. Colonel Charles Rowan addressed the regiment, and said, he did not think " those fellows would come near us, but that if they did we would give them a warm reception." Sir John Colborne was somewhere away in front at that time.

Almost immediately after the formation of the square, the 52nd advanced in square, up to, and over the British position. Some little time before it crossed the position, Cottingham, who was the first officer wounded, was struck by a spent cannon-ball on the right ankle. He had a trick of continually exclaiming "By Jove!" and was often joked about it. I had a little joke against him on the subject, as on our march up from Ostend, in describing to me an attack by a German regiment of cavalry on a body of French, he concluded by saying, "By Jove, they cut them up like sparrows." When he received this very severe contusion, he was immediately supported by one of the sergeants, and hopped about on his other foot, crying out "Oh, by Jove, by Jove!" One could hardly help smiling at the exclamation.

Plan 1

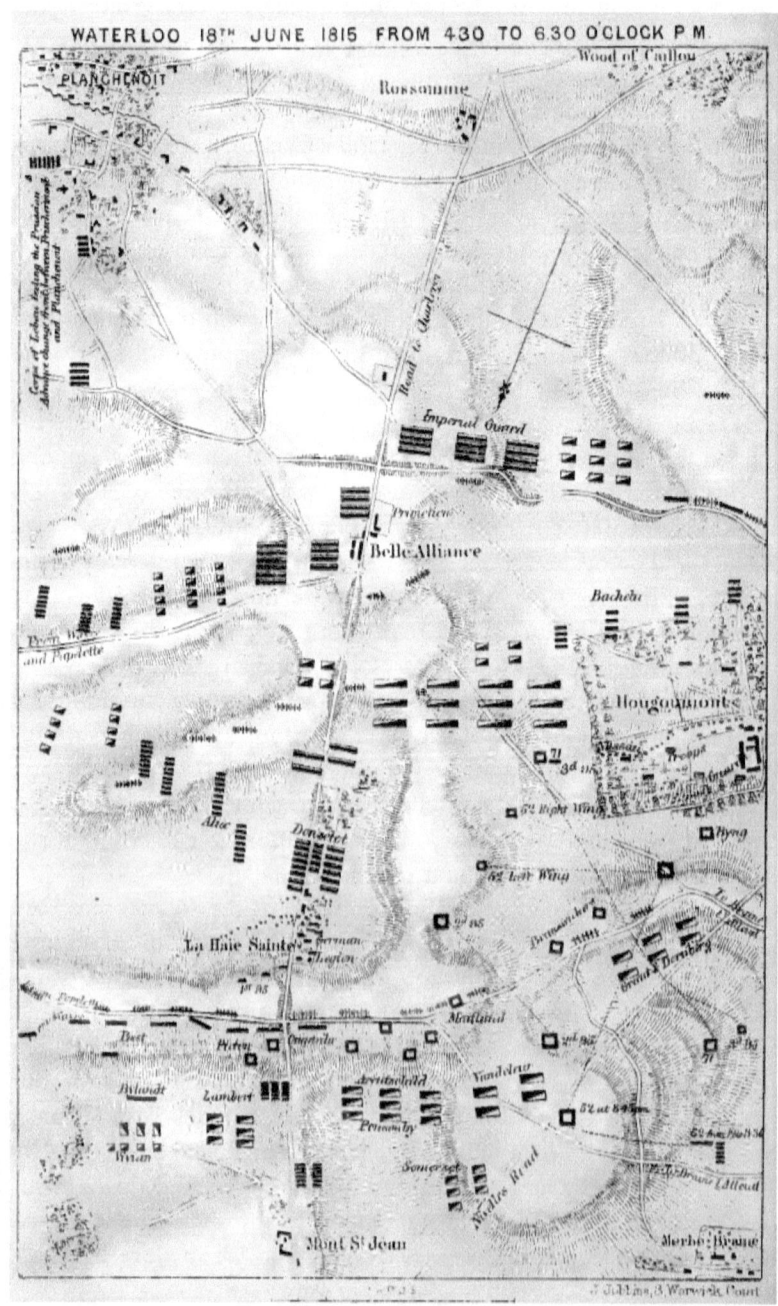

This shot must have been fired from the extreme left of the French Army, at the troops of Mitchell's or Du Plat's brigade, stationed on the higher ground in rear of Hougomont, and have first taken the ground near them. It passed over, or through the lengthened out right face of the 52nd square, and spent its strength on poor Cottingham's ankle. I was marching about five or six feet behind him; and first of all, thought it was a shell, but, on looking at it, I found it to be a round-shot, from one of the French twelve-pounder batteries.

On the position we passed over the spot on which one of the Brunswick squares had stood, and found lying there many of their killed and badly-wounded men. They had suffered most severely from round-shot and shells. It was one of the most shocking sights we saw even on that most bloodstained battlefield. One poor fellow, whose thigh was completely taken off high up, by the explosion of a shell at the moment it struck him, and who was black in the face, raised himself and caught hold of the hand of one of our men, and then fell dead. Another, who had not long to live, shook the hand of another 52nd man, as we were passing to the front, and cried "Brave *Anglais*."

Close to this was a Brunswick square, prepared to receive cavalry, with the front rank kneeling, as steady as a rock; but whether it was the square these wounded men belonged to, which had been removed out of its exposed position, or another square, I know not. We must have passed here near to the right square of Maitland's brigade of Guards, but we saw nothing of them. Our advance was just at the close of the first attack of the French cavalry on the Allied squares. I think, but am not sure, that we saw at this time, the 13th Light Dragoons, of Grant's brigade, ride down the slope on our left, to charge some French cavalry on their left front.

Immediately on descending the slope of the position towards the enemy, the regiment, almost concealed by the tall rye, which was then for the first time trampled down, formed two squares. I remember that when we formed these two squares, we were not far from the north-eastern point of the Hougomont enclosure, and on the narrow white road which, passing within 100 yards of that point, crosses the interval between the British and French positions in the direction of La Belle Alliance.

The squares of Adam's brigade advanced till the 71st were nearly half way down the enclosure of Hougomont, and about 300 yards from it; the right square of the 52nd was nearly 150 yards down the line of the enclosure and about 400 yards from it, the left square of the 52nd being on its left, and more up the British position, whilst the square of the 2nd battalion of the 95th Rifles, was the left square of the whole brigade, and was still further up the position.

When I was talking with Sir Colin Campbell on the subject of the Battle of Waterloo, he said he never understood why Adam's brigade was placed in that advanced and exposed position, and inquired if I knew what the object of it was. I told him that we had supposed we were placed there as a support to the troops in Hougomont. It has, however, occurred to me whilst I have been writing this portion of my book, that this brigade posted in squares in the manner above described, if it could maintain its ground, in spite of the tremendous cannonade to which it must necessarily be exposed, would so break the force of any fresh cavalry attack on the English guns and squares on the crest of the position, as to render it abortive; and also, that its maintaining its ground so far in advance of the other troops, many of whom were young battalions who had never been in action before, would tend to inspire them with confidence.

In the next chapter I shall bring before my readers many events of interest which occurred in connexion with the 52nd squares. Of the 71st and 95th squares I only know that they suffered very severely from the fire of the French artillery; and they appeared, as the French General Foy said of the squares of this brigade, to be rooted to the ground, so steady were they, under the tremendous fire to which they were exposed.

The old officers, who had served during the whole of the Peninsula War, stated that they were never exposed to such a cannonade as that which the 52nd squares had to undergo on this occasion for two hours and a half, from the French artillery planted about half a mile in their front. Our own artillery, on, or just under the crest of our position, were also firing over our heads the whole time, either at the enemy's troops or at their guns. Some shrapnel-shells burst short, and wounded some of the 52nd men; but the firing of these shells was discontinued, on our sending notice of what they were doing to the artillery above us.

In the right square of the 52nd, and I suppose it was the same in all the squares of our brigade, there was one incessant roar of round-shot and shells passing over or close to us on either flank; occasionally they made gaps in the square. The only interval that occurred in the cannonade, was when we were charged by the French cavalry, for they, of course, could not fire on our squares for fear of injuring their own squadrons, so that the charges of cavalry were a great relief to us all I believe, at least, I know they were so to me.

The standing to be cannonaded, and having nothing else to do, is about the most unpleasant thing that can happen to soldiers in an engagement. I frequently tried to follow, with my eye, the course of the balls from our own guns, which were firing over us. It is much more easy to see a round-shot passing away from you over your head, than to catch sight of one coming through the air towards you, though this also occurs occasionally. I speak of shot fired from six, eight, nine, or twelve-pounder guns. Some of the artillery above us were firing at one time, over our square, at a body of *cuirassiers* drawn up to their right and rear of the lower enclosure of Hougomont; one of the round-shot, which I caught sight of, made a regular gap, and occasioned some confusion in their front squadron.

After this, as the officer in command of the regiment was riding up and down about twenty yards in front of the leading squadron, I saw a round-shot which I thought would have struck his horse's head; it however appeared to pass about half a foot from his head, causing him to start back affrighted, and in a way calculated to have unseated his rider had he not been a superior horseman.

My position in the right square was in the rear of the centre of the front face. I have before stated that it is only very occasionally that a person can see a round-shot coming from a twelve-pounder gun, or from one of smaller calibre. After we had been stationed for more than an hour so far down in front of the British position, a gleam of sunshine, falling on them, particularly attracted my attention to some brass guns in our front which appeared to be placed lower down the French slope, and nearer to us, than the others; I distinctly saw the French artilleryman go through the whole process of spunging out one of the guns and reloading it; I could see that it was pointed at our square, and when it was discharged I caught sight of the ball, which appeared to be in a direct line for me.

I thought, Shall I move? No! I gathered myself up, and stood firm, with the colour in my right hand. I do not exactly know the rapidity with which cannon-balls fly, but I think that two seconds elapsed from the time that I saw this shot leave the gun until it struck the front face of the square. It did not strike the four men in rear of whom I was standing, but the four poor fellows on their right. It was fired at some elevation, and struck the front man about the knees, and coming to the ground under the feet of the rear man of the four, whom it most severely wounded, it rose and, passing within an inch or two of the colour pole, went over the rear face of the square without doing further injury. The two men in the first and second rank fell outward, I fear they did not survive long; the two others fell within the square.

The rear man made a considerable outcry on being wounded, but on one of the officers saying kindly to him, "man, don't make a noise," he instantly recollected himself, and was quiet. This was the only noise, except the "By Jove!" mentioned before, which I heard from any wounded man during the battle, although I must have been within hearing distance of many hundreds of the wounded, particularly later in the day, when we passed over the killed and wounded of the French Imperial Guard. The story one used to hear in one's boyhood, of the bands of regiments playing during the raging of a battle to drown the cries of the wounded, is a myth. The men of the band and some of the buglers generally make themselves useful in action, in attending to the wounded.

This cannon-shot coming through the centre of the front rank of our square without touching me was, I think, my narrowest escape up to that period of the action. I should not omit to mention that it was said, after the action, that a round-shot had expended its force in the solid square of the 71st Highland Light Infantry on our right front, and only stopped when it had killed or wounded seventeen men; I can easily suppose this to be possible from what I saw of the effects of the shot which passed so close to me.

We stood in the right square, not on rye, or wheat trampled down, but, I think, on clover or seeds which had been recently mown. I furnished information to Captain Siborne with regard to this crop, and to that on which we afterwards stood on the British position, when he was forming his beautiful model of the Field of Waterloo, and was very anxious to procure accurate information on the subject. It was generally supposed that there would have been a much greater loss in killed and wounded at Waterloo, if the heavy rain on the nights of the 16th and 17th had not well saturated the ground. Many of the shells which fell near the troops went so far into the ground, perhaps a foot or more, that they exploded without doing any injury. This was the case in and near our squares.

A company of the 95th Rifles were extended in front of the brigade at one time, that they might fire into the French *cuirassiers*, who were drawn up some three hundred yards from us. One of the files was about ten paces in front of our right square; they were both kneeling, and the front rank man was taking aim at the *cuirassiers*, when a shell pitched two or three feet before them; they hastily retired towards our square, when, from its not exploding, they supposed it was a round-shot, and returned to the spot and knelt down, and the front rank man was just raising his rifle again to take aim, when the shell exploded, covering them with dirt, and they retired, the front rank man having evidently been wounded.

It was said some little time after the action, but I did not observe it myself, that in one of the squares, probably the left, whilst Colonel Nicolay or some other officer who had come down from the position, was speaking to Colonel Charles Rowan, a shell fell in the midst of the square, when on Colonel Rowan saying, "Steady, men!" Colonel Nicolay observed, "I never saw men steadier in my life." The shell burst, and seven poor fellows were struck by the fragments.

Speaking of the left square of the 52nd, Colonel Hall writes:—

> A French half battery (*i.e.* two guns) about 600 yards distant from the farthest advance of this square, made it their especial object. They hit us several times whilst we stood halted, yet the casualties were not so numerous as might have been expected. I should say the enemy fired well but not with rapidity. Did you notice any of the cannon-shot wounds? While the left wing square stood under the cannonade, one of Shedden's company (Woods I think) was struck down by a ball full on the knee. He was removed into the centre of the square. I observed the limb above the knee quickly swell till it became the size of his body. The poor fellow was left upon the ground, I suppose to die there.

In addition to one or two advanced batteries, the brigade, being almost the only British infantry in sight, must have been cannonaded by a considerable portion of the artillery of the left wing of the French Army.

I have a very vivid recollection of the charge of the French cavalry. Those who advanced on the right square of the 52nd were *cuirassiers*, having not only a steel breastplate but the same covering for the back. As I observed before, the pleasing part of the charge was that, for several minutes, perhaps ten, we were relieved from the cannonade which the French had kept up upon us, except when their cavalry charged. They came on in very gallant style and in very steady order, first of all at the trot, then at a gallop, till they were within forty or fifty yards of the front face of the square, when, one or two horses having been brought down, in clearing the obstacle they got a somewhat new direction, which carried them to either flank of the face of the square, which direction they one and all preferred to the charging home and riding on to our bayonets.

Notwithstanding their armour many of the men were laid low, many horses also were brought down, and the men had a difficulty in disentangling themselves from them. The *cuirassiers* passed the square, receiving the fire of all the four faces, and proceeded up to the crest of the British position. They then re-formed, and came down the slope again upon us in the same way, and again avoiding to charge home upon the rear face of the square, as they could scarcely hope to penetrate the squares; possibly it was a reconnaissance ordered to be made by the emperor, who had no other means of ascertaining what force the Duke of Wellington had at that time on the reverse slope of the position. From the French position scarcely any of the British troops could at that time be seen, except our own and the other regiments of General Adam's brigade.

An interesting anecdote was mentioned to me not long ago, by the late General Sir Frederick Love, who was a captain and brevet-major in the 52nd at Waterloo:—

> Some years ago he and his brother were returning through the South of France, from a trip they had been taking to the Pyrenees, when they fell in with a nice gentlemanly Frenchman in one of the public conveyances, who, in the course of conversation, told them that he also had served at Waterloo; and it turned out, on their comparing notes, that he had been an officer of some standing in the very regiment of *cuirassiers* which had charged the right square of the 52nd in that action. Amongst other things, the French officer said that whilst the *cuirassiers* were re-forming, just under the British position, preparatory to renewing their attack upon us, he observed that the men had ordered their arms and were standing at ease, and that he said to a young officer near him, 'See how coolly those fellows take it; depend upon it that is one of the old Spanish regiments, and we shall make no impression on them.'
>
> This officer added, that on charging back again he rode close to the right face of our square, so close, that a young fellow sprang from the square and wounded him with his bayonet, on the left side of his

neck, it was a slight wound, but he showed them the scar which it had left. My attention, when the *cuirassiers* charged back upon us, was chiefly directed to those who were brought down by our fire, about twenty yards from the angle formed by the front and right faces; but I have a recollection of something having occurred at that time, without knowing what it was, in the front ranks of the right face of the square, not far from its junction with the rear face.

When we were in squares of wings, to the left of Hougomont, the French had two divisions, consisting of 12,000 men and some cavalry, in the neighbourhood of La Haye Sainte, from which, about six o'clock, they, after a severe fight, succeeded in driving the Germans under Major Baring, who had expended all their ammunition. The left square of the 52nd was not much more than a quarter of a mile from La Haye Sainte, and in much closer proximity to General Donzelôt's division, which was between La Haye Sainte and the square. At one time some skirmishers from Donzelôt's division crept up through the high standing corn and fired into this left square. There being some difficulty about the 3rd battalion of the 95th Rifles sending out skirmishers to drive them in, Lord Seaton ordered the front rank of the left face of the 52nd square to do so, thus leaving that face of the square with only three ranks for a short time.

Captain Yorke of the 52nd, who served at Waterloo as extra *aide-de-camp* to General Adam commanding our brigade, had his horse killed by a cannon-shot or a shell, when riding near the 52nd squares.

The following circumstance mentioned to me by Lord Seaton, when I was dining with him in London some years ago, will help to shew that the cannonade our squares were exposed to at Waterloo was something out of the common way. His words were:—

> I recollect a friend of mine, Beckwith of the 95th, riding down to the square in which I was, and when the men had opened out and let him pass into the square, he threw his bridle on his horse's neck, and said, 'I hope you are satisfied now, I hope you *are* satisfied.'

Major Beckwith was an assistant quartermaster-general, and, after leaving the square, lost his leg by the explosion of a shell. I recollect his dining with us, when we were encamped some miles from Valenciennes in the autumn of 1816, and keeping the whole mess in roars of laughter, with anecdotes relating to the light division in Spain. At one time Lord Seaton desired the right square to kneel, thinking, from the peculiar formation of the ground in front, that it would thereby be somewhat protected from the enemy's fire. We were told, when we arrived at Paris, that Napoleon had said of the British squares, that they stood like walls, and that the French cannon-balls seemed to make no impression on them.

About half-past six o'clock, the Duke of Wellington sent an order by his *aide-de-camp*, Colonel Hervey, to the commanding officer, that the 52nd should retire; but he replied that, if it was necessary, he could remain, for although the squares appeared very much exposed, the shot generally passed over them. Immediately afterwards, however, when the Nassau troops were driven back in the enclosures of Hougomont, the 52nd squares were ordered to retire up and over the position. Whilst this movement was taking place, the fire of the French artillery was more furious than ever, and several casualties occurred. In the left square Colonel William Rowan was wounded in the elbow by a shot which passed through his horse's neck and killed it, bringing its rider very heavily to the ground.

Poor Nettles, who carried the king's colour, was killed just before reaching the summit of the position, by a cannon-shot through his body; and it was said that his colour-sergeant was killed at or about the same time; and, in some unaccountable way, the colour was left under the body of poor Nettles till the next morning, when it was discovered by a sergeant of Captain Mercer's troop of horse-artillery. The other two sergeants attached to that colour, I presume, were in front of it when retiring in square, and poor Nettles, if he kept his relative position, would be just in front of the rear rank of what had been the front face of the square before it faced about to retire.

As we neared the summit of our position, it seemed as if the whole of the French artillery was firing round-shot at our devoted squares. Almost every shot which took effect, brought death or some dreadful wound to the person struck. It certainly was a pleasant relief from "one of the most murderous cannonades ever recorded in the annals of war," when, on passing the crest of the position, we found ourselves, at forty paces from it, out of fire on its reverse slope.

CHAPTER 8

Defeat of the Imperial Guard by the 52nd Light Infantry

It was now getting on for seven o'clock. The 52nd formed line four deep, the right wing being in the front line, and the left wing having closed up upon it. The regiment stood about forty paces below the crest of the position, so that it was nearly or quite out of fire. The roar of round-shot still continued, many only just clearing our heads—others striking the top of the position and bounding over us—others, again, almost spent and rolling down gently towards us. One of these, when we were standing in line, came rolling down like a cricket-ball, so slowly that I was putting out my foot to stop it, when my colour-sergeant quickly begged me not to do so, and told me it might have seriously injured my foot. Exactly in front of me, when standing in line, lay, at the distance of two yards, a dead tortoise-shell kitten. It had probably been frightened out of Hougomont, which was the nearest house to us, and about a quarter of a mile off. The circumstance led me to think of my friends at home.

For some little time, there was a lull in the battle all along the British line, excepting that the French artillery kept up their fire on the British artillery, almost the only force which could then be seen by them. No shells were at that time directed against the troops posted just behind the summit of the British position. Here was a most interesting scene! Everything was wild and strange, yet everything was quiet and natural. This is rather a bold paradox! Bounding our view, about forty paces in our front, was a bank not quite three feet high; there was a stunted hedge on it away to the right of our centre, but not so to the left. Under this bank and hedge to the right lay some twenty of our badly and mortally wounded men, covered by their blankets, which some of the poor fellows had got out from their knapsacks.

I particularly remember at that time two poor fellows passing through the line to the rear, who, I think, must have had their arms carried away by the same cannon-shot, for they were both struck exactly in the same place, about four inches below the shoulder, the wounded arm being attached to the upper part by a very small portion of skin and flesh, and being supported by the man taking hold of the hand of that arm with his other hand. About the same time, I made way also for one of the Rifles, who was seriously wounded in the head, to pass to the rear. Lieut.-Colonel George Hall, then a lieutenant in McNair's company, tells me that at that time most of the buglers had, with the permission of the officers, gone to the rear with wounded men; and that Captain Cross, at his request, allowed his last remaining bugler to take charge of and convey to the rear a severely wounded man of McNair's company.

In front of our left company were several killed and wounded horses; some of the latter were lying, some standing, but some of both were eating the trodden down wheat or rye, notwithstanding that their legs were shot off, or that they were otherwise badly wounded. I observed a brigade of artillery, coming from our left, pass over the bank into action in a very cool and gallant style. In doing this, some of the guns went over the legs of the wounded horses—the wounded men were out of their way. It often happens in action that, in charges of cavalry and in rapid advances of artillery, wounded men are ridden or run over.

It is mentioned that at the Battle of Ligny, two days before Waterloo, Blücher's horse fell, and that, before he could disentangle himself from it, the French and Prussian cavalry charged each other twice, passing over him and his horse without his being hurt. There was a peculiar smell at this time, arising from a mingling of the smell of the wheat trodden flat down with the smell of gunpowder.

Half an hour, or perhaps three-quarters of an hour, had elapsed after our return to the position, when a French *cuirassier* officer came galloping up the slope and down the bank in our front, near to Sir John Colborne, crying, "*Vive le Roi!*" He was a *chef d'escadron*, and took that opportunity of escaping from the French left wing, that he might shew his loyalty to Louis XVIII. He told Sir John Colborne that the French Imperial Guard were about to advance, and would be led by the emperor. I think the officer of *cuirassiers* was sent, under the charge of a sergeant, to the Duke of Wellington.

Soon after this, when it was nearly eight o'clock, the duke rode across our front from the left of the line quite alone, and spoke to Sir John Colborne, as they were both sitting on their horses observing the enemy. The duke's dress consisted of a blue surtout coat, white kerseymere pantaloons, and Hessian boots. He wore a sword with a waist-belt, but no sash, and had a small extended telescope in his right hand. He rode a chestnut horse. He rode across our front within fifteen paces of our centre, so that I had a complete view of him. I remember him and his cool, quiet demeanour as well as if I had seen him only yesterday. This was the first time the 52nd had seen him on the 18th. He wore no cloak, but Sir John Colborne wore then and during the whole of the action, as a short cloak, the cape and hood of my blue camlet boat-cloak, which I had lent him on the afternoon of the 17th. After speaking for a short time to Sir John Colborne, the duke rode quietly away again in the direction of the centre of the position, still unattended.

We heard what the officer of *cuirassiers* had said to Sir John Colborne about the attack of the Imperial Guard, and not long after we heard them advancing with continued shouts of "*Vive l'Empereur*" away to our left front. The drummers were beating the "*pas de charge*," which sounded, as well as I recollect, very much like this, "*the rum dum, the rum dum, the rummadum dummadum, dum, dum,*" then "*Vive l'Empereur.*" This was repeated again and again, till, in about a quarter of an hour or twenty minutes, we put an end to it in the manner mentioned a little further on.

The Imperial Guard advanced from the low ground in front of La Belle Alliance, and on the French left of the Charleroi road. At the same time a forward movement, in support of this attack, was made both by the right and left wings of the French Army, whilst the troops forming the centre of their left wing under Foy, made a corresponding advance within the enclosures of Hougomont. The French had maintained themselves in force for several hours to the right and left of La Haye Sainte, about 300 yards under the crest of the British position, and had taken that post from the Germans about six o'clock.

Thus, when the Imperial Guard were advancing from the low ground towards the right centre of the position, the duke could not withdraw any of his brigades of infantry from any other part of the line. A mass of skirmishers was sent forward from the Imperial Guard, who were joined on their right by skirmishers from Donzelôt's division; both sets of skirmishers getting, I believe, intermingled in some measure. Whether the Imperial Guard skirmishers fired into the right regiment of the 1st British Guards, that is, the 2nd battalion, and into the left of the 2nd battalion of the Rifles, I am uncertain, but the brunt of the attack from the French skirmishers fell upon the 3rd battalion of the 1st Guards.

Under these circumstances, when the leading battalion of the first column of the Imperial Guard was about 400 yards from that part of the British position occupied by Maitland's brigade of Guards, Sir John Colborne, who had been watching his opportunity, ordered No. 5 company of the 52nd, under Lieutenants Anderson, Campbell, and F. W. Love, to extend and move down and fire into the enemy's columns, looking to the regiment for support.

******

Note:—The left of the skirmishers of the 52nd and the left of those of the Imperial Guard could not have passed very far from each other, for only the four-deep line of the six companies of the 95th Rifles intervened, between the left of the 52nd and the right battalion of Maitland's brigade of Guards, yet the hostile skirmishers did not meet or even see each other; probably when the 52nd skirmishers advanced from the left of the regiment, which, owing to the formation of the ground, was more forward on the British position than the troops on its left, the French skirmishers were just surmounting the more retired crest of the position in front of the British Guards, and had commenced firing into them.

******

He then, without having received any orders from the duke or any other superior officer, moved forward the 52nd, in quick time, directly to its front. As we passed over the low bank and the crest of our position, we plainly saw, about 800 or 400 yards from us, in the direction of La Belle Alliance, midway between the enclosures of Hougomont and La Haye Sainte, and about a quarter of a mile from each of those places, two long columns of the Imperial Guard of France, of about equal length, advancing at right angles with the position and in the direction of Maitland's brigade of Guards, stationed on our left. The whole number of these two columns of the French Guard appeared to us to amount to about 10,000 men. There was a small interval of apparently not more than twenty paces between the first and second column; from the left centre of our line we did not at any time see through this interval; I think they were all in close column.

Plan 2

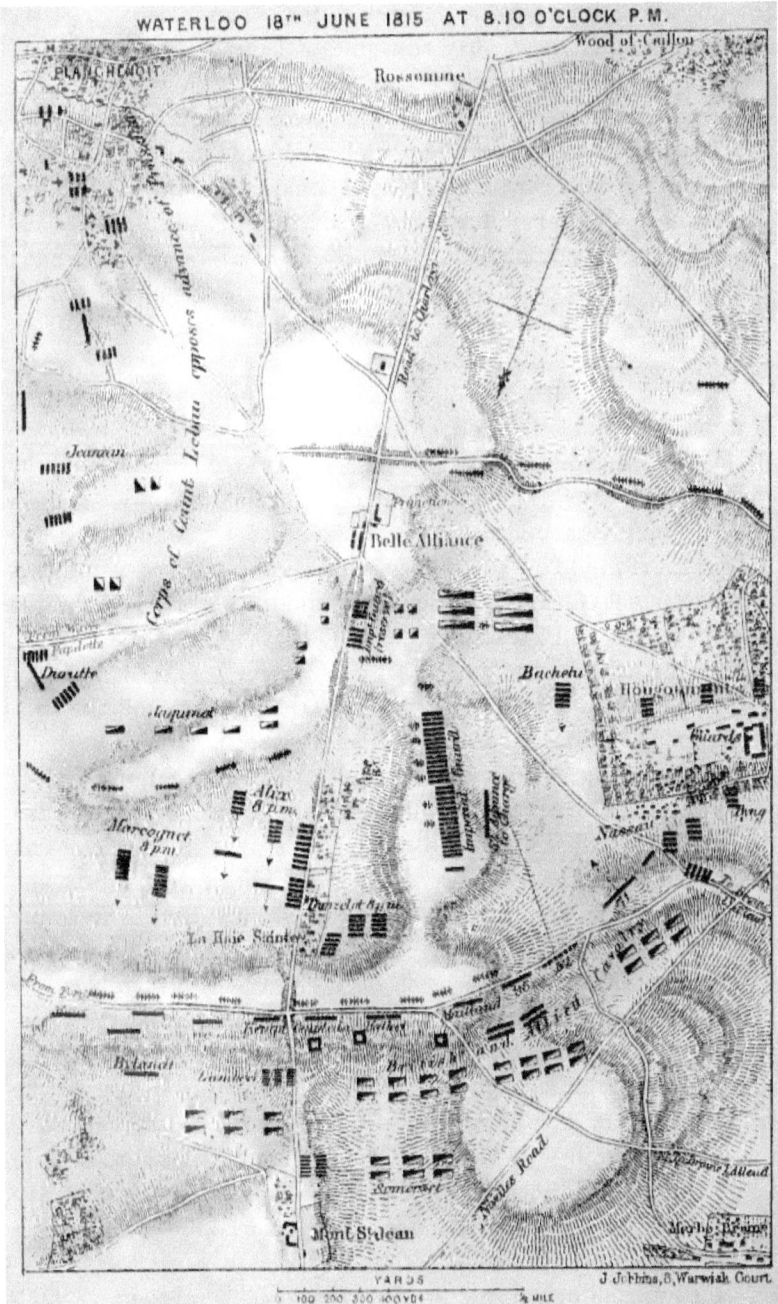

As the 52nd moved down towards the enemy it answered the cries of "*Vive l'Empereur*," with three tremendous British cheers. When the left of the regiment was in a line with the leading company of the Imperial Guard, it began to mark time, and the men touched in to their left, every one seeing the necessity for such a movement, and that, if they proceeded, they would be outflanked by the French column, which was then not quite two hundred yards from us. In two or three seconds the word of command, "Right shoulders forward," came down the line from Sir John Colborne, repeated by the mounted officers, and the officers commanding the front companies; the movement was soon completed, and the 52nd four-deep line became parallel to the left flank of the leading column of the French Guard, there being a slight dip and rise again of the ground between us and the enemy.

The 52nd was alone, the other regiments of Adam's brigade having been thrown out by the suddenness and peculiarity of the movement. In this dangerous and exposed advance Sir John Colborne was on the right of the regiment, anxiously watching a large mass of the enemy's cavalry, which was seen between us and the French position. From the left centre of the 52nd line we saw a numerous body of skirmishers of the Imperial Guard running towards, and then forming about 100 yards in front of, their leading column. (This was erroneously spoken of after the battle, as "an attempt at deployment.") These appear not to have been seen by the 52nd officers on the right; possibly the head of the French column intervened. I recollect seeing a French officer strike, with the flat of his sword, a skirmisher, who was running farther to the rear than the point at which the others were forming; at that time, I could see 300 yards up the slope of the British position to our left, and not a British regiment or a British soldier was in sight.

These skirmishers no doubt were the troops driven in from the British position, by the 3rd battalion of the 1st Guards, which was the left battalion of Maitland's brigade; Lord Hill was on the right of the 2nd battalion of the 1st Guards, which was the other and right battalion of the brigade, and it was "stationary and not firing." The 3rd battalion of this brigade of Guards was lying down in square, on the reverse incline of the position, to the left of their 2nd battalion and at some distance from it, when the duke, coming back from the centre of the position, and seeing how they were fired into by a large mass of skirmishers of the Imperial Guard, desired the commanding officer "to form line on the front face of the square, and to drive those fellows in," (this was the origin of "Up Guards, and at them," words which were never uttered.)

The duke's order was immediately obeyed, and the 2nd battalion of the Guards drove them some little distance down the slope, when there was a cry of "cavalry," and the Guards retired up and over the British position in some disorder. This agrees with Colonel Gurwood's statement, that as the 10th Hussars, in which he commanded a troop, were moving from the left to the right centre of the position, they saw the Guards retiring in some confusion. This, from all accounts, was the only movement made against the enemy by Maitland's brigade of Guards (and this was made by one battalion of it only) during the action. They suffered severely from the cannonade, and were charged, as all the troops were, by the French cavalry, and suffered very much from the fire of these skirmishers of the Imperial Guard, whom they drove in; but this was the only forward movement they made against the enemy.

Gurwood must have seen them at some distance down the reverse slope of the British position, just about the time that the 52nd were completing their right-shoulder-forward movement, and that the skirmishers of the Imperial Guard were forming in front of their leading column. I must not now stop to prove that the story of Maitland's brigade of Guards having attacked and routed the leading column of the Imperial Guard is a mere myth, and that this has been all along well known to every officer of the 52nd who was present at Waterloo, from Lord Seaton down to myself, the youngest ensign, but will hereafter devote a chapter or two to the subject.

This advance of the 52nd line and its right-shoulder-forward movement was seen from the height above, and was spoken of by Lord Hill as one of the most beautiful advances he had ever seen. Sir John Byng, who had succeeded to the command of the whole division of the Guards when General Cooke was wounded, and was at the time near Maitland's brigade, said of it to one of the 52nd officers that night, "*We* saw the 52nd advancing gloriously, as they always do." The Duke of Wellington also was much pleased with it, as I shall have to state more particularly in a subsequent chapter.

It is very difficult to calculate time during the progress of a battle; one officer told me that the whole action only appeared to him to last two hours, whereas it commenced exactly at twelve o'clock at noon, and lasted till a quarter after nine at night. It must have been nearly a quarter past eight when the 52nd stood parallel with the left flank of the Imperial Guard.

Our artillery on the British position, 300 yards above, had been playing upon the masses of the French Guard, but when we saw them there appeared to be no confusion amongst them; our advance put a stop to the fire of our artillery; it was not till the 52nd skirmishers fired into them that the Imperial Guard halted, then as many files as possible, on the left of each company of their leading column, faced outwards and returned the fire; as the 52nd approached, our skirmishers fell back to the regiment, two of the three officers being severely wounded, and many of the men being either killed or wounded. The regiment opened fire upon the enemy without halting; the men fired, then partly halted to load, whilst those in the rear slipped round them in a sort of skirmishing order, though they maintained a compact line, occupying, however, nearly double the extent of ground, from front to rear, which a four-deep line usually requires.

The French writer, Quinet, although his account of this action contains all kinds of mistakes, speaks of this attack of the 52nd on the flank of the Imperial Guard as follows:—

"*Le 52e régiment Anglais en profite pour venir audacieusement se déployer sur le flanc gauche. Quand le régiment Anglais l'eut débordée tout entière, il ouvrit son feu à brûle-pourpoint qui l'écrasait.*"
("The 52nd English regiment took the opportunity to boldly come and deploy on the left flank. When the English regiment had overwhelmed them, it opened fire point-blank which crushed them.")

Here was a most exciting as well as a most critical period in this famous battle. The far-famed Imperial Guard of France, led on by the gallant Marshal Ney, whom the French styled "*Le plus brave des braves,*" came into contact with that British regiment, of which Sir William Napier, the historian of the Peninsular War, had written that it was "a regiment never surpassed in arms, since arms were first borne by men;" and this regiment was commanded by Colonel Sir John Colborne (afterwards Field-Marshal Lord Seaton) one of the most experienced, steady, cool, and at the same time, gallant and dashing officers of the British or any other army.

The mounted officers rode to the front of the line. There were Colonel Sir John Colborne, Lieut.-Colonel Charles Rowan, Major Wm. Chalmers, Adjutant Winterbottom, and Assistant-Adjutant Nixon, also our general of brigade, Adam, who had just come up, and some of his staff, Lieutenant Campbell, 7th Fusiliers, and Major Hunter Blair, 91st regiment, Brigade-Major. Chalmers, in front of the right of No. 4 company, placed his cap on the point of his sword, and, standing up in his stirrups, cheered the regiment on. Here I saw Winterbottom badly wounded in the head, and brought by his horse through the line, without his cap, the blood streaming down him; the poor fellow managed to hold on by the pommel of his saddle.

Captain Diggle, commanding No. 1 company, had been desperately wounded just before on the left temple. Lieutenant Dawson was shot through the lungs; Anderson lost a leg. Major Love was severely wounded in the head, and afterwards, as he lay on the ground, in the foot and in two other places. Lieutenant Campbell, who had been skirmishing, came through the line severely wounded in the groin; General Adam was severely wounded in the leg, but did not quit the field. Colonel Charles Rowan was also slightly wounded; Sir John Colborne had his horse killed under him, and was grazed in the hand and on the foot.

Several of the other officers were very slightly hit, but were not returned as wounded; I consider that about 140 of our men were killed or wounded at this time, in the course of five or six minutes. I missed Sir John Colborne for two or three minutes, and felt very anxious about him, but presently he came quickly down the front on foot, giving directions, still wearing a portion of my cloak, and wiping his mouth with his white handkerchief.

As we closed towards the French Guard, they did not wait for our charge, but the leading column at first somewhat receded from us, and then broke and fled; a portion of the rear column also broke and ran; but three or four battalions of the Old Guard, forming part of this second column, retired hastily, in some degree of order, towards the rising ground in front of La Belle Alliance, with a few pieces of the artillery of the Guard, which must have been on their right flank when they advanced, as we did not see them, and those which were left by the gunners on the ground, until the French Guard had given way; indeed, had these guns been on the left flank of the columns of the Imperial Guard, when we were bringing our right shoulders forward, they might have plied our line with grape, and have caused us the most serious loss; or, possibly, had they been there, Sir John Colborne would not have ventured on the movement at all. With the exception of these battalions of the Old Guard, the whole French Army, as far as the eye could reach, appeared to us to be in utter confusion.

The 52nd still advanced by itself, in the direction of the lower enclosure of La Haye Sainte, towards the Charleroi road, and nearly at right angles with that part of the British position behind which, on the reverse slope, stood Maitland's brigade of Guards, and Sir Colin Halkett's, Count Kielmansegge's, and Colonel Von Ompteda's brigades, at a distance from the 52nd varying, as the regiment continued to advance, from 350 to 700 yards.

Immediately after the defeat of the Imperial Guard, the 52nd passed over their killed and wounded, who, poor fellows, were lying very thick upon the ground, where I passed on a breadth of about fifty yards; in some places I had to spring over heaps of them lying over each other. One of the 52nd officers, who has now been dead for many years, told me, sometime after the action, that an occurrence had taken place as we passed the killed and wounded of the French Guard, which had since given him at times some uneasiness. It was this:—As he was advancing in rear of the regiment, he saw a Belgian soldier, who was following us in pursuit of plunder, try to take money from a wounded Frenchman, who begged him to let him keep what little he had; on which the Belgian dealt him a heavy blow on the head with the butt end of his musket, which appeared to kill him, and that he was so indignant at this atrocity, that he immediately ran the Belgian through the body with his sword.

He asked me what I should have done under the circumstances, and I replied, that I most likely should have done the same; but that I was not sure it was the right thing to do; yet, as the scoundrel had left his own corps in search of plunder, and had under those circumstances taken away life, his own life seemed to be fairly forfeited. I saw a man of the 40th regiment about the same time, who also was probably on the same sort of errand, and I only mention him, because I observe that in Colonel Ponsonby's account of what happened to him when he was lying wounded on the ground, he mentions amongst other things that a soldier of the 40th came across him late at night, and took care of him till the morning of the 19th. This was probably the same man we had seen earlier in the evening. (See Appendix No. 5.)

The 52nd had only got a very short distance from the killed and wounded of the Imperial Guard, when suddenly, through the smoke, it saw a charge of cavalry coming upon its flanks and centre. They consisted of British and German light dragoons, mingled with French *cuirassiers*, before whom they were retiring at speed. We took them all for the enemy, and they were fired on and lost some men before it was discovered that many of them were English. Some went round the flanks, but many rode at the centre of the regiment, and, when they were about twenty yards off, the line opened about six or eight feet in the centre to let them pass.

I thought at the moment that the men were not right in making an opening for those whom we regarded as enemies, and should have received the charge on their bayonets; I, therefore, stood to the front, on the right of the formed line and to the left of the opening, and attempted to draw my sword from the scabbard that I might attack the leading horseman. It was hanging on my left side, hooked up to the waistbelt, as officers carrying the colours do not draw their swords in action, except in cases of emergency. To my great dismay, the looped sword-knot was entangled in the button of the scabbard, and I could not get my sword out, and therefore I instantly took the colour in both hands with the intention of using it as a lance against the foremost dragoon.

The poor fellow was, however, shot dead by our men, and fell headlong from his horse on his back, with his head towards us, about six feet in front of the opening; I then saw by his three stripes that he was a sergeant. The horse passed through the centre of the interval, and, as he was at speed, the stirrups flew out at right angles from the saddle, and the right one nearly struck me in the face. There was then a cry, "They are English," and the firing ceased. Opposite to the centre of the 52nd, the *cuirassiers* were seen to draw off in admirable order. On the right, one gallant *cuirassier* penetrated the line and was cut down, just as he got through it, by the sergeant-major.

Just clear of the right of our line, an encounter was witnessed between a *cuirassier* officer and a cadet, (answering to a volunteer in our service,) attached to one of the German light dragoon regiments of Dornberg's brigade. The latter was retreating at speed before his antagonist, with his head down on his horse's neck and his sword over his own neck. The German cadet was watching his opportunity, and on finding himself near his friends, on the right of our line, suddenly pulled his horse up upon his haunches, and dealt the *cuirassier* a blow across his face; he wheeled round and engaged the cadet in single combat, who managed to strike him again on his face, so that he fell over on one side, and was pierced under the arm and killed.

Colonel Hall, writes as follows, on the subject of this passage of the light dragoons through our centre:—

> The uniform of the light dragoons had just been altered, and they were dressed as the French *chasseurs*, so it was quite natural

that they should receive a volley. I remarked that but few fell in front of the line, but a considerable number in the rear. The coolness of our men in this unfortunate mistake was admirable; in the smoke and noise and confusion, no one knew if his comrade was cut down or not, but there was no thought of dispersing or of lying down for safety; they just faced about and prepared to fire on the supposed enemy in the rear. I believe some did do so before the officers, who had discovered the error, could stop them. Anderson told me that the dragoons who rode through our line, re-formed close to where he was sitting wounded, and that he heard the commanding officer exclaim, in a tone of vexation, 'It's always the case, we always lose more men by our own people than we do by the enemy.'

It was said that some of the 23rd Light Dragoons (and it seems there were German light dragoons with them) had attacked a body of French infantry, probably some of the defeated Imperial Guard, and that being consequently somewhat broken, they were charged by a formed body of *cuirassiers*, before whom they had to retire, in order that they might re-form. They did good service in engaging the enemy, but when they had to retire, they ought to have ridden round the flanks, and not through the line, of one of their own infantry regiments. I may remark that if all our soldiers, cavalry and infantry, wore the scarlet uniform, these unfortunate mistakes of taking friends for foes would be of less frequent occurrence.

Almost immediately after we had become disengaged from the above-mentioned cavalry, we suddenly found that some guns on our right, towards La Belle Alliance, were firing grape into the front of the regiment, and making some serious gaps in our line. One discharge came into the centre, and the rattle of the grape against arms, accoutrements, and men, was something very different from the roar of round-shot, the noise from the explosion of shells, and the whistling and humming of bullets, which we had hitherto been accustomed to. Sir John Colborne, who was not then mounted, anxiously exclaimed, as he went quickly towards the right of the line, "Where are these guns? they are destroying the regiment."

Lieutenant Gawler, who, after Captain Diggle was wounded, had taken command of the right company, told him they were not far away on the right, and asked if he should take the right section and drive them in; Sir John Colborne told him to do so, and he then wheeled the right section to the right, extended it, and advanced towards them. As soon as the French gunners saw the red coats through the smoke, they immediately limbered up and retired. Gawler found a considerable body of French infantry in front of him, at 200 or 300 yards distance, and collected his men and waited for the regiment, which in the meantime had brought its left shoulder rather more forward.

When the discharge of grape came into the centre, I saw a man spring behind to take the musket of one who was killed, as his own would not go off Another man near me said, in an undertone to his comrade, "the top of ——'s skull was taken off," mentioning the poor fellow's name, which I do not now recollect. Shortly after, as we were advancing, (there was no halt,) I found about a foot-and-a-half of my colour-pole was very wet with blood, about the height of my shoulder, and that there was blood on the buff cuff of the left sleeve of my jacket. It was not my own blood. The next morning, I found that the thumb of my left hand was black and sore. I think my left hand and the colour-pole must have been struck, without my perceiving it at the moment, by a part of the skull of the man mentioned above, for the contusion could not have been occasioned merely by blood.

I believe it was at this time that Lieutenant Holman had three musket-balls through the blade of his sword, without being touched himself. I have often seen the sword, and the holes made by the balls are connected with each other, as if they had been made by canister-shot; the thick rim of the sword holding the two parts of the blade so strongly together, that Holman used the sword for several years afterwards whenever he was on duty. He was the brother of Mr. Holman the blind traveller, whom I afterwards met at Nice and Rome.

I have mentioned that Sir John Colborne was on foot when the French fired grape into our line. Just before this, both he and the present Lieut.-General Sir William Rowan, G.C.B., now colonel of the 52nd, made an ineffectual attempt again to become mounted officers. I think I may venture to relate the circumstance in Sir William Rowan's own words:—

> I was mounted, and my horse shot under me by a grape shot, (I think it must have been a round-shot), which first grazed my right arm and then passed through my horse's head. The fall stunned me a good deal. Sir John Colborne's horse was also (afterwards) shot, which led to a laughable scene. On our coming up to an abandoned French gun, with the horses still attached

to it, Sir John and I mounted two of the horses, calling to our men to cut the traces, which they were unable to accomplish; and as the regiment was advancing rapidly, we had to dismount and follow as fast as we could. Shortly after we met plenty of horses with empty saddles.

It has been said that the guns which retired with the rear battalions of the second column, and which afterwards, as I have related, fired grape into us, were directed to open fire on the advancing 52nd line by the emperor himself; but I think it more likely they were directed to take up their ground by General Drouot, who was with the Imperial Guard when they gave way. The emperor was then on the height above, in front of La Belle Alliance. Drouot had commanded the artillery of the Guard in several of the former campaigns of the emperor, and had accompanied him to Elba, and afterwards went with him to St. Helena. At Waterloo he was the "*Général aide-de-camp de l'Empereur.*"

★★★★★★

Note:—It is recorded of Drouot that he always carried a small Bible with him to read, which constituted his chief delight; and he avowed it openly to the persons in the imperial suite, a peculiarity not a little remarkable on that staff, and the admission of which required no small degree of moral courage. Napoleon often placed him in the most exposed positions, so that his situation was full of peril. He was said to be somewhat superstitious, because in action he took care to wear his old uniform of general of artillery, as he had long worn it, and had never been wounded. The probability is, that he considered it unwise to draw the fire of the enemy upon himself by wearing a splendid uniform. He also always dismounted when near the enemy.

★★★★★★

Directly after the guns were driven in on our right by Gawler, we distinctly saw on our left, 300 or 400 yards up the British position, and on the Hougomont side of La Haye Sainte, four battalions in column, apparently French, standing with ordered arms. According to all accounts they were too far down the British position to be Dutch Belgians; they certainly were not English. It was thought they were French, and part of Donzelôt's division, who did not know how to get away, and therefore remained quietly where they were until the 52nd had passed. We were then about 200 yards from the Charleroi road, and I think a line in prolongation of our front would on the left have cut the farmhouse of La Haye Sainte, at 300 yards distance, and on our right the south-eastern point of the enclosures of Hougomont, at a distance of rather more than half a mile from us.

The 52nd was then, as before, quite alone, and had these four battalions of Donzelôt's division come down upon our left flank with a regular British charge, they would possibly have prevented the rout of the French Army from becoming so complete as it was. The brigades of Alten's division could not at this time have made any forward movement down a portion of the British position, which they did afterwards, when the duke ordered the whole line to advance, or we should have seen them. I think the 71st, the right regiment of our brigade, and the left regiment, the 2nd battalion of the Rifles, both of which had been thrown out by the sudden advance of the 52nd, and perhaps the Osnabruck *landwehr* battalion, under Colonel Halkett, were the only British troops which had left the crest of the British position at this time; and we saw nothing even of these till the next morning, though Captain Siborne and other historians of the battle place the 71st and Rifles in line with us in our attack on the battalion of the Old Guard, which will presently be described.

When we were about 200 yards from the Charleroi road, the Prussian round-shot, directed either at our line or at the French extreme right, began to strike near us, one about fifteen yards from the centre, but apparently none of them touched the regiment. The Prussians had come up on the right flank of the French from the direction of Wavre, and at that time were trying to drive them out of the village of Planchenoit; rather later they succeeded in doing so, at an immense loss to themselves. The Prussian guns were more than a mile from us; they soon discovered that we were friends, and ceased to cannonade us.

I well remember thinking, when I saw some of these Prussian round-shot striking the ground not far from us, that it would be very unfortunate to be killed or wounded just at the close of the action, when the enemy were in full retreat. I think it must have been at a rather earlier period of our advance, that my first thought occurred, of what would become of my soul in case I should be killed; I recollect I quieted the thought at once, by thinking that those who believed in the Saviour, the Lord Jesus Christ, would be saved; and that, as I believed in Him, all would be right if I should be killed that day.

PLAN 3

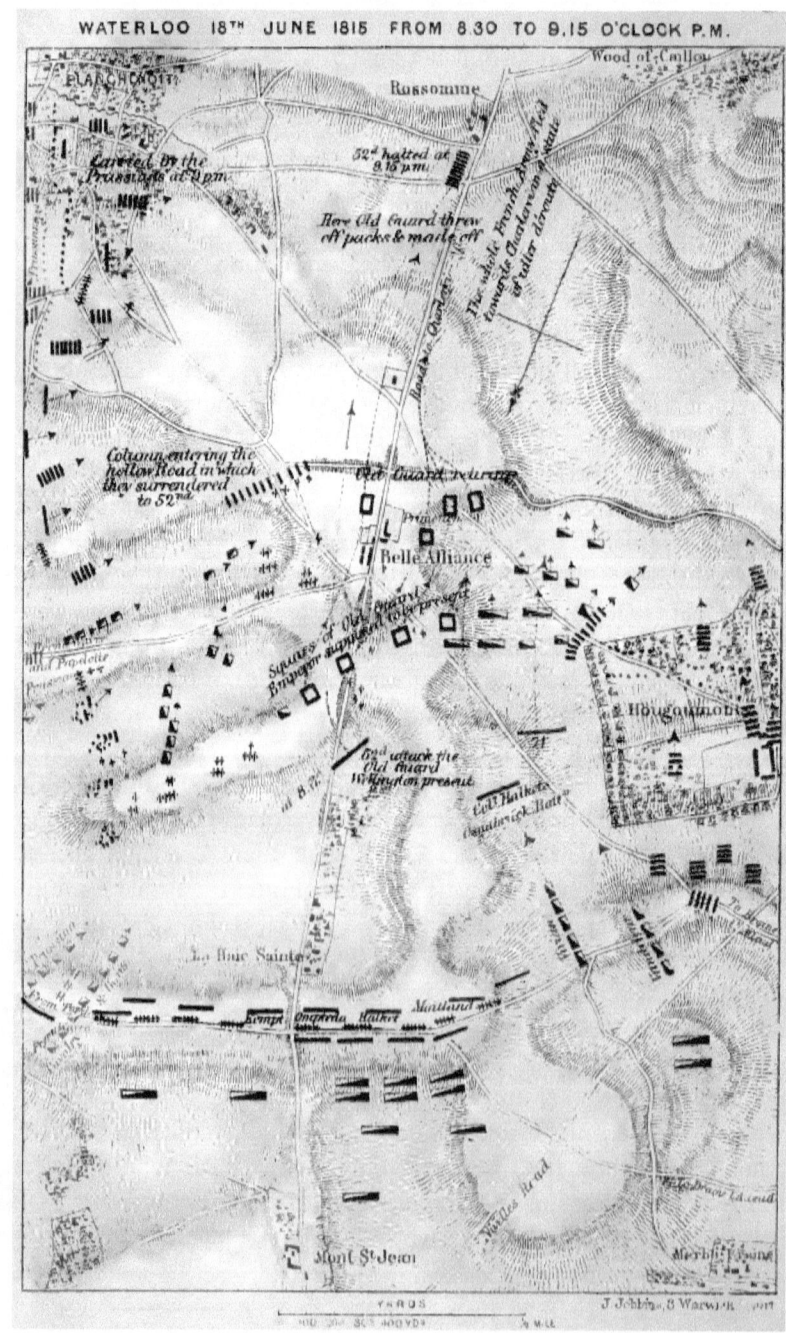

Chapter 9

1815: 52nd Attack and Defeat the Imperial Grenadiers

It was about twenty minutes after eight, when Sir John Colborne seeing a considerable body of troops in his front inclined to make a stand, halted the 52nd in the low ground close to the Charleroi road, for the purpose of dressing the line, which had then advanced more than half a mile without any halt from the time it had left the British position. The regimental colour and the covering-sergeants were ordered out, and Nixon, the acting adjutant, had just dressed them, when the Duke of Wellington, attended by Sir Colin Campbell, rode up to Sir John Colborne, who was in the rear of the centre of the 52nd, and I heard him say, as I looked back from my position in front of the centre, "Well done, Colborne! Well done! Go on, don't give them time to rally."

******

Note:—The duke, referring to this part of the action in a memorandum written in October, 1836, twenty-one years after the Battle of Waterloo, has shown perhaps a very pardonable forgetfulness of the exact circumstance here related. He writes, "The infantry was advanced in line. I halted them for a moment in the bottom, that they might be in order to attack some battalions of the enemy still on the heights."
This is altogether incorrect. The duke found the 52nd already halted, and said "Go on, don't give them time to rally." I find that after the lapse of several years, almost all those who were present at Waterloo forget many circumstances, which one is perfectly astonished at, whilst they are very clear about other points even of very minor importance. The being always able to

distinguish between what they themselves witnessed and what they have heard from others or read of, is a great difficulty with some of my friends, after the lapse of fifty years. I do not experience the same difficulty myself.

******

The French had then opened fire on our line at about 200 yards distance, and I well recollect that several bullets streaked the ground close to me, many others seemed to whiz very close to my ears, so that I suspected the French were directing more attention than was quite pleasant to me and my colour. It may however have been principally attracted by the duke, and Sir Colin Campbell and Sir John Colborne, who were immediately in my rear and about ten paces from me. The colour and the covering sergeants were immediately called in, without the line being dressed, and the regiment advanced and drove off the enemy. It was here that the Marquis of Anglesea, then Lord Uxbridge, rode up to the duke and said, "For God's sake, Duke, don't expose yourself so, you know what a valuable life yours is," and that the duke replied, "I'll be satisfied, when I see those fellows go." Lord Uxbridge was wounded by a grape or musket-shot in the knee.

I did not see it, nor was it observed by Sir John Colborne or by any of the officers of the regiment, our attention being engaged by the enemy's troops in our front. Sir Colin Campbell told me, several years afterwards, that, on observing that Lord Uxbridge was wounded, he rode up to him and laid hold of him by his collar and held him on his horse till his *aide-de-camp* took charge of him.

These troops, who acted as a rear guard to the French Army now retiring in the greatest confusion, were, it is said, three battalions of the Old Guard, a small body of *cuirassiers* of the Guard, and a few pieces of artillery, probably the same guns which had been driven off by the right section of the 52nd under Lieutenant Gawler. It has been stated and is supposed that the Emperor Napoleon was with these troops. If so, the emperor and the duke were at this time in closer proximity, than they ever were at any other time; and I am not sure that I have not a good claim to having been at this time, for a few seconds, for the second time the foremost man of the British Army, and the one nearest to the French Emperor; excepting of course the three or four persons who had been taken prisoners during the action and had been brought before him to see what information he could draw from them.

Here again was a most interesting period of the Battle of Waterloo, a battle of which the Duke of Wellington wrote, that:—

Being possibly the most important single military event in modern times, it was attended by advantages sufficient for the glory of many such armies, as the two great Allied Armies engaged.

Here the 52nd, certainly a most distinguished regiment in the British Army, and one of the regiments formerly composing the famous light division in Spain, were opposed to the Old Guard, which was recruited from the Young Guard and from the other French regiments, not a man being admitted into it, who had not seen twelve years' service and who was not distinguished for good and gallant conduct. No man was admitted into the Young Guard who had not been in the army for four years. These fine fellows had never met with any defeat before, unless such had happened to them in other corps of the French Army. Twenty minutes before this they had witnessed the defeat by the 52nd of the first column of their Guard and of the leading portion of their own column, from which they had hastily retired to their present position, where they were making something of a stand against us.

As I have observed above, here were the choicest troops of France, opposed to one of England's choicest regiments. Many fine and gallant officers had fallen on both sides, but here were on one side the Duke of Wellington, the Earl of Uxbridge, Commander-in-Chief of the British cavalry. Lord Seaton (then Sir John Colborne), an officer of the very highest repute in the English Army, and Sir Colin Campbell (not the one who was afterwards Lord Clyde), Chief of the Duke's staff. On the other side were the Emperor Napoleon, Marshal Ney, Prince of Moskowa, Bertrand, General Drouot, Count D'Erlon, and probably Soult.

From my point of view, I saw in front of us two or three bodies of men on the rising ground before us, but I could not see clearly their formation, for they were either kneeling, or no more of their bodies could be seen than to about a foot below their shoulders, owing to the ruggedness of the ground; they are, however, described by others of the 52nd as having been three squares, with a body of cavalry on their right; they had three guns on their left, which fired a round or two of grape at us. The 52nd did not return the fire of these troops of the Old Guard. On our advancing, the French retired in good order. The cavalry on their right faced about to cover the retreat of their squares, but, on our pressing on in pursuit, they prudently refused the encounter with our compact four-deep line.

Only one of their squares retreated by our left of La Belle Alliance and the Charleroi road; and this square the 52nd kept in view for nearly a mile further, until they lost sight of it about a quarter of a mile before it reached the farmhouse of Rosomme, where we brought up for the night.

Sir Colin Campbell told me that, when Lord Uxbridge was wounded, he himself again pressed the duke not to expose, as he was doing, his valuable life, and that he received the same reply which the duke had immediately before given to Lord Uxbridge, that "he would be satisfied when he saw those fellows go." He told me several other things about the duke, most of which I noted down the day after I had the conversation with him. He told me that, when the 52nd advanced, the duke and he went off to our right, which would probably be towards the lower part of the enclosures of Hougomont, and that some little time afterwards they crossed over some rising ground to their left, where they witnessed the unsuccessful charge by Major Howard and a party of the 10th Hussars upon a body of French infantry, and that the duke was very angry when he saw them make the attack without having any support.

Before he had accompanied the duke down to the rear of the 52nd and about twenty minutes after we had advanced from the British position, he had taken an order from the Duke of Wellington to Sir Hussey Vivian to bring forward his hussar brigade, consisting of the 10th, 18th, and 1st German Hussars. He met him coming down the slope of the position and Vivian told him his brigade was just behind him.

It appears from Vivian's correspondence with Gawler of the 52nd in 1833, that he must have come down the British position, through the interval made by the sudden advance of the 52nd, and that he saw no British troops as he advanced at right angles with the position, either to his right or left, and that his brigade came upon and charged a large body of cavalry somewhere in front of the 2nd French corps. These cavalry were mixed; there were *cuirassiers*, lancers, and guns with their horses attached. Colonel Gurwood, who had been in the 52nd, but at Waterloo commanded a troop in the 10th Hussars and was wounded, told me that, as he lay on the ground, he saw poor Howard's charge; that Vivian, after the charge of the 10th, observing some formed infantry in front, desired Howard to collect as many men as he could of those who had got into confusion in their charge on the French cavalry and to attack this infantry. This was looked upon as a very desperate service, as cavalry have rarely been known to defeat regularly formed and steady infantry.

Gurwood told me that a young officer said to Howard, "If I were you, Howard, I wouldn't do it," and that Howard replied, "You heard the general's order, and you know my position in the regiment." The charge was made and repulsed, Howard being killed. The infantry they attacked appears to have been one of the squares of the Grenadiers of the Imperial Guard, which had retired just to the right of La Belle Alliance and Primotion, when the square, followed by the 52nd, retired to the left of those houses, and to the left of the Charleroi road. As far as I can make out, this square and another were under Cambronne, and were closely followed, when he came near them, by Colonel Hugh Halkett with the Osnabruck battalion, one of the regiments of his Hanoverian brigade.

Halkett had seen the sudden movement of the 52nd, and having sent his brigade-major to order the rest of the brigade to follow, (the brigade-major was killed before he could deliver his order), he moved the Osnabruck battalion down the slope of our position from the right of the 71st, and came away to the right of the 52nd, when these squares of the Imperial Guard were attacked by us; Halkett with his Hanoverian battalion got so near to one of these, that he made a dash at General Cambronne, who was at some little distance from the square, and took him prisoner with his own hands.

✶✶✶✶✶✶

Note:—French writers assert that General Cambronne never exclaimed, "*La Garde meurt et ne se rend pas*" (The Guard dies and does not surrender), but that these memorable words were uttered by General Michel, "who was killed at Waterloo at the head of the square of the grenadiers of the Old Guard." In 1845, the two sons of General Michel addressed a request to the French king that a royal ordinance which authorised the town of Nantes to erect a statue to the memory of General Cambronne might be modified, that is to say, that the commission, charged with the erection of this monument, should not be authorised to cause to be engraven on the base of this statue those admirable words, "*La Garde meurt et ne se rend pas.*" In support of their request, the sons of General Michel brought forward many witnesses to prove that Cambronne himself had denied using these words, and others to prove that they heard General Michel use them.

Amongst these last was Baron Martenot, who commanded the

battalion in which the emperor took refuge "for a moment at the end of the battle." Bertrand presented to General Michel's widow a stone detached from the emperor's tomb, at Sainte Helena, on which he had inscribed these words and signed them:—

"*A la Baronne Michel, veuve du Général Michel, tué à Waterloo, où il répondit aux sommations de l'ennemi par ces paroles sublimes—'La Garde meurt et ne se rend pas*'!

"Pierre du tombeau de Sainte Hélèna. (*Signe*,) Bertrand."

✶✶✶✶✶✶

The other square, which Major Howard charged, was farther to the rear of the French position, and more to our right than the square which Halkett was so close to. Vivian, in his correspondence with Gawler, eighteen years after the action, mentions that he expected a regiment of Hanoverians, on his left and rear, to have advanced to attack the square that Howard charged, but that this regiment, instead of doing so, followed another square more to its left.

I must now return to the account of the advance of the 52nd in its pursuit of the square of the Old Guard to our left of the Charleroi road. It gradually brought its left shoulders more forward, till opposite to La Belle Alliance the line was exactly at right angles with this road, the British position being about a mile directly in our rear. We passed great numbers of guns and ammunition waggons, which had been deserted in consequence of our rapid advance. Lord Seaton stated that at this time we passed no less than "seventy-five pieces of French artillery, and that very shortly after the French columns dispersed."

Leaving La Belle Alliance and, farther on, the farm of Primotion on its right, the 52nd advanced in pursuit to the left of the Charleroi road, and at no great distance from it. It had been *quite alone* since it left the British position, and continued so till it halted for the night.

I think it was after passing the farm of Primotion that I remember seeing, on the other side of the Charleroi road about 300 yards to our right, a small body of cavalry riding to the charge, probably it was poor Howard's charge, before referred to. Sir Colin Campbell thought, on examining with me a plan of the Field of Waterloo, that this charge took place not far from Primotion; he remembered there were some trees there near to a house, and that it then wanted a quarter to nine by his watch.

✶✶✶✶✶✶

Note:—The following letter from the Duke of York to the Duke of Wellington is published in the tenth volume of the duke's supplementary despatches :—

"Horse Guards, June 30th, 1815.
"My dear Lord Duke—The family of the late Major Howard, of the 10th Hussars, have urged so earnestly that every possible measure should be adopted for finding the body of that officer, as to induce me to desire that the officer commanding at Bruxelles should be written to on the subject. I understood that two sergeants of his regiment were employed to bury him; and if you will give orders that one of them should be sent back to Bruxelles to give any information on the subject, the family will feel that both Your Grace and myself have done all that is practicable to effect their wishes.

I remain, my dear Lord Duke, yours sincerely,

Frederick."

("Let inquiry be made on this subject at the regiment for the two sergeants mentioned. Wellington.")

★★★★★★

One hundred yards to the south of the enclosures of Primotion, we being about the same distance to the left of the Charleroi road, the 52nd found itself on the edge of a deep hollow road with steep banks, in which were a large body of French infantry retiring from their right. In the centre it appeared to be a mutual surprise; they threw down their arms in token of surrender, and we rapidly passed through them. In the centre not a shot was exchanged. Captain McNair, however, made the men break some of the French muskets by knocking them against the ground, thinking it unwise to leave so large an armed body of the enemy in our rear, but there was no time for much of this, and probably not more than a dozen muskets were smashed. What took place on the right of the 52nd was thus graphically described by Colonel Gawler, in his *Crisis of Waterloo*, thirty years ago:—

> A hundred yards to the Allied left of La Belle Alliance, a hollow road runs, nearly at right angles towards the *chaussée*, up which a column of artillery and infantry was hastily retreating. The square (of the Imperial Guard) crossed the head of this body, but the high bank concealed the approach of the 52nd, until the distance became too small to admit of any but a hand-to-hand contest. The column seemed not sufficiently aware of its desperate circumstances to surrender without hesitation, and for a moment the scene was singularly wild. The infantry, before

they threw down their arms, made an effort either at defence or escape. The artillery dashed at the opposite bank, but some of the horses of each gun were in an instant brought down.

A subaltern of the battery, threw his sword on the ground in token of surrender; but the commander, standing in the centre of his guns, waved *his* above his head in defiance. A soldier sprang from the British ranks, parried his thrust, closed with him, threw him on the ground, and keeping him down with his foot, reversed his musket in both hands to bayonet him; when that repugnance to shedding of blood, which so often rises in the hearts of British soldiers even under circumstances of personal danger and prudential necessity, burst forth in a groan of disgust from his surrounding comrades; it came, however, in this case too late, the fatal thrust was sped, and the legion of honour lost another member.

On the left flank of the 52nd line, at no very great distance from it, a French officer brought up and formed about a hundred men from the hollow road, apparently with the view of making some attack upon us, but, on this being observed, the left company of the 52nd brought up its right shoulders to drive them in, when they retired back into the hollow road much faster than they came out of it; there was no firing on either side. I was the first up on the top of the opposite bank, and the regiment formed on the colour. It was then getting somewhat duskish, and must have been close upon nine o'clock. At a distance of about 200 yards we observed four French staff-officers. McNair who was on the right of No. 4, (his own company, No. 9, being in the rear) gave the word, "No. 4, make ready," when I, who was next to him on his right, begged him to "let those poor fellows off." He replied, "I dare not, I know not who they may be." He then completed the word of command, and No. 4 fired a volley; No. 3, on the right did the same. The "cease firing" sounded down the line from the right, and I believe these were the last infantry-shots fired at Waterloo.

The horse of one of the French officers fell, and we soon lost sight of them. I have thought it was probably Marshal Ney, who thus had his horse shot under him. It tallies with his own account; he speaks of lingering on the field, and of all his horses being shot. "When McNair said, "He did not know who they might be," he was thinking of Napoleon, and thought it was not right to let him get away, if he could prevent it. It is very possible that the emperor did form one of this group, for in the note earlier, he is spoken of as having *at the end of the battle* been, "for a moment," in one of the squares of the Old Guard. Now one of them was retiring before the 52nd, and the other two or three were in our immediate vicinity on the other side of the Charleroi road. He may have been in the square we pursued, and have left it when they halted for a moment to throw off their knapsacks. This they were seen to do I think before we reached the hollow road. Being thus lightened they gained on us and we no longer saw them when, from the top of the hollow road, the two centre companies, 3 and 4, fired on the four mounted French officers.

There was no pursuing-cavalry on our side of the main road. Vivian's brigade of cavalry came up into line with us, far away to the right, when we were somewhere abreast of Primotion. Vandeleur's brigade of cavalry, came up rather later in pursuit. Halkett, with the Osnabruck battalion, must have been not very far in our rear, on the other side of the *chaussée*; and I conjecture from Colonel Reynell's letter that when we were at Primotion, or at the hollow road beyond it, the 71st, one of the two other regiments of our brigade, must have been away on the other side of Vivian's brigade, in a line with us, but at a distance from us of nearly 700 yards.

The 71st, (perhaps the 2nd and 3rd Rifles,) and Halkett's Osnabruck battalion, afforded a most important support to the 52nd in its single-handed attack on the French Imperial Guard, but none of them nor any other regiment of the British or Allied troops were at all engaged with them. As far as I have been able to make matters out, the above-mentioned regiments were the only infantry which advanced that night beyond the low ground between the French and British positions. The rest of the infantry bivouacked on the lower part of the slope of our own position; the enemy having been fairly routed and dispersed, long before the rest of the British and Allied Army passed over the crest of that position. In the advance of the 52nd from the hollow road to the farm of Rosomme, where it halted for the night, it passed at one place within a quarter of a mile of the nearest houses of Planchenoit, but saw nothing of the French who nearly up to that time had been keeping the Prussians in check in that village, and had inflicted severe loss upon them. They had now made off, with the rest of the French Army who could get away, in the direction of Genappe and somewhat to their right of it, between it and Maison du Roi. About a quarter of a mile before we reached Rosomme we came upon the knapsacks of the square of the Old Guard.

My colour-sergeant took possession of a *havre-sac* and afterwards took from it a loaf, from which he cut a good slice of bread, and offering it to me said, "Won't you have a slice of bread, Mr. Leeke? I am sure you deserve it, sir!" I was very glad of the bread, for I had eaten nothing but one biscuit for more than twenty-four hours; and I was pleased also with the kind and approving words of the sergeant. Shortly after this we reached Rosomme, and forming column of companies on the northern side of the farm, we halted in the angle formed by the Charleroi road and the road leading into it from Planchenoit, and piling arms bivouacked there for the night. It was a quarter after nine o'clock.

The farm of Rosomme is three-quarters of a mile from La Belle Alliance, and exactly the same distance from the church of Planchenoit. On this ground we found the straw which the French Imperial Guard had collected for themselves, and slept on the night before. The duke himself must have ordered Sir John Colborne to halt there, for General Adam had not been with us since the defeat of the 10,000 men of the Imperial Guard, but had, notwithstanding he was severely wounded, been away to look after the 71st, who had been so much separated from the 52nd. I did not see the duke at that time, but I recollect hearing that when he came up to the regiment at Rosomme, he asked Sir John Colborne "if there was anything he could do for the 52nd," and that Colborne replied he should be very glad if the duke could send them a barrel of biscuits; which he promised to do.

As there has been so much controversy as to whether or not the Duke of Wellington and Marshal Blücher met, after the battle, at La Belle Alliance, the duke himself even having declared that they met first at Genappe, and his memory evidently having been confused about it, I will copy *verbatim* the note I made of the information I got from Sir Colin Campbell the very day after I had the conversation with him in 1833. It is as follows:—

> The duke, seeing where we (the 52nd) were to halt for the night, returned to La Belle Alliance and arranged with Blücher that the Prussians should undertake the pursuit.

> Soon after we halted a large fire was lighted, round which the officers stood, and talked over the events of the battle. Whilst we were thus engaged, we heard some cheering away in our rear, near La Belle Alliance, and May, of the 52nd, coming up shortly afterwards, told us that it proceeded from those who were present when Wellington and Blücher met.

******

Note:—The following is from the *Edinburgh Review* for April, 1864:—"In a letter to Mr. Mudford, dated June 8th, 1815, he (the duke) wrote:—'A remarkable instance of the falsehoods, circulated through the evidence of unofficial despatches, is to be found in the report of a meeting between Marshal Blücher and me at La Belle Alliance, (and some have gone so far as to have seen the chair in which I sat down in the farmhouse.) It happens that the meeting took place after ten at night, at the village of Genappe, and anybody who attempts to describe with truth the operations of the different armies will see that it could not be otherwise.'

"Captain Gronow has gone so far as to say that he was present, with other officers, at the meeting at La Belle Alliance. Confidently as the duke writes, there are strong reasons for suspecting that he was mistaken as to the precise place. It is clear, from French official accounts, that the French did not abandon Genappe till past eleven; from the Prussian, that Blücher and his staff did not reach it till near midnight."

******

One of the first duties attended to when the regiment had piled arms and were lying down in column, was the calling of the roll by a sergeant of each company. I observed that in almost every case of absence, some of the men could say what had happened to the man, whether they knew him to be killed or only wounded. We had left, including officers, exactly 206 of our poor fellows on the Field of Waterloo. Many of the wounded, I believe, but not all, got into houses at Merbe Braine or at the village of Waterloo.

The following was the return of the casualties of the 52nd at Waterloo:—

General Return.	Officers' Names.	
Killed.	*Killed.*	
1 Ensign	Ensign Nettles	
1 Serjeant	*Wounded.*	
36 Rank and File	Major and Bt.-Lieut.-Col. Charles Rowan	Slightly
	Capt. Charles Diggle . . .	Severely
Wounded.	Capt. and Bt.-Major J. F. Love .	Severely
1 Major	Lieut. and Adjt. John Winterbottom	Severely
2 Captains	Lieut. Charles Dawson . . .	Severely
5 Lieutenants	Lieut. Matthew Anderson . .	Severely
10 Serjeants	Lieut. George Campbell . .	Severely
150 Rank and File	Lieut. Thomas Cottingham . .	Severely

Major Hunter Blair, our brigade-major, who was in much concern about General Adam, whom he had not been able to find, came up to me about half an hour after we had halted, when I was near the men, and inquired if anybody had seen General Adam, and stated that he would reward any man who would find the general. This I made known, neither the brigade-major nor I thinking at the moment that by so doing we were giving an opportunity to any bad fellows, who might be so disposed, an opportunity of quitting the column for the purpose of plundering the killed and wounded they might meet with; I am not aware that any did so; but within half a minute, a man came to me in front of the general, who rode into the bivouac from the direction of Genappe, and said, "Here is General Adam, sir!" Neither Blair nor I thought him entitled to the promised reward, as the general had found the regiment and was within a few paces of it when the man saw him.

Adam had conducted himself with great gallantry in front of the 52nd when they took the French Imperial Guard in flank, and evinced his pluck also in not leaving the field, when severely wounded in the leg. As he sat on his horse for some little time near our fire, I heard him say that "he should never forget the honour of having commanded the 52nd on that eventful day."

The following is taken from the 52nd *Record*:—

On returning to England for the recovery of his wounds, the following extract of a letter from Major-General Sir Frederick Adam was communicated to the 52nd regiment:—

I request you will express in my name to the officers, non-commissioned officers and men of the brigade, (52nd, 71st, and 95th regiments,) how much I regret my separation from them. The expectation of being early enabled to rejoin, and the hope of doing so, (which till within these last few days I have continually entertained,) have alone prevented my sooner expressing to the several corps of the brigade the admiration I shall ever entertain of their intrepid and noble conduct in the battle of the 18th of June. To have had the good fortune of being at their head on so glorious an occasion will be to me a subject of increasing satisfaction. In proportion as I have regretted being separated from the light brigade, I shall look forward with anxiety to resuming that which through life it will be my pride to have held.

    (Signed)   Frederick Adam,
                                                   Major-General.

After our arrival at Rosomme I lay down for a few minutes on the flank of No. 9 company, and on my saying "Can anyone give me a drink of water," I was gratified with the kindness of the men, for there was no getting a supply of water where we were, yet four or five of them, directly they heard me, readily began to pass their canteens (wallets) towards me. I have always retained a grateful recollection of this little kindness. It is a rule with soldiers to go into action, if they can, with their canteens full of water, for, when a man is severely wounded, the desire for water is sometimes almost intolerable. I shall have to relate an instance of this presently.

About three-quarters of an hour after we had halted at Rosomme, the first column of the Prussians, by whom the pursuit was to be taken up, arrived from Planchenoit. As they marched round the column of the 52nd from Planchenoit into the Charleroi road, they broke into slow time, and their bands played, "God save the King." A mounted officer, who rode up the bank, and passed along the flank of the column, which was lying down, pulled up and asked me in French "if that was an English colour;" (I still kept it in my possession, to give some poor tired fellow a little rest before he was placed on sentry over it.) On my replying that it was, he let go his bridle, and taking hold of the colour with both hands, pressed it to his bosom, and patted me on the back, exclaiming, "Brave *Anglais*."

The 52nd *Record* relates the above occurrence as follows:—

> The Prussian regiments, as they came up the road from Planchenoit and wheeled round into the great *chaussée* by Rosomme, moved in slow time, their bands playing our National Anthem, in compliment to our success; and a mounted officer at the head of them embraced the 52nd colour, (which had been carried that day by Ensign William Leeke), to serve as the expression of his tribute of admiration for the British Army.

In a note from my name is the following:—

> Now the Rev. W. Leeke, of Holbrooke, near Derby. The king's colour was singularly lost for a time, buried under the body of Ensign Nettles, who was killed in retiring from the square near Hougomont, about 7 p.m. It was recovered on picking up the wounded.

Some few of the Prussian soldiers passed up the bank and along the flank of our column with strings of three or four horses each, which they had picked up between Planchenoit and Rosomme. They were apparently horses taken from the French guns and ammunition waggons. One man, to whom I spoke, I found very ready to part with a couple of horses for a few *francs*. Probably the thinking he would have considerable difficulty in conducting his prizes very far, in the confused state of the roads by which the Prussians were to advance, may have had something to do with his willingness to part with them at so small a price.

I had no defined object in the purchase, except that I thought it unfair that the Prussians should walk off with all the horses they came across, whilst we got none of them for our portion of the spoil. I took one of the horses for myself, and the other as a mess horse for the officers of the company. It turned out to be a very useful purchase; for half the officers of the regiment lost the whole of their baggage and baggage-horses, in the confusion which prevailed during the whole of the 18th on the road between Waterloo and Brussels. The officers of McNair's company were amongst the unfortunate sufferers. In a pocket on one of the saddles I found a quart bottle of brandy, which I suppose the Prussian soldier had not discovered. I do not think I tasted any of it myself, but I have no doubt it was properly appreciated by some of the more experienced officers, in the absence of anything else to drink or to eat.

Major Chalmers had a small straw hut constructed for himself just large enough to cover the upper half of his body. I took the liberty of lying down at the back of it with my head near to his and my legs stretched out in a contrary direction. I slept soundly and sweetly that night from eleven till about half-past two. How many thousands, within the space of two miles from us, British, Hanoverian, Brunswick, Nassau, Dutch, Belgian, Prussian and French, who bid as fair for life as any of us on the morning of the 18th, were now sleeping the sleep of death or lying desperately wounded on the field of Waterloo amidst what Marshal Ney described, as "the most frightful carnage he had ever witnessed!" Including the Battle of Ligny, between the French and Prussians, on the 16th, and that on the same day between the French and English, &c., at Quatre Bras, the English, Germans, and Prussians lost about 33,857 in killed and wounded, from the 16th to the 18th inclusive.

The loss of the French must have been much greater. Probably the whole amount of the loss on both sides during those three days would be about 75,000 men. Almost all the 52nd wounded officers were very "severely wounded." The late Lieut.-General Sir James Frederick Love, then a brevet-major, was wounded in the head in our attack upon the columns of the Imperial Guard. On falling, he lay on the ground stunned, for some moments; and, on recovering, he put his finger into the wound, and, in his confusion, it appeared to him to go straight down into his head, and, feeling convinced that no man could recover with such a wound, and seeing the 52nd advancing, he ran after them, thinking that he would die with his regiment, instead of lying to die where he was.

He, however, after making the trial, had to succumb. He remained on the ground and there received another severe wound in the foot, besides two other slight wounds. There was some serious intention at one time of taking off his leg, but Bell, the eminent surgeon who wrote one of the *Bridgewater Treatises*, to whom he was known and who had received some attention from him in the Peninsula, hearing that he was lying badly wounded at the village of Waterloo, went to see him, and by his advice the operation was delayed and the limb was saved.

Sir J. F. Love had two brothers in the 52nd, and they, hearing that their brother was severely wounded, obtained leave from Sir John Colborne, after the action, to go back and look for him. As people are so apt to do in the night, they completely missed their direction, and after wandering about for a considerable time, till they were regularly knocked up, they determined to remain for the night at a farmhouse which they had come to. Here the people, who were very glad of their protection, were very kind to them; and after getting something to eat, they had just laid themselves down on some straw in the large kitchen, when there was a loud knocking at the great gates of the farm, and, on these being opened, in stalked three grenadiers of the Imperial Guard with their firelocks and with bayonets fixed.

They would not have been pleasant opponents perhaps for two young officers, but on the elder Love saying to them " *Vous êtes prisonniers?*" they very gladly acquiesced in the proposal, and their firelocks having been placed against the corner of the room, after a little time the five wearied soldiers, who had so lately met in mortal strife, were lying side by side on the same straw, and there slept together till daylight. The French soldiers, no doubt, were most thankful for the protection thus secured to them; for soldiers of a defeated army can never feel quite sure that their lives will be spared by any of their enemies whom they may fall in with; and I suspect the French were that night especially, to make use of an elegant expression recently imported from Cambridge, "awfully afraid" of the Prussians.

I may here mention that General Gneisenau, who had the command of the Prussian advanced troops on the night of the 18th, gave the French no rest. When his infantry, who had been on the march or in action since daybreak, were unable to march any further, he mounted a drummer on one of the horses taken from Napoleon's carriage at Genappe, and made him every now and then beat his drum, to make the French, who did not care so much for the cavalry, think that the infantry were close at their heels. It is stated that in this manner Gneisenau drove the French from seven bivouacs which they had taken up, that he passed through Quatre Bras, which had been abandoned on his approach, and advanced beyond Frasne, a distance of eight miles from Rosomme, before he halted. The French Army, completely scattered and disheartened, fled beyond the Sambre without venturing to make the least stand against their pursuers.

Soon after the 52nd had halted at Rosomme, the present Sir William Rowan, then a brevet-major, received permission from Sir John Colborne to go and look after his brother, the late Sir Charles Rowan, K.C.B., who had been wounded. After passing beyond La Belle Alliance and the ground beyond it, he found Maitland's brigade of Guards between the British and French positions, with their arms piled, he thought. He fell in with an officer of the 1st regiment of Guards, whom he knew; whilst he was speaking to him Sir John Byng rode up and asked "Who is that?" and on the officer replying, "It is Rowan of the 52nd, Sir," Sir John said, "Ah, we saw the 52nd advancing gloriously, as they always do." Sir John Byng, in the early part of the action, commanded the brigade of Guards, composed of a battalion of the Coldstream and one of the 3rd Guards, which was posted in and to the rear of Hougomont.

When General Cooke was wounded, Byng succeeded to the command of the whole division of the Guards, and was with Maitland's brigade when the 52nd attacked the Imperial Guard and advanced in the manner described by him in such glowing terms. Now this conversation happened about a quarter past ten o'clock, two hours after the 52nd had crossed the whole front of the right wing of the British Army, 300 yards and more below the crest of the position; and the fact that Maitland's brigade was still at that late hour below the French position, helps to confirm the idea I have before advanced that scarcely more than four infantry regiments and two brigades of cavalry, Vivian's and Vandeleur's, advanced over the low ground towards the French position on the evening or night of the 18th of June, notwithstanding all that has been said about the duke's advancing his whole line in support of those troops.

I suppose that the greater portion of the British and Allied troops left their stations on the reverse slope of our position, and sought out for themselves ground on which to bivouac, more free, than that on which they had been stationed, from the melancholy sight of the slain and from the groans of the wounded and dying. I fear it was an unavoidable necessity that many of the wounded should be left for the night on the field of battle.

One of the 52nd officers who was ordered on duty to Brussels the next morning, on passing over the ground by which we had advanced, was called upon by name by some of the 52nd men, who had been lying wounded all night, to get something done for them. He was unable to assist them, but at a very early hour a strong fatigue-party was sent out from the regiment to place them under the care of the surgeons. Another fatigue-party was sent out to collect the arms belonging to the regiment. I think by far the greater number of the wounded on our side were removed into houses at Waterloo, Merbe Braine, and other villages, before it became dark on the evening of the 18th. Sir William Rowan proceeded to Waterloo and there found his brother and all the 52nd wounded officers, except Anderson, in the same house.

At daylight on the 19th all were stirring. It was some time before we left our bivouac at Rosomme, perhaps an hour or two. On the opposite side of the Charleroi road was a battalion of the 95th Rifles, whom we had not seen the night before; probably they were the 2nd battalion of the 95th, who belonged to our brigade, and had come up some time after we had halted for the night.

About a third of a mile from the 52nd bivouac, near the farm of Rosomme to the south-east, is the house in which Bonaparte is said to have slept on the night of the 17th. On the other side of the Charleroi road, we found at some little distance some dead bodies, and swords and *cuirasses* which had been thrown away. This would be the ground over which some portions of Vandeleur's and Vivian's cavalry brigades must have passed in pursuit the night before. In one place were a number of letters strewn about which appeared to have been taken from the dead body of a French officer; they were the letters of a young lady in Scotland, to her husband, a French officer, who had *recently* left her to join the French Army. They were just the tender affectionate letters which a young loving wife would write to a husband under such circumstances.

I well remember the following sentence in one of them, "How I pity the poor English." Portions of these letters were listened to with great interest by several officers who were present, and all felt distressed at the thought that such a bitter cup of sorrow awaited the poor young widow. It was observed that one of those present took a peculiar interest in the writer of these letters; he frequently spoke of them, and of her afterwards, and it turned out that he had taken down her name and address, and that on his going on leave to Scotland sometime after, he determined to go to the place in which she lived and to make enquiries about her. The sequel of the story is, that he was somewhat disappointed to find, that she and her husband were living most happily together. The husband had only been severely wounded at Waterloo, and had lost his letters.

If the French officer and his wife should be still living, (1866), and this should be read by them, the account of a matter, with which they were so closely mixed up, will be interesting to them, and it is hoped its public narration will not occasion them any annoyance. The Scotch officer died many years ago.

On moving from Rosomme, we passed through the burning village of Maison du Roi, about a quarter of a mile off, and joined the 71st on the other side of it. The following soldier-like letter to *The United Service Journal* from Sir Thomas Reynell, who commanded the 71st at Waterloo, will shew the good service that regiment performed when the 52nd moved down alone upon the two columns of the Imperial Guard. It also helps to shew that these columns were "*at the bottom of the declivity*" that is, *three or four hundred* yards from the crest of the British position, so that the 2nd battalion of the 1st Guards could not have come in contact with them, but only with their skirmishers:—

Sir Thomas Reynell on the Movement of the 71st during the "Crisis" at Waterloo.

Mr. Editor,—I am induced to address you in consequence of some observations on Sir Hussey Vivian's Reply to 'The Crisis of Waterloo,' that appeared in your last *Journal*, which leave in doubt whether the 71st regiment was not that 'regiment in red' represented to have halted and opened a fire more destructive to their friends than foes, instead of charging at a very critical moment, and thus 'contributing to prevent the complete success of the attack.'

Although Sir Hussey adds that the officer whom he sent to stop the fire of this battalion reported it to be a regiment of the Hanoverian Legion, and asserts, in another part of his reply, that the impression on his mind has always been that they were so, and not the 71st regiment, still something less questionable seems indispensable for the honour and character of the latter distinguished corps; and I trust that I shall be able, in a few words, to supply that something.

From having commanded the 71st regiment from the commencement to the close of that eventful day of Waterloo, and not having for a moment quitted its ranks, it may be presumed that no other person can speak with so much correctness as I can as to the part it performed during the battle.

After the deployment from square, the 71st regiment moved in line, the right wing to the front, the left wing to the rear, forming a third and fourth rank. We passed Hougomont obliquely, throwing the right shoulders a little forward, as stated by the author of 'The Crisis,' and experienced some loss in the companies nearest to the orchard hedge from the fire of the *tirailleurs* posted there. We had in view, *at the bottom of the declivity, two columns of the enemy's infantry*; and my object, and I believe the object of every officer and soldier in the corps, was to come in contact with those columns, but they did not wait our approach, or afford us an opportunity of attacking them.

I can positively assert that from the time the 71st regiment commenced this forward movement it never halted, but maintained a steady advance upon the only enemy in front, until it reached the village of Caillon, against the walls of which were deposited a considerable quantity of arms, as if abandoned by the soldiers composing the enemy's two columns. It was becoming dark at this period, and after scouring the village of Caillon, we retired to a field to the right of it, where we bivouacked for the night, near to our friends the 52nd.

I do not recollect to have seen in our advance any body of men, cavalry or infantry, to our front, but the *two columns of the enemy*; nor do I know that there was any on our right flank so much advanced as we were. I can well imagine that the movement of the 71st, conducted, as I trust it was, in a steady and soldier-like manner, must have afforded a very decided and important support to the troops acting to our left, who approximated closer to the point of the enemy's final attack.

I have no desire whatever to attract notice to the services of the 71st regiment in the Battle of Waterloo, firmly believing that every battalion and corps of the British Army engaged did the duty assigned to it fully as well; but I confess that I have every wish to remove the possibility of its being supposed that at any moment the regiment could have hesitated to attack an enemy opposed to it; and I only hope that this plain statement of facts will convince the readers of your valuable *Journal* that the 'regiment in red,' alluded to in Sir Hussey Vivian's Reply, was not the 71st Light Infantry.

I remain, Sir, your most obedient humble Servant,

Thos. Reynell, Major-General.

Devonshire Place, 18th July, 1833.

The 52nd remained for several hours on the morning of the 19th near Maison du Roi, before they marched to Nivelles. Meat was served out, and the men cooked. I recollect having there first eaten "beefsteaks fried at the end of a ramrod." My servant brought some water for us to drink from a pond in which he said there were the dead bodies of two French soldiers, and that he could not find any other water. Some of our men had some orders and other things, which they had picked up on the field of battle; probably the men had belonged to one of the fatigue-parties sent out to take up any of our wounded who had remained on the ground all night, and to collect arms belonging to the regiment. I bought a pair of brass-barrelled pistols from one of the men.

In a field about two hundred yards off, to the left of the *chaussée*, I found a French ammunition-waggon, and supplied myself with some cartridges, which fitted my pistols, for the purpose of putting an unfortunate horse, that had had its leg shot off, out of its misery. I did not succeed very well, as the horse, whenever I pulled the trigger, so suddenly moved his head that my aim did not take effect. Two Prussians coming up from Planchenoit, one of them a sergeant, shot the horse for me. After this I rode forward to a hamlet nearly half a mile in advance. I took three or four canteens with me to see if I could not get some water fit to drink; but one of our men whom I desired to fill them for me, told me when I was leaving the place afterwards, that he had filled them with beer, which he thought better than water.

I remained in a farmhouse at this place for some time, as there were several wounded men filling all the lower rooms, to whom I and some of our men tried to render some little services. One was a man. of the 7th Hussars who had received seven wounds when that regiment charged the French lancers, just to the north of Genappe, on the afternoon of the 17th. He described to me the manner and order in which he had received his wounds, all of which I do not distinctly recollect; but several of them, though not all, were lance wounds, inflicted whilst he was lying on the ground. There appears to have been much of this unnecessarily cruel work of piercing those lying on the ground wounded, carried on by the French lancers at Waterloo.

Some of our cavalry regiments have since that time been armed with lances; but it may be worthy of the consideration of our own military authorities and of those of other nations, whether the use of a weapon, which appears to be chiefly used for the unmanly and cruel purpose of putting the wounded to death, might not be altogether given up. This 7th Hussar man, who had not till then been discovered and visited by any surgeon, was, whilst I was at the place, taken away by his own regiment. How he had got so far away from the ground on which he was wounded I do not know; but I think the distance from Genappe must have been nearly two miles. I had some hope that the man would recover.

On the other side of the fireplace, on a bed or *mattrass*, lay a poor fellow belonging to the grenadiers of the French Guard. He had, I thought, a fatal wound from which the bowels protruded. When he saw one of our men washing the wounds of the hussar, he begged that he would bring the water to him also; and on this being done, he eagerly seized the basin, and quenched his burning thirst by drinking deeply of the bloody water which it contained.

On my return to the regiment, with my canteens hanging on each side of my saddle, and my pistols stuck through the straps which fastened on my boat cloak in front of me, I saw our general of division, Sir Henry Clinton, and some of his staff coming towards me. He looked all the more formidable from a fashion he had adopted of wearing his cocked hat, not in the usual way, "fore and aft," but with the small ends over either shoulder. I thought I must look so much like a marauder, that I was rather ashamed of being seen by him. I soon disposed of my pistols by pitching them over a hedge on my right, never to see them again, and thus freed from the chief appendage I was ashamed of, I passed the general without attracting his particular attention.

Whilst I was away, a French ammunition-waggon was blown up not far from the regiment, and two men of the brigade were killed. I think one belonged to the 71st and the other to the 95th Rifles. They were on the top of the waggon, hacking at it with a hatchet or billhook to get some wood for cooking. I am not sure that it was not the same ammunition-waggon from which I had been helping myself to cartridges some little time before.

When the regiment fell in for the march to Nivelles, an inspection of knapsacks took place and several things were thrown away with which some of the men had encumbered themselves. We formed square either before or after this inspection, and some men were paraded as prisoners, who had fallen out drunk at Braine-le-comte on the morning of the 17th, in consequence of getting access to some wine vaults in that town, and had thus missed being with their regiment at Waterloo. Sir John Colborne addressed them, and said he should forgive them, as he considered it was a sufficient punishment for them that they had been absent from their regiment *"when they had the honour of defeating the Imperial Guard of France, led on by the Emperor Napoleon Bonaparte in person."*

We supposed then, from what the French *chef d'escadron* had reported, that the emperor was with his guard when we attacked them; but it afterwards appeared from the French accounts that it was not so, and that after they had marched past him in the low ground between the two armies, he had gone back to the French position, from which he only retired with the squares of the Old Guard.

CHAPTER 10

1815: Defeat of the French Imperial Guard by the 52nd Alone

I must now, before I proceed to give the account of our march from Waterloo to Paris, enter upon the consideration of the following questions:—

1. Did the 52nd, as I have asserted in my account of what that regiment achieved at Waterloo, move down at least 300 yards from its position in the right wing of the Allied Army, and defeat, single-handed, by an attack on their left flank, the two heavy columns of the Imperial Guard, apparently consisting of about 10,000 men?

2. Did the 1st Guards on that occasion, or on any other on that day, do anything beyond receiving and defeating various charges made by the French cavalry, and driving off, by an advance of their left battalion in line, the mass of skirmishers of the French Guard, and perhaps of Donzelôt's division, who were firing into them?

I must endeavour to bring forward the various proofs I have of the correctness of my assertion relative to the defeat of the Imperial Guard by the 52nd alone, in the best order I can.

Every officer of the regiment who served at Waterloo has never had the least doubt of the correctness of the statement that the 52nd, and the 52nd alone, moved down upon the left flank of the Imperial Guard and defeated it, and when the Duke of Wellington's despatch reached us on our march to Paris, all considered themselves as most unjustly treated because Colborne's daring feat was not even alluded to.

Shortly after the 52nd reached Paris and were encamped in the

Champs Elysees, Sir John Colborne gave us the following account of what Sir John Byng had said, on meeting him a day or two before. He said:—

> How do your fellows like our getting the credit of doing what you did at Waterloo? I could not advance when you did, because all our ammunition was gone.

Some little time afterwards, when Sir John Colborne met Byng, and tried to lead him to speak on the subject again, he found him quite disinclined to do so. Many years afterwards, I think it was in 1850, when I was dining with Lord Seaton in town, one of his sons requested me to try and draw his father out to talk about Waterloo, saying that he often told them about his other battles, but they could not get him to speak much about that. I took an opportunity of asking him if he recollected much about Waterloo, and I suppose I particularised the charge of the 52nd on the Imperial Guard, for I remember he said, "Did you ever hear what Sir John Byng said to me at Paris?"

I replied that I had a very distinct recollection of it; but that I should be very much obliged if he would repeat to me what Sir John Byng had said, in order that I might see, if my recollection of it exactly tallied with his. Lord Seaton then gave me the account of what passed on the two occasions of his meeting Byng, just as I have related it above, and exactly as I remembered to have heard it from him five and thirty years before in the camp at Paris.

An old officer of the 52nd, who has now been dead for many years, wrote as follows in 1853, in reference to the advance of the 52nd on the French Guard and to the subsequent unjust treatment the regiment received, in that the credit of, and the reward for, their splendid charge was given to the 1st regiment of the British Guards, *who really had nothing at all to do with it*:—

> "The wheeling of a battalion in line, though under such circumstances the only practicable mode of changing front, was altogether unprecedented, just one of those promptings of inspiration that mark the mind of a great general. Executed amid a continued roar of artillery that rendered words of command inaudible, trusting chiefly to the further companies that they would be guided by the touch to their inward flank, it could hardly have been ventured at all, but for the previous precaution of the commanding officer, who, when the order was given by the duke, that all the regiments in the centre should form four deep, rather than loosen his files by that formation, had prepared

to double his line by placing one wing closed up in rear of the other; another instance, to show how the knowledge of details, and constant attention to them, are essential in order to enable an officer to apply his men to the best purpose.

"Owing to the skill with which the movement was made, the very *acmé* of time being seized, never perhaps was more signal service done by a body of troops so disproportionate in number to the force attacked; that force being composed of the *élite* of the enemy's army, the most veteran troops in Europe. A line on the flank of a column exhibits in the highest degree the triumphs of skill over number. The column has only the alternative of flight or destruction.

"This adventurous movement was undertaken upon his sole responsibility, by the commanding officer of a single battalion, and, from the first onset of the 52nd, that regiment and the 71st proceeded to the close of the day without receiving orders from any general officer, whether of brigade or division. (The movement of the 71st in support of the advance of the 52nd is described in Sir Thomas Reynell's letter, which will be found towards the close of the last chapter.)

"The successful charge and immediate pursuit of the broken columns carried Adam's brigade far ahead of the other troops, constituting them, as it were, an advanced guard to the main body of the British Army.

"We must not omit the admirable steadiness and intelligence of the men, mostly veterans of the Peninsula, enabling the commanding officer in the first place to rely on them for taking up, amid a deafening fire, such a movement as a wheel in line, which every military man knows would in general be an awkward business for the first time on a quiet parade-ground, and next exhibited in the cool way in which they treated the irruption of cavalry on them, causing the officers to remark, that with such self-possession, they need never be under any apprehension from a charge.

"The duke in his account of the battle entered but little into particulars. Of the period here referred to he says:—

> These attacks were repeated till about seven in the evening, when the enemy made a desperate charge with cavalry and infantry, supported by the fire of artillery, to force our left centre near the farm of La Haye Sainte, which, after a severe contest, was defeated.

"It is to be recollected that the despatch was written during the night succeeding the day of the battle in the house in which some of his staff were lying wounded and dying, and that it comprised also the action of Quatre Bras.

"These circumstances may account for its being somewhat brief, but certainly when the *Gazette* came out, a good deal of disappointment was felt that more detail had not been given. It was not only those who were engaged in that particular part of the fight we have been describing who were impressed with the importance of the service rendered in that conjuncture, but, two days after the battle, it so happened that sufficient means were afforded of learning something of the general sense of the army on the subject. Two officers from every regiment of cavalry and infantry were ordered back to Brussels to look after any missing soldiers, and among these, on their meeting there in the public rooms, discussing the events so fresh in their minds, it was the common consent that the charge of the 52nd was not only the decisive action of the day, but that it was one of the most gallant feats ever performed.

"And it may be said that a feeling stronger than disappointment arose, when it appeared that the defeat of Napoleon's last great effort was attributed to the Guards. The error was thus occasioned:—The battle commenced by the attack on Hougomont, which was occupied by a detachment of Byng's brigade of Guards, who held it during the day, had a hard service, and performed it well. So the duke in his despatch said:—

The Guards set an example which was followed by all.

"This therefore was true enough, but Lord Bathurst, at that time Secretary for War and the Colonies, having to make a speech on the occasion in the House of Lords, founded a romance upon it, and said that the British Guards had encountered the grenadiers of the Imperial Guard and overthrown them. Then too was invented the story of 'Up, Guards, and at them,' a myth of the same baseless character with the '*Meurt mais ne se rend pas*' of the French. It was a piece of gossip picked up in the camp by Sir Walter Scott on his visit to Paris, first appearing in his '*Paul's Letters to His Kinsfolk*,' and from thence gravely adopted by Alison as an historical fact.

✶✶✶✶✶✶

Note:—An instance of the common proneness to fiction respecting the events of great battles is to be observed in the repeated French assertions, that the British at Waterloo fought behind entrenchments. It had been proposed to the duke, when he looked over the ground a month before, to throw up some redoubts, but he refused, saying, "No, no, that would tell them where we mean to fight." The choice was decided rather by the junction of the great roads to Brussels, than by any great advantage of the ground: so that Picton, half an hour before the action began, said, "I have just ridden along the whole length of the line, and I never saw a worse position."

★★★★★★

"However, these fictions served as an excuse for making the 1st Guards grenadiers, and giving the ensigns of all three regiments precedence over those of the line by lieutenant's rank. And as most writers of narratives of battles think it is excusable to cover their ignorance of facts, by the use of inflated language and figurative descriptions of unrealities, so these inventions have become the staple of almost every subsequent account of Waterloo, and this trash has been handed on from one to the other till, by force of repetition, there is risk that at a future day, when none remain to contradict, it may be recognised as authentic; while the knowledge of such a piece of generalship as the charge of the 52nd, so full of interest and instruction to military men, is in danger of being altogether lost."

★★★★★★★★★★

The writer of the above says, in a letter I received from him in June, 1853:—

The Duke of Richmond, I mean the present one, was with the duke very near the Guards, and he says that until the 52nd began their movement the duke was very anxious; that his anxiety was to be seen in his countenance, and that he never saw such evident relief of mind as when the 52nd appeared moving across the ground so strong and steady.

★★★★★★

Note:—The Duke of Richmond was a captain in the 52nd at that time, but served on the staff of the Prince of Orange at Waterloo. After the prince was wounded, he attached himself it appears to the Duke of Wellington.

★★★★★★

I have mentioned before that all the officers of the 52nd who served at Waterloo were fully convinced that a very great injustice had been done to the regiment by the attempt to give to the British

Guards the credit of having repulsed the attack of the French Imperial Guard, or, as Captain Siborne has ventured to state, of having repulsed *the leading column* of the Imperial Guard.

In 1833 my friend and relative Colonel Gawler, then a major in the 52nd, published his admirably written work, *The Crisis of Waterloo*, and the wonder is how, with the few materials he had at command for such a work, he described so accurately, as he did, the movements of the two brigades of cavalry, and of the three or four regiments of infantry who were engaged at the crisis. From being on the extreme right of the 52nd he was not aware of the great distance (300 yards) of the left of our line from the British position, when it became parallel with the leading column of the French Guard, nor did he see, as we on the left and left centre of the 52nd line saw, the skirmishers of the Imperial Guard forming about a hundred yards in front of the leading battalion, when they had been driven down from the British position—no doubt by the 3rd battalion of the 1st Guards; he therefore fell into the mistake, which has been adopted by subsequent writers, of thinking and stating that:—

> The headmost companies of the Imperial Guard (those that the 52nd attacked) crowned the very summit of the position—their dead bodies, the next day, bore unanswerable evidence to the fact.

When he wrote *The Crisis* he was not aware, that the columns of the Imperial Guard had been preceded by a mass of skirmishers, and that the bodies he saw the next morning on the summit of the position, must have been the bodies of some of these skirmishers. But Colonel Gawler, although supposing that the head of the columns of the Imperial Guard had reached the summit of the British position, never for a moment had the idea that these columns were repulsed by the British Guards, but solely by the flank attack of the 52nd. His book was only written to refute the claim put forward on the part of the Guards, and he thus expresses himself on the subject:—

> All the accounts of the battle which have hitherto come before the public, including those by the standard writers of the day, (and general opinion even in the army has much followed the same current), assert more or less directly, that the attack of the Imperial Guard was repulsed and the French Army thrown into irretrievable confusion—either by a charge of General Maitland's brigade of Guards—or by an advance of the whole

line. But, if the leading points in the preceding account be, as they are maintained to be, correct, it follows, that the attack of the Imperial Guard was repulsed, and the French Army thrown into consequent irretrievable confusion by neither of these causes, but by a charge of the 52nd covered by the 71st regiment, without the direct co-operation of any other portion of the Allied Army.

For as the 52nd charged across the whole front of attack from right to left, a simultaneous successful attack from any other corps must have crossed the charge of the 52nd, and no such event took place. These points are not advanced in a spirit either of display or dispute, but simply for the purposes before described. If incorrect they are open to refutation; and no one will be more gratified than the writer to see correction or refutation ably and thoroughly, if candidly attempted by any, who, having been eye-witnesses of these events, may conceive they have sufficient grounds for establishing either. If injustice in any shape has been done to the corps, to whom the credit of deciding the crisis has been hitherto more or less imputed, it is altogether unintentional.

These battalions very hardly earned the honours justly due to them, not at the crisis and close, but by a most successful defence of their place in the position, during the reiterated attacks of the ordinary progress of the battle: they earned them well, and may they long, very long, continue to wear them untarnished. General Adam's brigade, posted during the early part of the day in reserve on the extreme right of the line, came up to the right centre at an advanced period of the action, principally to meet the fresh and desperate masses of the enemy which pressed on for the crisis; it was then their opportunity, and why should they not also wear the laurels they then as fairly gained?

★★★★★★

Note:—It will be perceived that Colonel Gawler has here omitted to mention the advance of Adam's brigade over the British position and a quarter of a mile down the slope towards the enemy, and our standing there for nearly three hours, exposed to a furious cannonade from the artillery of the centre and of a part of the left wing of the French Army.

★★★★★★

The battalions first referred to, possess too many indisputably their own, gathered on this and other fields, to require for the completion of their reputation a leaf to which they have no just title, while that leaf, torn as it was from the bearskin caps of imperial grenadiers at the grand crisis of the fate of Waterloo, of Napoleon, and of Europe, should not for ever be silently relinquished of those, by whom it was really won.

Eighteen years (Colonel Gawler published *The Crisis of Waterloo* in 1833), have elapsed without an effort to correct the error or to establish the claim, and if the attempt had further been deferred to any much later period, the generation of those who fought at Waterloo might so far have passed away, as to have left the question, without sufficient supporting evidence on either side, a standing subject of doubtful dispute and of historical obscurity."

It will have been observed from what has been stated, that those on the left of the 52nd line, when it was nearly parallel with the flank of the columns of the Imperial Guard, could see up the British position 200 yards beyond the ground on which the French skirmishers formed, when repulsed by the 3rd battalion of the Guards. This ground was entirely clear of anything in the shape of a defeated *column* of the Imperial Guard. And we were not a little astonished when we found that Siborne had stated in his *History of Waterloo* that the Guards had defeated the leading column of the French Guard. He was fully aware, when compiling his history, of what the 52nd claimed to have done; but yet, on weighing all the intricate and contradictory accounts which he received from officers of different corps, with whom he corresponded, he sought to reconcile them all by adopting this myth about a leading column having been defeated by our Guards.

The history of a great battle, especially if the materials for it are collected by one who did not see the principal events which he attempts to describe, must necessarily abound in mistakes. Captain Siborne took immense pains in collecting information, both when he first determined to construct his beautiful model of the Field of Waterloo, and afterwards when he was about to write the history of the battle, nearly thirty years after it was fought. Of course, after the lapse of so many years, the greater portion of those he consulted could not be expected to recollect much that they had witnessed with any great degree of accuracy, or to be able always to distinguish between what they themselves had witnessed and what they had heard from others or had read of in accounts of the action.

In the preface to his history, dated March, 1844, he says:—

> Anxious to ensure the rigorous accuracy of my work, (the model,) I ventured to apply for information to nearly all the surviving eye-witnesses of the incidents which my model was intended to represent. In every quarter, and amongst officers of all ranks, from the general to the subaltern, my applications were responded to in a most generous and liberal spirit, and the result did indeed surprise me, so greatly at variance was this historical evidence with the general notions which had prevailed on the subject. Thus, was suggested the present work. I was induced by the success of this experiment, to embrace a wider field, and to extend my inquiries over the entire battle, and ultimately throughout the campaign itself, from its commencement to its close.
>
> Having become the depositary of such valuable materials, I felt a duty to the honourable profession of which I am a humble member, to submit to it and to the world a true and faithful account of this memorable epoch in the history of Britain's military greatness.
>
> Though not so presumptuous as to imagine that I have fully supplied so absolute a *desideratum*, yet I consider myself fortunate in being the instrument of withdrawing so far the veil from truth. One of my Waterloo correspondents has humorously remarked that:—
>
>> If ever truth lies at the bottom of a well, she does so immediately after a great battle, and it takes an amazingly long time before she can be lugged out.
>
> The time for her emerging appears to have at length arrived, but, while I feel that I have brought to light much that was involved in obscurity, I cannot but be sensible that I may have fallen into errors. Should such be the case, I shall be most ready, hereafter, to make any corrections that may appear requisite, on my being favoured, *by eye-witnesses*, with further well authenticated information.

I find the following note written by me some years ago on the pages of my copy of Captain Siborne's work which contain the preface from which the above is extracted:—

Captain Siborne appears to have consulted more than one officer, and in some cases, several officers of the same regiment. Their accounts would of course vary as to the exact time and as to circumstances. In the case of the 52nd, and I think in the case of the 3rd battalion of the 1st Guards, he mentions things somewhat similar to each other, as having taken place on separate occasions, when in fact they only occurred once.

It may be well to remark here that in nothing have I found so much difference as in the ideas which people have formed respecting *the time occupied* by the several events, which occurred in connexion with the proceedings of the 52nd at Waterloo. Even under the long and severe cannonade we experienced, time passed much more quickly than it appeared to do. One intelligent 52nd officer, who, some years ago, was arguing with me about the time occupied by a certain movement or event—I forget now what it was—very soon gave way, saying:—

> I must not argue with you about the time it occupied, for I confess the whole of the Battle of Waterloo appeared to me only to last two hours.

The following are instances in which Captain Siborne has been led, in the arrangement of the immense amount of conflicting information supplied to him, to mention *the same event as having happened at two or three different times*. In the second volume of the second edition of his work, in speaking of events which took place some considerable time before the advance of the Imperial Guard, he gives the following description of an event which resembles in some of its principal features, what did afterwards really take place as regards the 3rd battalion of the Guards, (see my account earlier), with the exception that the skirmishers are not represented as being Imperial Guardsmen, but as having come from the hollow near La Haye Sainte:—

> A mass of *tirailleurs* now ascended by their left, from the hollow westward of La Haye Sainte, and pushed forward with great boldness against the advanced square of Maitland's British brigade formed by the 3rd battalion of the 1st Foot Guards. Their fire, concentrated upon the square, and maintained with astonishing rapidity and vigour, was most galling to the British Guards. Also, upon their left another portion of their numbers poured a destructive fire upon the left square of Adam's brigade,

formed by the 2nd battalion of the 95th Rifles. The exposed situation of the 3rd battalion of Guards, the fire from which in square was necessarily so vastly disproportioned to that by which it was assailed, caught the eye of the Duke of Wellington, who immediately rode up to the battalion, and ordered it to form line and drive the skirmishers down the slope.

Its commander, Lieut.-Colonel D'Oyley, wheeled up the right and left faces of the square—the right half of the rear face accompanying the former, and the other half the left face—into line with the front face, and charged the enemy down the hill. A body of French cavalry was now seen approaching, but the battalion re-formed square with great rapidity and regularity. The cavalry refused the square, but receiving its fire, and then dashing along the front of the 52nd regiment, it exposed itself to another vigorous fire by which it was nearly destroyed; whilst the 3rd battalion of the Guard retired, in perfect order, to its original position.

As regards the 52nd, all that is said in the above paragraph is mere moonshine; the 52nd never fired on the enemy's cavalry at the time referred to; indeed they never fired, *whilst in line*, on any cavalry excepting on a mixed body of English and French, immediately after passing the killed and wounded of the Imperial Guard, and both on that occasion and when in square they were charged by the French *cuirassiers*, they were some hundreds of yards from the 3rd battalion of the 1st Guards.

It must be remembered that the 2nd battalion of the 1st Guards, which was the right battalion of Maitland's brigade, was stationary and not firing at the time of the attack of the Imperial Guard. This was Lord Hill's statement, who was on the right of the brigade, and from the position saw the advance of the Imperial Guard and also the right-shoulder-forward movement and charge of the 52nd. The 3rd battalion of the 1st Guards only claimed to have advanced against the enemy once, and that was against what they called a column of the Imperial Guard, and that advance took place as I have before described it.

Not only the Imperial Guard skirmishers, whom we saw form in front of their leading column, were driven in by this advance, but also the skirmishers and their supports said to have been sent forward from Donzelôt's division to attack the right of Alten's division; this might account for their being called a column, and some of the skirmishers being Imperial Guardsmen may have led to its being called the *leading column of the Imperial Guard*; but as I have stated, and as will be shewn still more clearly hereafter, no column of the French Guard preceded those with which we came in contact.

In the second volume of Siborne's history, we have his account of the attack of the French Imperial Guard on the British Guards, and it will be seen from the following extracts, how it coincides, in various particulars, (such as the duke riding up, the square forming line on its front face, the driving the enemy down the slope, the alarm of cavalry, and the retiring to the position,) with the advance of the 3rd battalion of the 1st Guards related above as having taken place a considerable time before:—

> Pressing boldly forward, they had arrived within fifty paces of the spot on which the British Guards were lying down, when Wellington gave the talismanic call, 'Up, Guards, make ready!' and ordered Maitland to attack.
>
> ******
>
> Note:—Neither this, nor the more current expression of "Up, Guards, and at them!" was ever used by the Duke of Wellington. He merely told the commanding officer of the 2nd battalion of the Guards to "form in line on the front face of the square and drive those fellows in."
>
> ******
>
> The British Guards had continued their charge some distance down the slope of the hill, when Maitland perceived the second attacking column of the Imperial Guard advancing on his right, and exposing his *brigade* to the imminent risk of being turned on that flank.
>
> ******
>
> Note:—Who would gather from this description the fact, that the 2nd battalion of the 1st Guards never moved from their place on the position all this time, as there is abundant testimony to prove, besides that of Lord Hill and Sir John Byng? There were only two battalions in Maitland's brigade of the 1st regiment of Guards— the 2nd and 3rd battalions.
>
> ******
>
> He accordingly gave the order to face about and retire; but amidst their victorious shouts, and the noise of the firing of cannon and other arms, the command was imperfectly under-

stood, and the first sense of danger led to a cry of 'Form square' being passed along the line, it being naturally assumed that the enemy's cavalry would take advantage of their isolated position; which, however, was not the case. The flanks of battalions gave way as if to form square. Saltoun conspicuously exerted himself in endeavouring to rectify the mistake, but in vain; and the whole went to the rear.

Also in his second volume, Captain Siborne, in attempting a description of the advance of our brigade over the British position, four hours before the driving in of the skirmishers of the Imperial Guard by the 3rd battalion of the 1st Guards, makes statements and brings forward expressions, so similar, in some respects, to those used in relation to this latter event, that I cannot but look upon them as really belonging to that period. They certainly do not at all properly describe what happened to Adam's brigade on that occasion, for the duke was not then near them, nor were any French skirmishers attacked by them, and therefore the duke could not order them, as Siborne states in the following extract, to "drive those fellows away;" but all these things did occur to the 3rd battalion of the 1st Guards, and the very words just mentioned were uttered by the duke to Colonel D'Oyley, four hours afterwards, when they attacked and drove off the Imperial Guard skirmishers.

This I had several years ago from a very intelligent officer of the 3rd battalion of the Guards, who was present in the action. The extracts referred to above are as follows:—

> Suddenly the summit in front of Adam's brigade was crowded with the French skirmishers, who were almost as quickly concealed by the smoke from the rattling fire which they opened upon the Allied artillery and the squares. The gunners, whose numbers were fearfully diminished, were speedily driven back from their crippled batteries upon the nearest infantry, upon which the concentration of this most galling fire threatened the most serious consequences. But succour was at hand. Wellington, in the midst of a shower of bullets, had galloped to the front of Adam's brigade, ordered it to form line, four deep, and then, pointing to the daring skirmishers on the height, called out, with perfect coolness and unaffected assurance, 'Drive those fellows away.' With loud cheers the brigade moved rapidly up the slope, eager to obey the duke's commands.

The French skirmishers began to give way as the firm and intrepid front of the brigade presented itself to their view. Adam continued his advance, driving the French infantry before him.

I have thus endeavoured to point out how Captain Siborne has mentioned things as having taken place on two or three separate occasions, when in fact they only occurred once. In the case of the 3rd battalion of Maitland's brigade of Guards, they themselves only claim to have advanced and driven the enemy down the slope on one occasion, and that this advance was not an advance of the whole brigade, but only of one battalion, whereas Siborne makes them to have done so twice.

And he has also scattered some leaves of laurel on the 52nd which they are not entitled to, whilst at the same time he has treated them most unfairly by attempting to deprive them of that full share of honour and glory, and of that very large branch of the emblematic evergreen, which so justly is their due, for having so steadily and "gloriously," under their noble and gallant commander, moved down upon and defeated, without the direct help of any other regiment or portion of a regiment, ten thousand of the best and most veteran troops of Europe, led on by Marshal Ney, "the bravest of the brave," and others of the most experienced officers of the French Army, and accompanied by their artillery, and having large bodies of cavalry not far from them.

Perhaps this was one of the most dashing exploits ever performed by a single regiment;— and I trust the 52nd will no longer be deprived of the laurels they so nobly and fairly won on the bloodstained field of Waterloo. It must be remembered also that the defeat of the two columns of the Imperial Guard by the 52nd led immediately to the flight of the whole French Army. *The Prussians till then had been completely held at bay by the French at Planchenoit.*

Sometime after the completion of the model of Waterloo, and when it was about to be removed from London for exhibition in the large towns of England and Scotland, I went to see it for the first time, and met Captain Siborne there. I had given him information, in consequence of his having applied to me through Colonel Gawler, as to the crops growing where we stood in square to the left of Hougomont, and where we stood in line on the reverse slope of the British position just before we advanced to the attack of the Imperial Guard, and with regard to some other matters connected with that attack.

I therefore introduced myself to him, and spoke in terms of admiration of his beautiful model; but I told him that we of the 52nd were dissatisfied with the forward position he had given to Maitland's brigade of Guards, and to his representing a first French column as having been routed by them, and as flying in disorder towards and near to the Charleroi road, as we *knew both these things to be incorrect*. He merely shrugged his shoulders as much to say he could not now help it, and that there was no use now in discussing the matter. There was a sergeant there who was helping to exhibit the model: he had been in the 1st Guards at Waterloo; on my asking how far they had gone down the slope, from the British position, in pursuit of the French, he said "a few yards only, and that then they retired again."

It seems somewhat astonishing that when Captain Siborne must have known that only the 3rd battalion of the 1st Guards made the forward movement, and that the 2nd battalion of that regiment was stationary at the time, he should have ventured to place the latter on his model in a forward position, and on a line with the 3rd battalion within 100 yards of the French Guard, at the moment that he represents the 52nd as being at exactly the same distance from the flank of the same Imperial column. When the 52nd was within that distance of the column of the Imperial Guard, the French skirmishers had just been driven in, the 3rd battalion of the Guards, on the cry of "cavalry," had retired over the British position and some considerable distance down the reverse slope to the point at which Vivian's hussar brigade had arrived, for they were seen by that brigade retiring in some disorder.

They would have arrived at a point at some distance below the British position on its reverse slope, at the very time that the French skirmishers were seen by the 52nd to run in and form 100 yards in front of the leading column of the Imperial Guard, and 200 yards from the British position; these 300 yards being seen by us to be clear of all troops excepting these two or three companies of the Imperial Guard, containing perhaps three hundred men who had been skirmishing and firing into the square of the 3rd battalion of the Guards, and had then been driven off by them.

If there had been a *first* column of the Imperial Guards defeated and driven down the slope, as Siborne represents the case, how is it that the skirmishers, we saw, ran down to the long columns the 52nd attacked, and formed up in such a soldier-like and steady way a little a-head of that mass of troops? besides which, we must have seen such a defeated column, if there had been one at the time and on the ground indicated by Siborne both on his model and in his history of Waterloo.

In the *Life* of the late Lieut.-General Sir William Napier, the historian of the peninsular war, the following paragraph appears in one of his letters:—

Depend upon it, Waterloo has a long story of treachery and secret politics attached to it, which will not be made known in our days, if ever.

I have frequently wondered if Sir William Napier wrote this in connexion with the wrong, which he knew very well had been perpetrated on the 52nd, in what has somewhat the appearance of a systematic plan to deprive that regiment of the honour of having done, what the world never saw before, in having made single-handed the most glorious advance against, and the most successful defeat of, ten times their own number, of the best disciplined troops of any age or country, barring always our own gallant army.

I shall here introduce what I had intended to place in the appendix—a letter, taken from Sir William Napier's *Life*, on the regimental training of our young officers, written some time in 1853, in which he speaks of the defeat of the French Imperial Guard by the 52nd, under Lord Seaton, in connexion with Sir John Moore's system of training:—

To the Editor of *The Naval and Military Gazette.*
Sir,—Introducing the letter of 'Veritas,' you say, the late Duke of Wellington opposed, '*as contrary to our national feelings*' the having officers taught practically the whole routine of regimental discipline, from the first position of the drill-squad to marching in the ranks and mounting guard with the privates, which you nevertheless think would be useful.
Did the duke really object? He must have known that at Shorncliffe Sir John Moore introduced, and rigidly enforced that very system, and thus formed the British regiments of the light division, who were perhaps, or rather certainly, the best instructed, the most efficient military body in the field that modern times has produced—not excepting Napoleon's Guard, as Lord Seaton well proved with the 52nd regiment at Waterloo. The officers of those regiments, the 43rd, 52nd, and 95th Rifles, were never averse to, or mortified at, being made to acquire, amidst the private soldiers, a complete knowledge of what as officers they were to exact from, and superintend with, those privates. Never did the system lead to disrespect or undue familiarity on

the part of the soldiers; on the contrary, it produced the natural effect of knowledge, combined with power, willing and entire obedience from the soldiers, while the officers were proud of their acquirements, knew their men, and were known to them; knew when to exact and when to relax, and were in every sense commanders. This knowledge carried them through many a hard struggle, when ignorance would have gone to the wall.

Much, very much, now forgotten and unknown, did Sir John Moore do for the British Army, and I may perhaps here after recall some of it to public recollection. At present I halt at this point.

Whilst reading Sir William Napier's *Life*, I made also the following extract, as it bears upon my present object:—

What would become of mankind if the arena where must be fought out the great battle of right against wrong should be deserted by the champions of the good cause?

In accordance with this sentiment I have felt it to be my duty to endeavour to set forth in its right and true light the great event which took place at the crisis of the battle of Waterloo—the defeat of the French Imperial Guard. I believe there is no one now remaining of the 52nd officers, but myself, who has both the recollections and the materials necessary for bringing before the public the "wrong" which was perpetrated against that regiment immediately after Waterloo, and which has continued to be perpetrated, though not to the same extent, ever since.

I think I have observed before, that the officers of the 52nd always felt, with great indignation, the wrong which had been inflicted on the regiment.

Lord Seaton was very decided in his statements on the subject, though he always spoke about the charge of the 52nd with his usual modesty.

The late Lieut.-Colonel John Bentham, who served in the 52nd for many years, and afterwards did himself so much credit, and rendered good service to his country, when in command of the 3rd regiment of Lancashire Militia, and also by his unwearied efforts to introduce the use of the Minie rifle into the British Army, took a most enthusiastic interest in the 52nd, and especially in its glorious advance on the French Imperial Guard at Waterloo. In a letter on this subject, written to me in 1853, he shews his strong feeling about it, when he says, "I hope to live to see this matter made transparent." He entered into correspondence with many of the old officers of the regiment, and especially with Lord Seaton and Mr. Yonge, the latter a very intelligent officer who served in the 52nd, in the Peninsula and at Waterloo, and who also exerted himself for the introduction of the Minie rifle. The following testimonial was sent to Mrs. Bentham, sometime after the death of Colonel Bentham, by Lord Seaton:—

> At the request of Mrs. Bentham I have great satisfaction in stating that the late Colonel Bentham served under my command in the 52nd regiment; that he was one of the most active and efficient officers in that distinguished corps; and that by his "exertions and perseverance, for ten years, he accelerated the adoption of the Enfield rifle—having visited Vincennes frequently, and established by his inspections of the rifle-practice at that military station, the superiority and precision of the Minie Rifle.
>
> I am persuaded that the attention of the authorities at the Horse Guards was first attracted to this subject, in consequence of his strong representations, and of his having, in conjunction with the late Mr. Yonge, of the 52nd, published the report of Colonel Sir Frederic Smith of the trial of the old musket at Chatham, proving its defects.
>
> Seaton, Field-Marshal.
>
> London, May 16, 1860.

As some acknowledgment of the service thus rendered by Colonel Bentham to the army in the above matter, the Government have given his son an appointment in the War Office.

The following are extracts from a letter written to me by Bentham, in November, 1853:—

> I read with very great interest and satisfaction your reminiscences of Waterloo, forwarded to me by Yonge, and considering the intense excitement and bustle at the period chiefly dwelt on, it is marvellous how closely all the statements of 52nd men agree thereon.
>
> It can hardly be conceived that the duke, who witnessed the glorious swoop, and would not give the men time to inflate their lungs, but urged 'Colborne to go on,' could not only completely ignore this astounding flight, but allow others to have

the credit of it, by strong marks of distinction.

I can fully bear you out as to Gurwood's declaration about the Guards. He was always very strong on this point. I met Gurwood in London, about 1828; he was then staying at Apsley House, and I asked him why he never drew the duke out about the catastrophe at Waterloo. He said that he had repeatedly made the attempt, but that it was a subject which always excited great impatience. On the last attempt the duke said, 'Oh, I know nothing of the services of particular regiments; there was glory enough for us all.' But had he written his annals true, Baron Muffling would not, as he has done recently, have charged him with '*policy*' in advancing his weak battalions to prevent the Prussians coming in for the victory. Baron Muffling and the world would have known that the genius and daring of Colborne gave the panic and death-blow, before the French began to yield to the Prussians. Let us yet have the whole truth.

In a letter I received from Colonel Bentham, dated May 16, 1854, he gives the account of an interview he had with Lieut. Sharpin, of Captain Bolton's brigade of artillery, attached to our division; it was stationed just to the left of the 52nd, and not far from the right of the 2nd battalion of the 1st Guards. It must be borne in mind that Captain Siborne, in his history of the Battle of Waterloo, has stated, on what the 52nd knew to be incorrect information, that a *first column* of the Imperial Guard was repulsed by Maitland's brigade of Guards, and that I maintain no such column, (but only the *skirmishers* of the Imperial Guard) reached within three hundred yards of the British Guards, and that these skirmishers were driven off the British position, not by an advance of the whole of Maitland's brigade, but by the advance of the 3rd battalion of the 1st Guards, whilst the 2nd battalion remained stationary.

Captain Siborne has ventured to dress up his account of the supposed *column* ("which, as far as I can gather," writes Colonel Bentham, "was a column in buckram,") with several details, which belong to the advance of the two long columns of about 10,000 men, which the 52nd encountered and defeated. It must be borne in mind also that these two columns of the Imperial Guard were apparently of equal length, and were so close to each other that, although we could, in the left centre of the 52nd, see that there was an interval between them, we could not see through it. I should say that the interval did not exceed twenty paces.

Before I give the account of Colonel Bentham's interview with Lieutenant Sharpin, I must give the following extract from Siborne's history, in that part in which he is giving his account of what he calls a *first column* of the Imperial Guard:—

> Wellington rode up to the British foot battery, posted on the immediate right of Maitland's brigade of Guards, with its own right thrown somewhat forward, and addressing himself to an artillery officer, (Lieutenant Sharpin) hastily asked who commanded it. The latter replied that, Captain Bolton having just been killed, it was now under the command of Captain Napier. The duke then said, 'Tell him to keep a look out to his left, for the French will soon be with him.' The message had scarcely been communicated, when the bear-skin caps of the leading divisions of the column of the Imperial Guard appeared just above the summit of the hill. The cannonade, hitherto directed upon this point from the distant French batteries, now ceased, but a *swarm of skirmishers* opened a sharp and teasing fire among the British gunners. In the next moment, however, they were scattered and driven back upon the main body by a sudden shower of canister, grape, and shrapnel shells, poured forth from Napier's guns, which now kept up a terrific fire upon the column, within a distance of forty or fifty yards.
>
> Nevertheless, the French Guards continued to advance. They had now topped the summit. To the astonishment of the officers who were at their head, there appeared, in their immediate front, no direct impediment to their further advance. They could only distinguish dimly through the smoke extending from Napier's battery, the cocked hats of a few mounted officers, little imagining, probably, that the most prominent of these was the great duke himself. Pressing boldly forward, they had arrived within fifty paces of the spot on which the British Guards were lying down, when Wellington gave the talismanic call, 'Up, Guards, make ready,' and ordered Maitland to attack, &c., &c.

In contradiction of the above statement of Captain Siborne's, relating that Napier's battery fired into a *column* of the Imperial Guard which the British Guards had defeated, Colonel Bentham says, in his above-mentioned letter to me:—

> Since I wrote to you I ferreted out a Lieutenant Sharpin, of the artillery, who was attached to the battery in the angle made

by the Guards and 52nd. He tells me that, until he saw the statement in Siborne, he never saw or heard of two attempts on our centre by the Imperial Guard; and subsequently in a detailed description, he says that Siborne was wrong in making his battery fire on any column but the one taken in flank by the infantry on the right. He is an excellent witness on our side.

I now introduce *in extenso* a letter written by the late Field-Marshal Lord Seaton, (formerly Sir John Colborne) to the late Colonel Bentham, on the subject of the defeat of the Imperial Guard of France solely by the flank attack of the 52nd on their columns. I prefer giving it in full, although I think there are one or two slight mistakes in it, which I can rectify in a note. I copy from the letter in Lord Beaton's own handwriting:—

Deer Park, Honiton, October 15, 1853.

My Dear Bentham,

I forwarded to Lord Hardinge your letter addressed to him, and your suggestions relative to the extension of the system of education at Sandhurst. I do not, however, think that the authorities will encourage the establishment of an '*Ecole de Tir*' at that college on the scale proposed by you.

With reference to your letter of the 7th, it may be more satisfactory to you, instead of replying to your queries, to draw your attention to the principal movements which accelerated the termination of the Battle of Waterloo, and to the facts which would have been admitted as evidence in support of the claims of the 52nd, to the merit of having first checked the advance of the Imperial Guard at the crisis of the battle, and of having completed their *déroute*, by marching directly on their dense columns, and by a flank movement charging them so vigorously, that the whole gave way and retired in confusion. The statements of officers, engaged at Waterloo, I found were generally so different and conflicting, that it was impossible to draw up any correct account of them.

Captain Siborne, I believe, consulted every officer in command with whom he was acquainted, or to whom he was introduced, and endeavoured to make their versions correspond with the facts generally known relative to the movements of regiments, brigades, and divisions. I have never read his account. If you bring the 52nd into a contest with the Guards by attempting to prove from rumours that the latter were retiring at the time they are said to have charged and defeated the French troops, you will raise up a host of opponents to your account, which would rather injure the cause of the 52nd. I suppose the Guards must have made some forward movement, and that many officers must have seen it, but I contend that the French column had been checked and thrown into disorder before the Guards moved. I saw the column of the Imperial Guard steadily advancing to a certain point, and I observed them halt, which was *precisely* as the skirmishers of the 52nd opened fire on their flank.

My attention was so completely drawn to our position and dangerous advance—a large mass of cavalry having been seen on our right, exposed as it was, that I could see no movement whatever on the part of the Guards, and indeed, as we advanced, I believe, we were too much under the position to have been able to have them in sight. Sir John Byng's brigade remained in line without firing or making any movement, while we passed along its front, our line forming a right angle with that brigade, and being about two hundred yards nearer to the French.

******

Note:—It was Sir Peregrine Maitland's brigade, composed of the 2nd and 3rd battalions of the 1st Guards. Sir John Byng commanded the other brigade of Guards composed of the 2nd battalion of the Coldstream, and of the 2nd battalion of the 3rd Guards. This brigade was principally engaged in the defence of Hougomont. Major-General Cooke commanded the whole division, and on his being wounded, Byng succeeded to his command, and thus was with Maitland's brigade towards the close of the action. The whole of this brigade was not in line (possibly the right battalion was) when it was attacked and fired into by the skirmishers of the Imperial Guard; the 3rd battalion was at first in square, and was ordered by the duke to "form line on its front face, and drive those fellows in," which it immediately did, and the 2nd battalion remained stationary.

******

Sir John Byng told me afterwards at Paris, that he had his whole attention drawn to our movement, and that his brigade had no ammunition left. He gave us, at that time, full credit for our advance. Till the Duke of Wellington's dispatch was made known at Paris, we had never heard of the charge of the Guards; and I am inclined to believe that the attack of the French had been checked by the advance of the 52nd, and the movements afterwards of the whole of Sir H. Clinton's division, before any forward movement had been made by the brigade commanded by Sir P. Maitland.

******

Note:—Besides Adam's brigade, the Osnabruck battalion, under Colonel Hugh Halkett, was the only infantry regiment which advanced at that period of the close of the action. Vivian's hussar brigade appears to have come up with them somewhere between La Belle Alliance and Hougomont.

******

This account corresponds with that given to me by Lord Hill, who was close to the Guards and 'saw us moving across the plain.' When we followed the French towards La Belle Alliance, no troops from the part of the position occupied by the Guards were near us, and we passed eighty guns and carriages, a short time after the French had retired, which they had left on the road between La Haye Sainte and La Belle Alliance.

"I have written this, as circumstances have occurred to me to remind me of the part we performed, without method—but with these remarks and the facts mentioned in the enclosure, you may be able to judge correctly of the claims of the 52nd.

Yours very faithfully,

Seaton.

The following passages, bearing upon the defeat of the French Imperial Guard by the single-handed attack of the 52nd, are extracted from some remarks on Waterloo by Lord Seaton:—

The crisis may be called the period when the French columns, advancing with the intention of penetrating our centre, were checked and compelled to halt by the flank movement and fire of the 52nd. This was the very first appearance of a change in our favour. The attackers were attacked and checked in their assault, and driven from the ground they had gained before they could deploy.... The whole of the Imperial Guard advanced at the same time, and their flank was first attacked by the 52nd, before any forward movement was made to check them in front.... The Prussians could not have attracted the attention of the French, so as to cause the throwing back of their right wing, until after the Imperial Guard had commenced their attack on our centre .... No regiment except the 52nd fired on the flank of the Imperial Guard.

The late Mr. Wm. Crawley Yonge, of the 52nd, in a letter to Colonel Bentham written in November, 1853, says:—

"He (Lord Seaton) was saying here last week that after his conversation with the French *cuirassier* officer, he kept watching the heavy column advancing, saw it directed against a very weak part of the line, saw no attempt at preparation to meet it, and therefore, (making light of his own exercise of judgment and decision,) he said, there was nothing else to do, having such a strong battalion in hand, but to endeavour to stop them by a flank attack, for it seemed quite evident that, if something of that sort was not done, our line would unquestionably be penetrated. With a man looking on in this intelligent way, and acting on what he saw, how is it possible that all this fanfaronade, of Guards charging the head of this column, can have the smallest foundation in truth?"

The same officer writes:—

It is the dearest wish of my heart to see that affair put to rights in the eyes of the world. As to Lord Seaton, I think there never was a man so ill-used as he was—only fancy how many men were there at any time, who would have done what he did, being only the commanding officer of his own regiment, without orders or sanction from any superior officer, his own general of brigade yet on the field, to take upon himself such responsibility; first, in acting without orders, and secondly, daring to expose his flank to the enemy as he did? How few would have seen and caught the right moment; and was there another man in the army who would have ventured on it, if he had seen it? As for the regiment, if they had their rights, they ought to have more credit for their exemplary steadiness under heavy fire for a good while previous to the charge, than for the charge and pursuit itself. It was capitally done, and few regiments could have borne to be so handled without getting into confusion, but it was easy work compared with the other.

On another occasion he speaks of Lord Seaton's characteristic humility and modesty in the following terms:—

> Meeting him in London a little while ago at the house of a lady, a mutual friend, she, hearing us talk over some of the occurrences of the war, remarked, 'How proud you gentlemen may feel at the recollection that you had a share in those great events;' on which he replied very gently, 'Proud! No, rather humbled, I think.' How characteristic this is, is it not? It puts me in mind of two lines in *The Christian Year* on St. Philip and St. James's day. The *stanza* ends—
> *Thankful for all God takes away,*
> *Humbled by all He gives.'*

In *The United Service Journal* for 1833, Colonel Gawler published a letter from Colonel Brotherton, from which the following is an extract:—

> Some years ago, not long after the Battle of Waterloo, in conversation with a French officer of the staff, who had accompanied the column led by Marshal Ney at the close of the day, we were describing the relative merits of our different modes of attack. I observed to him that to us it seemed surprising and unaccountable that our gallant opponents should obstinately persist in a practice, which experience must have taught them to be so unavailing and destructive to themselves, *viz.*, their constant attacks in column against our infantry in line.
> I cited as a last and conclusive instance, the failure of the attack at the close of the day at Waterloo, where a column composed of such distinguished veterans, and led by such a man as Ney, was repulsed and upset by some comparatively young soldiers of our Guards, (for of such I understood the brigade in question to be composed,) adverting also to the singular coincidence of the Imperial Guard encountering our British Guards at such a crisis.
> Upon which he observed, without seeming in the least to detract from the merit of the troops which the column had to encounter in its front, who, he said, showed '*très bonne contenance*,' (this expression would fairly apply to the driving in of the skirmishers by the charge of the 3rd battalion of the 1st Guards), that I was wrong in adducing this instance in support of my argument, or in supposing the attack was solely repulsed

by the troops opposed to it in front; 'for,' added he, '*nous fumes principalement repoussés par une attaque de flanc, très vive, qui nous ecrasa.*' ("*We were chiefly repulsed by a very sharp flank attack, which destroyed us.*"

As far as I can recollect, these were his very words. I retain all the feelings of a Guardsman, in which corps I served several years, and should feel as jealous of its honours as if still in its ranks, &c.

Cavalry Depot, August 2nd, 1833.

These last words are the same as those employed by Quinet in describing the result of the fire of the 52nd, on the same occasion.

★★★★★★★★★★

Mr. Leeke's Replies to Certain Criticisms on His History of Lord Seaton's Regiment (The 52nd Light Infantry) at the Battle of Waterloo, &c., &c.

To the Editor of the *Army and Navy Gazette*.

Sir,—I feel much indebted to you for your kind review, in your paper of the 22nd of December last, of my "History of Lord Seaton's Regiment at Waterloo," &c. I should almost immediately have requested a short space in your columns in order to make a few observations on the two points in which you differ from me, but I thought it better to wait a few weeks, to see if any statements on the subject appeared in the *Army and Navy Gazette*, from any other quarter, and after that a most severe affliction prevented me for many weeks from giving any attention to these matters. I think it right thus to account for my having allowed several months to elapse without requesting you to insert the following remarks on the two points to which I refer:—1stly, that of placing on my plan. No. 2, the columns of the Imperial Guard too far down the slope of the British position at the moment of their being taken in flank by the 52nd; and 2ndly, the stating the numbers of these "dense columns" to have amounted apparently to about 10,000 men.

With regard to the distance, three hundred yards, at which I have placed the head of the leading column of the French Guard from the slope of the plateau in front of Maitland's Brigade of the 2nd and 3rd battalions of the 1st Guards, I will first mention what I observed myself, and what I have a most perfect recollection of. From the left centre of the 52nd four-deep line, when it was nearly parallel with the left flank of the Imperial Guard, and at right angles with the British position, on looking to see what support we had, I could see the whole of the ground between the head of the Imperial column and the outer slope of that part of the position behind which (Maitland's Brigade must have been stationed, and I had no doubt, when most anxiously considering the exact position which I should give on my plan to the head of the French column, nor have I now, that it should have the position which I have assigned to it, at the distance of three hundred yards from the point that I could plainly see, which must have been the outer part of the plateau.

I distinctly saw the Imperial Guard skirmishers form in front of the head of the column when they had been driven in from the position. Captain the Hon. William Ogilvy, an old Peninsular officer, with seven clasps, and who was towards the left of the 52nd line when it came on the flank of the Imperial Guard at Waterloo, wrote to me as follows, on the 1st of January last:—

> Today came a copy of the *Army and Navy Gazette*, which I have also to thank you for, containing a full and, as I think, a fair and honest estimate of your description, of the important part taken by Lord Seaton at the close of the field of Waterloo, but I cannot agree with the writer that your plan is inaccurate in showing the 52nd so far in advance of the rest of the Army, at least I am sure there was no force within our sight near enough to be considered a support in any degree.

General Sir William Rowan, after reading my account of the proceedings of the 52nd at Waterloo, in writing to me at the end of January, says:—

> So far as my memory serves me, your account of the several movements of the 52nd Regiment is correct.

Colonel Hall, in writing to me on the 4th of February says:—

> In reply to your question, if I can depend on my memory, I say you are correct; I could see beyond the head of the column; there was a considerable space between it and the brow of the British position. But in front of the column appeared a cloud of scattered men, probably its own skirmishers; even they had not nearly reached the summit of the hill.

Sir Thomas Reynell, who commanded the 71st at Waterloo, in writing to the *United Service Journal* in 1833, describes the Imperial

Guard, which the 52nd defeated, as "two columns of the enemy's infantry at the bottom of the declivity," by which expression he must mean that they were far down the slope. Lord Seaton says, when our skirmishers "had advanced a few hundred yards, the Imperial Guard halted, and opened fire upon them." Sir Hussey Vivian, who commanded the Hussar Brigade at Waterloo, and who kept a journal, from which most of the details given in a letter which he sent to the *United Service Journal* in July, 1833, are drawn, writes as follows:—

> When I went on the following day over the ground, I saw some few French infantry within our lines, but the mass of the enemy's dead and dying lay below the crest, extending away from the French left of La Haye Sainte, and rather in the rear of it.

He was speaking of the slope of the position in front of the ground on which Maitland's Brigade of Guards and his own Hussar Brigade were stationed, when the Imperial Guard were attacked by the 52nd. If any of your readers will draw a line from the buildings of La Haye Sainte to the north-western corner of the enclosures of Hougoumont they will find that it about cuts the head of the Imperial Guard column as placed on my plan. No. 2, therefore the mass of the French killed and wounded, stated by Vivian to have been seen by him rather to the rear of the head of the column, would be exactly where I have stated them to have fallen—more than three hundred yards below the British position.

The Imperial Guard in 1814 amounted to 112,482 men:—I have introduced a statement of the number of men of which the Imperial Guard consisted in each year from its formation in 1804, taken from a French history of that celebrated corps. They amounted in 1814, to 112,482: in 1815, the number was 25,870, of which 20,400 were infantry. Siborne states that there were only 12,000 infantry of the Imperial Guard at Waterloo, and twelve battalions of these, or 6,000, he mentions as having been detached to Planchenoit to oppose the Prussians; but I am inclined to think that he must either have made a mistake as to the number of battalions sent to Planchenoit or with regard to the numbers of which the several battalions consisted.

According to the Imperial Guard history, quoted above, each regiment of the *Tirailleurs* and *Voltigeurs* of the Guard consisted of 1,200 men, whilst the regiments of *Chasseurs* and Grenadiers of the Guard consisted only of 1,000 men each. But "much confusion exists in the accounts of these columns of attack, their number and formation," and the exactness of my statement, that the 52nd attacked 10,000 men of the Imperial Guard, may be fairly questioned. Colonel Gawler speaks only of eight battalions having been detached to Planchenoit. Baron Muffling states that sixteen battalions of the Imperial Guard made the last attack upon the British position; General Drouot also stated that there were sixteen battalions engaged in the last attack.

I believe the whole of the remaining infantry of the Imperial Guard advanced to this attack, and that there were no battalions left in reserve, but that the rear guard or reserve of the Imperial Guard who were found by the 52nd near the Charleroi-road twenty minutes after the defeat of the two heavy columns, had formed the rear portion of the second column, and retired hastily towards the French position on the defeat and flight of the battalions in their front, who were more immediately in front of the 52nd four-deep line.

Baron Muffling, in his despatch, says, "Some of the enemies' batteries cover with grape-shot the retreat of four battalions of the Guard." Now the only British infantry who had grape fired into them, at least at that period of the battle, were the 52nd, and it was immediately afterwards that Lieutenant Gawler drove in those three guns with the right section, and found himself as the smoke cleared off, with "three battalions of the Old Guard" two or three hundred yards in his front, "which having formed the rear of the columns of attack, had retired in tolerable order, and now stood in squares supported by a small body of *cuirassiers* on the first rise of their position." I am sorry to occupy so much of your space, but I have been anxious to show that I had no wish to exaggerate when I stated in the title page of my work that "the 52nd defeated, single-handed, that portion of the Imperial Guard of France, about 10,000 in number, which advanced to make the last attack on the British position."

The 52nd, from their appearance, always considered these two "dense columns," as Lord Seaton calls them, (which were in the very closest proximity,) and always spoke of them as amounting to about 10,000 men. Colonel Gawler, in his *Crisis of Waterloo*, written thirty-four years ago, speaks of them as 10,000, In my work I have called them "about 10,000," and in one place "8,000 or 10,000," by way of not exceeding the number, which we always supposed, from their appearance, that they amounted to. The later French writers appear, for obvious reasons, to have missed no opportunity of stating the number of the Imperial Guard attacked by the 52nd at the lowest possible figure. The defeat of a previous column of the Imperial Guard by the

British Guards I consider to be impossible. The 52nd found the "dense columns" of the French Guard apparently untouched. Lord Seaton says:—

> The whole of the Imperial Guard advanced at the same time, and their flank was first attacked by the 52nd before any forward movement was made to check them in front.

The old officers of the 52nd were not likely to make the great mistake of taking the "black, massive, solid columns" of the Imperial Guard, which we put to flight, to consist of 10,000 men if they only amounted to little more than half that number; even I, who had been only a few weeks in the army, was capable of forming something like a correct estimate of their numbers, for I had had opportunities of seeing together the whole of our division, Sir Henry Clinton's, which consisted of 6,833 men. At some future and not very distant time, I shall hope to reply, but not at this same length, to the several letters which the officers of the Guards and Sir Edward Cust have written to your paper and to the *Pall Mall Gazette* on the subject of my statements relating to the defeat of the Imperial Guard at Waterloo.—Very faithfully yours,

Holbrooke, May 30th, 1867.   William Leeke.

****

THE 52ND AND THE FIRST GUARDS AT WATERLOO.

To the Editor of the *Army and Navy Gazette*.

Sir, In my letter inserted in the *Army and Navy Gazette* of the 1st of June, on the subject of the position and numbers of the Imperial Guard defeated by the 52nd, as stated in my *History of Lord Seaton's Regiment at Waterloo*, &c., I mentioned my intention of endeavouring to reply, at no very distant time, to the letters which some of the officers of the Guards and Sir Edward Cust have written on the subject of my statement, that the 52nd "defeated, singlehanded, without the assistance of the 1st British Guards or any other troops, that portion of the Imperial Guard of France, about 10,000 in number, which advanced to make the last attack on the British position." As I have said in my former letter, "the defeat of a previous column of the Imperial Guard by the British Guards I consider to be impossible." Lord Seaton says:—

> The whole of the Imperial Guard advanced at the same time, and their flank was first attacked by the 52nd before any for-

ward movement was made to attack them in front. No regiment, except the 52nd, fired on the flank of the Imperial Guard.

Again he says:—

> I saw the column of the Imperial Guard steadily advancing to a certain point, and I observed them halt, which was precisely as the skirmishers of the 52nd opened fire on their flank.—(See *History of Lord Seaton's Regiment, &c.*, vol. 1 & 2.)

The following extract from a letter from Colonel (now General) Sir Thomas William Brotherton, G.C B., to Colonel Gawler in 1833, and published in the *United Service Journal*, completely disproves the statement made by Siborne in his *History of Waterloo*, that a first column, led by Ney, and Friant, and Michel, was defeated by the 1st Brigade of Guards, and it will be observed that this letter only speaks of one attack, and not of two separate attacks by two separate columns of the Imperial Guard, and also that it was addressed to Colonel Gawler, and published by him for the very purpose of proving that Ney's columns (which the 52nd saw to be in the very closest proximity, the rear of the one being about twenty paces from the front of the other) were not defeated by a front attack of the 1st Guards, but by the flank attack of the 52nd. Sir Thomas Brotherton says:—

> Some years ago, not long after the Battle of Waterloo, in conversation with a French officer of the staff, who had accompanied the column led by Marshal Ney at the close of the day, we were describing the merits of our different modes of attack. I observed to him, that to us it seemed surprising and unaccountable that our gallant opponents should obstinately persist in a practice which experience must have taught them to be so unavailing and destructive to themselves—*viz.*, their constant attacks in column against our infantry in line. I cited as a last and conclusive instance, the failure of the attack at the close of the day at Waterloo, where a column composed of such distinguished veterans, and led by such a man as Ney, was repulsed and upset by some comparatively young soldiers of our Guards, (for of such I understood the brigade in question to be composed,) adverting also to the singular coincidence of the Imperial Guard encountering our British Guards at such a crisis. Upon which, he observed, without seeming in the least to detract from the merit of the troops which the column had to

encounter in its front, who, he said, showed *très bonne contenance,* (This expression would fairly apply to the driving in of the mass of skirmishers and their supports by the 3rd battalion of the 1st Guards.—W.L.) that I was wrong in adducing this instance in support of my argument, or in supposing the attack was solely repulsed by the troops opposed to it in front; for, added he, '*Nous fumes principalement repoussés par une attaque de flanc, très vive, qui nous écrasa.*' ('We were chiefly repulsed by a very sharp flank attack, which destroyed us.') As far as I can recollect these were his very words. I retain all the feelings of a Guardsman, in which corps I served several years, and should feel as jealous of its honours as if still in its ranks, &c.—Cavalry Depot, August 2nd, 1833.

General Brotherton and the French officer were here speaking of the column of the Imperial Guard led by Ney. Siborne, (see his 14th chapter,) misled by all kinds of conflicting reports, and the other writers, who have followed in his wake, declare that a first column, led by Ney, was attacked, and defeated, and entirely routed by the 1st British Guards alone, whilst the French officer, in his conversation with General Brotherton, declares that Ney's column was defeated by "a sharp flank attack, which destroyed it;" and the 52nd know well that it was their flank attack which effected this remarkable defeat of the chosen troops of France, and that no column of the French Guard preceded those with whom they, the 52nd, came in contact?

When the 52nd four-deep line was becoming parallel with the left flank of the Imperial Guard, and at right angles with the British position, the left of the 52nd and the head of the Imperial column were both of them about 300 yards from that part of the position to the rear of which Maitland's brigade of Guards must have been stationed. The whole slope was clear of smoke and clear of troops, excepting the skirmishers of the Imperial Guard, whom I saw run in and form about 100 yards in front of their leading battalion. Lord Seaton says:—

> The whole of the Imperial Guard advanced at the same time, and their flank was first attacked by the 52nd.

The late Mr. Yonge, of the 52nd, wrote to Colonel Bentham in November, 1853, as follows:—

> He (Lord Seaton) was saying here last week that, after his; conversation with the French *cuirassier* officer, he kept watching the

heavy column advancing, saw it directed against a very weak part of the line, saw no attempt at preparation to meet it, and therefore (making light of his own exercise of judgment and decision") he said there was nothing else to do, having such a strong battalion in hand, but to endeavour to stop them by a flank attack, for it seemed quite evident that if something of that sort was not done our line would unquestionably be penetrated. With a man looking on in this intelligent way, and acting on what he saw, how is it possible that all this fanfaronade of Guards charging the head of this column can have any foundation in truth?—(See *History of 52nd at Waterloo*.)

Captain Siborne and those historians who have adopted his account of the defeat of a first column of the Imperial Guard by the 1st British Guards, have made a sad jumble of the whole affair. Amongst other statements he makes Captain Bolton's brigade of artillery to fire into this first column, and mentions Lieutenant Sharpin, who was attached to this brigade, as having been spoken to by the Duke of Wellington on the occasion. Colonel Bentham, in a letter I received from him in May, 1854, says:—

> Since I wrote to you I have ferreted out Lieutenant Sharpin, of the artillery, who was attached to the battery in the angle made by the Guards and 52nd. He tells me that until he saw the statement in Siborne he never saw or heard of two attempts on our centre by the Imperial Guard, and subsequently, in a detailed description, he says that Siborne was wrong in making his battery fire on any column but the one taken in flank by the infantry on the right. He is an excellent witness on our side.

It is very difficult to unravel all the apparently conflicting statements on the subject of a first column defeated by the 1st Guards, and then a second column defeated by the 52nd flank attack supported by an attack of Maitland's brigade of Guards in front. But the French officer's statement to General Brotherton, Lord Seaton's positive declaration, that of Lieutenant Sharpin, and what the officers on the left and in the left centre of the 52nd line saw of the strength of the two Imperial columns equal in length, and the rear column within twenty paces of that in front of it, and what they also saw of the 300 yards of ground and of the Imperial skirmishers between the head of the column and the British position, all make it a matter of certainty to my mind that skirmishers of the Imperial Guard, joined by their supports, and by quantities of skirmishers of Donzelôt's Division, and their supports, were massed together and fired into the square of the 3rd battalion of Maitland's brigade of Guards, stationed on the reverse slope of the British position, and that these massed and intermingled skirmishers, and possibly some of Donzelôt's battalions, seen at no very great distance away to their left front, as the 3rd battalion of the Guards passed over the summit of the position, were mistaken by them for a column of the Imperial Guard.

Several years ago, I received from an officer, who told me that he was sergeant-major of the 3rd battalion of the 1st Guards at Waterloo, and noted it down the day after, the following information with regard to what his battalion really did at the crisis of Waterloo. I copy a portion of it from my history of the battle (vol. 1):—

> They were attacked by a 'column' of twelve or fourteen hundred men, and that these troops opened fire upon them at a distance of fifty or sixty paces; that the duke coming along from their left, observed how this 3rd battalion of the 1st Guards was suffering from the heavy fire of the mass of troops in their front, and desired the commanding officer to form line on the front face of the square, and 'drive those fellows off,' which they did in very gallant style, and followed them for some eighty or a hundred yards down the slope; then there was an alarm of cavalry, and the 3rd battalion of the Guards, some of them thinking they were to form square, got into confusion and retired hastily over the crest of the position and beyond it on the reverse slope.

This officer told me most positively that this was the only movement the 3rd battalion of the 1st Guards made against the enemy's infantry at Waterloo, and that their 2nd battalion was not with them. It will be seen, therefore, that the two battalions of which Maitland's brigade consisted, could not at any time have advanced together, as Siborne and other writers have asserted, I observe that, in their letters to the *Army and Navy Gazette* and the *Pall Mall Gazette,* the officers of the Guards themselves speak of the two battalions of the Guards having advanced together in brigade and defeated the Imperial Guard. Their statements and the very positive declaration of the officer who was sergeant-major of the 3rd battalion at Waterloo are at variance. When the 3rd battalion of the Guards drove off from the British position the mass of skirmishers in their front, those belonging to Donzelôt's French division would run into the nearest battalion of that division away to their left front; the Imperial Guard skirmishers, running in front the front of both battalions of the 1st Guards and of the 2nd battalion of the 95th Rifles, would be those I saw form in front of the leading battalion of the leading column of the Imperial Guard, when the 52nd were becoming parallel with its left flank.

At that time the 3rd battalion of the 1st Guards had recrossed the position, as we saw nothing of them, although the slope of 300 yards between the Imperial column and the edge of the plateau towards us was clear of smoke. The 3rd battalion, being in square at the time, must have been at a considerable distance from the 2nd battalion on its right; when in a four-deep line there would, probably, be an interval of about 180 yards between each battalion which was on the right centre of the British position, so that I cannot at all understand how General Buckley's statement can be correct, that the 1st Brigade of Guards—i.e., both the battalions together—advanced over the crest and defeated a battalion or brigade (he does not know which) in grenadier caps and close columns; nor can I understand what General Buckley means when he says, "The men wheeled up their flanks, as it were, to enclose the columns."

Neither General Buckley nor any of the other officers of the Guards appear to claim the *two* advances and attacks which Siborne, in his history, on his sixth plan, and on his model, claims for them. He makes them to attack and route a previous column led on by Ney, and then to advance and fire into a second and larger column, which was taken in flank by the 52nd. Now, Sir Thomas Brotherton's letter shows that the column led by Ney was taken in flank by the 52nd. Lieutenant Sharpin's statement is that there was no previous column into which Bolton's battery fired. Lord Seaton, and other 52nd officers, saw that the whole of the Imperial Guard advanced together. The officers towards the left of the 52nd four-deep line saw that the British Guards, who were more than 300 yards away from the head of the column, and out of sight behind the crest of the position, never fired into it, and it, therefore, appears certain to me that the "swarm of skirmishers" and their supports massed together were the enemy which the Guards defeated.

It is hardly necessary that I should add any more than I have already written in reply to the letters of the Duke of Manchester and Colonel Maitland. I think the former, who was on Sir Peregrine Maitland's staff thirty years ago, and who mentions his recollections of what his general used to say about the battle, will, on consideration, feel sure that that gallant and respected soldier, in giving directions for the advance of his brigade, or, as I believe it to have been, of the 3rd battalion, never could have addressed them in such unsoldierlike words as those of "Up Guards, and at them." I do not quite see how Colonel Maitland knows the contents of a letter written by his father to Captain Siborne, and that it "described a previous movement of the 3rd battalion of the 1st Guards down the slope for the purpose of driving off some skirmishers," for he says, he "has not any written account by his father of the battle."

If he merely gathers from Siborne's *History of Waterloo* that Sir Peregrine Maitland must have written to him "describing a previous movement," &c., he relies on what I cannot rely upon, for not only had Siborne many conflicting accounts, as regarded both time and movements, from officers of the same regiment, but, as I have shown in the 5th chapter of my work, he mentions the same sort of thing about driving in skirmishers two or three times over, with nearly the same attendant circumstances—of the duke being present, the forming a four-deep line, and the words, "Up Guards," &c., or, "Drive those fellows off." There is good reason to believe that the three accounts, one mentioning Adam's brigade at four o'clock in the afternoon, all properly belong to the advance of the 3rd battalion of the 1st Guards, by the Duke of Wellington's order, at eight o'clock in the evening.

Although it is not necessary that I should reply further than I have already done to Colonel Ponsonby's straightforward and courteous letter in the *Pall Mall Gazette*, of December 26th, I hope that he and all the officers of the Guards will unite with me and others in an effort, not to deprive the officers of the. Guards of the brevet-rank which has been accorded to them in their several grades, but to have exactly the same rank given, in each grade, to the officers of all the other corps in the army, for it is evidently most injurious to the service, and most mortifying to the other branches of it, that the officers of the Guards should, as a rule, arrive at the higher ranks of the army at a much earlier age than that at which the officers of the rest of the army arrive at the same ranks. I have shown, by a calculation made some years ago, that, on an average, the officers of the Guards arrived at the rank of lieutenant-colonel in fifteen years, and the officers of the line in thirty years.

I am sorry to say that, as regards the crisis of Waterloo, General Sir Edward Cust, who quotes from his *Annals of the Wars*, in the *Army and Navy Gazette* of the 15th January, has fallen into all kinds of mistakes, one or two of which only I will take the liberty of mentioning. He brings forward the word of command, which, one would suppose, never could have been given by any officer in command, "Up Guards, and at them!" He says, "the duke, stationed near Bolton's battery, was heard to exclaim, 'Go on, Colborne.'" Now, even Siborne, with all his vexatious mistakes, makes the duke to utter these words where he did really utter something like them—at the Charleroi-road, 800 yards away from Bolton's battery.

Again, Cust makes Vivian's Hussar Brigade to come down the Charleroi-road to the help of the 52nd, when they really moved down the British position direct to their front, through the interval in the line, left by the 52nd, 800 yards away from the Charleroi-road, and never came near the 52nd. Sir Edward Cust not having been at Waterloo, and having Siborne and various other conflicting accounts to lead him, or rather to mislead him, was sure "to come to grief." I hope, in the next edition of the *Annals of the Wars*, he will do me the favour to be guided very much by my account of the crisis and close of the Battle of Waterloo.—Very faithfully yours,

Wm. Leeke.

★★★★★★★★★★

(From the *Army and Navy Gazette* of August 17, 1867.)

THE 52ND LIGHT INFANTRY, THE FIRST GUARDS, AND THE IMPERIAL GUARD OF FRANCE, AT WATERLOO.

To the Editor of the *Army and Navy Gazette.*

Sir—With your permission I wish to make the following remarks on Major-General Lindsay's letter, inserted in the *Army and Navy Gazette*, of July 27, on the subject of the defeat of the French Guard at Waterloo, General Lindsay says:—

> I do not propose here to reply to Mr, Leeke's letter, (*Army and Navy Gazette*, June 29,) nor to argue upon the movements of the two battalions which composed the brigade, (Maitland's,) nor upon the numbers of the Imperial Guard, but shall content myself with quotations from documents written by officers who were present, which assert as a fact the defeat of a column of the Imperial Guard by the 1st regiment of Guards. Major-Generals Sir John Byng and Sir Peregrine Maitland commanded the two brigades of Guards under Lieutenant-General Sir George Cooke. When the latter was wounded, the command of the division devolved upon Sir John Byng. On the day after

the battle both brigadiers wrote a despatch to the Duke of York as senior colonel of the brigade of Guards.

The following is the portion of Byng's despatch which relates to Maitland's brigade, consisting of the 2nd and 3rd battalions of the 1st Guards, and the attack of the Imperial Guard:—

I had also to witness the gallantry with which they met the last attack made by the Grenadiers of the Imperial Guard, ordered on by Bonaparte himself, the destructive fire they poured in, and the subsequent charge, which together completely routed the enemy. A second attempt met with a similar reception, and the loss they caused the French, of the finest troops I ever saw, was immense.

General Lindsay's extract from Maitland's despatch is as follows:—

It was at this period that Napoleon made his last effort against our centre, and advanced with masses of infantry, supported by cavalry and a blaze of artillery. At the command of the Duke of Wellington, our two squares formed into a line four deep. Napoleon himself led on his Imperial Guard against us to the bottom of the hill (or, rather, the small acclivity). The moment they appeared, and began to form about twenty yards in our front, we poured in the most deadly fire that perhaps was ever witnessed, as the field of battle abundantly testified the following day. The Imperial Guard retreated, &c. (This is the whole of the extract which General Lindsay gives from Maitland's despatch.)

It must be borne in mind that these extracts both from Byng's and Maitland's despatches refer only to Maitland's brigade, Byng's own brigade of Guards being at the time more than half a mile away, in or about the *château* and grounds of Hougomont,

I have already proved, as I believe, in my letter to you, (in the *Army and Navy Gazette* of June 29,) that there was no column in front of those led by Marshal Ney for the 1st British Guards to encounter, and that the troops they defeated on the British position must have been massed skirmishers from Ney's column of the Imperial Guard, and from Donzelôt's division, which was in force to the French left of La Haye Sainte. It may, however, be well for me to repeat, as your readers may not bear them in mind, the proofs of this, which I advanced in that letter. Lord Seaton says:—

The whole of the Imperial Guard advanced at the same time, and their flank was first attacked by the 52nd before any forward movement was made to attack them in front. No regiment except the 52nd fired on the flank of the Imperial Guard.

Again he says:—

I saw the column of the Imperial Guard steadily advancing to a certain point, which was precisely as the skirmishers of the 52nd opened fire on their flank.

These columns, apparently containing about 10,000 men, were in the very closest proximity, the rear of the one being about twenty paces from the front of the other. Colonel Bentham, in his letter to me in May, 1854, states that Lieutenant Sharpin, of the artillery, stationed in the angle made by the Guards and 52nd, says that "till he saw Siborne's statement, he never saw or heard of two attempts on our centre by the Imperial Guard." He says, "Siborne was wrong in making his battery fire on any column but the one taken in flank by the infantry on the right." Colonel Bentham adds, "He is an excellent witness on our side."

General Sir Thomas Brotherton's letter to Colonel Gawler, in 1833, mentions that in his conversation, not long after Waterloo, with a French staff officer who accompanied the Imperial Guard column led by Ney, the officer stated that "they were chiefly repulsed by a very sharp flank attack, which destroyed them." This was the single-handed attack of the 52nd. The officers of the 52nd, who were towards the left of the 52nd four deep line, saw that the British Guards who were more than 800 yards away from the head of Ney's column, and out of sight behind the crest of the position, never fired into it; but they did see skirmishers of the Imperial Guard retire down the British position, and form in front of the head of the column.

As I observed before, these various circumstances, which I have stated more particularly in my letter to you of the 29th of June, make it a matter of certainty to my mind that skirmishers of the Imperial Guard, joined by their supports, and by quantities of skirmishers of Donzelôt's division and their supports, were massed together and fired into the 3rd battalion of the 1st Guards, stationed on the reverse slope of the British position, and that these massed and intermingled skirmishers, and probably some of Donzelôt's battalions, seen at no very great distance away to their left front, as the 3rd battalion of the 1st Guards passed over the summit of the position, were mistaken by them for a column of the Imperial Guard.

When the 3rd battalion of the 1st Guards formed line, by the Duke of Wellington's order, on the front face of its square, and drove off from the British position the mass of skirmishers in their front, those belonging to Donzelôt's division would run into the nearest battalion of that division away by their left front; the Imperial Guard skirmishers, running in from both battalions of the 1st Guards, and from the 2nd battalion of the 90th rifles, would be those I saw form in front of the leading battalion of Ney's columns, when the 52nd were becoming parallel with their left flank; the left of the 52nd line and the head of the Imperial Guard being both of them 300 yards from the British position. When the 3rd battalion of the 1st Guards advanced over the position in pursuit of the mass of skirmishers, they would probably see the nearest of Donzelôt's battalions about 250 yards away to their left front, and the head of Ney's column about 350 yards from them to their right front.

I must now make some observations on the extracts contained in General Lindsay's letter from Byng's and Maitland's despatches to the Duke of York. Having proved that there was no *column* in advance of the column of the Imperial Guard led by Ney, Michel, and Friant, which was routed by the flank attack of the 52nd, and which the British Guards never attacked, I can still only understand the statements of Byng and Maitland as referring to the repulse of the swarms of massed skirmishers of the Imperial Guard and Donzelôt's division by the two battalions of Maitland's brigade, but not by the two battalions in one almost contiguous line, but by each battalion separately.

There is the very best authority for stating that the 3rd battalion of the 1st Guards, when lying down in square on the reverse slope of the position, were attacked by a "column" (as the officer, who was sergeant-major of that battalion at Waterloo called it) of twelve or fourteen hundred men, and that these troops opened fire upon them at a distance of fifty or sixty paces; that the duke, coming along from their left, observed how this 3rd battalion of the 1st Guards was suffering from the heavy mass of troops in their front, and desired the commanding officer to form line on the front face of the square, and "drive those fellows off," which they did in very gallant style, and followed them for some eighty or a hundred yards down the slope; then there was an alarm of cavalry, and the 3rd battalion of the Guards, some of them thinking they were to form square, got into confusion, and retired hastily over the crest of the position, and beyond it on the reverse slope. (Colonel Gurwood, then with the 10th Hussars, stated that they saw the Guards thus retiring in confusion.)

> The officer told me most positively that this was the only movement the 3rd battalion of the 1st Guards made against the enemy's infantry at Waterloo, and that their second battalion was not with them.

Siborne erroneously speaks of this as a separate and previous attack, after the taking of La Haye Sainte, by *tirailleurs* from that quarter, who not only fired into the 3rd battalion of the 1st Guards, but "also, upon their left, another portion of their numbers poured a destructive fire upon the left square of Adam's brigade, formed by the 2nd battalion of the 95th Rifles." Then he mentions the duke coming up to the 3rd battalion of the Guards, and ordering the commanding officer to form line on the front face of the square and drive the skirmishers down the slope, which they did. He says on the approach of cavalry:—

> The battalion re-formed square with great rapidity and regularity. The cavalry refused the square, but receiving its fire and then dashing along the front of the 52nd Regiment it exposed itself to another vigorous fire, by which it was nearly destroyed; whilst the 3rd battalion of the Guards retired, in perfect order, to its original position.

Here is an instance of the confusion which a writer of the history of a battle, who himself was not an eye-witness, may be led into both as to time and circumstances, by the varied accounts given to him by several officers of the same regiments: The 52nd did not at that time fire on any body of cavalry; the officer of the 3rd battalion of the 1st Guards, as I have just stated, gave me very much the same account with regard to the repulse of a "column" as he called it, of the Imperial Guard; but he did not say the battalion formed square and fired into the cavalry, but there was a cry of "cavalry," and that, some thinking they were to form square, they got into confusion, and retired over the summit of the position again.

The two generals, Maitland and Byng, do not mention this affair. Maitland appears to allude to Siborne's statement, when he says, in his letter to him in 1847, "the formation in line four deep, which you must have had in mind, belongs to a later hour of the day, when the Imperial Guard were advancing," &c.

The extract from Byng's despatch speaks of "a second attempt which met with a similar reception;" this I suppose must have reference to the repulse of the massed skirmishers, who, we are told, fired into the 2nd battalion of the Guards and the 2nd battalion of the 95th Rifles. Sir Peregrine Maitland speaks only of one attack made by the French on his brigade. He says in his despatch, "at the command of the Duke of Wellington, our two squares formed into a line four deep." There would be an interval between the two squares; and when both of them were in a four-deep line, there would still be a very considerable interval, as the lines would only occupy half the space which they would require in a two-deep line; and I suppose that the 3rd battalion of the 1st Guards, after having recovered its order on the reverse slope of the position, took ground towards the 2nd battalion on their right, and that this is what Lord Saltoun meant when he wrote as follows:—

> The left shoulder was then brought forward, and we advanced against the second column of the Imperial Guard, but which body was defeated by General Adam's brigade (it was defeated by the 52nd alone) before we reached it, although we got near enough to fire if we had been ordered to do so, and, as far as I can recollect, we did fire into that column.

As I have stated before, the 52nd knew well that the Guards were never in a position to fire into the column, which they (the 52nd) took in flank; yet from such loose and conflicting statements as these, Siborne, and many other historians of Waterloo, who have followed his account, have been forced to draw the materials for their histories. When the third battalion of the 1st Guards drove in the swarm of massed skirmishers in their front, and followed them for a short distance down the slope, no doubt they would, many of them, see the heavy columns of the Imperial Guard, which the 52nd took in flank—their officers on the look-out must have seen them before—but how, after the retiring of the 3rd battalion in confusion over the crest again, and some distance down the reverse slope, the two generals and other officers could fancy that they defeated the columns of the Imperial Guard, led on by Ney, and so decided the fate of Waterloo, it is very difficult to understand.

It may partly have had its origin in the fact of the separation of the two battalions of the Guards at the time of the advance of the Imperial Guard and its skirmishers, so that, when the accounts of what each battalion saw were collected, in order to the preparation of Byng's and Maitland's despatches for the Duke of York and the Duke of Wellington, there might be a greater liability to strong expressions, and to mistakes as to what was really done by the 1st Guards at the close of the action, and with regard to the fate of the French columns seen by them below the position. I think it is to be regretted that the two generals and other officers have confused their accounts by speaking of the whole brigade having resisted or made attacks, which it is clear were only made or resisted by each of the two battalions separately.

In the memorandum of Sir Peregrine Maitland in 1834, in the possession of the late Captain Siborne, he says:—

> As the attacking force moved forward it separated, the *Chasseurs* inclined to their left, the Grenadiers ascended the acclivity towards our position.

With regard to most persons, I have not much confidence in the accuracy of their recollections about Waterloo after the lapse of many years, as it is difficult for them to distinguish between what they themselves saw and what they have read in histories, or have heard from others; but I have no doubt that these were the skirmishers seen just before they extended, one body inclining to their left towards the 2nd battalion of the 1st Guards, and the 2nd, 95th, and the other advancing towards the 3rd battalion of the 1st Guards.

Major-General Lindsay mentions that he has "brought forward information which could not be in my possession," and that he has many letters and documents from many other officers, who were personally engaged, corroborative of what he has advanced. I have also in my possession, but I cannot at the moment lay my hand upon them, extracts from letters from several officers of the 1st Guards, who were at Waterloo, written soon after the action, in which they fully claim all the honour of the defeat of the Imperial Guard, and the consequent victory. But what does all this amount to? The two generals and the senior officers came to the conclusion that when they drove off the massed skirmishers the victory was gained; whilst Ney's columns were still untouched, and probably would have penetrated the British line of battle but for the flank attack of the 52nd.

If the senior officers made such a mistaken claim, no wonder that the others, in the excitement consequent upon the victory, should write home to their friends and claim the honour of having defeated the far-famed and choicest troops of France. No wonder that Lord Bathurst, on the 23rd of June, 1815, only eight days after the action, made use of the following words in the House of Lords:—

Towards the close of the day Bonaparte himself, at the head of his Guards, made a desperate charge on the British Guards, and the British Guards immediately overthrew the French.

No wonder that the following order appeared in the *Gazette* of the 29th of July, 1815:—

His Royal Highness has been pleased to approve of the 1st Regiment of Foot Guards being made a regiment of grenadiers, and styled 'the 1st or Grenadier Regiment of Foot Guards,' in commemoration of their having defeated the Grenadiers of the French Imperial Guard upon this memorable occasion.

But all who know the circumstances have greatly wondered that the Duke of Wellington should, in the manner he did, so completely ignore the remarkable defeat of Ney's columns by the 52nd, under Lord Seaton. Colonel Ponsonby states that, "it was he who recommended the 1st Guards for the distinction it enjoys, and he could scarcely have done so, had Mr. Leeke's version been correct." When the duke had directed the advance of the 3rd battalion "to drive those fellows off," (an expression, by the way, hardly applicable to a strong column, but quite so to skirmishers *en masse*,) he must almost immediately have seen Colborne's (Lord Seaton's) right-shoulder-forward movement, and have sent Colonel Percy to desire him to continue it.

The duke, therefore, must have been fully aware of Colborne's exploit, as appears also from the words which I heard him address to him, when he rode up to the 52nd, close to the Charleroi-road, twenty minutes after we had put to flight the "black massive solid columns" of the Imperial Guard. The words were "Well done, Colborne! Well done! Go on; don't give them time to rally." During the half hour before, Colborne had taken his regiment by itself down on the flank of the Imperial Guard, had thoroughly defeated it, had then led it over the thickly-strewed killed and wounded of the Imperial Guard; then it was ridden at by *cuirassiers*, and our own cavalry, one flying from the other; then it had grape fired into it, from the three guns of the Old Guard; it had traversed by itself eight hundred yards from its place on the position, and when the duke came down to it it was preparing, after a minute's halt for the purpose of dressing the line, to advance against the reserve of the Old Guard, which had retired to the first rise of the French position.

The duke might well exclaim "Well done, Colborne!" &c. But the duke owed also a great deal of his success in the Peninsula war to

Colborne and his gallant regiment, where they and the 43rd and 95th Rifles (the three regiments of the Light Division) so often led the way to victory in many a general action, and so greatly distinguished themselves also in equally hard-fought divisional engagements.

How was it then, that the duke allowed the great services of Colborne and the 52nd at Waterloo to be ignored, and how came he to allow the 1st Guards to be honoured and rewarded for "having defeated the Grenadiers of the French Imperial Guard," when the feat was really performed by the 52nd? If the duke did not inform himself on the subject of course his conduct would be most censurable. The reviewer of my *History of the 52nd at Waterloo*, in the *Pall Mall Gazette*, makes the following observations:—

> Perhaps the question of most general interest mooted in our author's pages is the charge of injustice on the part of the Duke of Wellington towards the 52nd in reference to Waterloo, in evading the distinct recognition of the deciding influence which that regiment exerted on the issue of the battle, and, indeed, in countenancing the error which attributed to the 2nd and 3rd battalions of the 1st Guards a share in the exploit which was really achieved by the 52nd alone. . . . .It is possible, too, (for the duke was decidedly human,) that he felt he owed the 52nd too much. It may have been uncomfortable to enter into the examination of the circumstances which gave that regiment a chance of coming (like a *Deus ex machina*) to the rescue of the British Army. It has always been our opinion that the duke was not particularly proud of his conduct of the great battle. . . . Perhaps a part of his known dislike to conversing on the subject of Waterloo may be attributed to his own dissatisfaction with a performance which nearly all the world was agreed in considering faultless.

The following is an extract from a letter written to me by Colonel Bentham in November, 1853:—

> I can fully bear you out as to Gurwood's declaration about the Guards. He was always very strong on this point. I met Gurwood in London, about 1828; he was then staying at Apsley House, and I asked him why he never drew the duke out about the catastrophe at Waterloo. He said that he had repeatedly made the attempt, but that it was a subject which always created great impatience. On the last attempt the duke said, 'Oh! I

know nothing of the services of particular regiments; there was glory enough for us all!'

Although I have greatly exceeded the proper limits of a letter, I must beg of you to permit me, before I close this, to make some few observations on the following extract which General Lindsay brings forward in support of his claim that Maitland's Brigade defeated the attack of the French Imperial Guard at Waterloo. It is an extract from Captain Powell's journal:—

> A close column of grenadiers, of *La Moyenne Garde*, about 6,000 strong, were seen ascending the rise *au pas de charge*. They continued to advance till within fifty or sixty paces of our front, when the brigade was ordered to stand up.

He then mentions that this, or the tremendously heavy fire thrown into them, stopped the French Guard, and forced the head of the column back. He then says:—

> We charged down the hill till we passed the end of the Orchard of Hougomont, when our right flank became exposed to another heavy column, which was advancing in support of the former. This circumstance obliged us to retire to our original position.

Captain Powell published this part of his journal upwards of thirty years ago, and there are several other statements in it besides those which General Lindsay has sent to you, and there are also two or three things in the extract which differ from the printed statement which I have mentioned. Captain Powell's printed statement mentions that the column was a close column of the Moyenne Guard (it does not mention "Grenadiers" as the extract does), "*about 8,000 strong, led by Marshal Ney.*" General Lindsay's extract, published in his letter to you, does not contain this line which I have italicised. The line seems to indicate that Ney's column of "eight or ten thousand men," which was taken in flank by the 52nd, was *seen* by the 3rd battalion of the Guards, when it drove in the skirmishers from the position.

Had General Lindsay been at Waterloo he would have understood how impossible it was that the Guards could set down near the enclosures of Hougomont, that is unless they were going out of the fray, for the tide of battle, at the time spoken of, ran quite the other way.—
Very faithfully yours,

Wm. Leeke.

Holbrooke, near Derby, August 8, 1867.
****

As I am circulating many thousand copies of my replies to certain criticisms on my *History of Lord Seaton's Regiment (the 52nd Light Infantry) at the Battle of Waterloo,* I think it desirable to fill up this remaining space, in the second pamphlet, with the following extracts, &c.:—

General Sir William Rowan, now colonel of the 52nd, in a letter written in December last, says:—

My dear Leeke—You seem so anxious to attach the extracts from my letter of the 31st of January last to other papers which you are about to publish, that I cannot resist giving my consent, though I have a great horror of appearing in print; but you have taken so much trouble and have incurred so serious an expense to clear up any doubts, which may have existed with regard to the 52nd Regiment at Waterloo, that I feel every person connected with the regiment, is bound to render you all the assistance in his power. You fought bravely to maintain the position you had taken up at Waterloo; I suppose now the war is over. Had I known of your intention to visit that celebrated spot, I think I should have proposed joining your party: I have not been there since the 18th of June, 1815; it was my birthday. (He was then twenty-five, and a Brevet Major for Orthes.)

The following is the extract above referred to, from Sir W. Rowan's letter to me of the 31st of January, 1867:—

The fact that the 52nd had the glory of attacking and defeating the principal columns of the Imperial Guard, and that the decisive movement was the spontaneous act of Sir John Colborne, had become matter of history, was abundantly proved by the remarks of the press on the death of Lord Seaton. Of that fact no individual of the regiment ever entertained a doubt, which was the cause of their taking no notice of the remarkable omission of their exploit in the Duke of Wellington's despatch. Gawler's *Crisis of Waterloo* published it to the world many years since. So far as my memory serves me, your account of the several movements of the 52nd Regiment is correct!

At the end of September last I went with my two eldest sons to Brussels, and spent two days on the Field of Waterloo: I was very much pleased to find, that in the various positions occupied by the 52nd—

when in reserve in front of Merbe Braine; when in square a quarter of a mile in front of the whole army, and to the left of Hougomont, where, as Sir Henry Clinton, in his despatch says, the manner in which they, with the 71st and 2nd and 3rd 95th, "discharged their duty was witnessed and admired by the whole army"; and when also, after retiring from square they stood, from seven till eight o'clock, just out of fire, forty paces below the position, on its reserve slope, preparatory to their advance on the French Imperial Guard—I was much pleased to find that the ground in these positions tallied with my recollections of it fifty-two years before. On my arrival at Paris from Brussels, I wrote at ten o'clock at night a very hasty note to a relative in England from which I copy the following remarks;—

> I was very glad to go a second time to Waterloo, two days ago, and to follow the exact course of the 52nd four-deep line in its advance against, and defeat of, the Imperial Guard, and over the ground on which their killed and wounded lay: and that on which we were charged by the mixed cavalry; and that from which the three guns, driven off by Gawler, made such holes in our line with grape. We saw, also, how short the distance was of the first rise to which these French guns had retired. We then found about the exact spot on which I stood to the right of the lower enclosures of La Haye Sainte, when the duke came up. The guide pointed out the spot on which Shaw, the Life Guardsman was buried, which was not far from that on which the Marquis of Anglesea was wounded, about half-past eight, just in rear of the 52nd line."

After crossing the Charleroi road and driving off a square of the Old Guard and some cavalry on the height above, the 52nd advanced well to the left of La Belle Alliance and Primotion, and came upon a French Division, which surrendered to them in a hollow road, 100 yards beyond the latter place. I was able to pick out the exact spot at which the left centre of the 52nd four-deep line passed the deep part of that road, 300 yards to the left of the point at which it crosses at right angles the Charleroi road, and about fifty yards from where it turns up to the right to Planchenoit. From the top of this bank the two centre companies had fired the last infantry shots fired at Waterloo, at, I believe. Marshal Ney and his staff. From thence they had advanced in pursuit nearly three quarters of a mile farther to the farm of Rossomme, where they bivouacked for the night on the straw used the night before by the Imperial Guard.

The two guides, who were with us at Rossomme, were much pleased when I picked out the very ground on which I had slept on the night of the battle. The guides I found to be intelligent, pleased to have what they knew confirmed, and to receive further information on which they thought they could depend. I think visitors should not fail to visit the Hotel de Lion, at the foot of the Belgian mount; they will find Sergeant-Major Cotton's niece very obliging, the fare good, and the museum worth seeing.

I have now accomplished to my own satisfaction, and I believe to that of the great mass of the readers of my *History of Lord Seaton's Regiment at Waterloo* and of these supplementary pamphlets, the object with which I commenced writing that work—that object being, as I have stated in the title-page, to prove that:—

> Lord Seaton and the 52nd had the honour of defeating, single handed, without the assistance of the 1st British Guards, or of any other troops, that portion of the Imperial Guard of France, about 10,000 in number, which advanced to make the last attack on the British position.

Even the 1st Guards, I think, must recognise the fact that the exploits of the 52nd at Waterloo were ignored, and that though a mistaken claim the Guards had the honours and rewards thrust upon them, which in a tenfold degree belonged to the 52nd. Never before had the 52nd "surpassed in arms" what they achieved at Waterloo.

I may venture to observe that every 52nd officer and man, who was with the regiment from the beginning to the end of the action, had a fair greater opportunity of seeing the details of that great battle than any other officer or man in the whole army.

My readers will see what further object I have in view, if they will turn back to the first of these pamphlets. I believe it would be of much benefit to the service, if the officers of every regiment in it held the same rank in each grade, which the officers of the Guards hold, so that the latter should not, as a rule, arrive at the higher ranks and commands of the army at an earlier age than is the case with regard to the officers of all the other regiments. The officers of all the other regiments of the army would no doubt be satisfied with such an arrangement, without any consequent present increase of pay, supposing that to be a difficulty in the way of carrying out such an arrangement. It would, perhaps, be difficult for the officers of the rest of the army to take the initiative in making such a proposal, however much they may see the injury inflicted on the service by the present state of things, but it would be a noble and graceful thing for the officers of the Guards to do.

Wm. Leeke.

Holbrooke, near Derby, February 15th, 1868.

Chapter 11

1815: Siborne's, Alison's, and Shaw Kennedy's Mistakes Refuted

In reading over the numerous accounts, both printed and in manuscript, both English and French, of the *Crisis* of Waterloo, that is, of the advance of the two long columns of 10,000 men of the French Imperial Guard, towards the British position, supported by a forward movement of a great portion of the remainder of the French Army, and of the total defeat of these columns, followed by the flight of the whole of the French Army, one has been almost struck down with a feeling of despondency and of utter despair of being able to unravel the confused and complicated mass of detail, into which the various writers on the subject have together managed to work the history of that event.

Many of these writers have followed in the wake of Captain Siborne, who, not having had the good fortune; to be at Waterloo, and not having witnessed the attack, was sure, as I have before shewn, to fall into the most terrible mistakes with regard to persons and time, in working up all the conflicting information which he received, so many years after the battle, from great numbers of officers who were present at it.

The Duke of Wellington, whose own memory, with regard to many things which occurred at Waterloo, has been found to be exceedingly defective in after years, wrote as follows to a person whom he wished to deter from attempting to write a history of the Battle of Waterloo:—

Paris, 8th August, 1815.

I have received your letter of the 2nd, regarding the Battle of Waterloo. The object which you propose to yourself is very difficult of attainment, and, if really obtained, is not a little invidious. The history of a battle is not unlike the history of a ball. Some individuals may recollect all the little events, of which the great result is the battle lost or won; but no individual can recollect the order in which, or the exact moment at which they occurred, which makes all the difference as to their value and importance.

To another person he writes, in 1816:—

The Battle of Waterloo is undoubtedly one of the most interesting events of modern times, but the duke entertains no hopes of ever seeing an account of all its details, which shall be true.

Again in 1816, he says:—

The people of England may be entitled to a detailed and accurate account of the Battle of Waterloo, and I have no objection to their having it; but I do object to their being misinformed and misled by those novels called *Relations, Impartial Accounts*, &c., &c., of that transaction, containing the stories which curious travellers have picked up from peasants, private soldiers, individual officers, &c., &c., and have published to the world as the truth I am really disgusted with and ashamed of all that I have seen of the Battle of Waterloo. The number of writings upon it would lead the world to suppose that the British Army had never fought a battle before; and there is not one which contains a true representation, or even an idea, of the transaction; and this is because the writers have referred as above quoted, instead of to the official sources and reports.

Alas! the official reports are very meagre, and the duke's own despatch is particularly so, and I must say, and every 52nd officer who fought at Waterloo, from the gallant Colborne (Lord Seaton) to the youngest ensign, always felt that that despatch was most unjust towards that man and that regiment, which very probably had saved himself and his army from an ignominious defeat.

The duke surely knew the great exploit which had been performed by Lord Seaton and the 52nd, when he rode down with Sir Colin Campbell to the rear of the centre of the 52nd line, near the Charleroi road, eight hundred yards from their original position on the right of the 1st Guards, and found them there by themselves preparing to attack the three battalions of the grenadiers of the Old Guard, and when he exclaimed, as he rode up to us, "Well done, Colborne! Well done! Don't give them time to rally."

In after years the duke's recollections of what took place at the crisis of Waterloo were most confused, as will be seen from a memorandum written by him in October, 1836, one-and-twenty years after the battle, which I shall take the liberty of extracting from the despatches and memoranda published by his son. I shall also number the several paragraphs, and give my commentary upon some of them in brackets:—

MEMORANDUM UPON THE PLAN OF THE BATTLE OF WATERLOO, WRITTEN IN OCTOBER, 1836.

1. I have looked over the plan of the ground of the Battle of Waterloo, which appears to me to be accurately drawn.

2. It is very difficult for me to judge of the particular position of each body of the troops under my command, much less of the Prussian Army, at any particular hour.

3. I was informed that the smoke of the fire of cannon was seen occasionally from our line, behind Hougomont, at a distance, in front of our left, about an hour before *the British Army advanced to the attack of the enemy's line*. (The Italics are mine here, and in the succeeding paragraph.)

4. The attack was ordered possibly at about half-past seven, *when I saw the confusion in their position upon the result of the last attack of their infantry*, and when I rallied and brought up again into the first line the Brunswick infantry.

> (The hour was much later than "half-past seven," at which the Duke of Wellington ordered the whole of his troops, then in position, to move forward, "when he saw the confusion on the French position upon the repulse of the last attack of their infantry." It must have been a quarter past eight o'clock when the 52nd repulsed this last attack of infantry, which was made by the 10,000 men of the Imperial Guard. It will here be seen that the duke himself makes a distinction between the repulse of this last attack of the French Guard by the 52nd, followed by the advance of the 71st and of the Osnabruck battalion on the right, and the subsequent advance of his cavalry and infantry from the British position. He calls this last advance an "attack," but it will have been seen that after the return of the

3rd battalion of the 1st Guards from driving off the Imperial Guard skirmishers, and the defeat of the columns of the Imperial Guard by the 52nd, and the flight of the French Army, there were no remaining French infantry to be attacked, except the three or four battalions of the Old Guard, who had retired hastily, without breaking, from the rear of the columns repulsed by the 52nd, and had brought up, 500 yards to their proper right and rear, on the rising ground situated about midway between the lower end of the enclosures of La Haye Sainte and La Belle Alliance, and which is crossed by the Charleroi road; and these battalions were attacked and driven off by the 52nd; and it would appear from Sir Colin Campbell's and Sir Hussey Vivian's statements that one, if not two of them, was afterwards followed and fired into by Halkett's Osnabruck battalion, and that one of them was that charged by Major Howard and a small party of the 10th Hussars. Vivian's and Vandeleur's brigades of cavalry found and "attacked" the retiring French on and beyond the French position.)

5. The whole of the British and Allied cavalry of our army was then in the rear of our infantry. I desired that it might be collected in rear of our centre; that is, between Hougomont and La Haye Sainte.

6. The infantry was advanced in line. I halted them for a moment in the bottom, that they might be in order to attack some battalions of the enemy still on the heights.

(There is much confusion in the statements made in the whole of this memorandum, but this 6th paragraph must refer to the 52nd and 71st, who were each in a four-deep *line*, and the duke says, in the 9th paragraph, "the infantry was formed into columns, and moved in pursuit in *columns* of battalions," which 9th paragraph must therefore refer to the infantry which advanced after the repulse of the Imperial Guard by the 52nd. What the duke means, when he says these columns advanced in *pursuit*, I do not quite understand; but they probably moved down the British position some distance, and bivouacked on the lower slope of it, when it was ascertained that the whole French Army was in utter *déroute* far beyond the French position.

The infantry, which the duke says he halted for a moment in the bottom, was the 52nd by itself, which Lord Seaton had halted for a moment close to the Charleroi road—*immediate-*

ly before the duke rode up—in order to dress the line before he attacked the battalions of the Old Guard in his front. The duke never halted the regiment, but on the contrary, found it just halted, and said, "Well done, Colborne! Go on, &c." One does not altogether wonder at mistakes on the part of the duke when speaking of movements which had been made by portions of his army at Waterloo one-and-twenty years before, but they help to shew that his statements with regard to the events, and with regard even to the *very great events*, of that battle, must be received with caution.)

7. The cavalry halted likewise. The whole moved forward again in very few moments. The enemy did not stand the attack. Some had fled before we halted. The whole abandoned their position.

8. The cavalry were then ordered to charge, and moved round the flanks of the battalions of infantry.

(I believe scarcely anyone but myself could possibly discover what movements the duke had in his mind when he wrote down paragraphs 7 and 8. I think, after some amount of puzzling, I have found the clue to his meaning. No. 8, which should have preceded No. 7 paragraph, must refer to the advance of Sir Hussey Vivian's hussar brigade, from the British position round the flank of the Guards or of the 2nd battalion of the 95th Rifles the left battalion of our brigade, which, if it had not then left the position, would be in line to the right of the 1st Guards.

✶✶✶✶✶✶

Note:—I am exceedingly sorry not to be able to speak of the position or movements of our gallant friends of the 2nd battalion of the 95th Rifles after the 52nd moved down from the British position on the flank of the Imperial Guard. They were, of course, thrown out by our sudden movement, and were not with us when we defeated the 10,000 men of the French Guard; nor when we afterwards drove off the battalions of the grenadiers of the Guard from the height in front of La Belle Alliance. We were alone from the time we left the British position till we halted for the night at Rosomme, at about a quarter past nine.

✶✶✶✶✶✶

In a note made the day after a conversation I had with Sir Colin Campbell in 1833, I find the following entry:—

Sir Colin Campbell told me distinctly that he did not go with the order to Sir Hussey Vivian *until twenty minutes after our advance against the Imperial Guard*; that he went before the three squares of the Old Guard and the *cuirassiers* gave way before us; that he met Sir Hussey coming down the hill, who said his brigade was close at hand in his rear.

"The cavalry halting likewise," in paragraph 7, refers to Vivian's disposition of his brigade on the rise of the French position, before they made their charge on the intermingled French cavalry of all arms, somewhere in a line with La Belle Alliance, away to our right.

9. The infantry was formed into columns, and moved in pursuit in columns of battalions.

Wellington.

(This 9th paragraph I have endeavoured to explain under paragraph 6.)

What the duke has said of the inaccuracies and mistakes of others, and of the confusion they would be sure to fall into, in attempting to give a history of the Battle of Waterloo, I have found, to my very great disgust and annoyance, to be perfectly and painfully true; but I think my readers will agree with me, that the duke, in his memorandum of 1836, which I have just quoted and commented on, has shewn himself not to be a whit behind the writers of the *Relations*, *Impartial Accounts*, and *Histories* of Waterloo, whom he so properly denounces, in the inaccuracies, mistakes, and confusion of ideas which he himself has fallen into.

It may be asked, Are the histories of all battles equally incorrect? Perhaps never were there anything like so many histories of any other battle written, either before or since, as have been written about Waterloo, I must, however, for myself confess that my confidence in the accuracy of history in general, which was never very great, has received the very rudest possible shake from all that I have read, both in English, German, Prussian, Belgian, French, and Spanish accounts concerning this great battle.

I feel that I must not leave the subject I am endeavouring to elucidate, without introducing one or two specimens of the manner in which persons, professing to describe the leading events of the crisis at Waterloo, have made the most egregious mistakes. The following is one in which much credit is given to General Adam's brigade, consisting of the 52nd, the 71st, and the 2nd and 3rd battalions of the 95th

Rifles, for repulsing the French Imperial Guard. I will mark those portions of the account, which I know to be incorrect, in italics, and afterwards advert to it within brackets. It is called. *An extract from a letter from an eye witness*:—

After various hot and desultory attacks of the day, the last and most dreadful was made by the Old Imperial Guard, grown grey in an uninterrupted career of victory. In black, massive, solid columns, supported and covered by the fire of a numerous artillery, they advanced in spite of the most desperate resistance. *Lord Hill*, who had seen the approaching storm, *having formed General Adam's brigade a little 'en potence' on the enemy's left, placed himself at its head*, and advanced with dreadful regularity to the assistance of the Guards. General Adam's veterans of the Peninsula, after one terrible volley within a few yards of the Imperial Guard, cheered and charged. These gallant troops (the Imperial Guard) for the first time fled, although encouraged to the last by the conduct of the brave but unfortunate Ney. *Lord Hill* followed with his usual rapidity, *the British Guards supporting him*, and *at the same instant* our great duke ordered the general and decisive advance of the whole army.

(Lord Hill, and the British Guards, and the 71st, and 2nd and 3rd battalions of the 95th, were not engaged in the attack on these "black, massive, solid columns" of the Imperial Guard. It was made by the 52nd alone. The name of Sir John Colborne—Lord Seaton—should be substituted for that of Lord Hill. General Adam came up at the exact moment of the charge, and behaved most gallantly in front of the 52nd line, and was severely wounded, but he did not at all interfere with the command of the 52nd, which was left entirely to Colborne. After the Imperial Guard had fled, we saw no more of him until he rode into our bivouac at Rosomme, towards ten o'clock. With regard to the "general advance of the army," I have shewn a few pages back, under the paragraph in the duke's memorandum which I have numbered 6, that it could not have taken place till about twenty minutes after the 52nd had routed the French Imperial Guard.)

I have shewn that Siborne, in his account of the crisis of Waterloo, has made most terrible mistakes. Alison, in his history of Europe, has followed him and taken much of his version of the crisis from

Siborne. The Chaplain-General, Gleig, whilst following the account of a French writer, has written a work on the Battle of Waterloo, and dedicated it to the queen, which appears to me to be about as full of errors as it is possible for any work to be. Hooper, in his history of the campaign of 1815, has followed Siborne, and gives the myth of the British Guards having defeated a first *column* of the Imperial Guard, very much in Siborne's own words.

Mr. Hooper has evidently taken much pains to give a correct account of the battle and of the defeat of the French Guard; but he not only speaks of a first column of them, but even makes the British Guards, as Siborne does, both on his model and in his history, to assist in the defeat of a *second column*. Mr. Hooper candidly acknowledges in a note appended to his account of the defeat of the Imperial Guard, that "*much confusion exists in the accounts of these columns of attack, their number and formation,*" but adds, "the conclusions in the text are derived from a study of the best accounts on both sides."

★★★★★★

Note:—I would here ask, If the British Guards sent a column of the Imperial Guards flying down the slope, how was it that the 52nd, who were at that time 300 yards in a direct line in front of the British Guards, and at right angles with them; how was it that the 52nd never saw this column, but that they did see the skirmishers of the Imperial Guard run in and form 100 yards in front of the "black, massive, solid columns of the French Guard," which they (the 52nd) took in flank and overthrew, whilst the whole slope of the British position, above and in front of them, was quite clear of troops of any kind for 300 yards?

★★★★★★

The following account, from Hooper's work, of the advance of the 52nd, may be taken as nearly correct, if it be recollected that the British Guards were not there, but 300 yards away; that the 71st never reached the enemy, but were away to the right, near the enclosures of Hougomont; that the 95th were not in line with the 52nd, and were not seen by them, and that the column said to have been defeated by the 3rd battalion of the 1st Guards still formed a portion of the "black, massive, solid columns," attacked by the 52nd, and that even the Imperial Guard *skirmishers*, driven back from the British position by the advance of the 3rd battalion of the 1st Guards, had returned to swell the numbers of the enemy, which we believe were fairly estimated as amounting to about ten thousand men.

******

> Note:—Baron Muffling, who was present with the British Army, says, respecting the strength of the columns of the French Guard, defeated by the 52nd, "The enemy's Guard began to move, and with sixteen battalions, leaving La Haye Sainte a little to the right, at half-past six o'clock advanced towards the platform." (There is a great mistake here about the time of their advance; it must have been nearly eight o'clock when they reached the first ascent of the British position.)
>
> Muffling states also, "Some of the enemy's batteries cover, with grape-shot, the retreat of the four battalions of the Guard." (These battalions were the battalions of the Old Guard which, on the flight of the rest of the Imperial Guard, drew off hastily towards the French position.)
>
> Sixteen battalions of 800 men each give an amount of 12,800 men, besides the officers and the artillery, and some cavalry of the Guard; so that allowing for any casualties or mistakes as to the numbers, there must have been, as it was always stated by the 52nd officers, about 10,000 of the Imperial Guard, when we attacked and defeated them. Ney, in his letter to the Duke of Otranto, speaks of four regiments, that is eight battalions, of the Middle Guard, and four battalions of the Old Guard.

******

It must also always be borne in mind that the arena, on which this conflict between the 52nd and the 10,000 picked and veteran soldiers of the Imperial Guard took place, was not towards the *crest* of the British position, as has been related by Siborne and others, but 300 yards below it. Lord Seaton calls it "the plain," Sir Thomas Reynell, of the 71st, speaks of it "as the bottom of the declivity." Hooper writes as follows:—

> At this moment Sir John Colborne, who had steadily observed their progress, wheeled the 52nd upon its left company, and brought it nearly parallel to the left flank of the attacking column.

******

> Note:—Sir John Colborne had at first, for a moment, the idea of changing in some degree the direction of the 52nd line, by wheeling back the right companies, (No. 1 and No. 6 in its

rear,) on their right a few paces only, so as to throw back the left of the regiment before he brought them over the crest of the position, but it was immediately given up, and they advanced directly to the front, afterwards bringing their right shoulders forward as they moved down the slope, in the manner before described.

******

What was he going to do? was the inquiry of his superior officer. 'To make that column feel our fire,' was the prompt answer. The duke and Lord Hill had seen and approved of the movement, and the next moment the 52nd was over the brow, and its full fire was brought to bear upon the heavy masses before it. (The duke and Lord Hill only saw the 52nd when it had moved some distance down the slope, and then sent to desire Sir John Colborne to continue the movement.)

The Imperial Guardsmen faced this new and terrible foe, and began to fire from the flank. For a brief space the combat was one of musketry. 'A thick, white smoke enveloped the contending parties.' Napier's guns double-shotted, the muskets of the British Guards, the rifles of the 95th, and the rapid fire of the 52nd, shook the column from front to rear. (The artillery had ceased to fire on the Imperial Guard, the left of the 52nd being in their way; and, I think, the French were then rather sheltered by the ground from Napier's guns. The British Guards were on the reverse slope of the British position, 300 yards away; the 95th were not there; the 52nd had it all to themselves, with the exception, that their truly gallant general of brigade, Adam, and his staff, arrived in time to get into the thick of the fight in front of the 52nd four-deep line.)

******

Note:—General Adam's spurs were well won on that glorious occasion. He was made a Knight Commander of the Bath; and so was Sir Thomas Reynell of the 71st; Sir John Colborne had obtained that distinction, and several other honours, at the close of the Peninsular War in 1814.

******

Hooper thus continues his account:—

Reduced to an unsteady crowd, it yielded and fled, when, at Colborne's command, the 52nd brought down their bayonets to the charge, cheered and dashed on. This splendid regiment, supported on the right by the 71st and on the left by the 95th, did not halt in its career in the track of the fugitives until it had swept, from right to left, along the front of the British centre. When the regiment halted, its left flank was in the hollow on the *chaussée* to Genappe, in advance of the orchard of La Haye Sainte, 800 yards from the ground at which the charge commenced.

Colborne had led it from the little hollow above the north east angle of Hougomont, working through the furrowed and muddy ground, trampling amidst the dead and the wounded, a bright beam of red light streaking the sombre and misty field until the left flank of the brigade (of the 52nd) nearly touched the edge of the Charleroi road. Before its steady march the broken Imperialists withdrew without a halt; but not without looking back fiercely and grimly upon their pursuers, whose bayonets glittered in the yellow glare of the setting sun.

Hooper continues:—

The battle was won; it was now the time to reap in ample measure the fruits of victory. The British leader, watchful of the course of the fight, had been patient and persevering for nine hours. It was now his turn to attack. He had been stricken long. It was now for him to break out from his fastness and strike. The charge of the 52nd, so magical and so decisive, begun at the right moment, and carried forward by the right kind of daring, was speedily sustained. At the order of the duke, Vivian's untouched light horsemen broke from the cloud of thick smoke, which hung over the ridge, and wheeling round the right flank of the British Guards poured down the slope, through the space left vacant by the light infantry brigade, (52nd, 71st, and 95th,) and, ably led by its consummate chief, swept onward over the field.

Since the foregoing portion of this volume was written, a work has come out, entitled *Notes on the Battle of Waterloo, by the late General Sir James Shaw Kennedy, K.CB.* Captain Shaw, at the time of the battle, was a captain in the 43rd Light Infantry and deputy-assistant quartermaster-general attached to General Baron Alten's division, the 3rd division of the British Army. He was an old peninsular officer, and was much distinguished for his gallantry and intelligence. He afterwards took the name of Kennedy. He appears to have seen nothing of the 52nd during the action, though he speaks most highly of their advance; nor does he appear to have seen the 3rd battalion of the 1st Guards drive in the skirmishers of the Imperial Guard. What he saw himself is very interesting. In almost everything which he did not see he acknowledges that he has followed Siborne's account.

I propose to select some of his observations and to comment freely upon them, for as Captain Siborne was not at Waterloo, and Shaw Kennedy did not leave the British position, they cannot speak of what happened to the 52nd and to the Imperial Guard 300 yards below that position, with the same authority with which I and other 52nd officers can speak, who saw, and participated in, the remarkable encounter which took place between the 52nd, then about 950 strong, and their renowned adversaries. I repeat here again, that the Imperial Guard was in two columns of *equal* length, apparently consisting of, and always mentioned by us as containing, 10,000 men.

All that has been said about a first column of the French Guard having been separated from the other column, and having been defeated by Maitland's brigade of Guards, is a myth. And I repeat again, the 2nd battalion of the 1st Guards, never advanced from the British position, when the 3rd battalion drove in the Imperial Guard skirmishers and probably some skirmishers and their supports of Donzelôt's division, and then, after following them a short distance down the slope, retired in some confusion, and did not come in contact with the enemy again, though Siborne states erroneously that both battalions did so.

Sir Shaw Kennedy says of Siborne and his history of Waterloo:—

Captain Siborne's history of the campaign has very great merit, I doubt if, as to any other battle, there ever were so great a number of facts brought together, or more care, industry, and fidelity displayed in their collection, so that all other accounts of the battle, to be correct, must, for a great portion of the details, borrow from Siborne, as he had access to sources of information that no historian following him can have.

As regards the 52nd and the French Imperial Guard, my information, derived from Lord Seaton and other 52nd officers, and from my own very accurate recollection of every movement of the 52nd, must be allowed to come from sources very superior to those from which Siborne or Kennedy derived their information. And even as regards the movements of the 2nd and 3rd battalions of the 1st Guards, I know my information is more accurate than that of either of them. Will the surviving officers of the 2nd battalion of the 1st Guards maintain that their battalion advanced against the Imperial Guard skirmishers or against *a first column* of the Imperial Guard when Lord Hill, who was on their right, and Sir John Byng, (afterwards Lord Strafford,) who had succeeded to the command of the whole division of the Guards, both declare that they did not? And when it is declared, on the part of the 3rd battalion of the Guards, that the 2nd battalion did not advance with them?

In the *Life* of Sir William Napier, we are told that in a matter of dispute as to whether a howitzer was taken from the French by the 43rd or the 52nd at Sabugal, speaking of his informants of the 43rd, he wrote:—

> They know what they have written and said to me, and I expect them to respond to my appeal. If they do not, the 43rd regiment must bear the stigma of having accepted from the Duke of Wellington the credit of an exploit belonging to another regiment.

Awkward as it may be, should not the 1st Guards even at this late period, when more than fifty years have passed away since the famous battle was fought, listen to my appeal, and no longer "accept," I do not say, "from the Duke of Wellington," for he never assigned that credit to them, but from Captain Siborne, Alison who has copied Siborne, and other mistaken historians of Waterloo, a portion of "the credit of an exploit belonging (entirely) to another regiment?" Should they not even lend their assistance towards rectifying the representation of a column of the Imperial Guard routed by them, and the position of the 1st Guards on Siborne's beautiful model, so that they should no longer be represented as firing into a column of the Imperial Guard which the 52nd single-handed attacked in flank and completely defeated?

Some of the officers of the Guards did much towards rescuing the model from being lost to the public, and no doubt have much in their power, respecting the alteration of the position of troops on the model, in any case in which a most glaring injustice has been perpetrated against one gallant regiment, and undeserved honour has been thrust upon another gallant corps. Siborne himself caused a considerable alteration to be made in the positions he had assigned to several of the Prussian corps, on the representation of some of the superior Prussian officers; thus alteration appears to be possible, without injury being done to the model.

A 52nd officer remarks in a letter, written to me in the year 1853, that:—

> In addition to the honour yet due to the regiment, the crisis and close of the action of Waterloo is a matter of importance, historically, nationally, and professionally.

The French historians of the battle, who have written of late years, have not been at all unwilling to adopt Siborne's (to the 52nd vexatious) account of the *successive* defeat of the columns of the Imperial Guard; because in a national point of view, there is not so much discredit in the rout, first of all of six battalions of the Imperial Guard by Maitland's brigade of the 1st British Guards, supported by the 33rd and 69th regiments, and then ten or twelve minutes afterwards in the defeat of the remaining battalions of the Imperial Guard by the flank attack of the 52nd assisted by Maitland's Guards in front, as in the defeat of the whole of the Imperial Guard of about 10,000 men, as I have before described it, by the 52nd alone at the distance of 300 yards from any other British or Allied regiments.

The defeat, by the advance of a single British battalion, of 10,000 or even 8,000 of the finest troops in Europe is an honour to the regiment, and an honour to Lord Seaton who commanded it, and an honour to the British Army and nation, which must not be tamely relinquished whilst there is any British blood and old 52nd Waterloo spirit remaining, combined with the possession of sufficient amount of material and detail to justify one in advancing almost single-handed to meet the many shafts, which I must expect to be levelled against me and my attempt to rescue one of the most daring exploits I believe ever performed in war, from the mass of confusion and error with which succeeding historians have, unwittingly I presume, almost ingulfed it.

When I was going into action at Waterloo, I was very anxious to know how I should feel and conduct myself under fire; I perhaps am not less anxious now as to the point of how I may feel, when I and my work are exposed to the very formidable artillery of the Press levelled against all my inflated and presumptuous pretensions, both military and religious, as they may perhaps consider them. Did my readers ever stop to see what would be the fate of a little dog who goes yelping and barking at a great big mastiff? I have often witnessed such a scene, and have invariably observed, that the little cur, directly the large dog comes up to him throws himself upon his back in token of submission, and the large one never hurts him, but stands over him for a second or two and perhaps licks him and wags his tail. Well, my readers, I am the little dog; the mastiff is the Press; and though I don't mean to knock under, unless I am convinced, I am wrong in any point, yet I do humbly deprecate any angry feeling or criticism on the part of the Press.

Baron Muffling, who was attached to the British headquarters by the Prussian commander-in-chief, and was present at the Battle of Waterloo, says in his history of the campaign of 1815, when speaking of the advance of the Imperial Guard towards the close of the action, that the columns consisted of sixteen battalions.

The following statement of the number of men of which the Imperial Guard consisted in each year from its first formation, is taken from a French history of that celebrated corps.

In 1804	9,798	men.
" 1805	12,187	"
" 1806	16,656	"
" 1807	15,361	"
" 1808	15,392	"
" 1809	31,203	"
" 1810	32,130	"
" 1811	31,960	"
" 1812	56,169	"
" 1813	92,472	"
" 1814	112,482	"
" 1815	25,870	"

The following table, taken from the same work, gives the composition and amount of the Imperial Guard in 1815.

HEAD QUARTERS			20
STAFF			200
INFANTRY.			
Grenadiers	3 Regiments	3,000	
Chasseurs	3 Regiments	3,000	
Tirailleurs	6 Regiments	7,200	
Voltigeurs	6 Regiments	7,200	
		20,400	20,400
CAVALRY.			
Grenadiers	1 Regiment	800	
Chasseurs	1 Regiment	800	
Dragoons	1 Regiment	800	
Gendarmerie	1 Company	100	
Light Dragoons, Lancers	1 Regiment	800	
		3,300	3,300

ARTILLERY.

Old Guard, 6 Foot Batteries	
Old Guard, 4 Horse Batteries	1,500
1 Company of labourers, 1 squadron of the Military Train	
Engineers and Sappers	250
Waggon Train, 1 squadron	200
Total	25,870

Mr. George Hooper, in his history of the campaign of 1815, a pleasing and well written book in which the author follows Siborne's mistakes as to the 1st Guards, makes out that altogether there were twelve battalions of the Imperial Guard brought forward by Napoleon to make his last attack on the British right centre, and that two of them were formed in reserve midway between La Belle Alliance and the southern end of Hougomont.

This last statement of the two battalions being left in reserve I doubt, because the two columns of equal length having not an interval of 30 paces between them, both gave way before the 52nd, but whilst the leading column of the two fled in utter confusion, and a portion of the rear column also, leaving some of the guns of the Old Guard with the horses harnessed to them, yet it is said that some of the rear battalions of the rear column fell back hastily but in comparative order to the French position; their immediate rear, at the time they gave way before the 52nd, being the spot indicated by Hooper as that at which Napoleon left two battalions of his Guard in reserve—I am inclined to think therefore that these two battalions of the fine Old Guard advanced with, and retired from, the rear column of the two.

Hooper observes in a note:—

Much confusion exists in the accounts of these columns of attack, their number and formation. The conclusions in the text are derived from a study of the best accounts on both sides.

I wish Hooper and Siborne and Alison had been with the 52nd at Waterloo, and they would have understood plainly that no column of the Imperial Guard could possibly have advanced upon, or have been defeated by, any portion of the British Guards without their seeing it; and that all three of them, Siborne at their head, have been robbing the 52nd of a portion of the honour belonging to them, by advancing this "column in buckram," or this mythical column, up the British position to the attack of the Guards.

Colonel Gawler, as I have before observed, from being on the extreme right of the 52nd line, and from seeing the dead bodies of Imperial Guardsmen on the summit of the British position the next morning, not reflecting that they might be those of their skirmishers only, fell into the mistake of supposing that the head of the column of the Imperial Guard had reached that point, when in reality it was 300 yards or thereabouts from the position. But Colonel Gawler speaks of the 52nd when it cleared the ascent being "under a furious fire (this however was further down the position than he supposed) *from the long flank of the columns.*" and his book, *The Crisis of Waterloo*, was written in 1833 on purpose to maintain:—

> That the attack of the Imperial Guard was repulsed, and the French Army thrown into consequent irretrievable confusion, by a charge of the 52nd covered by the 71st regiment without the direct co-operation of any other portion of the Allied Army.

Colonel Gawler reckoned the columns attacked and defeated by the 52nd at 10,000 men, and he had as good a view of them as any other 52nd man had.

Siborne says in his first preface, dated March, 1844:—

> One of my Waterloo correspondents has humorously remarked, that, 'if ever truth lies at the bottom of a well, she does so immediately after a great battle, and it takes an amazingly long time before she can be lugged out.'

I have good reason to believe that the following is the truth with regard both to the advance of the 3rd battalion of the Guards, and to the defeat of the two columns of the Imperial Guard by the 52nd:—That the mass of skirmishers of the Imperial Guard and their supports were joined by the skirmishers and their supports from the French troops massed to the left of La Haye Sainte, and that the whole of the intermingled skirmishers and their supports were still further supported by the advance of the battalions themselves of Donzelôt's division, which, with many other divisions of the French Army, is spoken of, as moving forward at this time in support of the advancing columns of the Imperial Guard. These skirmishers extended along the front of both the battalions of the Guards who are stated by Kennedy to have been lying down in square, though I do not feel sure of this as regards the right or 2nd battalion; the skirmishers extended also along the front of Sir Colin Halkett's brigade, which was on the British left of Maitland's brigade of Guards, for both these brigades maintain that they were opposed to troops wearing the bear skin caps of the Imperial Guard.

And the 2nd battalion of the Guards declared that they were attacked by a "column" of twelve or fourteen hundred men, and that these troops opened fire "upon them at a distance of fifty or sixty paces; that the duke coming along from their left, observed how this 3rd battalion of the 1st Guards was suffering from the heavy fire of the mass of troops in their front, and desired the commanding officer to form line on the front face of the square, and "drive those fellows off," which they did in very gallant style, and followed them for some eighty or a hundred yards down the slope; then there was an alarm of cavalry and the 3rd battalion of the Guards, some of them thinking they were to form square, got into confusion and retired hastily over the crest of the position and beyond it on the reverse slope, to where the 10th Hussars and all Vivian's brigade were, on their way from the extreme left of the position to the interval made by the advance of the 52nd from the position.

The 2nd battalion of the 1st Guards took no part in this charge, but was stationary. The only conclusion I can come to is that the mass of troops seen and defeated by the 3rd battalion of the Guards, were, as I have before observed, the skirmishers of the Imperial Guard and of Donzelôt's division and their supports; and that when the Guards passed over the top of the position they saw also, away to their left, some of Donzelôt's battalions. Any other troops than skirmishers, whom they saw, must have been other than troops of the Imperial Guard.

The skirmishers of the Imperial Guard came down the slope running towards the leading battalion of the French Guard, and formed about 100 yards or rather more in front of it, just as the 52nd was completing its right-shoulder-forward movement and becoming parallel to the left flank of the Imperial columns. There was no smoke, there was a gleam of sunshine on the skirmishers, as they were forming, and I could see them most completely, and 200 yards or more beyond them up the British position. Of any other troops driven in by the 3rd battalion of the 1st Guards we could see nothing, nor of the Guards themselves, therefore they could not have come far down the position in pursuit. Donzelôt's skirmishers and their supports, when they gave way, must have run towards their own division in the direction of La Haye Sainte. This formation of the retiring Imperial Guard skirmishers was afterwards spoken of in mistake, by some writers, as an attempt at deployment on the part of their leading battalion.

The 52nd fired into and charged the Imperial Guard, as I have before related, and it gave way and fled in utter confusion, with the exception, it was said, of two or three of the rear battalions of the rear column, who gained the French position hastily and in comparative order.

The 52nd never met with or saw any British troops from the time they left their position till they halted for the night at Rosomme, excepting the English and German cavalry—beforementioned, as having ridden at speed round the flanks and through the centre of the 52nd, when retiring before the *cuirassiers*—and with the exception also of those whom I suppose to have been engaged in poor Howard's charge.

If there was a second column of the Imperial Guard defeated, as the historians try to make out, partly by the 52nd, and partly by Maitland's brigade of Guards, how came it that Maitland allowed the 52nd to go on by themselves to, and over, and a mile beyond, the French position, in pursuit of the enemy, when there were tens of thousands of French infantry, and thousands of cavalry still in the field?

Sir John Byng, who said "we saw the 52nd advancing gloriously, as they always do," and who thought it necessary to say to Sir John Colborne, "I could not advance when you did, for our ammunition was exhausted," would he, if he had been near the 52nd, and been engaged with them in defeating the same column, would he, ammunition or no ammunition, have allowed them to be exposed, single-handed, to all the dangers to which, by their isolation from the rest of the army, they were really exposed? Must he not, if he had been so near them as is represented, have brought down Maitland's brigade of Guards to their support, instead of keeping them in rear of the crest of the British position until the duke, long after, made a sort of forward movement from the position of some portion of his troops, which was called an advance of his whole line?

I wish not, nor do I mean, to say one word in disparagement of any individual or of any regiment, but as I feel certain the 52nd came in contact just below the British position with all the remainder of the Imperial Guard, after the half of it had been sent to Planchenoit to hold the Prussians at bay, that is, that they engaged and defeated two heavy columns of equal length, apparently containing 10,000 men, and as this was always the opinion of the 52nd officers who were present, and as the greater portion of these officers have passed away, and I am almost the only person left who could take this matter in hand, I think it right not to shrink from doing so, though I may conjecture that much unpleasantness and annoyance to myself may possibly be the result of my undertaking it.

Another idea occurs to me, and I think it will approve itself to the minds of all military men. "A column" of twelve or fourteen hundred men or more of the Imperial Guard bent on penetrating the British line, and especially if they were backed up by other advancing troops, would never have contented themselves with reaching the crest of the position, and then halting that their front company might fire on a British square, lying down at sixty or eighty yards distance from them on the reverse slope of the position. It is exactly what a swarm of daring French skirmishers *would do*, especially if the Imperial Guard skirmishers and Donzelôt's were intermixed and vying with each other.

It must be remembered that the square of the 3rd battalion of the 1st Guards, was about 150 yards to the left of the 2nd battalion, and probably at nearly double that distance from the nearest square of Halkett's brigade on its left, so that the skirmishers, intended to occupy ground 300 yards or more in length, would as a matter of course close more and more to the points from which they might fire into the front and flank faces of the square of the 3rd battalion of the Guards. It is most probable also that their supports had joined them. Hence, I suggest, there were enough of skirmishers congregated in a space perhaps not exceeding fifty yards in length, to give them the appearance through the smoke of being a formed body of men.

Although Kennedy, following in Siborne's wake, makes the vexatious mistakes about the defeat of a first column of four battalions of the Imperial Guard by Maitland's brigade of Guards, and about the head of a second column of the Imperial Guard being fired into by Maitland's brigade at the same time that Colborne charged it in flank, (all which is a regular myth,) yet he gives the 52nd as much honour and credit for their share in the rout of the 2nd column of four battalions, *as would have quite satisfied, them, for what they really did do, for the defeat of the whole of the ten or twelve battalions of the French Guard, without* any other British regiment being within 300 yards of them. Kennedy says:—

> The French column, feeling the severity of the fire of the 52nd, wheeled up its left sections and commenced firing, but the fire from the 52nd threw it into great disorder, and the combined fire and formidable advance in line of the 52nd caused the entire rout and dispersion of the four (twelve) battalions of the French Guard which were opposed to it.

Again, Sir Shaw Kennedy says:—

> The march of the 52nd has thus been traced continuously, without referring to other incidents of the battle during its advance; for its progress was the leading and distinctive feature of the action during that period; and it will thus be more easy, by reference to the progress of the 52nd, to understand what was done by the rest of the Anglo-Allied Army, and the Prussian Army, during this most highly interesting part of the action.

Again, he says:—

> It is perhaps impossible to point out in history any other instance in which so small a force as that with which Colborne acted, had so powerful an influence on the result of a great battle, in which the numbers engaged on each side were so large.

Now there is great truth in this last observation, if applied to the real exploit of the 52nd at the crisis and close of the Battle of Waterloo, but for which exploit. Sir John Colborne thought, the columns of the Imperial Guard would be likely to penetrate the British line of battle.

In consequence of the sad mistake of La Haye Sainte being allowed to fall into the hands of the enemy, Donzelôt was enabled to establish himself in force, within 100 yards of the centre of the British and Allied Army, and exceedingly to harass Alten's division, which occupied the British position for a quarter of a mile or more, between the centre of the position and the left of Maitland's brigade of Guards.

★★★★★★

> Note:—This took place only at six o'clock in the evening, according to Kennedy, at about the same time that the last of the great cavalry attacks was repulsed. Major Baring, who commanded the 2nd light battalion of the King's German Legion at La Haye Sainte, and the reinforcements subsequently sent there, slept on the ground with Kennedy, on the night of the action, close to the Wellington Tree.

★★★★★★

Had Napoleon sent his Imperial Guard to attack the British centre by La Haye Sainte it has been thought by some that he would have succeeded in defeating the troops at that point, harassed and reduced in numbers as they were.

When the Imperial Guard was ordered to advance towards the

right centre of the British line, opposite to the spot where the 3rd battalion of the 1st Guards was lying down in square, orders were at the same time given that all the French infantry should advance in support of their attack. Sir Shaw Kennedy, who be it remembered was with Alten's division during the whole of the engagement, says:—

> The attack of Donzelôt's division from La Haye Sainte preceded that by the Imperial Guard, as that attack had never ceased from the taking of that farm, and increased in intensity as the grand general attack progressed...... The attack was preceded along the whole line by a furious cannonade; and the whole front of attack was covered by a swarm of skirmishers.

Farther on in his work Kennedy adds:—

> The effect of the defeat of the ten battalions of the Imperial Guard, and of Colborne's diagonal march, was electrical on Donzelôt's division, which was in fact compromised by the advance of Adam's brigade.

******

Note:—Kennedy is wrong, the 52nd were alone; the 71st were far away, not far from the enclosures of Hougomont and advancing towards the French position; the other part of the brigade, six companies of the 2nd battalion of the Rifles and two of the 3rd battalion, were not with the 52nd during their advance.

******

Its attack, which had up to that time been violently severe on Alten's division, was at once slackened and very soon suspended, and a retreat commenced.

The loss of the 2nd battalion of the 1st Guards at Waterloo was as follows:—

	Killed.			Wounded.		Total.
Officers.	Serjts.	Rank & File.	Officers.	Serjts.	Rank & File.	
1	—	50	5	7	80	143
Of the 3rd battalion as follows :—
3	2	79	6	7	238	335

If we deduct 143, the total loss in killed and wounded of the 2nd battalion, from 335, the total loss of the 3rd battalion, we find that the loss of the 3rd battalion exceeded that of the 2nd battalion by 192. This excess of loss on the part of the 3rd battalion, perhaps helps to prove the truth of what I have advanced, that the 2nd battalion was not engaged to the extent that the 3rd battalion was, and that it was stationary when the latter, by the duke's order, formed line on the front face of its square, and drove off the mass of skirmishers assembled on the crest of the position before it.

I have already, in a quotation from a work printed and circulated by a very intelligent Peninsular and Waterloo 52nd officer, mentioned that the 1st Guards were made grenadiers, and that the ensigns of all the three regiments of Guards were given precedence over all the ensigns of the line by lieutenant's rank, for their good conduct at Waterloo. All the regiments of the Guards did good service at Quatre Bras and Waterloo, as I have observed before, but the singling those regiments out for these particular rewards was unfair towards the rest of the army. And it was particularly awkward that the 1st Guards should be made grenadiers for defeating the grenadiers of the French Imperial Guard, when all they really did, *as regards the Imperial Guard,* was to drive in their *skirmishers.* There was no harm in their being made a regiment of grenadiers, but it was an awkward mistake that the thing should have been mismanaged as it was.

The giving to the ensigns of the three regiments of Guards the brevet rank of lieutenant, was afterwards followed up by depriving several of the regiments of the Line of little distinctions, some of which were an advantage to them, others merely prized by them as distinctions, probably conferred upon them for services rendered, or supposed to have been rendered to their country, and the being deprived of which occasioned perhaps in some cases only a little annoyance at the time, but in others very considerable hardships. Still if it was an advantage to the service, that there should be no invidious distinctions, then of course the change might be necessary; but why should it not be equally necessary that there should be no invidious distinction in favour of the three regiments of Foot Guards?

It was not till the year 1854, that the Fusilier regiments, the 5th, 7th, 21st, 23rd, and 87th, and the 60th Rifles and the Rifle Brigade had the rank of ensign given to their junior officers instead of that of 2nd lieutenant. In the case of the 7th Fusiliers all their subalterns were, till that time, full lieutenants. All this appears to have been fairly done, and without infliction of hardship on individual officers; but still the only reason for it appears to have arisen from a desire to make all the infantry regiments, except the guards, alike, as to the appellation of their junior subalterns.

In the light infantry regiments, it appears, from the following document addressed to the lamented Sir John Moore, that an additional lieutenant was appointed for each company as far back as 1803:—

War Office, 18th October, 1803.

Sir,—In pursuance of a communication from His Royal Highness the Commander-in-Chief, I have the honour to acquaint you, that as the 52nd Regiment of Foot under your command, being a light infantry corps, requires a greater proportion of officers and non-commissioned officers than a battalion of the Line, His Majesty has been pleased to order that an augmentation of one lieutenant, one sergeant, and one corporal per company, shall be made to the establishment thereof from the 25th instant inclusive.

I have the honour, &c.,
(Signed) C. Bragg.
Major-General Moore, 52nd Regiment.

I cannot trace the whole detail of circumstances which led to the injustice and hardship perpetuated on some of the officers of the 52nd, and of the other light infantry regiments, in connexion with some of the reductions which took place after Waterloo and the return of the army of occupation from France. There were ten captains with the 52nd at Waterloo (besides Lord March and Yorke who were on the staff) thirty-five lieutenants including the adjutant, and eight ensigns. On the return of the 52nd, then only consisting of one battalion, from France, the establishment of subalterns was reduced to ten lieutenants and ten ensigns, and on the 25th of August, 1822, it was reduced to eight lieutenants and eight ensigns.

On the first of these reductions taking place, the junior lieutenants beyond the ten remained on the list of lieutenants, receiving only ensign's pay, until by death-vacancies the two supernumerary lieutenants were absorbed, and in the meantime the ensigns could only become lieutenants by purchase. The grievance created by this paltry and shabby arrangement was very great in the 52nd, and ought to be a lesson to all admirers of Mr. Joseph Hume's views of economy, to consider well the amount of annoyance and disgust which they may occasion to many deserving officers, before they proceed, for the sake of saving the veriest trifle of expense to the country, to recommend and carry out reductions which interfere, in so great a degree as those I speak of did, with the feelings and prospects of individuals.

The hardship inflicted upon one of the officers of the 52nd, the late Lieutenant Yonge, was that he was put on ensign's pay, after having received the extra pay of a seven years' lieutenant. In mentioning this in a letter to the Secretary of War some years ago, he also spoke of the injustice it was, that :—

> While the ensigns of the Guards were made lieutenants on the pretence of the 1st Guards having repulsed the Imperial Guard, the lieutenants of the regiment that actually did that work were made ensigns.

In a subsequent letter to the same Secretary of War, he wrote thus:—

> But I was led to speak more particularly of the 43rd, 52nd, and Rifle Brigade, because being the originally-formed light corps, and constituting as they did the light division, to them especially fell the outpost duties of the Peninsular Army, and the practice of the system, of which they had acquired the theory from Sir John Moore. How they acquitted themselves is sufficiently known. Their losses were proportionately severe. The merit of their services had been continually acknowledged, and to my own regiment, the 52nd, the commander-in-chief had repeatedly accorded a quite unusual amount of promotion, professedly on account of the high character it sustained.
>
> It was a strange turn of affairs that, as soon as the war was over, they should have thus been placed in a more disadvantageous position than any of the ordinary regiments of the Line, and this on the miserable pretext that they had no flank companies, whereas it should rather have been held, that theirs were all flank companies. The detached services required of them had been tenfold more numerous than could ever be required of the flank companies of any Line regiment..... No one who is made aware of it can, I am sure, refuse to acknowledge that the light regiments have not been fairly treated, and it appears still more glaring, when we look at the Fusiliers, differing in no respect but in name only from the other Line regiments—yet in these, in the place of the ten lieutenants and ten ensigns of the light corps, the subalterns of the 7th are all 1st lieutenants and the establishment of the 21st and 23rd is twelve 1st lieutenants and eight 2nd lieutenants.

Mr. Yonge, who received ensign's pay as a supernumerary lieutenant, after having received extra pay as a seven years' lieutenant, was a very intelligent and good officer. His services are enumerated as follows, in the 52nd record:—

Lieutenant William Crawley Yonge entered the 52nd in 1810, served with the regiment at the Nivelle, the Nive, Orthes, Toulouse, and the intervening affairs. He also served in the campaign and Battle of Waterloo. He has received the Peninsular War medal with four clasps.

These supernumerary lieutenancies, which were to be absorbed by death vacancies, interfered very much with the promotion of the ensigns. The only hardship besides my own which I recollect was that of Ensign Bentham, who stood next to me on the list and remained an ensign twelve years. My own case was a very trying one. My money was lodged all along for the purchase of my lieutenancy, and yet, very much owing to this treatment of the light regiments, I was more than eight years and a half an ensign. And when in November, 1823, I purchased my lieutenancy, the delay that had been occasioned by the falling in of the supernumerary lieutenancy, which had not been filled up when Brevet-Major Shedden died in 1821, was the means of my tardy promotion coming just too late to enable me to avoid the very great mortification of having an ensign four years my junior, by the purchase of a half-pay lieutenancy, and by a subsequent exchange, pass into the regiment again as my senior in the list of lieutenants.

I perhaps should just mention that all the ensigns of the Guards who were at Waterloo, and who remained long enough in their regiments, were lieutenants and *brevet-captains* before I obtained my lieutenancy.

I have always felt that the favour and distinctions accorded to the three regiments of Foot Guards in the way of a step in advance of the officers of the other infantry regiments, in the several ranks of ensign, lieutenant, and captain, so that all the ensigns are brevet-lieutenants, the lieutenants captains, and the captains lieutenant-colonels, is not only very annoying and galling to the other officers of the army, but also exceedingly injurious to the service.

And so much did I feel this, that, in December, 1855, when the Guards were making some stir about a disadvantage which they considered their senior officers were labouring under, and expressed a desire to be placed on an "equality with their more fortunate brethren of the Line," I went out of my way as a clergyman and took some trouble in drawing up the following letter and explanatory columns, which were published by *The Times*, and I think led our friends of the Guards to see that, with regard to the further agitation of the point they aimed at, "the better part of valour was discretion."

****

The Guards.

"To the Editor of 'The Times.'

"Sir—The accompanying columns are taken from the *Army Lists* for April, 1824, and January, 1841, which are the oldest *Army Lists* I have at hand. If you think well to publish them in *The Times*, they will help to point out what the officers of the Guards will obtain if they really are placed on an 'equality with their more fortunate brethren of the line.'

"I have taken the names and the dates of the commissions of the ensigns of the Guards mentioned in the *Army List* of 1824, who subsequently obtained the rank of lieutenant-colonel, and have shown from the *Army List* of 1841 when they arrived at that rank. I have also taken from the same *Army Lists* the names of the officers of the first thirty regiments of the Line and of the light infantry and rifle regiments, which occur in both these lists, and have shown the rank which they respectively held in 1824, and in 1841. The average time, from their first entrance into the army, in which the 19 officers of the Guards have obtained their lieutenant-colonelcies, is as nearly as possible fifteen years.

"Of the 76 officers of the Line, mentioned in the two *Army Lists*, only 16 had arrived at the rank of lieutenant-colonel in 1841, and of these not less than 12 were on an average 20 years and six months after they got their companies in obtaining their lieutenant-colonelcies. If we make the moderate calculation that, on an average, they were 10 years in getting their companies, then it appears that all the officers of these Line regiments who reached the rank of lieutenant-colonel were, on an average, 30 years in doing so—just twice the average time that it took the officers of the Guards to attain the same rank. But if your readers will look at the columns, they will perceive greater hardships than these. For instance. Ensigns Muller and Richardson, of the 1st Royals, were still only subalterns in 1841, after 21 years' service.

"These peculiar privileges of the officers of the Guards have always been obnoxious to the other officers of the army, and in the opinion of many are not only unjust, but also injurious to the best interests of the service. If the brevet rank in each grade is a desirable thing, let it be extended to the whole army; if not, then let it be abolished as quickly as possible in the regiments of the Guards. But the present system pushes forward many men in the Guards to the rank of major-general who know but little of the handling of a battalion, or of its internal economy and requirements. If it is to be retained and extended, then some plan must be devised by which no man shall pass on to the rank of major-general without "having an adequate acquaintance with the whole regimental system.

"The Guards did their duty as well as other regiments at Quatre Bras and Waterloo, but they have never done anything to entitle them to peculiar privileges, and, unfortunately for one of these truly gallant regiments, it was by mistake rewarded for that which was actually performed at Waterloo by regiments of the Line. I write advisedly, and allude to the defeat of the heavy columns of the French Imperial Guard by the 52nd Light Infantry, supported by the 71st Light Infantry, and "by the 2nd and part of the 3rd battalions of the 95th Rifles.

"*QUAEQUE IPSE MISERRIMA VIDI.*"
****

It would probably be better for the officers of the Guards themselves, and certainly more pleasant to the officers of the rest of the army, and for the benefit of the service generally, if these distinctions were abolished, perhaps not by taking away the rank which the officers of the Guards hold, but by giving exactly the same rank to the officers of all the other corps in the army. There would not be any very tremendous difficulty in finding out appropriate titles if the present titles for the several grades were considered unsuitable; and the army rank of those who became brevet-lieutenant-colonels, might be so adjusted by antedate (and why should this not be done?) as no longer to allow the regimental captains of the Guards to be of higher standing in the army than captains of other regiments, whose regimental commissions might be of an older date.

I suspect, if it should be once conceded that it was injurious to the service that the officers of the Guards should as a rule arrive at the higher ranks of the army at a much earlier age than that at which the officers of the rest of the army should arrive at the same ranks—then some of the various difficulties, which may now appear to loom in the distance, would soon be got over.

One obvious disadvantage of the present system, of the officers of the Guards having invariably a step of army rank in advance of their regimental rank, is this that, both in garrison and camp, and on active service, it may be often happening that considerably younger men will take the command of their seniors and of men of many years' more experience than themselves. The system may probably foster a spirit of pride and conceit in the guardsmen, and a feeling of disgust and annoyance in the minds of the other officers of the army, who suffer from the invidious distinctions heaped upon the Guards. I should suppose it must frequently happen that officers of the latter service, really feel pained, when called upon to command those older and more experienced than themselves.

It may be desirable that there should be a body of men, accustomed to the duties required from the troops usually stationed in London or at Windsor, but their position should be rendered as little invidious in the eyes of the rest of the army as possible. They should be let off taking their turn of duty in the East and West Indies, and in China, and in other distant places; no one would begrudge them those little distinctions:—gallant fellows as they are, and as they have ever shewn themselves, they would always wish to take their turn of *active* service.

Chapter 12

1815: March to Paris

In 1859 I drew up, for the regimental record, a very short account of the march of the 52nd from Waterloo to Paris. I will, in introducing it into this work, endeavour to mention several details, which may possibly add to its interest.

I believe it was between twelve and one o'clock on the 19th, when we left our ground near Maison du Roi, and marched to Nivelles, which, by the road we took, was about nine miles off. We had now fairly started on our triumphant march to the French capital, and all were in the highest state of delight at our glorious victory, in the gaining which the 52nd had been fortunate enough to take such a leading part, and in our glorious prospect of immediately entering France, and eventually Paris itself. We bivouacked about a mile beyond Nivelles, on the left of the *chaussée*, and about a hundred yards from a beautiful little stream, at which we washed our hands and faces, not having been able even to wash our hands since the morning of the 16th.

Hearing that there was an opportunity of sending letters to England, I got some paper from the colour-sergeant of the company, and wrote two short notes, one to my mother and sisters, the other to a kind friend much interested in the 52nd. My letters, which I am sorry to say, have been long ago lost, though short, were to the point, and very astounding no doubt. I well recollect telling them that we had gained a glorious victory, and that the 52nd had "defeated the Imperial Guard of France, led on by the Emperor Napoleon Bonaparte in person," using the same words which I had heard Sir John Colborne use in the morning.

My letter did not reach my mother for several days. She was very ill, and confined to her bed with rheumatic fever. The news, that a great battle had been fought, and that there had been great numbers of killed and wounded on both sides, reached every corner of the land some days before the long list of killed and wounded made its appearance. These were days of great suspense and anxiety to my young sisters, who had kept all mention of the battle from their poor mother. They have often given me the account of their proceedings. At last they got the newspaper containing the fearful list. They tremblingly spread it out on the sideboard, that all three might read it together.

As everyone knows, there was first of all a long list of those who had been killed. They looked down it to the 52nd, and there they read Ensign William ———, and they had time for a moment of agony, before they found that the surname was not mine, but that of my poor brother-ensign. The longer list of the wounded was then examined with almost equal anxiety, and when my name did not appear there, the eldest exclaimed, "Thank God, he's safe;" and they went to my mother, and after telling her quietly that I was safe, they told her of the "bloody battle and glorious victory of Waterloo," and then they all cried together, and felt very thankful for God's great kindness to us.

My brother, who arrived from the Cape a few days after, as a young commander, first heard the news of the victory at Spithead, or on landing at Portsmouth, and first heard that I was in the army, by being told that I had been in the action and was safe. I recollect he wrote me a letter on the occasion, in which he said he always thought that I had "a great desire to smell powder," which I suppose somewhat flattered my vanity.

On the 20th of June we readied the neighbourhood of Binche, and I think it was not far from our halting-place that I went down a coal-pit of considerable depth. I had to put off *all* my own clothes and to dress myself in the very thick flannel shirt and trowsers which the colliers use; and thus clothed, and with one of their old felt caps on my head, into which a short iron spike was run, with a socket at the end for the lighted candle, I followed my guide down the ladder fixed to the side of the pit, to the depth of, I think they told me, 1,100 feet. All the way down there were wooden platforms, at about every forty yards, completely filling up the whole area of the pit, with the exception of the hole which we had to pass through, in our descent from each platform, so that there was some comfort in thinking that if I got giddy I could not fall to the bottom of the pit.

After descending some not very considerable distance, the water began to trickle down the sides of the pit, and my candle was frequently put out before we reached the bottom. My guide, whenever this happened, was very attentive in relighting my candle or starting me with a fresh one. When I got amongst the colliers at the bottom of the pit, they were very curious to know who I was, and made many inquiries about me of my guide, some suggesting that I was a deserter, endeavouring to conceal myself from those in pursuit of me. One advantage of my expedition was that I had to wash from head to foot before I could get into my own clothes again. The officers of the company were rather surprised at my little adventure, for they had not missed me.

On the 21st of June, between Binche and Bavay, we passed the frontier, and entered France from Belgium. We bivouacked in a very pleasant orchard, within half-a-mile of Bavay, and an order was given that no one was to enter the town. However, I was soon despatched with a *havre-sac,* as caterer for the company's officers' mess; they all insisting upon it, when I pleaded the order, that it was not intended to apply to the officers. On getting into Bavay, I tied up my horse and got into a cabaret, the lower rooms of which were filled with English and German soldiers, all intent on getting anything they could meet with in the shape of eatables. I considered myself very fortunate, when I managed to purchase some small loaves, and two or three very small cheeses, about six inches by four, and one-and-a-half thick; and also, a dozen of eggs, which I boiled for a good quarter of an hour.

Having put all into my *havre-sac,* I started off for the bivouac; but whom should I fall in with, as I rode out of the town, but Sir John Colborne, who, however, as he rode by my side, to my great relief did not mention the order, either because it was not intended for the officers, or from a very kind feeling which all persons in authority find it desirable to exercise at times, and which leads them to appear not to notice things, which if noticed at all, would render it necessary that they should speak or act in a way which would be more productive of harm than good. I rode rather fast over part of the way from the auberge to the bivouac, and the consequence was that all my eggs, which I thought were hard-boiled, were smashed, and made a regular mess of the cheese and the bread in the *havre-sac,* to the no small annoyance of my mess friends and myself Knowing nothing about egg-boiling, I had neglected to make the water boil before I put the eggs into it.

On the 22nd we marched from Bavay to Le Cateau Cambresis. I think it was on this march, at one of our halts, that I found one of our men washing a nasty-looking wound on his breastbone, at least half-a-foot square; on my inquiring how he had got it, he told me that it was occasioned by a musket ball striking his breastplate, as we advanced on the Imperial Guard; and that he had determined not to mention it, as he did not wish to be left behind in hospital. But for the breastplate, he would have been a dead man.

We remained at Le Cateau till the morning of the 25th, and the regiment had a very agreeable bivouac in a large, square grass-field, which, as I recollect it, had on two or three sides the ruins of old walls, partly covered with grass. It was close to the town.

Louis XVIII arrived at Le Cateau on the 24th, and was received by the Duke of Wellington.

The duke halted his advanced troops at this place for several purposes. Some of the French fortresses near the frontier were to be taken possession of Cambrai was taken on the 24th, and its citadel on the 25th, and Louis the XVIII entered the town on the 20th. Peronne was taken on the 26th. On all these occasions there was but trifling loss.

The duke wrote as follows, two days afterwards, to Lord Bathurst:—

> The armies under Marshal Blücher and myself have continued their operations since I last wrote to Your Lordship. The necessity which I was under of halting at Le Cateau, to allow the pontoons and certain stores to reach me, and to take Cambrai and Peronne, had placed the marshal one march before me; but I conceive there is no danger in this separation between the two armies.

He wrote to Lord Liverpool on the same day:—

> You will see in my letter to Lord Bathurst the account of the state of things here, which I hope we shall bring to the conclusion we wish for, without firing another shot. I hope to be in Paris on the 1st of July.

On the same day the duke, in writing to the Duke of York, the commander-in-chief, made the following recommendation relative to the Companionship of the Bath, and to the gold medal, and to a medal for Waterloo:—

> I confess that I do not concur in the limitation of the order to field-officers. Many captains in the army conducted themselves in a very meritorious manner, and deserve it; and I never could see the reason for excluding them, either from the order or from the medal. I would also like to suggest to Your Royal Highness the expediency of giving to the non-commissioned

officers and soldiers, engaged in the Battle of Waterloo, a medal. I am convinced it would have the best effect in the army; and, if that battle should settle our concerns, they will well deserve it.

The medal for Waterloo was given to every officer and man in the field, and was distributed to each some little time before the first anniversary of the battle.

The non-commissioned officers and men were allowed two years' time towards any claim for increase of pension; and the Waterloo subalterns were allowed two years for Waterloo towards getting the additional shilling per day which they before received after seven years' service.

The 1st Guards were made "Grenadier Guards," for defeating the grenadiers of the Imperial Guard of France; and the ensigns of all the three regiments of the Guards, were for the future to be ensigns and lieutenants; the ensigns thus having precedence given them over all the ensigns of the British Army.

The following are extracts from a general order, dated Nivelles, 20th June, 1815:—

> The field-marshal takes this opportunity of returning to the army his thanks for their conduct in the glorious action fought on the 18th instant. With a view to preserve order, and to provide for attendance at the hospitals at Bruxelles, the commander of the forces desires that one officer, one non-commissioned officer, and three private men, for 100 men sent to the hospital, wounded in the late actions of the 16th and 18th instant, may be sent from the several regiments to Bruxelles tomorrow, and place themselves under the orders of the *commandant* there.
>
> No regiment need send officers and men for more than 100 men, and in case any regiment has not sent more than fifty men to the hospital, such regiment will send only one non-commissioned officer and two men to take charge of them.

During the two clear days that we remained at Le Cateau, our hope of seeing our baggage come up was greatly diminished. I rode out several times on the Brussels road, and at times thought I had caught sight of it in the distance; but it always turned out to be the baggage of some other corps. The baggage of half the officers of the 52nd was entirely lost, and it was reported that it was plundered on the 18th, on the road to Brussels, by some foreign cavalry, who were running away from the action. Sometime after Waterloo, but I cannot recollect the exact time, I determined on sending in a claim for remuneration for the loss of my baggage; and this I did, notwithstanding that all the officers told me it was perfectly useless for me to prefer such a claim, as remuneration was never allowed unless the baggage had been taken by the enemy.

I thought it was a gross piece of injustice that officers should be fighting the battles of their country and risking their lives in its service, and incur such a serious loss without any fault of their own, and that the country should not bear them harmless from it. My claim was accordingly made out; and Colonel Charles Rowan certified that it was correctly and justly stated, and forwarded it to the proper quarter. It included the value of my baggage-horse and saddle, a bearskin bed, and a canteen, and all the clothes, regimentals, &c., &c., which I had not on my back and in a small valise fastened behind the saddle of my riding-horse. The things were all new since the 1st of May, and my outfit had cost me about £200. However, I could only recollect the articles and their prices, which had to be specified, sufficiently to enable me to make out a claim for £77, 14s. 0d. I believe the claim was referred by the Duke of Wellington to the proper board in England.

After some time, the commanding officer received information that the claim was allowed to a certain extent, and that the sum of, I think it was, £63 was to be paid to me. Then, of course, all the other officers of the regiment who had lost their baggage sent in claims for remuneration; but, notwithstanding my success, all their claims were rejected. I, of course, was rather proud of having displayed more generalship than any of them.

However, the matter did not quite end there, for Colonel Rowan wrote a letter of expostulation on the subject, in which he stated that some of the officers claiming were in the same company with me, and their horses in the same string of horses with mine; that I had received remuneration for my loss, and that it would, of course, be considered a very great hardship if they should not be remunerated also. I was rather joked and twitted about the probability of my having to refund the money which I had received; but, as I thought it well to have some answer to this threatened and very probable disaster, I used to say, "Oh! that's impossible, for I have spent it all."

In due time a reply came to Colonel Rowan's letter, and then I had a regular crow over all my friends. The reply was, that:—

If Ensign Leeke had received remuneration for the baggage which he lost at Waterloo, all the Duke of Wellington could say was, that he knew nothing at all about it.

And thus, it all ended. We heard at the time that one other officer in the army had obtained remuneration for loss of baggage.

We afterwards learnt the true fate of the baggage of some of the officers. Two of the batmen, of which the man having charge of the string of horses belonging to McNair's company was one, reached Brussels, and had the rascality to pass themselves off as wounded English officers, having managed to rig themselves out with the officers' clothes which had been entrusted to them; they managed to obtain billets from the proper authorities. This was not likely to last long, when there were upwards of 170 wounded officers and men of their own regiment in Brussels, besides the officers and men who had been sent there to look after the wounded; so in the course of three or four weeks they were denounced to the officers, and I recollect our man was sent up to the regiment, and tried by a general regimental court-martial, and was sentenced to be transported for seven years.

Amongst the clothes which this man had not got rid of—and he had sold the greater part of the things—there were articles of clothing discovered belonging to all the other officers of McNair's company except myself. After the court-martial I asked him how this happened to be the case, and he told me that in the great confusion which there was amongst the baggage, it was almost impossible for one man to take care of a string of four or five horses, and that much baggage was lost in consequence; that my horse was the last, and that he saw a Belgian peasant cut the rope which fastened him to the horse before him; that he could not leave the leading horse, and that whilst he was loading his firelock to have a shot at the Belgian, some increased confusion took place, and the man succeeded in getting off with my horse and baggage. Very possibly this account was correct. I forget what became of the other delinquent, but he was not tried at the same time with our batman.

I believe it was not unfrequently the case in the Peninsula, that officers on baggage-guard at the time of a general action, ran the risk of getting into a scrape, and left their guard and went up to the front, to their regiments, to see the fun, as it was termed. I think I understood that our subaltern on the baggage-guard did this at Waterloo; and probably, had he not done so, much of the confusion and loss I have described would have been avoided. But I dare say there was not an officer, who sustained the loss of his baggage on that occasion, who would not rather have done so than that this poor fellow should have missed the pleasure of being present with his regiment at Waterloo. And yet the practice cannot be defended, and I do not mean to defend it, but merely to describe the feeling on the subject.

It is related in the 52nd regimental record that the late Duke of Richmond, The Prince of Orange, and Lord Fitzroy Somerset (afterwards Lord Raglan) entered the breach at Ciudad Rodrigo with the 52nd storming party, and that on the following morning, when taking their places at breakfast in Lord Wellington's tent, "they received a gentle reproof for adventuring into a position which, being officers of the staff, they were not called upon to undertake by the customs of the service."

I believe it was at Le Cateau that we had notice that there was a sale of the effects of some of the German officers who had been killed at Waterloo. I went to it, as some of us were very much in want of a change of linen; somehow or other I only succeeded in securing two shirts, the best of which fell to the lot of one of my brother-officers. It was either when we were at Le Cateau or a day or two afterwards, that Sir John Colborne, on finding that my boots were in a most dilapidated state, very kindly made me a present of a new pair of his own.

On the 25th of June the 52nd marched from Le Cateau to the neighbourhood of Joncour; on the 26th they were near Beauvoir and Lanchy; on the 27th close to Roye; on the 28th at Petit Crevecoeur, on the road to St. Just; on the 29th near Clermont; on the 30th near La Chapelle.

On the 30th I think it was that Captain McNair's company (No. 9) was sent, in consequence of an application from Marshal Monçey, Duke of Cornegliano, to occupy for the night and protect his *château*, about a mile from the bivouac of the regiment. The grounds of this *château*, and the *château* itself, were in excellent taste, and we considered ourselves very fortunate in being quartered there for the night. The servants provided us with a very nice dinner, but the greatest luxury was to be able for the first time since the 16th to undress ourselves and sleep in a bed. They told me that the room selected for me was Mademoiselle Monçey's.

I must not neglect to mention, that one of the officers of the company having met with an accident and injured his shin, some time before we arrived at Waterloo, the wound became so troublesome that his trowsers stuck to it, and got into such a state on the outside that, when the battle was over, he sent back his servant to search for another pair for him, and he succeeded in bringing him a pair drawn from the body of a dead Frenchman. It happened that the Frenchman was what is termed "Dutch built," and the officer was taller and thinner than his predecessor in the property; and so, after bearing for twelve days with the inconvenience arising from the unfitness of the trowsers for him, and finding that there was no chance of the baggage turning up, he took advantage of our occupying the *château* to lie in his cloak for some hours, whilst a tailor belonging to the company reduced the trowsers to dimensions suited to the wants and taste of their new proprietor.

Sir John Colborne also took up his quarters at this *château*, but I did not come across him. The next morning, when the company had marched about a hundred yards from the gates, we met a very gentlemanly-looking elderly man on a handsome long-tailed grey horse, whom we supposed to be the duke, but he passed us without taking any notice of us, or we of him. He might have thanked us for taking care of his property, but we could not well take any notice of him, as we were not sure that he was the duke.

Some days before this it was currently reported in the army that Marshal Blücher had declared most positively, that if the Prussians got hold of Bonaparte, he would hang him. And he was equally determined to destroy any monuments in Paris which recorded any of the victories gained by the French over the Prussians in former years. Some days after our arrival at Paris, I saw the Prussian engineers very busy under one of the arches of the bridge of Jena, which received its name to commemorate a victory gained by the French in 1806.

There was also a strong report that Blücher would destroy the splendid column in the Place Vendôme formed out of the brass cannon taken by the French from their enemies during their long course of victories in former years. He intended also to impose a heavy contribution on the city of Paris. The Duke of Wellington had some difficulty in restraining Blücher's angry impetuosity until the course of action as to these and other matters should he decided by all the Allied powers.

The following letter from Lord Castlereagh to Lord Liverpool, written June 20th, will give some idea of the state of affairs at this time:—

The papers of the 23rd just arrived.

Bonaparte has abdicated in favour of his son. The assemblies have accepted the abdication unconditionally. They have nominated a provisional government of five, of which Fouché, Carnot, and Caulaincourt are three, and determined to send commissioners to the Allies to negotiate.

The Minister of War states in the House of Peers, that they have still an army of 60,000 men to cover the north; Ney contradicts this, and says it does not exceed 25,000; and that there is nothing that can prevent the advance of the enemy to Paris. He tells them they have no choice but to negotiate with the Allies. The French Army is admitted to have been entirely dissolved in the battle of the 18th. Vandamme seems to have got with 10,000 men in the rear of the Allies, and to be thus cut off.

Sir C. Stuart writes from Mons, the 23rd, to which place Louis XVIII had removed:—'Wellington at Cateau Cambresis; Blücher at Avesnes. We have parked 172 cannon; the Prussians 62.' I have called a cabinet council. Ever yours,

Castlereagh.

On the 1st of July, when we were not many miles from Marshal Monçey's *château*, the 52nd first saw Paris, and the splendid dome of the hospital of the Invalides in the distance. It was a beautiful day. The regiment moved off the road to the right to a rising ground, called the Jardin de Paris, finding large quantities of fruit-trees covering an immense extent of ground. Here they looked down on St. Denis, rather towards the left, and the hill of Montmartre, between them and the French capital. Montmartre appeared very rugged and to be strongly fortified, and our feelings got on to the war establishment again, as we fancied we might very probably have to storm this not very pleasant-looking fortified hill on the morrow.

It was when we arrived at the Jardin de Paris that we first saw the French troops again after their defeat at Waterloo, they having sent out from St. Denis along the high road a few skirmishers to fire at one of the English videttes. It was not a very pleasant post for him to be on sentry in, as he had some thirty or forty fellows blazing away at him for some considerable time at a distance of about 250 yards. As he walked his horse up and down on his post, he occasionally returned the fire of the skirmishers by giving them a shot from his carbine. Sir John Colborne, who had commanded the brigade since the action, Adam and Reynell being wounded, sent down a party of the 71st, who drove the French skirmishers off.

I remember we very much enjoyed the ripe currants and cherries on the slope to the right below our bivouac. At the bottom of the slope, about half-a-mile off, I found a deserted village, in which there were a great number of gentlemen's houses completely plundered, and every atom of furniture destroyed in the most wanton manner by the Prussians. Mirrors and chests of drawers, &c., &c., were smashed to atoms. This was the first time that we had come across the Prussian line of march. They were determined to retaliate upon the French civilians all the suffering and cruelty they had experienced at the hands of the French soldiers in by-gone years.

On the 2nd of July the 52nd were alone at Argenteuil on the Seine. Here we found the village had been plundered by the Prussians. Three of them who had to turn out of the village, when we arrived there, not being well pleased at being interfered with, did us the favour, when they had proceeded about two or three hundred yards on the road, to send three musket-balls whistling through our bivouac; they rather astonished us, but did no harm; and I think the fellows were not followed and punished.

In the afternoon of the 2nd McNair's company crossed the Seine in boats, and took possession of and loopholed a gentleman's house on the other side, to protect the formation of a pontoon bridge across the Seine; the French troops being about a mile off, but not shewing themselves. The next morning another company of the 52nd joined us, and pushed on an officer and some men to a village in front, from which a few French soldiers hastily retired as they entered it. On the 2nd and 3rd of July the Prussians were twice attacked by the French under Davoust, and the latter were defeated, the Prussians following them nearly to the walls of Paris.

On the same day a convention was signed, Napoleon having abdicated and fled, by which, amongst other arrangements, it was agreed that there should be a suspension of arms, that the French Army opposed to us should evacuate Paris in three days, and retire behind the Loire, and that, within the same space of time, all the barriers of Paris and also Montmartre should be given up. The English and Prussian commissioners. Colonel Hervey and Baron Muffling, were fired at in the streets of Paris, shortly after entering it by the barrier of Villette; which might have led to very disastrous consequences, but an ample apology was made by the Prince of Eckmühl and the French commissioners charged with the execution of the convention, and the affair was passed over.

On the afternoon of the 3rd of July, the 52nd crossed the Seine on the pontoon bridge, and proceeded to the bridge of Neuilly. We observed places along the side of the road where the Prussians and French were buried who had been killed there, I think, the day before. Sir John Colborne had received orders to cross the bridge of Neuilly; but the French refused to retire from the strong barricade, which had been built across the centre of it. The two front companies of the 52nd (10 and 9) were advanced a very short distance in front of the column of companies, on the road by the side of the river, with fixed bayonets. Sir John Colborne coolly took out his watch and allowed five minutes to the French commander in which to give up the bridge or to have it stormed; in two or three minutes it was given up, some few men coming over and shouting "*Vive le Roi!*"

The village of Neuilly, within a short distance of one of the barriers of Paris, was occupied, and the 52nd passed the night in the walled graveyard of that place. The only things I recollect as occurring on that night were the getting some bread and cheese in a cabaret; and, with the assistance of one of the officers, getting late at night a truss of hay for our horses out of the hayloft belonging to a gentleman's house, which was either deserted, or the inhabitants declined to "shew up."

On the morning of the 4th of July, we saw the last of the French troops, two videttes close to the gate of the graveyard, having two English videttes within twenty paces of them, and a French infantry picket about half-a-mile off on the road to Paris. They soon retired, and the French Army began to evacuate Paris that day, and, I think, it was on the same day, that the National Guard of Paris relieved the guard of the troops of the Line at the Barrière de l'Etoile. The 52nd proceeded to the Bois de Boulogne, to the right of the road from Neuilly to Paris, and remained there till the 7th. On the 5th Montmartre was given up to the English, and on the 6th, I believe, some of our brigade took possession of the Barrière de l'Etoile.

On the morning of the 7th of July General Adam's brigade (52nd, 71st, and 95th) had the honour of entering Paris by the Barrière de l'Etoile. They marched down the centre of the road leading through the Champs Elysées, to the Place Louis Quinze, (now the Place de la Concorde) and the Tuileries. A brigade of artillery, with lighted matches, was posted close to the barrier on either side of the *chaussée*. It was a proud and happy moment, when, with bands and bugles playing, we thus took possession of, and entered, the capital of France. At least I am sure it was the proudest moment of my life, when I found myself riding down the centre of the avenue of the Champs Elysées, bearing in triumph, into the enemy's capital, that same 52nd regimental colour which I had the honour of carrying to victory on the eventful and glorious day of Waterloo.

The whole brigade halted and piled arms in the Champs Elysees, to the right of the main road and between it and the Seine, and not far from the Place Louis Quinze. These were the British troops which occupied the French capital; almost the whole of the rest of the Allied Army remained in the Bois de Boulogne, although some were at Montmartre. Before the 52nd band was dismissed, Sir John Colborne ordered it to play "*Vive Henri Quatre*," one of the principal royalist tunes, but it did not appear to attract any number of people. Indeed, there were not many more persons stirring at that hour—it was between eight and nine—than one would see at the same hour in Hyde Park, between Apsley House and the Marble Arch.

Mr, Hollond, an English gentleman, who had a house in Paris, had ridden out to see the arrival of his compatriots, and having entered into conversation with me, invited me to go and breakfast with him in the Rue de Mont Blanc. I willingly accepted his invitation, and having deposited my colour, I rode with him into Paris and along the beautiful boulevards to his residence. With the exception of Colonel Hervey, the commissioner, I suspect I was the first individual of the British Army who entered the streets of Paris.

******

Note:—I at one time used rather to boast of three things, that *very probably* I had the honour of being the youngest officer at Waterloo, of being the nearest British officer to the Emperor Napoleon in that battle, (I mean when the 52nd colour was in front of the 52nd line with the covering sergeants, at the moment that the duke and Lord Uxbridge were in our rear, and Bonaparte was, as it was afterwards reported, with the Old Guard in our front,) and thirdly, as I have mentioned, that I was the first officer who entered Paris. I lately heard of a Waterloo officer, who was my junior by about six weeks.

******

Mr. Hollond was exceedingly kind, and I remember that, amongst other things, when on inquiry he found I had only a few *ducats* in my pocket, he insisted on becoming my banker and on lending me ten *napoleons* till I should get a bill on England cashed. McNair begged of me, directly I got back to the Champs Elysées, not to lose a day in getting a bill cashed by the paymaster and in repaying the money. This I did the very next day. I was not aware, till he told me, that I had done anything wrong, or *infra dig*, in thus allowing a stranger to become my banker for a few days. Just as we had finished breakfast, a Prussian general and his *aide-de-camp* arrived with a billet on Mr. Hollond's house, which must have been a considerable nuisance to him, but not so great a one as it would have been, had he not been a bachelor. The Prussian officers were remarkably quiet and gentlemanly in their demeanour.

On my way back, as I walked my horse along the boulevards, some boys did me the favour of throwing stones at me, but as I thought that, on that occasion at least, "the better part of valour" was discretion," I contented, myself with quietly cantering away from them.

The 52nd, in the course of the morning, crossed the main road and encamped on the other side of the Champs Elysées, leaving the 71st and 95th on the side nearest to the river, and throwing its sentries forward about 140 yards to the low rail separating the Champs Elysées from the Place Louis Quinze, where the unfortunate Louis XVI and Marie Antoinette were executed in 1783. For a day or two the whole regiment was together, encamped in a large open square place bordered on the four sides by rows of trees.

The Champs Elysées consisted of a series of these large square openings; there was the main road from the Arc de Triomphe and the Barrière de l'Etoile in the direction of the Tuileries, down which we had marched, and about half-way up it was crossed at right angles by another main road, leading from the Rue du Faubourg St. Honoré, and the palace called the Elysée Bourbon, to the Seine. On the other side of the river were the Champs de Mars, the Ecole Militaire, and the hospital of the Invalides facing the Champs Elysees. The bridge of Jena, which was near the barrier, and which Blücher wished to destroy, led from the Champ de Mars towards the Champs Elysées.

Close to the large open space in which the 52nd encamped there was a decent *restaurateur's*. There were several of these places, and also dancing houses, in different parts of the Champs Elysees.

CHAPTER 13

1815: Paris, the 52nd Encamped in the Champs Elysées

Either the day after we entered Paris, or on the following day, No. 9 and No. 10 companies of the 52nd were ordered to encamp nearer to the Place Louis Quinze, and near to where the quarter-guard already was, close to the wall of the Duke of Wellington's garden. The cords of the officers' tents were close to the short palings, which fenced off about ten feet of garden-ground between them and the wall. My tent was against the little gate in the palings which led to the garden-door, and close up to it, so close that one day, about a week or fortnight after we arrived, I heard somebody floundering about and stumbling over the cords, and, on looking out, found it was the duke himself, who sometimes, but not often, came out that way. He desired that the tent might be moved a few feet forward.

The whole brigade remained encamped in the manner I have mentioned till the 2nd of November, a period of nearly four months. Lieut.-Colonel W. Rowan of the 52nd was made *commandant* of the first *arrondissement* of Paris. We, who belonged to No. 9 and No. 10, considered ourselves as an especial guard to the duke. There was a sergeant's guard at the entrance to the courtyard of his residence, in a short street leading out of the Place Louis Quinze. I think it was on the afternoon of the 8th, that two of the King's *Garde du Corps* took refuge with this guard, having been pursued by a street mob.

Bonaparte, after lingering at the Elysée and then for several days at Malmaison, in the vain hope that something might occur, which would afford him a chance of retrieving his broken fortunes, was persuaded, if not forced, by the provisional government, to take the road to Rochefort, where they had placed two French frigates at his disposal, with the view of his escaping to America. He embarked in the Saale on the 8th of July, but in vain did some of his devoted friends endeavour to obtain a promise from Captain Maitland of the *Bellerophon*, the blockading English ship, that he would allow the French frigates to pass with Napoleon on board. In a few days he found it necessary to take refuge in the *Bellerophon*, and before he readied the quarter-deck of that ship, the French frigates had both hoisted the white flag.

The *Bellerophon*, on her way to Torbay, which she reached on the 15th, astonished the captain and crew of an English frigate on their way to Spithead from the Adriatic, who were quite unacquainted with recent events in France, by signalling "Napoleon on board." The Bellerophon was ordered to Plymouth, where Bonaparte was transferred to the *Northumberland*. He was not permitted to land either at Torbay or Plymouth. It was decided, after some little time, that he should be sent as a prisoner of war to St. Helena, for which island the *Northumberland* sailed on the 8th of August.

The king, Louis XVIII, reached Paris on the 8th of July, the day after we entered the city. I was present in the Tuileries on the afternoon of the day of his arrival, and I think no one could have desired to have a greater display of enthusiasm and loyalty than was manifested on the occasion of his presenting himself to the people on one of the balconies of the Tuileries looking towards the Champs Elysées. There must have been from fifteen to twenty thousand persons assembled. When the king came forward there was a cry for the people to take their hats off, which almost all appeared to do, and, being tall, I had a good view over the whole assembled people. I was in the midst of the crowd, and whilst they knocked off the hats of one or two obstinate fellows near me, they treated me with marked civility, one patting me on the back, as the Prussian officer did on the night of the Battle of Waterloo, and calling me "Brave *Anglais*." As an officer in uniform I of course kept my cap on. I saw two other English officers at a distance in the crowd.

I must now record something more about the proceedings of the Imperial Guard. It must be remembered that it consisted in 1815, of 25,870 men. There were 20,400 infantry, 3,300 cavalry, and 2,170 artillery, sappers, waggon train, &c. Of these 25,870 men, after deducting for casualties on the 16th and 17th, probably nearly the half were engaged with the Prussians at Planchenoit. After the defeat of the whole of the Imperial Guard at Waterloo, "Generals Morand and Colbert succeeded in rallying some remnants of companies of them at Beaumont," about five-and-twenty miles from Waterloo, and from thence they proceeded towards Paris, and made a considerable stand against the Prussians at the village of Vertus, near St. Denis, and afterwards made good their retreat from that place when forced out of it by very superior numbers.

The French historian of the Imperial Guard states that this affair of the 30th of June was the last in which they were engaged. During the 4th, 5th, and 6th of July, the whole French Army marched from the neighbourhood of Paris on the road to Orleans, and retired behind the Loire. Great numbers retired to their homes. On the breaking up of the army, many of the officers of the Imperial Guard emigrated, some to Turkey, others to Greece, others again to America. Several of the chief officers. Marshal Grouchy, and the Generals Clausel, Vandamme, Lefèvre-Desnouettes, Rigaud, and a great many officers of rank, were at New York and Philadelphia in 1817, and a large portion of them, under the direction of General Lallemand, attempted to found a colony in Texas, but it did not prosper, and after losing three-fourths of their numbers, the remainder of these poor fellows returned to New Orleans and settled there.

The encampment of Adam's brigade in the Champs Elysées was about the same thing, as regarded Paris and its inhabitants, as would be the encampment of 2,500 men in Hyde Park, between the entrance gate near Apsley house and the statue of Achilles, to London and its inhabitants; or the same number in the Green Park, near Piccadilly; or in St. James's park, between the Horse Guards and Dartmouth street; it was also the same sort of thing to us. We were not troubled with any orders about not appearing in the streets except in uniform. We generally wore the blue surtout coat, when in undress, and had but to exchange a foraging-cap for a round hat, and spring over the low rails in front of our quarter-guard near the Café Ledoyen, and we found ourselves in Paris, *en bourgeois*, in less than two minutes after we had made up our minds to go there.

We were within four or five minutes' walk of the principal entrance to the Tuileries, which was just across the Place Louis Quinze. The men could only pass the cordon of sentries under certain regulations. There was no regular officers' mess whilst we were in Paris, but the officers of each company messed together in one of their tents, and I remember that I continued to be the caterer, and a very inexpensive mess it was, for we none of us cared much about eating and drinking.

A considerable number of the Parisians visited our camp from the first, and some of them I know were ladies belonging to superior Bonapartist families; such confidence had they in the discipline and good behaviour of the British soldiers. Crowds of persons came to see us play at cricket, which we sometimes did in the 52nd. It was a game to which the French were unaccustomed, and one speech which was overheard was that, "no wonder the English were not afraid of cannon-balls, when they could so fearlessly meet and stop those dreadful cricket balls coming towards them with such terrific force." It was a current report at Paris, that the emperor had said, that "at Waterloo the English squares had stood like walls, and the French cannon-balls could make no impression on them."

Out on the same open place on which we played at cricket, beyond the 52nd encampment, our regular drill was carried on, and as I had done very little in the way of drill before the campaign commenced, I had much to learn after we reached Paris. I perhaps was the only British officer who had the honour of finishing his drill in the French capital. We had many spectators who, of course, were much interested in the light infantry movements, and the bugle sounds. We had some forty men who had to go through the same amount of drill that I had. The 52nd drill instructors were always required to be most particular in the marching drill, from the goose-step upwards; and it was to this great attention paid to the balancing of the body in marching, and the avoiding of all flourishing of the foot as it came to the ground, that we used to attribute the good marching of the 52nd, and especially their beautiful advances in line, for which they were very remarkable in my 52nd days, and for years afterwards; I hope they are so still.

About ten days after our arrival in Paris, Sir John Colborne (Lord Seaton) very kindly invited me to dine with him at his lodgings, or billet, somewhere to the left, in a line with the principal entrance of the Tuileries from the Place Louis Quinze, and in the street leading down past the end of the Rue de la Paix. I met there only three or four of the senior officers of the regiment, and I well recollect his telling me, before them, that I might consider myself one of the most fortunate fellows in the whole army; for I had only been in it two months, and had, in that short space of time, not only taken part in the glorious action at Waterloo, but had also been present at the taking of the capital of France.

I kept no journal at that time, and not till about four years afterwards, and then only occasionally during the next four or five years, so that in describing the circumstances that occurred at Paris and elsewhere, I have to trust to my memory, which I have good reason to think is particularly retentive and accurate.

The French commanders, as is well known, had during a long course of years, wherever their arms were successful, brought away from the museums of the several countries, and from other places where they were to be found, great numbers of the choicest paintings and statues. Vast numbers of these paintings, etc., were found in the Louvre when the Allies took possession of Paris. The French ministers, and also the king, were very unwilling to restore these improperly acquired treasures of art to their rightful owners, more especially perhaps as they knew such restitution would be very unpalatable to the French people. The following extracts from a letter from the Duke of Wellington to Lord Castlereagh will show how the affair ended:—

Paris, 23rd September, 1815.

Shortly after the arrival of the sovereigns at Paris, the minister of the King of the Netherlands claimed the pictures, etc., belonging to his sovereign equally with those of other powers; and, as far as I could learn, never could get any satisfactory reply from the French government. After several conversations with me he addressed Your Lordship in an official note, which was laid before the ministers of the Allied sovereigns assembled in conference, and the subject was taken into consideration repeatedly, with a view to discover a mode of doing justice to the claimants of the specimens of the arts in the museums, without hurting the feelings of the King of France.

In the meantime the Prussians had obtained from His Majesty not only all the really Prussian pictures, but those belonging to the Prussian territories on the left of the Rhine, and the pictures, etc., belonging to all the allies of His Prussian Majesty; and the subject pressed for an early decision; and Your Lordship wrote your note of the 11th instant, in which it was fully discussed.

The minister of the King of the Netherlands, still having no satisfactory answer from the French government, applied to me, as the Commander-in-Chief of the Army of the King of the Netherlands, to know if I had any objection to employ His Majesty's troops to obtain possession of what was his undoubted property. I referred this application again to the ministers of the Allied courts, and no objection having been stated, I considered it my duty to take the necessary measures to obtain what was his right.

I spoke to Prince de Talleyrand on the subject . . . . and begged him to state the case to the king, (of France,) and to ask His Majesty to do me the favour to point out the mode of effecting the object of the King of the Netherlands, which should be least offensive to His Majesty.

The Prince de Talleyrand promised me an answer on the following evening; which not having received, I called upon him at night, and had another discussion with him on the subject, in which he informed me that the king could give no orders upon it; that I might act as I thought proper, and that I might communicate with M. Denon.

I sent my *aide-de-camp*, Lieut.-Colonel Fremantle, to M. Denon in the morning, who informed him that he had no orders to give any pictures out of the gallery, and that he could give none without the use of force.

I then sent Colonel Fremantle to the Prince de Talleyrand to inform him of this answer, and to acquaint him that the troops would go the next morning at twelve o'clock to take possession of the King of the Netherland's pictures; and to point out, that if any disturbance resulted from this measure, the king's ministers, and not I, were responsible. Colonel Fremantle also informed M. Denon that the same measure would be adopted.

It was not necessary however to send the troops, as a Prussian guard had always remained in possession of the gallery, and the pictures were taken without the necessity of calling for those under my command, excepting as a working party to assist in taking them down and packing them. . . . . . .

The Allies, having the contents of the museum justly in their possession, could not do otherwise than restore them to 'the countries from which, contrary to the practice of civilized warfare, they had been torn during the disastrous period of the French Revolution and the tyranny of Bonaparte.

It has never appeared to me to be necessary that the Allied sovereigns should omit this opportunity to do justice and to gratify their own subjects, in order to gratify the people of France.

It is on many accounts desirable, as well for their own happiness as that of the world, that the people of France, if they do not already feel that Europe is too strong for them, should be made sensible of it.

The duke argues, in conclusion, that it would not only be unjust in the sovereigns to give way in this matter, but also "impolitic, as it would deprive them of the opportunity of giving the people of France a great moral lesson."

I was at the Louvre once or twice when this taking down and packing the pictures was going on; whether or not I was there on duty I do not recollect, but I remember seeing a fatigue-party of the 52nd there. There was no particular excitement observable amongst the French on that occasion.

But about that time the 52nd remained fully accoutred and ready to fall in at a moment's notice, for eight-and-forty hours, and on one of those two days, we were marched up, and remained for two or three hours on the Place Louis Quinze, in front of the gates of the Tuileries; I think it was when the Austrians were taking down the horses dedicated to the sun from the top of the gateway leading into the Place du Carrousel. They had been taken from Venice. It was expected that much discontent would be manifested by the French, and perhaps some violence on that occasion. Each horse was taken away separately, and was escorted by a whole regiment of Austrian dragoons. I was the orderly-officer on the day that the last horse was removed and was sent that evening by Sir John Colborne to report to General Adam, who had recovered from his wound and taken command of the brigade again, that all had passed off quietly.

We had one or two reviews on rather a large scale on an extensive plain near Paris, in which we passed over immense quantities of beet-root, which is grown there in order to produce sugar from it. I fear a large amount of damage was done to the crops, as we could scarcely take a step without each person treading on, and breaking in two, one of the roots; but the reviews were especially memorable for the clouds of black dust in which the troops were enveloped during nearly the whole time they were marching and manoeuvring.

We must have been terrible warriors to look at, as on our return to camp we marched through the streets of Paris covered from head to foot with this dust, and with our clothes and accoutrements, our faces, eyes, and ears, and our hair and whiskers, (at least of those who had any of the latter,) completely blackened by it. A considerable amount of time was consumed in getting all right again, to say nothing of the possible injury done to the clothing and appointments of both officers and men.

Sir John Colborne took the 52nd several times to the Champ de Mars, which was a very extensive and good exercising-ground. There we first practised the half-face movement in column, which I think was taken up from the Prussians, and was afterwards found to be a most useful movement. One day we came across the Emperor of Russia and his staff, in the Champ de Mars, and Sir John very neatly threw the regiment into close column just as the emperor was arriving in front of the flank company, and saluted him with carried arms. As the emperor was merely riding across the Champ de Mars, and as we were only there for drill, the salute with carried arms in close column was the only available method, under the circumstances, of shewing him any attention. It was the Emperor Alexander who received and acknowledged this salute.

I think it was not many weeks after our arrival in Paris that there was a review of several thousands of the Russian Guards in the Champs Elysées, on the road leading from the Barrière de l'Etoile to the Tuileries. They were a very fine body of picked men. The Russian soldiers of the Line appeared to me to be shorter and smaller men than the ordinary soldiers of any of the other armies who were in the neighbourhood of Paris at that time. On returning from this review I met with a rather severe fall, when galloping round one of the sunk plantations enclosed by balustrades in the Place Louis Quinze. My horse's legs flew from under him and he came down heavily on his side on my left leg, by which my knee and shoulder were cut. It was rather a nuisance, too, to be thus sent sprawling in uniform on the paved square in the presence of a good number of spectators; and I was very glad to slink off into our camp, which was close at hand.

Two or three hundred yards from the 52nd encampment towards the barrier there was stationed a troop of Cossacks of the Don, whom we occasionally used to visit. They were fine men and very orderly. Their horses were tied to the trees in the Champs Elysées, four or five round the same tree. Whenever there was any disturbance amongst them in the shape of biting or kicking, the Cossacks reduced them to order by thrashing them severely with the flat part of their naked swords. It was no uncommon thing among the Cossacks, though we saw nothing of the kind at Paris, for the officers to order their men to receive the same description of punishment for not very grave offences. One of the members of an English family which was thrown very much among the Cossacks, when the Russians marched on Paris in 1814, told me that on complaints being made to the officers of any infringement of the rules laid down, they would tell them in French that the delinquent should forthwith receive "*vingt-cinq coups de plat de sabre.*"

When I was in Paris in 1817, I observed that great numbers of the trees which the Cossack horses had barked in 1815, had been thereby destroyed and that fresh trees had been planted in their place.

There was a very good swimming-bath on the Seine, not far from our camp, called in French the "*Ecole de Natation.*" I learnt to swim there, and used it very frequently during the whole time of our occupation of Paris. I think it was on the first occasion of my visiting it, that I was in some danger of being drowned, by foolishly jumping into deep water, about six feet from the nettings, to try and solve the question, "Why, as every other animal will swim, if thrown into water, should not man do the same?" My attempts to swim were abortive, and I had gone under water twice, when six or eight of the bathers jumped in, and one of them saved me from going down again by pushing me against the netting at the side. Before we left Paris, I could swim and float very fairly.

There was always plenty of excitement for us, encamped as we were so far within the barrier of Paris, and so close to the Tuileries and other public places; the Champs Elysées were a favourite resort of the Parisians, and, although scarcely any of us had any opportunity of entering into French society, yet the meeting with numbers of the better classes in the public walks, and in the various places of public amusement, and the numbers of things we had to see, always prevented the time from hanging heavily on our hands. Besides which, some of us had friends from England staying there, who helped to make our occupation of Paris very pleasant to us.

I recollect only a few of the tricks which we used to play each other; a very approved one, now and then practised, was the quietly loosening the cords and loops of a tent from their stakes on a very wet night, and then letting the wet tent down on the helpless and infuriated occupier; the perpetrator generally managing not to be discovered. I did hear of one man, who undertook to take a portmanteau from under the walls, or lower canvass of a tent, but the occupant heard him and attacked him with his sword, very reasonably taking him for a thief, when the attacking party after seizing the sword, and getting his hands cut, found it necessary to beat a retreat.

The only practical joke I remember to have played at Paris, occurred as follows; and as far as the joke went it was a very innocent one:—Two of us came into camp from Paris one very dark night, and, after replying to the sentry's challenge, we passed the tent of the officer of the quarter-guard, whom we saw fully accoutred lying on his back on his guard-bed, very fast asleep with his mouth open: there were eight or ten rather large books on the table, and going into the tent I piled them up on a chair, one above another, till the top one touched the tent just over our friend's head.

I then went round to the back of the tent, where, by the light of the candle inside, I could easily see the upper book, and giving it a push I sent the pile on to our victim's face, having done which I quietly and quickly got round to the darkness, pervading the trees of the Champs Elysées, at a very short distance, opposite to the tent door; from this we saw the officer coming out of his tent, hardly aware of what had exactly happened, and we heard the following short dialogue between him and the sentry. *Officer calls out:*—"Sentry!" *The Sentry replies:*—"Yes, Sir!" *Officer:*—"Has anyone just come into camp?" *Sentry:*—"No, Sir!"

We then made off, leaving the officer of the guard to renew his slumbers. This was the officer who, when the 52nd were pursuing the French at Vera, about two years before, went over a short mountain path with Sir John Colborne and four soldiers, and rushed down on to the road, into the middle of the 9th French light infantry, and summoned them to surrender, which those who were thus cut off did, to the number of two or three hundred. This officer, Lieutenant Cargill, received on the spot, and tucked under his arm, the swords of fourteen of the French officers. I have frequently heard it mentioned as a fact, that one of these officers having hesitated to deliver up his sword, Cargill struck him a blow in his face with his fist which made his mouth bleed, and had the effect of making him tractable. In these days such acts of daring would be deservedly rewarded by the grant of the Victoria Cross.

The anecdote just related brings to my remembrance an occurrence which took place at Paris a few weeks after we had left it. Some detachments sent out from England, just at the time that the army was about to proceed to take up its cantonments in the north of France, arrived in the neighbourhood of Paris, and several of the officers, amongst whom were two of the 52nd, availed themselves of the opportunity of seeing something of the French capital. One of the places they visited was the Palais Royal. As they were walking along the covered pavement, near the shops, they met several persons, who had all the appearance of being half-pay French officers; one of these, as they passed them, kicked against the foot of one of the 52nd officers with the evident design of insulting him; the 52nd officer immediately started round and inquired what he meant, but he not knowing much of French, the other 52nd man began to interpose, when the Frenchman gave him a smart box on the ear, asking him at the same time, what he had to do with it?

This of course was responded to in the shape of a heavy blow planted on the Frenchman's mouth, which made his teeth both rattle and bleed: before the row had proceeded to any greater length, the guard appeared, and marched off both parties to the prefecture, where the whole case was gone into. The Frenchmen were adjudged to be the aggressors, and the English officers were freed from all blame in the transaction. Insults offered to the English were seldom heard of during the three years of our occupation of France.

I went with three or four artillery officers, whom I knew, to the fair of St. Cloud, and we rather enjoyed it, and got on very well, till we were just coming away, when we got into a considerable unpleasantness through the stupidity, and possibly also the rascality, of the driver of the carriage which we had hired for the occasion. When we were about to return, he insisted upon it that he should be paid before we started: possibly somebody had done him out of what he considered his fare on some former occasion. However, that may have been, he positively refused to drive us back to Paris, unless we first settled with him; this we considered very impertinent on his part, and determined not to give way to it.

A crowd of eighty or a hundred persons were gathered round us, and on our attempting to take possession of the carriage, an altercation ensued with some of them, and then, without its actually coming to a fight, they began to interrupt our proceeding. A friend of mine, a very nice fellow, by the name of Heisse, belonging to one of the Hanoverian Jäger Corps, to whom I had been speaking during the day, happening to pass, saw our difficulty, and ran down to the bridge of St. Cloud, where a German picket was stationed, and brought up a few men to our assistance just at the right moment. They very unceremoniously made the mob stand back by striking at their legs with the butt ends of their muskets. The Prussians were to leave the neighbourhood of Paris the next morning, and our driver, who appeared to have a very wholesome fear of them, was considerably alarmed by hearing some of our party say, that it would serve him right, and do him good, if we could manage to get him pressed into their service, on the occasion of their march northwards.

Paris, of course, had many temptations for the officers of the British Army. One was that arising from the gaming-houses, of which there were many, especially in the Palais Royal. I never heard, whilst we were there, of anybody having suffered very severely from them; but yet I have no doubt that many were inconveniently fleeced, to say the least of it, by occasionally visiting them. I do not think it will be injurious to my readers, if I briefly mention what I saw of them. I had been to one of the theatres with a captain of the 52nd, and when it was over, I found he was not going back to camp, but going to look into one of these gaming-houses at the Palais Royal.

I had never seen a gaming-house, and begged that I might accompany him; but he said, Colborne would never forgive him, if he took me to such a place; however, on my pressing him, and shewing him that I had not above two *napoleons* in my pocket, so that I could not lose much, he gave way, and I went with him. The way to the first and second floors of these houses was up a very wide and substantial staircase, lighted with one gloomy lamp on each landing, the whole appearance of which led one's mind to associate with these places scenes of violence and assassination. There were about forty or fifty persons standing, and several of them playing at a roulette table in one room, and about as many more at a *rouge-et-noir* table in another. If I recollect rightly, I won a few *napoleons* that night by playing with two-*franc* pieces, which I think was the lowest sum which by the rules of the place was allowed to be hazarded.

On a subsequent evening I took with me about seven *napoleons*, thinking that if I had been able to win a tolerable sum by playing with two-*franc* pieces, I might perhaps gain ten times as much by playing with *napoleons*. On this second night I seemed to have what is termed, a great run of luck, and at last I found my two waistcoat pockets to be so full of *napoleons* that it was not safe to put any more into them, and I began to stow away my winnings in my trowsers pockets. I could make no proper calculation of the amount of my "ill gotten wealth," but I observed at last that I had attracted the attention of most of the persons present, and especially that of the croupiers who received and handed out the money.

I now began to think of making good my retreat, but how to do it decently I did not know. However, having made up my mind to leave the place, I very quietly, though unexpectedly to them, walked to the door, and went tolerably quickly down the stairs, but, quick as I was in my movements, a man who followed me was on the landing-place at the bottom of the first flight of stairs before I had quitted it. He begged me to give him some money, as he was a person in distress; this I declined to do, not only because I thought it was not quite safe to be parleying with him under all the circumstances, but also because I felt annoyed that a person should pursue the degraded course of watching the gaming-tables for the purpose of demanding charity from the successful players.

As I crossed the Palais Royal, I roughly calculated that I had two or three hundred *napoleons* in my pocket, and thought that these would soon be gone and would do me no permanent good, whereas, if I could make the sum up to a thousand, I could, in some way, make it do me some more lasting benefit. With this idea in my head I went into another house on the opposite side of the Palais Royal, and played away as largely as I had done before; my pockets were very nearly emptied again. I determined, however, not to return to camp without taking back with me a small roll of *napoleons* which I felt were still remaining in my pocket, and which I judged to amount to about the sum I had started with. I was surprised, on reaching my tent, and counting over my remaining *napoleons*, that I had thirty-nine, instead of seven, remaining. This led me to think that I had been greatly mistaken as to the sum which I had at first gained, and that it must have amounted to three or four times as much as I had roughly calculated it to be.

This was a great ordeal for a boy under eighteen years of age to go through; but it was a very great mercy that I lost the money which I had gained. As it was, my taste for play continued, to an extent, for some years, (until I saw that it was decidedly wrong and sinful, and evidently a breach of the tenth commandment, to desire to win another person's money,) and if I had carried away with me the large sum above mentioned, it would probably have been more injurious to me than one can well imagine. I went three or four times after that to these *maisons de jeu*, but I was careful not to lose my money to any great extent; yet I did lose it, I am now thankful to say.

I have hesitated to write down the foregoing account, lest it should possibly do harm, in the way of exciting in any one an "itch for gambling." I may possibly not publish it; if I do so, I wish it to be accompanied by my protest against a practice which I believe is not so prevalent now in the houses of our gentry as it was fifty or sixty years ago; I mean the allowing children to play at cards or other games of chance, by which they may win money. I trace much evil that arises in the way of ruinous betting at races, or in playing at cards or billiards, for large sums of money, to this practice. I recollect it was the custom to set a dozen or more of children to play at commerce, when each put down a shilling, and the winner of the game took the whole of the money.

It was this sort of thing, which led to an immense deal of gambling in a small way at schools, where the boys played at marbles and with tops, and at other things, for money; this easily paved the way for attendance and betting at public billiard-tables and races. I never but once made a bet at a race, but I knew a youth most respectably connected, who was utterly ruined both in character and fortune, who told me that his evil courses commenced when a near relative took him to a racecourse, and encouraged him to bet there.

Many years ago, when I little thought of publishing a book, I used to say, half in joke, "If ever I publish a book, it shall be against allowing boys at school, or in the streets, to play at marbles for money," so convinced was I of the importance of endeavouring to check any disposition to gamble at an early age, or, what is still better, as far as possible not to let children or young people be at places, or amongst persons, where anything of the sort is practised. I have always enjoined on my children never to play at any game for money, and never on any account to make even the smallest bet, and I have never had a card in my house. I consider myself to be fully justified in stating, that all desire to win anything belonging to another, at a game of chance or skill, is contrary to that which God enjoins upon His people in the tenth commandment.

I must apologise to my readers for this digression from the account of the various occurrences which took place whilst we were at Paris; but I do sincerely hope that all parents, and heads of schools, and others who may read it, will use their best efforts to nip in the bud that taste for gambling, which is yet so prevalent amongst both rich and poor, and which I believe, in nine cases out of ten, commences in early youth. It is obvious that everything in the shape of a lottery or raffle is of evil tendency.

I must not attempt to speak of the execution of Marshal Ney and Colonel Labédoyère, which all of us were much grieved at; nor of the remarkable escape of Lavalette from prison, by putting on some of his wife's clothes, she remaining behind whilst he passed out of the prison, nor of his escape from Paris, disguised as an English general, by the help of Sir Robert Wilson and two other Englishmen. These things took place whilst we were at Paris, and the accounts of them may easily be obtained.

A very sad and exciting business occurred, whilst we were at Paris, in connexion with the mutinous behaviour of one of our own men, when coming to join the army with detachments under the command of a captain and other officers belonging to other regiments; I think I recollect the circumstances very clearly, they were these:— Several of the men of these detachments had got drunk, and this man, when ordered by Captain ——— to be silent, or to perform some duty, refused to obey, as he was not a 52nd officer, and swore at him, calling him a d——d; the officer drew his sword, and cut the drunken mutineer very severely across the shoulder. For this the officer was afterwards brought to a court-martial and honourably acquitted.

The Duke of Wellington, on reading the proceedings of the court-martial, ordered the 52nd soldier to be brought to a general court-martial for mutinous conduct towards his superior officer; he was accordingly tried, found guilty, and condemned to be shot. The duke, who always felt the vast importance of upholding the discipline of the army, determined that the sentence should be executed. I saw at a little distance, not far from my tent, an interview between the duke and Sir John Colborne, which I had reason to believe was connected with this man's execution. The duke had come into our camp from his garden door, and as Colborne almost immediately joined him, I fancy the interview had been arranged before.

The duke, who generally appeared to be a person of very quiet demeanour, seemed on this occasion to speak with some considerable earnestness, and Colborne, who was most anxious, as we all were, that the man's life should be spared, was equally energetic. The conversation did not last more than seven or eight minutes, and I did not learn the result, until the order for the execution appeared in orders. I think the next morning, the regiments of the brigade marched to some ground near the walls of Paris, to see the sentence carried into effect.

The regiments were drawn up so that each occupied one side of a large square, the man to be executed being placed in the middle of the fourth side of the square with his coffin behind him, and the firing party, consisting I think, of a sergeant and twelve rank and file, a few paces in his front. The brigade-major, or some other staff-officer, then rode forward and read the charge against the soldier, the finding of the court-martial, and the sentence. When this was done, an *aide-de-camp*, the bearer of a reprieve, rode into the square; I think it was an order from the duke, granting the man a pardon, and stating, amongst other reasons for doing so, that it was partly in consideration of the high character of the regiment to which he belonged, that the duke was induced to take this course.

I have an idea that some of us were aware the night before that the man would be pardoned, but the man himself, and the men of the regiment and of the brigade generally, expected the execution to take place. I met him close to the camp, in the course of the afternoon, walking with one of the men, and I recollect that the poor fellow sobbed as he passed and saluted me. I cannot quite bear in mind whether I spoke to him or not; but I am sure I must have shewn him, in some way, how much I felt for him.

Two or three other recollections which I have of Paris at the time of our encampment there, are of a much lighter character than the occurrences I have just mentioned. Great numbers of English families came out to Paris during the summer and autumn of 1815, and the costumes of many of the women, who, according to the most approved English fashion of that day, wore very short waists and very long bonnets, appeared very odd and ridiculous, even to us who were their countrymen, when contrasted with the neat and elegant style of dress of the Parisian ladies. We used to think that our fair countrywomen, as a general rule, greatly excelled the French females in beauty, whilst the latter carried away the palm with regard to dress.

The caricatures of the English visitors, exhibited in the shop windows, were very good, and did not go far beyond the reality. A large stout John Bull, weighing from sixteen to eighteen stone, was generally the principal figure, and there were generally Mrs. and some Misses Bull with their short waists, &c., and sometimes a Master Bull or two, staring about, as one saw them do every day, at everything they came across. Sometimes the whole party were represented as standing out in the middle of the street, curiously examining the tops of the tall houses, at other times walking along the streets, staring at everything and everybody.

But the French were not satisfied with exhibiting caricatures of our females, dressed in the inelegant national costume of that day, but they brought forward a comedy at one of the theatres, called "*Les Anglaises pour rire*," in which the same sort of characters and costumes were represented on the stage. I once saw the play acted, and could not but join in the general laugh at the ludicrous exhibitions made of the curiosity, and want of taste in dress, of our fair countrywomen.

One evening some English officers determined to oppose the acting of the play, and there was some skirmishing between them and the police before the opposition ceased; shortly afterwards the piece was given up.

There was also another very laughable piece, which was brought forward at one of the theatres, and which met with great success. It was intended as a burlesque on the drapers' and other shopkeepers' assistants, many of whom were in the habit, on Sundays and *fête*-days, of dressing, and passing themselves off, as military men. The farce was called *Monsieur Calico*.

Monsieur Calico himself was represented, in the caricatures and on the stage, as a young man of three or four-and-twenty, about five feet high, dressed, I think, in a tailed coat and round hat, and manifesting considerable pretensions also, as regards the hair, whiskers, front of shirt, and stock. But the most remarkable appendage was a pair of steel spurs, about four inches in length, attached to the heels of his boots. The linen drapers' assistants, and numerous other young men, who felt themselves aggrieved, were furious at the representation, and at the success which it met with, and for several nights they endeavoured to take possession of the theatre, and to put down the obnoxious piece. I believe it was withdrawn after some little time.

CHAPTER 14

1815, 1816: The 52nd quartered at Versailles, St. Germain, and Clermont

On the 2nd of November, 1815, we broke up our agreeable encampment in the Champs Elysées, and went into quarters at Versailles, which is about fourteen miles from Paris. Versailles is a beautifully built town, and I was quartered in a very good house belonging to Madame Courtin, a very nice old lady, who was very kind to me, and gave me three neatly-bound volumes, containing Voltaire's *Histories of Peter the Great, of Russia,* and of *Charles XII, of Sweden;* they now lie before me, as I write this, fifty years after I received them.

We had not much to do at Versailles, where we remained about six weeks, and I spent much of my time in the palace, and in the adjoining beautiful gardens and grounds. In this palace of Versailles Louis XVI and Marie Antoinette were attacked five-and-twenty years before, by the Parisian mob, accompanied by soldiers under La Fayette, and treated with great indignity; they were forced to accompany them the next day to Paris, and I believe never returned again to Versailles.

About the middle of December, the 52nd marched from Versailles to St. Germain. The men were in the palace, and the officers were quartered on the inhabitants. I was on guard the first night, and passed one of the most wretched nights I ever passed in my life. By some accident there was no proper officers' guardroom, and when it was too late, I found myself with a whole suite of magnificent rooms, on the first floor of the palace, for my guard-rooms, without one single article of furniture in them; there were some logs of wood, but no other means had I of igniting them, or of keeping any heat in my body during that very cold night, than by collecting from time to time, and burning, quantities of straw, which had been swept out on to the balconies extending along the whole of the suite of apartments.

Sir John Colborne went on leave, during the short time that the 52nd was at St. Germain. On my calling upon him shortly before I started, he gave me some good advice on the subject of the importance of my improving myself by reading, &c., &c., and kindly told me he might very probably have it in his power to be of use to me in the service, but that of course my getting on well in the army must depend chiefly on my own attention to the reading and studies necessary in order to my becoming a good and useful officer. He was travelling in Germany during most of the time that he was absent from the regiment, and I think he joined us again about June or July, 1818, at the camp near St. Omer, when I was much pleased by his saying that Colonel Charles Rowan had given him a good account of my endeavours to improve myself during his absence.

In order to strengthen the government of Louis XVIII, and to give him time to reconstruct his army, and to feel increasing security against any attempts which might be made again to overthrow the newly established order of things in France, it had been determined by the Allied sovereigns that an army of 150,000 should remain in the north of France for three years, and that certain fortresses should be held and garrisoned by them during that period. The troops were to be paid, clothed, and provisioned at the expense of France.

✶✶✶✶✶✶

Note:—Will it be believed, that under these circumstances the officers of the British portion of the army of occupation had to pay an income-tax of ten *per cent.?* I well recollect that it was deducted from my ensign's pay of about £95 a year. There must have been some meanness or rascality somewhere. The amount thus deducted from the British officers, certainly would not find its way into the French Treasury.

✶✶✶✶✶✶

The leading powers of Europe sent their several quotas of troops, and the whole Allied Army of occupation was placed under the command of the Duke of Wellington.

The 52nd marched from St. Germain, I think, on Christmas-day, towards the cantonments which they were to occupy in the Pas de Calais. All the necessary arrangements appear not to have been completed at that time, for we were quartered in the town of Clermont, about thirty miles from Paris, and in some of the neighbouring villages, for about a month before we proceeded to our destination. I have very little recollection of Clermont and of the village about a mile and a half from it, which I occupied with about forty or fifty men. I well remember that I first tried to smoke a cigar as I walked out from the town one night, and that it made me dreadfully ill; I also remember that on the 21st of January, the anniversary of the death of Louis the XVI, in 1793, a guard of honour, accompanied by the King's colour, was allowed to be present in the church at Clermont: at a particular moment, I suppose on the elevation of the host, the colour was lowered, and the guard presented arms, at the same time each man coming down on one knee.

The whole scene appeared to me to be exceedingly ludicrous, and this arose especially from the awkward business the men made of saluting in a posture which they were of course unaccustomed to. We thought nothing at the time of the sin of thus joining in an idolatrous ceremony. I trust the practice, which prevailed so many years, of requiring our officers and soldiers to take part in the idolatrous ceremonies of the Roman Catholic and Greek churches, has now been entirely given up.

On our way from Clermont to our cantonments, we halted for two days at Amiens. On the first day I was on guard. When relieved from guard the next day, I went to the house I was quartered on; it was occupied by a very quiet, gentlemanly man and his wife; but in finding me accommodation they shewed an extreme ignorance of the relative positions of officer and soldier in the British Army, for I found at night that they had actually made up a stretcher-bed for my servant in the small room which I was to occupy; I had the greatest difficulty in getting them to understand that this arrangement would never do. After some considerable parley, it ended in my servant and I carrying the stretcher-bed into a sitting room on the other side of the passage; they all the time thinking me a most unreasonable person, and maintaining that as the arrangement was only for one night, we might as well submit to it.

CHAPTER 15

1816: Cantonments in the North of France

About the beginning of February, 1816, we reached our cantonments in the north of France. The regiment occupied six-and-twenty villages. They were within a circle of which the ancient town (now only a village) of Thérouenne might be considered as the centre; the diameter of the circle would be about seven miles. Thérouenne was besieged and taken by our Henry VIII, in 1514; it is situated about seven miles south of St. Omer, and is on the Lys, a very small river, fordable in many places below the town, but not above it. The first village we arrived at was Estréeblanche, which was my quarter during the greater part of our occupation of France; but I was stationed first of all, for several months, at Enguinegatte or Guinegatte, a village about two miles from Estréeblanche, and the same distance from Thérouenne, a quarter of a mile to the left of the road, the Chaussée Brunehaut.

My first quarter was at the house of the principal man of the village, a most respectable farmer, by the name of Ledoux, I think. He was one of the finest men I ever saw; his son and daughter also were fine, handsome young people, of about twenty-one and nineteen. I had a large square room, the principal room in the house, which served me both as a sitting and a bedroom; the windows were towards the garden, and the lower part of them, where there was a ledge of nearly the breadth of the wall, was about four feet from the ground; I should say they were four feet square. I have been thus particular in describing the room on account of a somewhat alarming occurrence which took place on the very first night of my arrival at Enguinegatte. I must premise that I am rather ashamed of relating the occurrence, but I do so more particularly for the benefit of my younger readers.

My narrow iron bedstead was placed in one corner of the room, close under one of the windows, and there was just room for a chair between the bedstead and an old-fashioned fireplace, which was on the same side of the room with the head of my bed and the chair; the fireplace projected about twenty inches from the wall. As I was in a strange place and amongst strangers, I thought it desirable before I went to bed to examine the fastenings of my doors before, I retired to rest. As usual, there was no fastening to the main door communicating with the farmhouse kitchen, and the other door was locked or bolted on the other side.

On going to bed, I laid my sword, in the scabbard, along the sill of the window, which was above my bed to the left. I soon fell asleep, and slept soundly for some hours; in the middle of the night I awoke, and was conscious that I had been awakened by some noise in the room. I listened for some seconds, and quietly taking my sword from the window, I drew it, and having a good hold of it so that I could use it, if necessary, I laid it along the outside of the bed clothes, and listened very anxiously for any sound which might discover to me who or what it was that had disturbed me. I could hear no footstep or other sound for a minute or two, but after a little time, I distinctly heard what appeared to be the breathing of a person standing by the side of my bed, with his head a foot or two above my face.

Without any consideration, I immediately made a horizontal cut, with all the force I could use in my horizontal position, in the direction of the fireplace: to my great astonishment, I only cut through the air, and my sword made a tremendous clatter against the projecting wall of the fireplace. I lay quietly for a minute or two, and then heard the breathing again, but closer to me; and then I thought it possibly proceeded from a rat either on my bed or on the chair; in order to dislodge this enemy, I took the pillow, and making a dash at him with it, upset the chair, and altogether made so much noise, that it disturbed my host and hostess, who, I then found, from a peculiar cough of one of them, were my neighbours, in the room the door of which was fastened on the other side.

They probably began to wonder what the young English officer, who had just taken up his residence with them, was up to, in making all these terrible noises in the middle of the night. I did not hear any rat scamper away, but wishing to find out, if I could, what had led to all this disturbance, and recollecting that possibly there might yet be some small remains of fire in the wood ashes on the hearth, I felt my way to the fireplace, and found the bellows, a long iron tube about two feet and a half long, and more than half an inch in diameter in the inside, and blowing through this tube, I produced enough light from the dying embers to shew me, not a fairy, but a poor quiet tabby cat sitting and warming herself in the chimney corner.

I had about seventy men of No. 9 company with me at Enguinegatte; the remainder of them were at Estréeblanche with the two other officers: when the weather permitted, the two parties met about ten o'clock each day, two or three times a week, on the company's parade ground, which was between the two villages, and about a mile from each; the whole regiment was occasionally assembled at Thérouenne, but the frequent assembling of the regiment during the winter was not necessary, as in the summer months the whole division was encamped at Racquingham, not far from St. Omer, and each autumn we marched to Valenciennes, and its neighbourhood, and joined the rest of the British and German troops for the purpose of engaging in sham fights and other field movements.

In 1816, and in 1817, towards the end of October, the 52nd returned from Valenciennes to their old cantonments, but after proceeding to Valenciennes in 1818, and being encamped on the glacis there for some time, they occupied the citadel of that place for several weeks, till they marched on the 19th of November to Calais, to embark for England, being the last remaining regiment of the British Army of Occupation.

When the alterations were made in the various brigades and divisions after the battle of Waterloo, and before the army of occupation marched to the north of France, the 52nd was placed in Major-General Sir Denis Pack's brigade with the 4th regiment and 79th highlanders; and in the division commanded by Lieut.-General Sir Charles Colville. Pack inspected us in the long meadow near Thérouenne early in June, 1816, and afterwards issued the following:—

Extract from Brigade Orders, June 11th, 1816.

> Major-General Sir Denis Pack feels much pleasure in recording his opinion that the appearance of the 52nd regiment, on his late inspection, justified all he heard in praise of the system established in that corps. He thinks particular praise is due to the officers for the good example they set by their strict uniformity of dress and officer-like appearance in every respect.

I believe it was on this occasion that he halted the regiment, and inquired of one of the officers "where was the place for the covering-sergeant of a company, when the battalion was in open column of sections, left in front?" The 52nd practice was not exactly in accordance with his view of what was correct, and after asking the same question from a second officer and not getting the right answer, he told us "that the place for the covering sergeant, under the circumstances, was on the right of the rear section, that, when the company wheeled into line, he might be in his proper place."

After the movements, &c., were ended, the general and the officers proceeded to the paymaster's quarter at, I think, the north-eastern extremity of the meadow. While we were there, bearing in mind what had occurred about the covering-sergeant's post, he desired an officer, who I think was on his staff or acting on the staff for the day, to look the thing out in Dundas; and when he had turned over the pages for some time, the general said "how can you be so stupid, Major ——?" and took the book himself. He was quite as unable to find the place as the other officer had been, and had to relinquish his task with rather a bad grace.

As my plan is to record my recollections of most of the things which can be properly recorded without giving annoyance to any one, I must mention a circumstance which occurred either then or at some other time in the garden of the paymaster's quarter. Two of us were amusing ourselves, and whiling the time away by playing at pitch-and-toss with five-*franc* pieces, when one of the pieces, which had been pitched not more than five yards, on to the centre of the gravel walk, disappeared in a most remarkable manner. We had both seen it pitched to the mark, and had then lost sight of it, to our very great astonishment.

We hunted for it and searched everywhere and everything for it, within several feet of the mark, for a good quarter of an hour or more, but it was all in vain; and we seriously, and not at all laughingly or in a joke, felt constrained to come to the conclusion that it had disappeared through the agency of Satan himself. It made a great impression on me at the moment, and the thoughts passed my mind, that it had possibly been permitted on account of our sins, or that it foreboded some impending evil. After we had given up every idea of finding the five-*franc* piece, on turning up a leaf, which appeared to be flat on the ground and to be no larger than the piece itself, there it was, to our very great surprise.

I believe there was scarcely anything that could be considered religion, or even the appearance of religion, amongst us at that time. Some years afterwards I heard that, whilst we were in those cantonments, an agent from some Bible Society, I believe it was the Naval and Military Bible Society, had sold or given bibles to a few of our men. Long afterwards one of the soldiers, who had become quite a religious man, said that this great change had taken place in him, solely through his having read one of these bibles, whilst he was quartered on a Roman Catholic family near Thérouenne, without his having had any communication with them on the subject of religion.

It was the only means of grace he had at the time; chaplains' visits to the regiments were almost unknown in those scattered quarters. When we were in these separate villages, I do not recollect that any attention was paid to the observance of the Lord's Day, either as regarded ourselves or the men. There was no instruction for them in anything of a religious nature; nor indeed did it occur to us to endeavour to employ and amuse them by giving them any other kind of instruction. When encamped at Valenciennes, service was performed by the chaplain, but whether he was attached to the brigade or to the division I forget.

CHAPTER 16

1816: Amusements in Cantonments

Our amusements were not much varied, yet we managed to pass our days very pleasantly. I think it was after our return from Valenciennes, in the autumn of 1816, that we started a pack of fox-hounds in the regiment; they were a very nice pack, and were well managed under the superintendence of one or two of the officers. When we returned to England at the end of November, 1818, ten couples were sold at Tattersall's at a high price. I was very fond of hunting, and will mention a few anecdotes connected with our proceedings in that direction. Almost the whole of the country was unenclosed; the woods and villages being the exceptions. When we were clear of them, the chief impediments to a straightforward gallop were deep hollow roads; and steep banks. There was a long bank, some miles from my quarters, which, on more than one occasion, was a sore trouble to a sailor friend of mine, by the name of Charles English, who was staying with me and others of the 52nd for some time.

I mounted him; and as he was not a first-rate horseman, the difficulties he frequently got into, afforded his friends much amusement; and after he had got safely back to our quarters, the recounting them afforded him also much gratification. This high bank was perhaps about seventeen feet deep, and certainly very steep, but still it was what those who were used to such things would take their horses down on their haunches, yet it was a real trouble to our friend, and I recollect looking back for him several times, in the space of about two miles that we had ridden away from him, and still seeing him riding backwards and forwards on the top of the bank, doing what we termed "life-guardsman's duty," searching for some more promising-looking place of descent than he had hitherto discovered.

One day, when I was the officer of the day, I had to go to make a report to Colonel Charles Rowan, who was quartered at the Château d'Uppen, about a mile from Thérouenne. On coming away, after making my report, I found that our hounds had just run a fox into the adjoining wood, and, as my duty was performed, I at once joined them, although, as I was in full regimentals and had my sword hanging by my side, I was not very suitably equipped for hunting. As soon as the fox had broken cover again, a greyhound joined in the chase, and threatened to spoil our sport, so as I was well mounted, and could, when I chose, ride from the rear to the front of the hounds, I rode ahead to drive him off.

Having done this, I kept my place at the head of the party, as we entered the enclosures of a village, with the hounds well up to the fox. After passing two or three fields, in taking a fence, my cap was knocked off my head by the bough of a tree. Of course, as I was before everybody, I could not stop to pick it up, but, noting the place, I rode on till in a short time we killed our fox. This being accomplished, I began to think of recovering my cap, and returned to the fence, at which I felt quite sure I had lost it. The cap, however, was nowhere to be seen. Our caps or shakoes were at that time ornamented, or rather disfigured, by a very broad band of silver round the top, a very unsuitable appendage to the cap of a light infantry officer.

I thought I could not have made a mistake about the fence, and became convinced that somebody, tempted by the silver lace on the cap, had walked off with it. On raising myself in my stirrups and taking a survey, as well as I could, of the fences of the adjoining fields, I saw the head of a woman through the higher branches of one of them, about two fields distant from me. On riding up to her and inquiring if she had seen my cap, she strenuously denied knowing anything about it; however, notwithstanding that she endeavoured to keep in a position to prevent my discovering that she had something bulky under her clothing, I at once perceived that such was the case; and on my accusing her of having my unfortunate cap there, she was forced to hand it out, and I was only too glad to recover and ride off with it, after giving her a good scolding for her dishonesty.

I have forgotten to mention an occurrence which took place at the first meet of our hounds. My recollection of the ground leads me to think that we met abreast of Enguinegatte, near to the south-eastern corner of that long village, nearly on the reverse side of it from that on which the Battle of Spurs was fought. I am not quite sure that this was the place, but I mention it, as perhaps some of the surviving officers of the 52nd may recollect it. I believe almost all the officers of the regiment, and no others, were present on the occasion. The thought crosses my mind as I write, and I feel disposed to give my readers the benefit of it—If these recent warriors and heroes of Waterloo could have met at this place the warriors and heroes who had fought and conquered at the Battle of the Spurs, what an astonishing interview it would have been.

How, after this digression, I am to get back to the trifling anecdote I was about to mention, I know not:—The officers of the 52nd were all assembled to see their new hounds throw off. The hounds had never hunted together, and were of course very wild. As we were all sitting very carelessly on our horses, one of the horses got loose and galloped away. This was a great deal too much for the sobriety of the new hounds, and they set off in full cry after the horse; and this sudden start made many of the horses set off also.

I was sitting in my saddle, with my bridle lying on my horse's neck, and my horse, "Norman," (not the one before mentioned,) a horse well known in the regiment as something very superior to a baggage-horse, and whom I saw last in the stables of the posting-house at Calais, this horse made a sudden start away, which threw me quite backwards before I could touch the bridle, and from his back I fell off on the left side without being able to disengage my foot from the left stirrup; I was consequently dragged a short distance, and, either accidently in his gallop, or purposely by a kick, he gave me a heavy blow on my jaw, close to my chin, which covered me with blood, and the mark of which I carry to this day.

I was desperately afraid that my jaw was broken, and sought out our assistant-surgeon, who was on the ground. It seems but yesterday, so vividly do I recollect the scene, although it took place as nearly as possible fifty years ago from the day on which I am writing this. The following short dialogue took place:—"Macartney! I fear my jaw is broken."

He then took hold of my chin and giving it a slight shake, said, "Oh, your jaw is not broken." I think no other person was thrown. I forget what sort of a run we had that day, but I remember my horse got planted in some ploughed land, and that I thought he was at last paid off for all his ill behaviour at the start.

I don't know if any other regiment in the army of occupation kept a pack of hounds, though I think the brigade in which the 29th was kept a pack. We once by arrangement took our hounds to the cavalry quarters to the north of St. Omer, to give the cavalry officers a day's sport. Lord Combermere, who had taken the command of the cavalry, after Lord Uxbridge (the Marquis of Anglesea) had lost his leg at Waterloo, went out with us, and many other cavalry officers.

✶✶✶✶✶✶

Note:—The great disappointment of the gallant Sir Stapleton Cotton, (Lord Combermere,) at not being allowed to proceed to Flanders in 1815, as Commander-in-Chief of the Cavalry, is mentioned in very strong terms in his *Life*, which has just been published by Lady Combermere :— "All was of no avail. Both his personal claims and the representations of the Duke of Wellington failed to induce the prince regent to forego his revenge or partiality for the sake of the public service, and at Waterloo Stapleton Cotton's sword flashed not in the van as it was wont to be. The disappointment was grievous, and to the end of his days he never could bear to speak on the subject of the Battle of Waterloo. On the 15th of July, 1815, in a letter from Paris, he wrote:—'I regret more than ever not having been at the famous battle which decided the fate of Europe.'"
(*Vide Wellington's Commander of Cavalry: the Early Life and Military Career of Stapleton Cotton* by Mary, Viscountess Combermere, W. W. Knollys & Alexander Innes Shand: Leonaur, 2018)

✶✶✶✶✶✶

The French general and his staff came out from St. Omer, in full uniform, to see the fun. In order to avoid disappointment, a bag-fox had been provided, which was turned out about a mile or more to the northward of St. Omer, on the *chaussée*, along which it went for perhaps half a mile. When it had had sufficient "law," the hounds were laid on. It was a brilliant day, and there was a good and well-mounted field. As we galloped after the hounds, none appeared to enjoy the sport or to ride faster than the French general and his staff; but as they were not at all used to hunting after our English fashion, their pleasure soon came to an end.

The fox after a time was headed, and crossing a tolerably wide ditch to the left of the road, took to the open country. The ditch was altogether too much for our French friends, as it would have been for my sailor friend of whom I wrote before, but all the rest of the party thought nothing of it. Before I had gone half a mile from it, I had the misfortune, when I was well placed, to break one of my stirrup-leathers, and I thought the best plan was to pull up and see what I could do to remedy the disaster.

Fortunately, it had broken exactly at the buckle, so that by shortening my stirrups one hole, which I could well afford to do, I avoided the, to me, great annoyance of riding the rest of the day without stirrups. I was not very long in getting all to rights, and at once began to fetch up my lee-way in pretty good style; and it certainly was a considerable pleasure when I found myself steadily advancing upon, and then passing Lord Combermere, who of course was well mounted. After some time, I found myself ahead of everybody, and I rode for several minutes nearly abreast of the two leading hounds, being about thirty yards on their right, and they gradually gaining on the fox, which I had in full view all the time, till we came to the enclosures of a village. There we had to gallop at speed up the most muddy lane I ever galloped through in my life.

One of the 52nd came next to me and rode within about eight yards, and got his face and the whole front of his body regularly plastered with thick mud, after a fashion which I never saw equalled either before or since. The fox took to a large piece of water in the village, and was caught by our huntsman in a boat, and given to the hounds, after having afforded us a very excellent run. I think it was recollecting, several years afterwards, the miserable plight in which I had seen this poor wretched fox, that first determined me to give up hunting, of which amusement I was exceedingly fond. There may be other reasons why a man who fears God might avoid hunting—for instance, he might think it calculated to lead him on other occasions into the society of persons not of congenial habits and feelings with himself; but it appeared to me (I have never forced these opinions on others) that I had no right to inflict pain on any of God's creatures—my fellow-creatures, for such they are—merely for my amusement.

In Hooper's *Waterloo* is the following anecdote, which I venture to borrow from him; I omitted to do so in the more suitable part of my work:—

> A trumpeter-boy of the 2nd Life Guards, Thomas Beamond, was riding through the field when a *cuirassier* rushed at him, with his sword's point levelled at the boy's breast. Discovering he was a mere lad, the gallant Frenchman dropped his point, spared him, and passed on. Sad to relate, in sight of the poor boy, a comrade, who had not witnessed the noble act of the *cuirassier*, fell upon him and slew him. When the boy, grown a man, told the story to my informant, he was, even after years had passed by, affected even to tears.

CHAPTER 17

1816: Amusements and Incidents in the North of France

We had not a very great variety of amusements during the time of our occupation of the North of France. I received from time to time during several weeks, as a present, from our regimental pack, those hounds which, from their being rather small or for any other reason, our managing committee wished to part with; and thus I collected, I think, seven hounds, for my kind friend Captain Frederick English, of the Engineers, who was quartered with his family at the *château* of Callone, near St. Pol, about seventeen miles from us. Whilst I was collecting them, two or three of us got a little private hunting of our own occasionally. At Callone they were considered a great acquisition, and I several times went there for two or three days, and enjoyed hunting with them very much.

On one occasion I remember riding ahead with a drag, which afforded us very good sport. There was in existence at one time, several years after our return from France, a very spirited sketch, by Captain English, of the officers, horses, and hounds of that hunt; I think he never mustered more than five horsemen, even when I made one of the party. Captain English and his horse, and I and my mare, were amongst the figures; and I should have liked to have brought away with me the sketch, if they could have parted with it, when I last saw my kind friends in England some thirty years ago.

The Duke of Wellington, whose headquarters were at Cambrai, between fifty and sixty miles distant from our cantonments, on one occasion sent his boar-hounds for a day's hunting in our direction, and four of the 52nd officers went between twenty and thirty miles the day before in order to hunt with them. They threw off not very far from the inn at which we slept, in a forest, the name of which I have forgotten, but we had scarcely any sport. The hounds found a boar, and hunted him for a considerable time, and we rode up and down the rides of the forest; at last he broke cover, but merely to run about half a mile across an open space to another part of the forest. There was a tremendous and awkward leap out of the forest, which my mare managed very cleverly.

The boar is said to be a fast runner when hunted, but I had not the pleasure of seeing him during the whole day. Lord Hill and his brother. Colonel Hill, of the Blues, were out, and I think not more than half a dozen other people, besides ourselves, one of whom was Colonel Fremantle. Lord Hill and his brother carried boar-spears, as did one or two of the others. Soon after we got into the forest, as I was walking my horse along, about 150 yards behind the other 52nd men, Lord Hill overtook me, and coming up alongside, asked me "How are Sir John Colborne and the 52nd, Sir?" He *might* have heard that some 52nd officers were to be out that day, but I remember my impression then was, that he had not had the opportunity of hearing that we were to be there, and that it was a case of remembering, after having only once or at the most twice, seen me before; the one occasion being when he rode very close upon me in the standing corn, half an hour or an hour before the commencement of the Battle of Waterloo; the other, in passing along the front at a review, when the troops were standing in contiguous close columns, and when I think I carried one of the colours.

Some of our officers got some good coursing; I only occasionally joined them. The shooting was very bad, the birds being very wild on the extensive cultivated lands between the villages. Sometimes, for want of something else to do, I recollect firing ball from my double-barrelled gun at partridges, which I could often see running on the rise of the ground 200 yards off, when I could not get within half that distance of them. I need scarcely add, that this ball-practice of mine did not inflict any serious injury on the enemy in my front.

Some spirited officers, quartered in the neighbourhood of St. Pol, belonging to our division, proposed, in the spring of 1816, I think, the establishment of a gymnastic club, at which those of the officers of the division who were so disposed, might meet at stated times to play at cricket and other games. The meetings were to take place some few miles to the northward of St. Pol. This was at a great distance from our brigade, but two of us from the 52nd attended the first meeting. The

71st, belonging to another brigade, were close to us at Estréeblanche to the eastward; and inclining towards the south, and in the direction of St. Pol, were the 6th regiment, I think, at or near Lillers, and beyond them the 29th regiment; and nearer to St. Pol, and beyond it, there was another brigade and some artillery. These being nearer to the place of meeting than Pack's brigade, were enabled to contribute a goodly number of members to the institution.

I forget what games were played at the first meeting, but after dinner, Captain McDonald, the Hon. Secretary, came to where I was sitting, and said it was proposed that our brigade should play the rest of the division at cricket, at the next meeting of the club, and asked if I would undertake, on the part of the brigade, to accept the challenge; I was foolish enough to reply, that I could not answer for the rest of the brigade, as I knew nothing of them, but that I would undertake that the 52nd should play the rest of the division, I dare say I should just as readily have said that they would play "All England." I have no doubt it created some smiles when this was announced, as it immediately was.

On my giving an account, on my return to the regiment, of all that had taken place, they told me that I had acted very foolishly in what I had done, but that as the thing was considered as fixed, they would endeavour to turn out in sufficient force to try and do some credit to the expectations which I might have raised of their prowess as cricketers. We did not take any men with us, but eight of the officers including myself went, and some of them must have ridden upwards of forty miles there and back; for I was the nearest to the place of meeting, and I reckoned that my quarters were about sixteen miles from it.

We found a numerous assemblage of the officers of the division there. It was arranged that there should be only eight on a side. We were not overmatched, and had a most excellent game. They paid us the compliment of saying, that they never saw better fielding in their lives. They had a major in the artillery on the other side, who got fifty-two runs. We consoled ourselves with saying, that had he been an ordinary batter, and had not made more than half that score, we should have carried away the laurels.

But I have a sad addition to make to this account. We heard a few days afterwards, that this poor major of artillery, I am sorry I cannot recollect his name, who had been full of health and spirits, and who was the hero of the day, was killed on his return to his quarters that evening, by the upsetting of the gig, in which he and another officer were riding, at the turn of a road. How often do the solemn warnings come to us—"*memento mori!*" and, "there is but a step between me and death!"

One moonlight evening, as four of us, including a young acquaintance of mine, a fine young fellow by the name of Barnett, of the 71st Highland Light Infantry, were returning along the Chaussée Brunehaut, from our mess at Thérouenne, to Estréeblanche, four miles distant, the 71st officer and another of the party determined to ride a race, from the top of the ascent from Thérouenne , in the direction of Estréeblanche. I always thought those races on roads extremely dangerous and disagreeable, and being mounted on a small Galloway, contented myself with trotting smartly along the road.

When I had proceeded about a mile, I heard a voice crying out, "Hold hard, hold hard!" The first object which I saw was one of the horses fixed in a ditch to the right of the road, two feet wide and two feet deep, with his back at the bottom of it, and the four feet up in the air. The two racing horses, in some curious way, had got their fore feet entangled and had both fallen. The 52nd officer and his horse had not taken much harm; but my poor 71st friend was insensible, having fallen most heavily on his head; his horse was in the ditch, as I have described. The 52nd officer was sitting down with the head of the other on his lap.

The fourth man of the party was up immediately after me; they left me with poor Barnett, and one of the other two rode off to a village two miles off, for an assistant-surgeon, and the second, after giving notice to some of our men at Enguinegatte, a third of a mile off, to come to my assistance, went in another direction. As I sat supporting our injured friend, I desired the last officer, as he was moving off, if he had a knife in his pocket, to leave it with me, intending to get some blood from his temples or some other part, if Barnett should appear to cease to breathe.

I was often joked afterwards about this. It was not a very pleasant position to be in, for I thought it most probable that my companion would die before assistance came. When we had been there about twenty minutes, I was for a moment startled by four of our men rushing down some broken ground behind us, with drawn bayonets, one exclaiming, as he saw our figures, "Where's Mr. Leeke?" They were the men quartered at the first farmhouse, and had misunderstood the hasty notice given by the officer, that they should lose no time in going to my assistance. They gathered that there was a dying man on the

Thérouenne road, and that I was there, and probably thought that we had been attacked by some party. Two or three others came to our assistance, and we placed Barnett, still insensible, upright on one of the horses; and, two men holding him on and I leading the horse by the bridle, we proceeded to my quarters at Estréeblanche.

A small river, called the Laquele, flowed along the road of the village for eighty or a hundred yards, completely filling it and being nearly knee deep, the footpath going along the bank on the right. On our arriving at this water, Barnett astonished me by taking hold of the bridle and pulling the horse up, and saying that I must not go through the water. Here was a momentary consciousness. Of course, however, I did this. He was put into a bed at my quarters, and our assistant-surgeon attended him. The day after, the surgeon and the assistant-surgeon of the 71st arrived, and said he had received a severe concussion of the brain; they were anxious to get him into their neighbourhood, and he was removed to his own quarters on the third day, where he gradually recovered. I wonder whether he is still living. Perhaps one fourth of the officers who fought at Waterloo, still survive at this date, December 8, 1865; at least that is about the proportion of survivors of the 52nd Waterloo officers.

There were sixty-three officers present on that occasion, including the surgeons and two *aides-de-camp*, of whom it is ascertained that about forty-five are dead. I only know of fourteen that survive, now at the end of fifty years. Three of these were captains at Waterloo; William Rowan, James Frederick Love, and Charles Yorke, now lieutenant-generals and G.C.B.'s. Ten of them were then lieutenants: George Hall, (now lieutenant-colonel,) George Gawler, (now colonel,) George Whichcote, (major-general,) Hon. William Ogilvy, (captain,) E. R. Northey, (lieutenant-colonel,) Hon. W. Browne, Edward Scoones, (major,) W. Austin, (major,) Charles Holman, (captain,) G. E. Scott. One only was then an ensign, William Leeke.

Just before the 18th of June, 1816, the medals for Waterloo were served out to all those who had been present, and on the anniversary of the victory two of us thought well to ride into Aire, which was about six miles from Estréeblanche; it was the nearest fortified place to our village, and was garrisoned by the French. None of our non-commissioned officers or soldiers were admitted into St. Omer or Aire without a pass from the officers commanding the company to which each belonged, but officers in uniform might enter without any pass. It must be recollected that there were very few soldiers remaining in the French Army who had been at Waterloo, and that they were now the soldiers of our ally Louis XVIII, for whom we had fought and some thousands of our comrades had shed their blood, but, nevertheless, our riding into one of the French garrisons on the first anniversary of a victory gained over French troops, would perhaps have been better avoided. My companion, on the occasion, thus speaks of it in a letter which I received from him not very long ago:—

> Do you remember how you and I rode into Aire, on the first anniversary of Waterloo, wearing the medals just issued, and laurel in our shakos. The guards at the gate scowled, but we met with no adventure. Kenny, a very correct and rather censorious person, thought we had been extremely unwise—it was all your doing too—I, so many years older, ought to have tried to dissuade you, instead of being led away by you as I was.

In reply, I told him that I perfectly well recollected the whole affair, and that it certainly was much more like me than like him to engage in such an adventure. I felt rather confident that it was on this occasion that the following, in some little measure redeeming, occurrence took place, but my friend says he has not the least recollection of it, so it is probable that it happened when I rode into Aire on some other occasion with some other officer. As we rode across the large square of the town, an old woman, carrying one of those small tin boxes with lighted charcoal, which the older French women are so constantly seen with, suddenly fell down in what appeared to be a fainting fit; we immediately jumped off our horses, and letting them loose, carried the poor woman into the nearest house: on our seating her in a chair, her lower clothes were found to be slightly on fire from the charcoal-box, and she was quite dead.

A fine old soldier, a corporal in the 23rd Fusiliers, recently told me that their grenadier company, in which he was, adopted a singular method of parading their medals on the first anniversary of Waterloo. Two of their comrades were, for some not very serious offence, confined in the guard-house at headquarters, not very far distant from their colonel's quarters; so they made one of their number put on his red jacket and all his regimentals, and having fastened the whole of their medals all over the front of his jacket, they borrowed an ass, on which he rode to their headquarters, accompanied by the whole of the grenadier company.

When they arrived, they asked permission to see the colonel, and he immediately came out to them, and on his asking what they wanted, they told him that they had come to ask him to do them a great favour on the anniversary of the great victory, and it was that he would have the kindness to forgive their two comrades, who were in disgrace. He smiled at their gallant cavalier bedizened with medals, and good naturedly told them that their comrades should be at the village they were quartered at, before the company could get there themselves. The two men joined them in a very few minutes after they left the colonel's quarters.

Monsieur Robichez, the owner of the *château*, at Estréeblanche, at which Captain McNair was quartered, on one occasion pressed me very much to go with him to a ball, at Betune, a French fortress, about ten miles from Aire. I was the only Englishman there; indeed, all the rest were French, and many of them French officers in uniform, and although there was nothing uncivil in their conduct, yet there was a certain constraint, which was almost sure to arise under the circumstances, and which made me feel I had been very foolish in allowing myself to be placed in such a position.

Although I was too far from St. Omer to have any acquaintances amongst either the inhabitants or the few English residents there; yet, on one occasion I, with many 52nd officers, joined the other regiments of Pack's brigade, and the cavalry quartered to the north of St. Omer, in giving a grand ball to the people of the town and neighbourhood, both English and French; which was attended, including the entertainers, by about four hundred people. The supper-tables, it was arranged, were first to accommodate the one half of the assemblage, and when they had been duly feasted, then the other half were to be admitted, and the only thing I now remember of that ball is, that when the second detachment of supper-eaters arrived, every bonbon, and every other pocketable eatable, had been carried off by those who had been invited to make the first attack upon the abundant provision, which had been intended to be more than sufficient for the whole party.

As I was returning from the ballroom to the hotel at which I was to sleep, at a very badly lighted spot I made some wrong turn, and lost my way for a minute or two; I heard someone coming, but could not, as it was very dark, see more than the figure of a man approaching. I took him to be a Frenchman, and asked him which was the way to the hotel. He answered in French, and gave me some directions, which, although I had in some degree lost my way, I felt very confident were incorrect, and, as I thought he was leading me wrong on purpose, I gave him somewhat of a scolding for his conduct in my best French, which he took very quietly, and then said good naturedly in English, "Oh come with me and I'll shew you the way *à l'ancienne poste*," I walked with him twenty or thirty yards, when he put me into the right direction, for which I thanked him. I could not see his face, but I discovered from his voice that it was the commanding officer of the 4th English regiment. I cannot at all understand how it was that, in a fortified place of some extent, the streets, or at least some of them, were left in such a state of darkness.

I think the army was very healthy during the time of the occupation of France. We had two sad accidents at Estréeblanche, and whilst we were there one of our men was mortally wounded by a retired French officer, who lodged in the village.

I have mentioned that at one time we regularly dined at the *château* at which Captain McNair was quartered. It was surrounded by a moat about thirty feet broad, over which there was a bridge about five or six feet wide, formed of planks, resting on four or five walls built up from the bottom of the moat; there was no railing on either side of the wooden bridge. It communicated with a vaulted passage, which passed under some of the rooms to a small open court within, surrounded by the buildings on three sides, whilst on that side which was opposite to the passage to the bridge, we looked over the moat to the field beyond it. There was a massive door between the end of the passage and the bridge. We often crossed this bridge on the darkest nights without the least apprehension of danger, although the water was deep all round the *château* except at the edge.

One dark night my servant, whose name was George Soones, with another soldier, was passing through the doorway close to the bridge, and, as it was blowing hard through the passage from the opposite direction, he found some difficulty in keeping the door open, and at the same time in keeping alight a piece of candle which he was carrying between his fingers. The other man was nearly across the bridge, and heard Soones say, "If this light goes out, I'm done."

At that moment the door was blown heavily to upon him, and the light went out, and before he had reached the middle of the bridge he fell over, striking his neck, it was supposed, against one of the buttresses on which the bridge was built; he was a good swimmer, and, notwithstanding the hurt he received, which was shown by an extensive bruise on the side of the neck, he swam about five-and-thirty yards, but not towards the shore of the moat. His body was not found until about two hours afterwards, under the walls of the *château*.

I was away from Estréeblanche on that evening, and was very much grieved to hear of poor Soones's fate. He and his two brothers had volunteered into the 52nd from the South Hants Militia, and his friends, I found, lived within two miles of my home, though I had never known them; and possibly this made me feel his death all the more. It was truly melancholy for me to enter my bedroom at night. He had been the last person there, and had turned down my bed, and laid out my things. It was impossible to get to sleep, and I felt very wretched. Divided from my room by a thin lath and plaster partition was the servants' room, in which they kept their firelocks and accoutrements, and slept. Holman's servant, a nice fellow by the name of Blackman, slept, or rather dozed there on the night in question. I heard him all night tumbling about on his bed, and more than once I heard him say, "I'm coming, George, I'm coming!"

The next morning, in good time, I sent a man to the next village, about a mile and a half off, occupied by Shedden's company, in which Soones's brothers were, to break the melancholy intelligence to them. On his return, he told me that he had met one of them before he reached the village, and on his saying that he was come to look for him, he at once exclaimed, "You have no occasion to tell me what you are come for, I dreamt last night that my brother was drowned".

Now I am sure, so much did everyone feel the melancholy death which had occurred, that the man would tell me exactly what passed between him and the brother, and I perfectly remember it all. However, I should probably not have thought so much about this dream, had it not been for the additional circumstance which I am going to mention. I wrote home to my mother to request her to inform George Soones's family of his death. She could not go to their house, and therefore sent to request that one of them would come and speak to her; the poor mother came, and on being informed that her son was dead, immediately said, "Was he drowned, Ma'am?" and on being told that he was, she replied, "I thought so, for I dreamt several nights ago, that he was drowned."

I well remember how melancholy I felt, as we marched along a long pathway, by the side of a high hedge, following poor Soones's remains from the *château* to the Roman Catholic church at Estréeblanche, on the north side of which he was buried. The "Dead March in Saul," which I had never heard before, was sounded very nicely, by our two buglers, who preceded the corpse, and had a very solemn effect. I have no recollection of the service being read over his remains, though I suppose it was read by McNair or Holman; nor do I recollect the firing the three volleys over his grave, though that must have been done. So curious is memory! Some very trifling words or circumstances we remember with the greatest accuracy, when somewhat more important things, which happened at the same time, we entirely forget.

But I have another very sad event to relate, which happened a week only after poor Soones's death. The whole company, or the Estréeblanche portion of it, I forget which, were at ball-practice, about half a mile above the village, under the command of Holman. I was not present, and I have some idea I was at Euguinegatte. One of the men's firelocks would not go off, (it was the same man who was just in front of Soones when he fell off the bridge,) he went to the rear of the firing-party to hammer the flint with his turnscrew, but instead of pointing his musket to the rear, he thoughtlessly pointed it towards the men standing in line in front of him. It went off, and the ball went through the arm (breaking it) and through the lungs of a corporal in the rear rank, and lodged in the body of poor Blackman, Holman's servant, who was in the front rank.

The corporal recovered, but Blackman was mortally wounded. He was taken to the nearest cottage, and placed on a chair, and lived about three-quarters of an hour. I think no surgeon could get to him before his death. They told me, he was quite aware that he had not long to live, and said he should "soon be with poor George;" and again, immediately before his death, "I'm going to poor George." He was buried by the side of poor Soones, and I often think of their last resting-place. Blackman also was a Hampshire man, and I think the man who accidentally shot him, also came out of the South Hants Militia. This man afterwards became my servant, somewhat I believe to the astonishment of people, as they thought "he was so unlucky." I do not think I took him as a servant out of bravado, but out of compassion in some measure, for he felt how unfortunate he had been in the matter of these deaths, and how blameable for his great carelessness as regarded that of poor Blackman. He was a clean, smart soldier, and one likely to make a good servant.

We were sitting at our mess one evening after dinner, and Brisbane, one of our assistant-surgeons, was with us, when a messenger came from the village, to say that Corporal Gilpin had been stabbed by a Frenchman. We found, on going to the public house, that the intestines being wounded there was scarcely any hope of his recovery. His wound was dressed and sewn up, and he was the next day sent to the hospital, where he died within the week. Gilpin and this retired French officer were great friends, and they studied a little together; the Frenchman assisting Gilpin, I think, in French and arithmetic; but they also drank together, and on this occasion they were both in liquor, and a quarrel arose between them, when Gilpin struck the other severely with his fists. The French officer took up a chair to protect himself with it, at the same time opening his knife, and when Gilpin again advanced upon him, he stabbed him under the chair. Corporal Gilpin was one of our finest men, and was the right-hand man of the company.

The Frenchman made his escape into Belgium, and was afterwards, if I recollect right, condemned to death, "*par contumace*," I think they call it. He was very nearly taken, for he jumped out of a window with his double-barrelled gun in his hand, just as our village guard, of a corporal and three, came to the other side of the house in which he lodged, and they pursued him down the garden, but lost sight of him. I remember his once being examined as a witness at a court-martial, at Estréeblanche, and I met him once afterwards as I was returning from shooting, where, as he passed me at about sixty yards distance, he saluted me by taking off his hat, which of course I returned. Captain McNair had to attend with some others at the trial, when he was found guilty.

McNair also had to give evidence on another occasion. The circumstances were these, and although there was nothing very particular in what occurred, they were well remembered because they afforded us some little excitement for the moment in the midst of our rather monotonous life:—We were sitting quietly one moonlight evening after dinner, when Angelique, M. Robichez's housekeeper, came into the room, and told us she had just watched some men who had gone into her master's barn, about eighty yards from the *château*, no doubt for the purpose of stealing the wheat, and requested us to come and try and secure them. We did not at first pay much, attention to what she said, but presently she returned in a very excited state, saying she had seen people going into the barn, and reproached us with being unwilling to take any trouble to prevent her master from being robbed.

On this we sallied out, and one or two of the servants came also. McNair stopped to take a pistol with him, so that I got downstairs and over the bridge the first, and picked up a switch, for want of something more suitable, as I ran along. Just as I came to the barn door it was partly opened, and then shut to again hastily; so, giving it a smart cut with the switch, I ran round to a door, which I knew was on the other side; on my arriving at it, the persons within had got it half open for the purpose of getting away, but on seeing me they closed it again, and I could not move it when I pushed heavily against it, nor could all our party together make any impression on the doors; so one of the men was sent to the village, a quarter of a mile off, for the corporal's guard.

Just then we heard voices about fifty yards off, and recognised amongst them the voice of one of our own men, who was a drinking, troublesome fellow, and we immediately feared that he and his companions were in some way mixed up with the proceedings in the barn. Leaving two of our party, one of them with his musket in his hand, to look after the barn doors, and to prevent the escape of the men within, McNair and I proceeded to reconnoitre the party whom we heard talking at a little distance. They turned out to be the man, whose voice we had recognised, and six soldiers of the 71st. They were on the footpath leading from Estréeblanche to the nearest 71st village, which was rather more than a mile off, and they were all out after hours.

On our coming up to them they made no attempt to run off, and at once obeyed McNair's order to follow each other in single file. He told me to keep by the rear man and bring them all along. I was greatly afraid that finding themselves brought along by only two persons, they might be tempted to break away from us, for I knew, if they did so, that McNair would certainly shoot one of them, he being a most determined man. However, they walked quietly along till we came abreast of the gable end of the barn, and a little beyond, when they were ordered to halt and remain there. They then saw that something was up at the barn.

The guard had by this time arrived, and we proceeded to force open the principal door, which had been barricaded with beams by those within. Angelique bravely volunteered so to hold the lantern that we might see those within, when the door gave way. It opened inwards, and was about four feet wide; and it shut to against a sill at the bottom, about fourteen inches high. The four men of the guard with their bayonets fixed, with my help added, soon made the props yield a little, and two or three of us got each a foot over the sill, and the butt ends of two or three muskets were in, and the door had opened nearly two feet at my end, when the brave Angelique ran right off with the lantern, leaving the small open space in darkness; so, for a few seconds, we allowed the door to close to upon us again.

I took the lantern from Angelique, and we again made good our footing within the sill, and the door went right back on its hinges, all of us going forward almost on our faces; and then, I confess, I felt somewhat ashamed, for we found in the barn only two poor frightened Frenchmen, who fell on their knees, crying "*Misericors, Misericors.*" I think they were afraid that our soldiers would bayonet them. Angelique's courage returned, and, mounting a wheelbarrow which was in the barn, she harangued them vehemently for their ingratitude in robbing so kind a master as M. Robichez. They were afterwards condemned to five years' imprisonment. The seven soldiers, when it was found that they were not mixed up with the attempt to rob the barn, were, I think, allowed to go to their quarters. I believe all our characters rose wonderfully in the estimation of Angelique.

We had a court-marshal on one of our men at Estréeblanche, for being drunk on guard, when he was found guilty, and received one hundred lashes. Winterbottom, our adjutant, who had risen from the ranks, told me, when the sentence was executed, that the poor fellow had been his comrade when first he entered the regiment, and added, "I feel very sorry for him. He took to drinking ways, which has brought him to this degradation and punishment. I avoided drinking, and tried to do my duty, and am now adjutant, and nearly the senior lieutenant of the regiment."

I had a curious complaint made to me by one of the men, when the new clothing of the company was being fitted on at Thérouenne. He came to me and said, "If you please, Sir, sergeant ——— (the master tailor) has cut my chin with his scissors."

I told him it must have been done accidently. He replied, "No, Sir, I believe it was done out of spite. He has always had a spite against me, since I brought up his wife, when I was sentry on the quarter-guard at St. Omer camp, and she tried to pass into camp without answering, when I challenged her."

I immediately went with the man, who I think was the same man who had his pouch knocked off at Waterloo by a cannon-shot, to the master tailor, and told him of the complaint, when he said, "I was trying on his jacket, Sir, with my scissors in my hand, when he fidgeted about so much, that he made me impatient, and I said, 'do stand still,' at the same time putting up my hand, when the point of the scissors caught him accidentally on the chin."

There was nothing to be done but to accept this excuse, and to tell him quietly to be more careful in future. The master tailor of the regiment was attached to No. 9 company, and was in the rear of it as a sergeant on inspection and review days. He tried to have himself looked upon as a privileged character, on those occasions, with regard to his military bearing, &c., but this I never permitted. There was no great harm in him, but he was rather conceited in his undress and in his walk, and attempted to be a bit of a dandy.

I recollect on the occasion of one of the older officers joining at the citadel of Valenciennes, after having been away from the regiment for some very considerable time, he was shaking hands very cordially with all the officers who met him, when the master tailor passed along, dressed in a blue surtout coat which he was allowed to wear, and an undress cap, somewhat resembling those of the officers, and before he could salute the major, the latter, knowing his face and taking him for one of the officers, put out his hand and gave it a hearty shake, saying, "I'm very glad to see you, my good fellow;" which my unmilitary readers must understand was, under the circumstances, rather contrary to military etiquette. On finding out his mistake, and getting a little laughed at for it, the major uttered something in which the words "scoundrel," and "put him in the guard-house," were distinguishable.

It is a general feeling, I believe, in the army, that officers cannot be too particular in their behaviour to sentries, when challenged by them. The sentry may be placed in very awkward circumstances, particularly with regard to officers, when enforcing the orders of his post. At the camp near St. Omer, one night when I was the officer of the guard, as I lay on my guard-bed, I heard one of my sentries challenge someone who was passing near his post without receiving any reply, and the "Halt, who comes there?" was repeated several times without the question being answered.

At last he crossed the path of the person, who proved to be an officer of another regiment encamped beyond us, and stopped him, when he gave the answer, "officer," and I heard the sentry say, "Then, Sir, you should have said that you were an officer." I was just going to the sentry's assistance, when I found that the officer made no further reply, and was allowed to pass on. But I had no idea of allowing sentries to be improperly treated by anyone.

CHAPTER 18

1816, 1817, 1818: Leave to England and Paris. Return of the Army to England

In the autumn of 1816, I obtained three months' leave of absence to go to England. We were told afterwards, that on the very night of our departure, there was a very heavy gale with rain; and that great numbers of the tents were blown down. There were two other officers went on leave at the same time, but I forget who they were. We started on a Sunday morning from Dover, in a postchaise, for London. I was voted the paymaster for the journey, and at one of the turnpikes I recollect I had a bad shilling given to me in the change for a pound note, and that it gave us some trouble, as we went along, so to shy it out of the window that no one might be likely to find it.

I well remember the delight and pleasure I felt that morning, on finding myself again in our own dear country. I have always felt that one great advantage to be derived from travelling in other parts of the world, was the learning from it to love and value one's own country all the more. As it was Sunday, all the people were very nicely dressed, and in our eyes our fair countrywomen carried off the palm of beauty, when compared with the nice and kind-hearted females on the other side of the channel. I had not then learnt to value the Sunday as a day set apart by Almighty God as a day of rest, and of holy observance, and, consequently, if rightly observed, of spiritual benefit to man.

I recollect nothing more of the journey, than that I found myself on the afternoon of the next day at Cheltenham, where my family were staying. I was not expected, and was not at first recognized by my mother and sisters, when I was ushered into the drawing room, without being announced. Each looked at the other, as much as to enquire who the stranger was. I was now more than eighteen years and a half old, and fifteen months had made some considerable alteration in my appearance. At last one of them ventured to mention my Christian name, and then we enjoyed one of those happy meetings which occur so seldom in the course of our lives.

I have not much to relate about Cheltenham; but one of the first things I discovered was, that the Duke of Wellington and I were still nearer neighbours there, than we were when my tent was close to the garden door of his house at Paris. He was in the next house to us; but all I remember of him was, the seeing him attending to the present duke, and, I think, his brother, when they were put on a couple of ponies, apparently for the first time, on the other side of the fence which separated the drives up to the two houses. There was a great deal of gaiety going forward at that time at Cheltenham, which we entered into very freely. One of our chief friends, with whom we first became acquainted there, was Captain Sir Edward Tucker, of the navy, who early in 1817, married my eldest sister.

★★★★★★

Note:—Admiral Sir Edward Tucker was one of our most gallant officers, and was made a K.C.B. in 1814, for distinguished services rendered in the capture of several of the Molucca Islands, when in command of H.M. Ship *Dover*. He died in 1864, at the age of 86, humbly trusting in the righteousness and atonement of the Lord Jesus Christ.

★★★★★★

After spending about a month at Cheltenham, and a very agreeable week at Malvern with a very large party, we went into Hampshire, and I returned to the north of France in the early part of November. One day at Cheltenham an old gentleman accosted me, and told me he had been in my regiment at the Battle of Bunker's Hill; but I never fell in with him afterwards. He did not mention his name, but I think it very likely that he was General Hunter, who I know served at Bunker's Hill in 1777, and whose journal of what took place with regard to the services of the 52nd in America and India, is largely quoted in the early part of the regimental record.

Towards the end of the summer of 1817, Colonel Charles Rowan very kindly applied for three months' leave for me to go to Paris, to improve myself in French. I lived in the family of a superior French officer, who had suffered a great reverse of fortune and prospects by the overthrow of Bonaparte, and the restoration of the Bourbons. They were very nice people, and were very kind to me; but they were very strong Bonapartists. I picked up a good deal of French whilst I was there, and tried to make a start in German. I also did something, but very little, in the way of military surveying. Several other persons usually dined with the family with whom I had taken up my quarters; amongst them was a French *chef d'escadron*, who had served at Waterloo in the *cuirassiers*. He was now on half-pay.

He generally sat at a distant part of the table from me, so that I knew little of him; we were however on very good terms. I only remember two circumstances connected with him, one of which shewed rather strongly his dislike to the English, a dislike very natural, and, I suspect, almost universal amongst Bonaparte's officers and soldiers, many of whom had met with such signal defeats at the hands of the English in the Peninsula and at Waterloo. The circumstance was this:—We were sitting at dinner one day, when I heard some considerable laughing at the other end of the table, and found, from several of the party looking towards me, that they rather wondered if I had heard what had just been said by the French officer. On my requesting that he would repeat it, he did so, and said, good humouredly:—

"I was saying, 'we dislike very much the Prussians, the Prussians, and the other dogs, (meaning the Austrians) but with regard to these English we *detest* them.'"

The words "*autres chiens*," (in English, *other dogs*,) sound very much like the word "*Autrichiens*," which is the French word for Austrians. I think this play upon the words was common amongst the French at that time. I took the speech very quietly, and merely said, that "there was no love lost between us."

The other circumstance connected with the proceedings of this French officer was as follows:—We went with a party to the cemetery of Père la Chaise, and as I followed them I found our friend the *cuirassier* writing something on one of the tombs in pencil. On my asking, if I might read what he had written, he made no difficulty in allowing me to do so. The words were very treasonable, and had he been denounced to the government, no doubt they would have cost him his liberty, if not his life. They were to the following effect:—

> Rise, Frenchmen, and avenge yourselves on this executioner of a king, (*ce bourreau du roi*) who has deprived of life the noble Labédoyère.

✶✶✶✶✶✶

Note:—On the return of Napoleon from Elba, Colonel Labédoyère was one of the first sent, at the head of his regiment, to oppose his progress towards Paris; but instead of doing so, he, and the troops he commanded, went over to the late emperor. After serving at Fleurus and at Waterloo, he retired, at the capitulation of Paris, with the French Army behind the Loire. He was soon afterwards arrested, brought to Paris, tried by a court-martial, and condemned to death. He was shot on the plains of Grenoble, on the 19th of August, 1815, when he was not yet thirty years of age.

✶✶✶✶✶✶

I think some few years afterwards I saw an account in the papers of some trouble which this officer had got into, in connexion with a disturbance in front of the Chamber of Deputies.

I had several English friends at Paris, which enabled me to spend my time there very pleasantly, although I did not allow my intercourse with them to interfere with my study of French, for which I had principally gone to Paris. I recollect a very pleasant picnic to Malmaison, with a large party of English and French; and the going to a ball at the English ambassador's. As some of the French royal family were to be there, it was necessary to go in a court dress; I had no regimental court dress with me, and, therefore, as was customary, hired a civilian's dress. It consisted of a chocolate-coloured coat and waistcoat, with cut steel buttons, black satin knee-breeches, with buckles, white silk stockings, shoes and buckles, sword, and cocked hat.

On my return from Paris, I found the 52nd at Valenciennes. On my way thither with the mail courier, I encountered, near Denain, the most tremendous thunderstorm I was ever exposed to. We were afterwards encamped for two or three weeks, and the army was reviewed, on the plains of Denain. Two of us put one of our tents over the other, which helped to keep out the cold. We had a brother-officer in the next tent to us, whose horse's name was "Chance," and having, on two or three mornings, heard him ask his servant, when he called him, "How is old Chance?" (he pronounced the name in a peculiar manner) we, during the remainder of our encampment there, made a point, the first thing every morning, of inquiring after the health of his horse, in the same words, and with the same peculiarity in pronouncing the animal's name.

Every morning, for a fortnight, might be heard the following colloquy; for although after a few days it was very difficult to get him to answer when we called to him by name, yet we always persisted, sometimes in a coaxing way, till we made him do so, which latterly he did, by saying, somewhat impatiently, "Well, what do you want?" when we immediately replied by asking, "How is old Chance?" I fear I have not been able to make the anecdote so amusing to my readers, as the little daily inquiry after the horse's welfare was to us. The words are often quoted by my sons; when, at cricket or any other game, I have made some lucky stroke, or have had some lucky escape, they to this day often exclaim, "How is old Chance?"

Lieut.-Colonel Beckwith, whom I have mentioned in my account of the Battle of Waterloo, dined with us one day in our large-mess marquee, in the neighbourhood of Denain, and kept the whole mess in roars of laughter, when talking over, with his old Peninsula friends, many of their adventures of former days. He was a great favourite in the light division.

******

Note:—He afterwards became a very religious man, and took a great interest in the Vaudois, amongst whom he lived for many years, and to whom he rendered many services, by his influence with the Sardinian Government.

******

We returned to Estréeblanche and Thérouenne, late in October, 1817, and I think I have nothing to recount of the ensuing winter and spring, which has not been already mentioned.

Early in June, 1818, we occupied our old encampment-ground to the south of St. Omer. Sir John Colborne joined us there, and I remember his telling me, he was glad to hear from Colonel Rowan, that I had not been idling away my time, during his absence from the regiment, but had been trying to improve myself. His establishment of horses was not complete, and someone mentioned that I had a horse to part with, which it was thought might suit him.

On the first day on which he appeared on parade, mounted on his new purchase, the horse behaved very well for a time. But on our forming square, and Sir John Colborne, who was on the outside, giving the word of command, "Prepare to receive cavalry," the horse bolted, and carried him off the common, and down the hill to his quarters a mile and a half away; and we saw no more of him till the next morning. His right arm had been disabled at Ciudad Rodrigo, and he had consequently no proper command of the horse.

About the middle of August, we marched to Valenciennes, and encamped on the glacis and in the ditch; one officer per company having to remain in camp, and the others being quartered in the town. In October the 52nd marched into the citadel. On the 23rd of October the army was reviewed by the Emperor of Russia, the King of Prussia, and their chief commanders, and I was left on guard in the horn work of the citadel, with some thirty or forty men, for eight-and-forty hours. I think there were no other troops in the town; I had some particular orders, but I forget now what they were, but no one was likely to endeavour to gain possession of a fortress, which, in less than a month, was to be handed over to the French. After the review the 52nd returned to the citadel, and held possession of it till the rest of the British Army had embarked.

The following came out in general orders, just as the army was breaking up:—

Cambrai, 10th November, 1818.
Upon the return to England of the troops which have so long served under the command of the field-marshal, he again returns his thanks for their uniform good conduct, during the period in which they have formed part of the Army of Occupation.

The field-marshal has in another order, addressed to the army of occupation at large, expressed his sentiments regarding the conduct of, and his obligation to, the general-officers and officers of that army. These are especially due to the general officers and officers of the British contingent, and he begs them to accept of his best acknowledgments, for the example they have given to others, by their own good conduct, and for the support and assistance they have invariably afforded him, to maintain the discipline of the army.

After a service of ten years' duration, almost without interruption, with the same officers and troops, the field-marshal separates from them with regret; but he trusts that they will believe that he will never cease to feel a concern for their honour and interest.

I think it desirable to insert here what the duke said of the British Army when leaving Spain and France in 1814. It is extracted from his evidence given before the royal commission for inquiring into military punishments:—

I always thought I could have gone anywhere, or done anything with that army. It was impossible to have a machine more highly mounted and in better order, and in a better state of discipline than that army was. When I quitted that army upon the Garonne, I do not think it was possible to see anything in a higher state of discipline; and I believe there was a total discontinuance of all punishment.

I do not know the exact order in which the British troops were withdrawn from France, or the exact time of the embarkation of each corps at Calais. Sir Robert Arbuthnot of the Guards, who was *commandant* of Valenciennes, left the place some little time before we did. I went to make some report to him one morning, and found him in his shirtsleeves, very hard at work packing some wine, which he was starting for England. Two or three hundred Sappers and Miners, with the Engineer officers, were the last troops to leave us. When they had fairly started, I recollect a passing thought of loneliness passed over my mind, at the idea of the 52nd being the only English regiment left in France.

The night before the Sappers left Valenciennes, the Engineer officers dined at our mess. I was president or vice-president, and I well remember having a very long and interesting conversation with the officer on my left, about the truth of the Christian religion. I was not very capable of arguing correctly on the subject, and I now wonder how I managed at all, in attempting to combat his sceptical ideas. He was quartered in the town, and I went with him to see him safely out of the citadel and over the esplanade into the first street. I never read the last sentence but one in Acts xii, 10, without thinking of him. When we were about to separate, I said, "I wonder when we two shall meet again?"

He replied "Perhaps in heaven." I understood, several years afterwards, that he had accompanied Mr. Owen, of Lanark, to America.

Colonel Hall has given me the following account of our giving over the town and citadel of Valenciennes to the French civil authorities, which I think we did on the 22nd of November, 1818:—

> The authorities wished to embody some of the National Guard to receive over the place, but Colborne would allow no Frenchmen in arms until we had quitted it. The regiment marched out, and halted on the glacis, leaving the main-guard under Clerke, in the Grande Place. When the citadel had been given over to the civil authorities, the town was also formally surrendered. Clerke and his guard joined us on the glacis, and we marched to Auberchicourt, a coaling village, for that night. Some hours

after we left Valenciennes, a French garrison of the line entered the town. I forget for what reason, Clerke returned to pass the night there. We heard from him that the town had been illuminated on the occasion of our departure. He remarked, either in lamps, or on a transparency, the words, 'The more we see of strangers, the more we like our own countrymen:' base, if only to curry favour with the new garrison; and ungrateful, if a true sentiment.

The English had been great benefactors to Valenciennes, and we never experienced the smallest symptom of dislike from the inhabitants. The tradesmen, I am sure, regretted us. A good woman who kept a shop of pastry and comestibles, seemed inconsolable at our departure. She made it known that she wished we would all come and take leave of her the day before we left, and help ourselves *gratis* to the best she had. So, we did all go in the course of the day, and ate some little thing to please her, of course without offering payment. The poor woman was sitting with her handkerchief to her eyes all day, in the greatest distress. This was something more than interested sorrow for the loss of custom.

The mention of the main-guard in the foregoing account reminds me that shortly before our departure from Valenciennes the Emperor of Russia slept there one night. We had notice that it was his intention to do so, and that he wished that no attention should be shewn to him beyond that of placing a couple of sentries at the gate of the house in which he took up his quarters, and, to supply these sentries, a few more men were sent to join the guard some little time before the Emperor (Alexander) was expected. I commanded the main-guard that day, and determined to give him a salute, if he did not pass through the Grande Place too quickly. Although the *Place* was rather crowded and noisy, (I think it was about eight o'clock at night on the market day,) and he passed along the other side of it, at a distance of about fifty yards from us, we managed to turn out and salute him in time.

He was travelling in an open *caleche*, drawn by four post horses, and had three other persons in the carriage with him, and two attendants on the seat behind. He did not at first, on account of the noise of the carriage and people, observe the salute, or hear the accompanying bugle sound; but I observed that one of the officers with him pointed out the guard to him, when he immediately acknowledged the salute in the usual foreign style, by placing the two first fingers of his right hand against the forward point of his cocked hat. Soon after the emperor's arrival, Sir John Colborne saw General Winzingerode for a minute or two to see if the arrangement made was what was desired, and I visited the sentries as a part of my guard. The emperor went away early, having left a small but handsome sum of money to be given to those who had been actually sentries at his house.

We made seven days' march from Valenciennes to Calais. I think it was after we had halted on the third day, that I heard Sir John Colborne telling someone that he was just going to write to the *commandant* of St. Omer to request that the regiment, or a portion of it might, when it arrived in his district, be quartered within the *territoires de la place*, so as to avoid the fatigue and annoyance to the men of being taken two or three miles from the line of march to the several villages from which they would have to return the same distance the next morning.

On the 26th I was ordered to go forward to see that proper arrangements had been made with respect to the quarters, and found that no orders had been given that we should be quartered within the territories, but that the old plan was adhered to, which involved much additional fatigue to the men; I therefore took upon myself to ride into St. Omer, and to see the *commandant*. (I could not recognise him as our fox-hunting friend.) I told him that I came on the part of the Chevalier Colborne, who, I understood, had written to him to request that he would allow the regiment, or a portion of it, to be quartered for the night within the *territoires de la place*. He said he had not received any letter from Colborne, but immediately granted the permission requested, and issued the necessary orders.

When I reached the column of march, I found that one or two companies had already branched off from the main road to occupy the distant quarters intended for them; they were greatly pleased when I quickly overtook them, and thus saved them some considerable extra fatigue, and Sir John Colborne was pleased with my having taken upon myself to call on the *commandant* of St. Omer.

We embarked at Calais on the afternoon of the 28th of November in about thirty small sailing craft, and reached England the next morning. There are some strange mistakes about some of these points in the 52nd record: it makes us to have been only five days on the march from Valenciennes to Calais, and three nights and two days between Calais and Dover. The wind was contrary, but there was not much of it till the next morning, and the night was tolerably clear. We had about half the company in the vessel in which I was with another officer. As each vessel of the flotilla sailed independently of the others, they soon got well separated; but as we tacked about, we occasionally came near enough to some of them to give them a hail.

With the help of the master's speaking-trumpet we contrived to give ourselves some considerable amusement, by keeping up a little talk with them in the following fashion. *Self*:—"What ship is that?" *Reply*:—"The *Harriet*, of Ramsgate." *Self*:—"What have you on board?" *Reply*;—"Troops." *Self*:—"What troops?" *Reply*:—"Part of captain's company, of the 52nd Light Infantry." *Self*:—"Ar'nt you ashamed of yourselves, you lubberly set of fellows?" In the morning the breeze freshened a good deal; almost all the vessels got into Ramsgate; two were on the Goodwin sands for some hours, and the one I was in, and another, put into Dover. Thus, the last portion of the Army of Occupation reached England on the 29th of November, 1818.

CHAPTER 19

Sundry Matters Connected with Waterloo, and with the 52nd at Waterloo

There are some further matters connected with Waterloo, and several of them connected with the 52nd at Waterloo, which I wish not to omit from this work, and to which I have determined to devote one of its concluding chapters. I must not, however, attempt to place them in any order.

Some months ago Professor Selwyn, of Cambridge, did me the favour to send me a copy of his beautiful poem entitled:—

WATERLOO: A Lay of Jubilee for June 18, a.d. 1815.

'It was a day of Giants.'—Wellington.

On the leaf before the title page, he had kindly written:—"To William Leeke, one of those who helped to win the victory of Waterloo, with the Author's grateful respects. Christmas, *A.D.* 1865."

I hope my readers will inquire for this poem. I can promise them great pleasure in its perusal. It occupies, with a few notes, about ninety quarto pages. One Waterloo officer, whom I know, and his wife were moved to tears as they read it. Professor Selwyn has sent it to every Waterloo officer whose address he could discover. He says he has followed Captain Siborne's account of the history of the battle, and consequently he has, as a matter of course, been led into the two mistakes—of the 1st Guards having defeated a first column of the Imperial Guard of France, and of the 52nd having been accompanied by the other regiments of Adam's brigade when they defeated the two columns of the Guard, and also when they subsequently drove off the rear-guard of the enemy.

The whole work is full of heart-stirring passages, which may help to prove that martial ardour and the love of daring deeds burn not alone in the breasts of those who have chosen arms as their profession.

In a letter from Mr. W. Crawley Yonge, I find the following eulogy of the staff-officers of the British Army by Lord Seaton, who, contrasting them with the staff of the general officers of one of the foreign armies, of which an officer of high rank had just been speaking in terms of disapprobation, observed, "What a contrast to our service, when, with so much less pretence at order, there is so much more reality;" and he added:—

> That he could do our staff-officers the justice to say he had never seen an occasion when there was the same want that had been described—that there never was a moment of hesitation, always a readiness to carry orders, whenever a communication might be wanted, into the hottest fire.

Mr. Yonge relates with much feeling the following instance of quiet, unpretending heroism of an old corporal of the company in which he and I were:—

> He appeared to be quite worn out and ill, and suffered greatly from fatigue in the long march before Waterloo, and McNair pressed him to go to the rear, considering that he was not at all equal to another day's work; but he refused, saying, in the quietest manner, that, having gone through a good deal of service with the regiment, he would rather not leave it on the eve of an action—he was sure it would be his last, but he thought he should be able to keep up during the day, and so he did, but he went into hospital directly after, and from thence was invalided, so that we never saw him again.

Little more than six months before his death in 1854, my poor friend Yonge visited the field of Waterloo. In a letter to Bentham he mentions that:—

> In order to make the Belgic mound, which was formed on the crest of the British position, not far from the left of the 52nd when in line, about 800 yards of round, extending along the crest of the position from the Charleroi road to the back of Hougomont, had been scooped out, fifty yards wide and seven feet deep......It is very grievous, for perhaps no other so effectual a mode could have been devised for mutilating so interesting an historical record, as the place itself would otherwise have always afforded.

One of the guides told him, that in trenching the ground on the ridge a little deeper than usual, the bones of poor Nettles had been turned up. They were recognised by the 52nd officer's buttons, and the man said, it was evident, from his appearance, that he had been buried just as he fell; the spot he pointed out tallied very well.

The following most confused account of the defeat of the Imperial Guard at Waterloo, was given by Count Drouot, *Aide* Major-General of the Imperial Guard, in the Chamber of Peers, at Paris, on the 24th of June, 1815, only six days after the action. It is translated from *The Moniteur:*—

> The emperor regards this moment as decisive, he brings forward all his Guard: orders four battalions to pass near the village of Mont St. Jean, to advance upon the enemy's position, and to carry with the bayonet whatever should resist them. The cavalry of the Guard, and all the other cavalry at hand, seconded the movement. The four battalions, when they arrived upon the plateau, were received by the most terrible fire of musketry and grape. The great number of wounded who separated from the columns, make it believed that the Guard is routed. A panic-terror communicates itself to the neighbouring corps which precipitately take flight. The enemy's cavalry, which perceives this disorder, is let loose into the plain. It is checked for some time by the twelve battalions of the Old Guard, who had not yet charged, but even these troops were carried away by the inexplicable movement, and follow the steps of the fugitives, but with more order.

✶✶✶✶✶✶

I must make a few remarks on this speech of Drouot's. In the first place he probably means La Haye Sainte, and not Mont St. Jean; La Haye Sainte is called Mont St. Jean in the French official account. The thought has only just struck me, whilst I am writing this, "Is it possible that Drouot is correct in stating that four battalions of the Guard did, according to the emperor's order, advance towards the British position along the western side of the enclosures of La Haye Sainte, and could these be the four battalions seen by us, who remained steady with ordered arms, 300 or 400 yards up the British position on our left, close to the enclosures of La Haye Sainte, when the whole of the rest of the French Army had given way? If so, Drouot was misinformed, and does them very great injustice. The 52nd never saw or encountered any but about twelve battalions of the Guard, and those they defeated single-handed. These twelve battalions of the Guard were the first that gave way, and then the whole army fled, with the exception of four battalions close to La Haye Sainte, who may have been Germans. I wonder whether Siborne took from Drouot his idea of a first column of four battalions of the French Guard having been defeated by the 1st British Guards!

We know, however, from the Guards themselves, and from other sources, that the right battalion of Maitland's brigade of Guards was stationary when the mass of skirmishers of the Imperial Guard, and from Donzelôt's division, were driven in by the left battalion of the brigade, and when we saw the Imperial Guard skirmishers run down the position, and form about 100 yards in front of their leading column, at the time that the 3rd, the left battalion of the 1st Guards, retired to the rear of the British position in some confusion, where they were seen by Vivian's Hussar Brigade.

The Guards do not claim, (although Siborne, and many who have copied him, claim it for them,) that the 2nd, the right battalion of the brigade of Guards, joined in any attack upon the French Infantry at Waterloo, excepting always their light company, which, nearly up to that time, had been engaged with the light company of the other battalion in helping to defend Hougomont. The 2nd battalion was stationary, and the 3rd only made the one advance and attack before spoken of.

✶✶✶✶✶✶

It is very difficult to avoid repetition in speaking of the various mistakes which both English and French writers have fallen into in describing these events, but I will avoid it, as much as possible, in the few additional remarks which I wish to make on the subject of the defeat of the French Imperial Guard.

The more I think of it the more it appears possible, that the four battalions we saw up to our left when the 52nd were nearing the Charleroi road, were the four battalions of the Imperial Guard, spoken of by Drouot. If they quietly advanced along the outside of the western enclosure of La Haye Sainte to strengthen Donzelôt, and to be prepared, with his division, to attempt to penetrate the British line of battle in advance of that post, at the same time that the two heavier columns should attack our line, 400 yards away in the direction of Hougomont, they would have arrived at the spot where we saw the four battalions (with ordered arms and facing towards the French position) about the time that the two heavy columns, always computed at 10,000 men, gave way before the charge of the 52nd.

One difficulty in this theory is, that these four battalions, if French, should not have taken to their heels at the same time that the rest of the French Army fled. But then, as they were at the distance of 400 or 500 yards from the British position, there was no cause for any immediate panic, and, if they were battalions of the Guard, their *esprit de corps* especially if they had confidence in their principal officers, might be expected to lead to the steadiness so manifested in them. When the 52nd passed near to the lower corner of the La Haye Sainte enclosure it was fully 800 yards distant from any part of the British position, and these columns were 300 or 400 yards above them.

I saw them most distinctly, they certainly were not English, from their uniform, nor were they likely to be Germans. What should keep them there, 400 yards or more from the British position, if they were either? And would they be likely to be there, when Donzelôt's division, which had been harassing Alten's troops for two or three hours at least, could not have left the spot more than ten or, at the most, fifteen minutes before? If they were our Allies, why did they not come to our help, when they saw a regiment in red all alone, and must have seen the squares of the Old Guard only 200 or 300 yards in a direct line beyond us? And one may say again—If they were French, why did not these four battalions (notwithstanding that they had seen the flight of the Imperial Guard, and of the whole of the French troops) rattle down upon the left flank of the 52nd, and try to help their friends of the Old Guard to cover the retreat of their army.

I cannot conceive that any English general, commanding four steady battalions, would have missed such an opportunity as that which here presented itself, either of advancing to the assistance, or to the attack, of a regiment circumstanced as the 52nd was. But I may inquire, who but Colborne would have ventured on, and would have carried to such a successful issue, such a feat of daring as was the whole of his advance from the time that he first moved his regiment down the British position to attack the heavy columns of the Imperial Guard, till he brought it across the Charleroi road and led it onward, and up the French position, against the last remaining troops that made a stand—

the renowned Imperial Guard, the Old Guard, of France?

But Colborne knew his men, and they knew him, and knew each other, and all had confidence in each other! But I must forbear, and apologise for having allowed myself to be so carried away by my *esprit de corps*. My only excuse is, that I should have done just the same, had I belonged to any other gallant regiment which had so distinguished itself. I must however add one word more. Is it not common justice, that, if matters happened as I have related them, Lord Seaton and the 52nd should no longer be deprived of the credit and honour which are their due? "Should not those, who won the laurels, wear them?"

But to return for a moment to those four battalions, which we saw standing, with ordered arms, close to the western enclosure of Hougomont, I would just say, that I think they must have been a French brigade of Donzelôt's division, or possibly of the Imperial Guard, waiting, as I said before, after they had seen the flight of the heavy columns of their Guard and indeed of the whole French Army, and the daring advance and attitude of the 52nd, to see how they could quietly get away, without having to lay down their arms; which by the way, as they were not disposed to try their strength with us, was perhaps the wisest thing they could have done.

****

Drouot, in his speech six days after the battle, although his account is most inaccurate with regard to details, speaks of the emperor ordering *four* battalions of the Imperial Guard to advance towards the British position, and then he speaks of the advance of an additional body of troops consisting of *twelve* battalions of the Old Guard, making out that there were altogether sixteen battalions of the Guard engaged in the last attack.

Baron Muffling, the Prussian Commissioner, who was with the British Army during the battle, says, in his *History of the Campaign of 1815:*—

> The enemy's Guards began to move and with sixteen battalions at half-past six o'clock advanced towards the platform. (Muffling makes a terrible mistake with regard to the time, which was very much later.)

Marshal Ney, in his letter to the Duke of Otranto, dated Paris, June 26th, 1815, says:—

> A short time afterwards I saw four *regiments (i.e. eight battalions)* of the Middle Guard arriving, conducted by the emperor him-

self... He ordered me to lead them on.

He speaks afterwards of "four squares of the Old Guard, who protected the retreat."

"A French eye-witness" states that the emperor's column of attack "was almost entirely composed of the Old Guard."

It will be seen from all these accounts that the 52nd officers, in addition to their own calculation that the two heavy columns of the French Guard, which they defeated, amounted to about 10,000 men, have the testimony of the earliest French accounts, to shew that more than that number of the French Imperial Guard were in that part of the field, and were engaged at, what has been very properly called by Colonel Gawler, Lord Seaton, and numbers of other gallant and experienced officers, "the crisis of Waterloo."

The mistakes which have been previously mentioned, which Captain Siborne first fell into, and which the French writers were only too glad to follow, and which so many English historians have adopted, were, that there were two columns of the Imperial Guard, which separately advanced to make the last attack; that the first was charged and defeated by Maitland's brigade of Guards, and that the second was defeated by a flank attack of Adam's brigade, consisting of the 52nd, 71st, and the 2nd and 3rd battalions of the 95th Rifles, Maitland's brigade attacking them at the same time in front; and it has been further asserted that both these columns reached the summit of the British position.

I assert that all this is entirely incorrect, and that:

1. The two columns were seen by the 52nd in close proximity, as shewn in Plan 2 of this work, the head of the rear column being within thirty paces of that which preceded it.

2. That the head of the leading column was 300 or 400 yards below the crest of the British position.

3. That not a man of these columns advanced a single step towards the British position after they were fired into by the 52nd skirmishers.

4. That no other troops but the 52nd attacked, fired into, charged, and defeated these columns.

5. That we, who were in the left centre of the 52nd, distinctly saw the skirmishers of the Imperial Guard run down from that part of the British position occupied by Maitland's Guards, and form in front of the leading battalion of the Imperial Guard columns just as the 52nd four-deep line was nearly parallel to the left flank of the leading column, as shewn in Plan 2.

6. That when the 3rd battalion of Maitland's 1st Guards were lying down in square, some distance on the reverse slope of the British position, and were suffering from the fire of a mass of skirmishers of the Imperial Guard, (it is said also that a number of skirmishers from Donzelôt's division joined them,) the Duke of Wellington desired the commanding officer of that battalion to "form line on the front face of the square, and drive those fellows in." That this was immediately done; that the 3rd battalion fired into them, killing and wounding numbers of them, and that they then charged and drove them off the crest of the position, and followed them a short distance down the slope; that then there was a cry of "cavalry," and that some attempting to form square, whilst others had not heard any command to do so, the battalion got into some confusion, and retired in disorder over, and some distance beyond, the crest of the British position, where they halted, and recovered their order.

7. That this was the only forward movement against the enemy made by the 3rd battalion of the 1st Guards at Waterloo.

8. That the 2nd, that is the right battalion of the 1st Guards did not join the 3rd battalion in this movement against the Imperial Guard skirmishers, nor did they make any other forward movement against infantry at Waterloo; and that they were at this time "stationary and not firing."

9. That when the skirmishers of the Imperial Guard were forming in front of their leading column, the 3rd battalion of the 1st Guards must have just re-crossed the British position, as there was a clear view of the ground from the 52nd left centre for 300 yards above the leading company of the Imperial Guard columns, and no troops were visible.

10. That it was a great mistake which my friend and relative Gawler made, when he assumed that the leading column of the Imperial Guard reached the crest of the British position in front of the 1st Guards, because the dead bodies of Imperial Guardsmen were found lying there the next morning. He did not reflect, when making the statement, that they might be only the dead bodies of skirmishers, but he had no idea of admitting the 1st Guards to a share of the honour of defeating the Imperial Guard. Colonel Gawler was on the extreme right of the 52nd when they advanced from the position, and brought

their right shoulders forward, so as to take the Imperial Guard in flank, and consequently he was at a distance from, and, as he states, "did not see the front of the Imperial column."

Hence the *mistake*, which has probably helped to lead Siborne and others into the idea that, if the headmost companies of the Imperial Guard reached the crest of our position in front of Maitland's brigade, it was probable that that brigade should have had a hand in defeating them, particularly when the 1st Guards, and also Sir Colin Halkett's brigade, spoke of having been opposed to troops wearing the bear-skin caps of the French Imperial Guard.

Siborne's correspondent might well remark, that:—

> If ever truth lies at the bottom of a well, she does so immediately after a great battle, and it takes an amazingly long time before she can be lugged out.

I am endeavouring to lug out some of the truth, respecting the defeat of the Imperial Guard at Waterloo, from the mass of conflicting statements under which it has remained encumbered, if not altogether buried, for so long a period.

There are, as might be expected, many and varied difficulties in the way of arriving at the truth in this matter; one of the chief of which, has been mentioned before, namely, that of the impossibility which some officers find to distinguish, after the lapse of many years, between what they recollect to have seen, and what they have read of, or have heard from others.

One difficulty, which the 52nd laboured under for years, when individuals amongst them were anxious to substantiate their claim to the full honour due to them for having defeated, single-handed, the heavy columns of the French Guard, arose from their not being able to make out what the 1st Guards really did at Waterloo beyond their having, in common with a great portion of the right wing of the British and Allied Army, received and beaten off, in good style, several charges made by strong masses of the French Cavalry.

Immediately on our arrival at Paris, we knew what Lord Hill had said about the Guards being "stationary and not firing," (he was on the right of the Brigade of Guards,) and we knew Sir John Byng had told Sir John Colborne that he could not bring the Guards forward when the 52nd advanced, because all their ammunition was gone, (rather a lame reason, by the way, for which the 1st Guards would not thank him,) and knowing also that we had, far away from the British position, defeated, in the lower ground, two columns of the Imperial Guard, containing about 10,000 men, we could not at all reconcile matters.

Sir John Byng probably only referred to the 2nd (the right battalion of the Guards), and possibly knew nothing of the 3rd battalion having been ordered by the duke to "drive those fellows off" the position.

Lord Seaton, in writing to Colonel Bentham, as late as October, 1853 says:—

> I suppose the Guards must have made some forward movement, and that many officers must have seen it; but I contend that the French column had been checked and thrown into disorder before the Guards moved. I saw the column of the Imperial Guard steadily advancing to a certain point, and I observed them halt, which was *precisely* as the skirmishers of the 52nd opened fire on their flank.

I think it well to mention here further observations of Lord Seaton's:—

> The whole of the Imperial Guard advanced at the same time, and their flank was first attacked before any forward movement was made to check them in front. The Prussians could not have attracted the attention of the French, so as to cause the throwing back of their right wing, until after the Imperial Guard had commenced their attack on our centre ... No regiment except the 52nd fired on the flank of the Imperial Guard.

Let me request my readers to look at the letter of Sir Thomas Reynell, who commanded the 71st, (the right regiment of our brigade,) at Waterloo, and say if, after reading that, and after considering also what Lord Seaton has written on the subject, they can come to any other conclusion than this: that the whole of the Imperial Guard advanced at the same time, as Lord Seaton declares, that neither of the two heavy columns of the Imperial Guard reached the summit of the British position, but that they were both defeated at "the bottom of the declivity," as Sir Thomas Reynell terms it, by the 52nd alone?

In bringing this subject to a close, I must beg leave to observe that it is very evident to me that none should venture to become historians of battles, but those who have been present at, and have seen some considerable portion of, the events which they profess to relate.

None but those who, like myself, have some considerable acquaintance with the various movements and incidents which most of the writers on Waterloo profess to relate, and even to give in detail, and which they often give in beautiful and heart-stirring language, can have any idea of the amount of annoyance and disgust I have experienced in reading so many relations and details which I know to be utterly untrue.

My belief in the truth of history in general has been most rudely shaken and almost destroyed by reading, in Siborne's account of Waterloo, and in the accounts of others, many statements respecting the 52nd and other regiments, which have no foundation in truth whatever as regards the regiments with which the writers endeavour to connect the movements, or incidents, or exploits, which they record. I do not intend to accuse any of these historians of wilfully mis-stating facts; but the varied information as to events and time which they receive from different persons was sure to lead them into all kinds of error, particularly when they are endeavouring to reconcile, in the best manner they can, these often very contradictory statements.

Possibly it might be a good plan to appoint several officers in each regiment whose especial business it should be to chronicle its proceedings, and more especially when it is on active service. The want of a regularly kept document recording the services of the 52nd, was much felt by different officers who were requested to undertake to write the "Record" of the regiment. The details of circumstances, written down nearly at the time that they occurred, are, of course, more to be depended upon than those recollected many years afterwards. I believe that in a naval action, all the principal events are regularly entered in the ship's log, and why should there not be something of the same sort in the army?

It appears to be the practice in the British Army that, after a general action, only the officers in command of corps, divisions, and brigades, should send in reports for the commander-in-chief. The 52nd was in Sir Frederick Adam's brigade, and his brigade was in Sir Henry Clinton's (the 2nd) division, and the 2nd division was in Lord Hill's corps; so in the tenth volume of the supplementary despatches of the Duke of Wellington, edited by his son, we have a report from Lord Hill to the duke, enclosing Clinton's report of the proceedings of his division, and he again encloses General Adam's report of his brigade, mentioning it at the close of his report as follows:—

I beg, too, that Your Lordship, in making your report to the commander of the forces, will have the enclosed letter from Major-General Adam laid before His Grace.

The italics are mine. I would observe that it is a great pity General Adam's letter or report is not given in this volume of the despatches. He was the only general officer who was engaged in the attack and defeat of the Imperial Guard, and it is most probable that his report contained a correct account of its defeat by the 52nd alone. In the following passage Sir H. Clinton refers, I think, to Adam's brigade, when it was posted in squares to the left of Hougomont, from four o'clock till half-past six:—

> It then fell to the share of General Adam's brigade to take its share of the same honourable service. The manner in which the several regiments—the 52nd, under Colonel Sir John Colborne; the 71st, under Colonel Reynell; and the 2nd and 3rd 95th, under Lieut.-Colonels Norcott and Ross—discharged their duty was witnessed and admired by the whole army.

Sir H. Clinton afterwards says:—

> When the handsome repulse of the enemy's last attack afforded the opportunity to become ourselves the attacking body, so judiciously taken advantage of by Major-General Adam's brigade, under Your Lordship's immediate direction, I directed Colonel Halkett to reinforce the attacking line with the Osnabrück battalion.

Clinton says, also, that the Osnabrück regiment "drove the enemy from four guns on the right of the Genappe (*i.e.,* the Charleroi) road," and that, "during its advance they got possession of two pairs of colours;" but he omitted to mention—probably he had not heard of it—that Halkett took the French general (Cambronne) prisoner with his own hands.

Sir Thomas Picton's division, which was posted on the left centre of the British position, and to the left of the Charleroi road, consisted of Sir James Kempt's brigade, containing the first battalions of the 28th, 32nd, 79th Highlanders, and 95th Rifles, and of Sir Denis Pack's brigade, containing a battalion of each of the following regiments:— The 1st, 42nd Highlanders, 44th, and 92nd Highlanders; Colonel von Vincke's 5th Hanoverian brigade also formed part of Picton's division, the command of which, after Sir Thomas Picton's death in the early part of the action, devolved on Major-General Sir James Kempt. I copy the following extracts from his report to the Duke of Wellington, as they give a concise account of one of the most glorious events of the day:—

Bivouac, near Genappe, 19th June, 1815.
In consequence of the lamented fall of Lieut.-General Sir Thomas Picton, (who was unfortunately killed early in the battle of yesterday, at a very critical moment, while nobly animating the troops,) the command of the 5th division, and the troops which had been placed under his orders, devolved upon me, and it is quite impossible for me to convey, by words, to Your Grace the feelings of admiration with which I beheld the invincible spirit displayed by the British troops in repulsing every attack which was made upon the position where I had the honour to command. The troops were formed in two lines, supported by Major-General the Hon. Sir W. Ponsonby's brigade of cavalry. (The 1st Royals; 2nd Scots Greys; and 4th Inniskillings.)

The first line was composed of Dutch and Belgian troops, with the 1st battalion of the 95th Regiment, under Sir Andrew Barnard, posted on a knoll on the right. The second line was composed of the 8th and 9th brigades of infantry, under Major-General Sir Denis Pack and myself, and the 4th and 5th Hanoverian brigade of militia, commanded by Colonels Vincke and Best. The enemy having concealed his attack till the last moment, advanced rapidly in three immense columns of infantry, covered by 30 pieces of artillery, directing their heads on the right, centre, and left of the position to the left of the *chaussée*.

Our first line, acting as light troops, gave way as the columns approached; but the 8th and 9th brigades of infantry instantly advanced, and charged the heads of the columns just as they had gained the crest of the position: a struggle of a few moments ensued, but the invincible spirit and determination of the British troops were such, that these immense masses, directed with the greatest fury, were absolutely put to flight by two British brigades, weakened as they had been most materially by the severe action which they had fought two days before. Major-General the Hon. Sir W. Ponsonby instantly availed himself of this, and charged in the most gallant manner at the head of his brigade. Many prisoners were taken, and three eagles.

(I suspect that the three regiments of kilted Highlanders, in these two brigades, astonished the French in no slight degree. W. Leeke.)

Shortly after this handsome repulse of the French attack, Lambert's 10th British brigade was sent to strengthen these troops, and those on the other side of the *chaussée*, who were very much harassed by Donzelôt's French division, and by other troops, who were allowed to maintain themselves in the immediate neighbourhood, and to their left of La Haye Sainte, the whole afternoon, and up to eight o'clock, when the Imperial Guard was defeated by the 52nd. The French, as has been mentioned, took La Haye Sainte at six o'clock: the troops in their front suffered most severely, and the 27th Regiment, of Lambert's brigade, which, Kempt says, was unavoidably exposed more than the other troops, lost an immense number of men.

I see by the returns that, out of 18 officers present, they lost 14 killed or wounded, and, out of 698 rank and file, they lost 96 killed and 348 wounded; making a total of 444 killed and wounded, out of a total of 698 rank and file present; and to these 444 may be added 34 officers, serjeants, and drummers; making the whole amount of killed and wounded in the regiment to be 478. This gallant regiment must have suffered an immensely greater loss than was experienced by any other regiment at Waterloo.

The ground occupied and passed over by the 52nd at Waterloo, gave to its officers peculiar advantages for observing many of the principal events which happened during the latter part of the action, from four o'clock in the afternoon till a quarter past nine in the evening.

A reference to the three plans will assist the reader in understanding those leading points of the close and crisis of Waterloo, which I have endeavoured faithfully to describe.

It will be seen, by referring to Plan 1, that from twelve o'clock to 3.30 the 52nd was in reserve a quarter of a mile in front of the village of Merbe Braine, and that they then moved a quarter of a mile to their left and formed square; this was just at the time that the first great charge of the French cavalry took place, and the 52nd saw them scouring the British position and driving the artillerymen from our guns. The 52nd then moved *in square* over the position, and descended it a short distance, to within 150 yards of the northern enclosure of Hougoumont, where it halted on the narrow cross road to La Belle Alliance and formed squares of wings, which proceeded immediately to take up their forward positions between the 71st and 2nd 95th;

here they remained between two and three hours, when they were ordered to retire over the British position, which they reached about seven o'clock, and having formed a four-deep line by closing the left wing up upon the right wing, they remained in that position (shewn on Plan 2 by a short dotted line) for about an hour.

Here the regiment could see nothing of the field of battle, being forty yards below the crest on the reverse slope of the position; but during the whole of that period their commanding officer, Sir John Colborne, sat on his horse, partly covered by a bank two feet and a half high, with an excellent view of the whole of the ground between him and La Belle Alliance, watching the formation of the columns of the Imperial Guard, and their subsequent advance in the direction of the right centre of the British line. He appeared to have his eye on them the whole time, as he himself states was the case, except when the officer of *cuirassiers* rode down the bank and spoke to him, and when, afterwards, the Duke of Wellington rode across our front from the left, and conversed with him for a few minutes, as they both sat on their horses partly covered by the low bank.

At about eight o'clock Sir John Colborne moved the 52nd over the position, and, passing the brigade of guns immediately in their front, they saw, away in the direction of La Belle Alliance, the two heavy columns of the Imperial Guard. The 52nd line did not march straight on these columns, but proceeded some distance down the slope, nearly straight to its front, and then the whole line brought its right shoulders rapidly forwarded, and, about ten minutes after eight, it must have been on the flank of the leading column of the Imperial Guard, as shewn in Plan 2. We saw the Imperial Guard skirmishers run in and form in front of the column. The 52nd did not halt, but advanced firing. The French returned the fire, and the 52nd lost there about 140 men, killed and wounded, in the course of five or six minutes.

They saw the whole French Army run in utter confusion, and advanced, as I have before described it, over the masses of the killed and wounded; they were then charged by a mixed body of cavalry. Some French guns fired grape into, and made some havoc in, our advancing line; then some Prussian or French round-shot struck near the centre of the line, and, immediately after, Sir John Colborne halted the regiment in the low ground, below the enclosures of La Haye Sainte, close upon the Charleroi road, as shewn in Plan 3, for the purpose of dressing the line. Some of the Old Guard here made a stand, and opened fire upon us. Lord Uxbridge was wounded. The colour and covering-serjeants were called out and dressed by Nixon, the acting adjutant, but the line was not dressed, for the duke rode up at the moment and told Sir John Colborne to "go on, and not give them time to rally."

The 52nd advanced to its left of the Charleroi road and of La Belle Alliance, in pursuit of one of the squares, and, after passing through a French column in the hollow road beyond Primotion, who surrendered, they advanced to the farm of Rosomme, three quarters of a mile beyond La Belle Alliance, and there halted for the night, on the very spot on which the Imperial Guard had bivouacked the night before.

There was something interesting in the fact, that the 52nd and the Imperial Guard of France were both in reserve in the early part of the Battle of Waterloo, and about as far distant from each other as they well could be—the one being near Merbe Braine, the other at Rosomme—and that, after the battle had raged for seven hours, they should meet in the centre of the field, between the two positions and the two armies, and there decide the fate of the day.

I have always attributed, in some measure, my very clear recollection of the movements of the 52nd at Waterloo, and of so many of the circumstances which occurred at that time, to the fact of its being the only action I was ever in, and that I had no recollections of other battles, as my chief companions, Mc Nair, Hall, Holman, and Yonge had, to interfere with my recollections of Waterloo. Very often when dining and spending the evenings together at Estréeblanche, in our cantonments in the north of France, did they talk over their Peninsular battles and campaigns, and, when Waterloo took its turn, I recollect that I well made up for my only having been a listener to their interesting Peninsular accounts, by taking more than my full share of the discussions which took place with regard to all its remarkable and ever-changing incidents.

I just wish to mention, before I leave the subject of Waterloo, that General Gneisenau, who wrote, by Blücher's order, the Prussian account of their actions on the 16th, 17th, and 18th of June, confirms that the Duke of Wellington and Blücher met, after the battle, at La Belle Alliance. He writes, speaking of La Belle Alliance:—

> It was there also that, by a happy chance, Field-Marshal Blücher and Lord Wellington met in the dark, and saluted each other as conquerors.

CHAPTER 20

The Appendices

No 1.

Taken from the "Gentleman's Magazine" for December, 1810.

"Lieut. Samuel Leeke was the eldest son of the late Samuel Leeke, Esq., of Havant. A fleet of the enemy's armed vessels were discovered entering Puerto Santa Maria, near Cadiz, November 2nd, 1810, and a signal was made for the British gun-vessels to attack. Lieut. Leeke commanded one of them, and most gallantly led the way into the centre of the enemy's fleet.

"This example of bravery proved fatal to him, he being wounded by a musket-ball, which soon occasioned his death, and deprived his friends of a beloved, good young man, and his country of a valuable officer, whose good conduct ever secured to him the approbation of his superiors in rank, and whose past actions gave great hopes of a brilliant career in the profession he had chosen. He had just completed his twenty-first year. To have been thus early cut off, is the source of great affliction to his mother and family. To alleviate in some measure their distress, and as a memorial of Lieut. Leeke's bravery, his next brother has been promoted to the rank of lieutenant."

Mr. Yorke, the First Lord of the Admiralty, when he heard of his gallant conduct and death, said that, had he survived, he should have been made a commander at once.

No. 2

Death of Captain Bogue at Leipsig.

Letter of Mr James, (son of Sir Walter James, Bart.,) *Aide-de-camp* to General Sir ('has. Stewart, K.B., to John Hanson, Esq., communicating the melancholy particulars of Captain Bogue's death.

"Dear Sir,

"A duty most melancholy in its nature, and peculiarly painful to myself, has devolved on me, in making you acquainted with the death of Captain Bogue, which melancholy event happened on the 18th of October, in the victory gained by the Allies over the French in the neighbourhood of Leipsig.

"Out of respect to the feelings, and for the sake of the family of Captain Bogue, I have to regret that this melancholy task has not fallen to the lot of one, who, in entering into the mournful particulars, would be better able than I am, to shew in the strongest light those drops of consolation that are most undoubtedly to be derived from an exit the most honourable—even the most glorious. But, if the afflictions of relatives, and the regret of friends, are to be soothed by the reflection that a duty has been honourably performed, by the conviction that every act of posthumous justice must be rendered to those exertions which contributed in no slight degree to the success of that memorable day, then are the friends of Captain Bogue in possession of a consolation so often wanted in similar events.

"The Rocket Brigade, under the command of Captain Bogue, had been attached, in its general movements, to the body-guard of the Crown Prince of Sweden, under the command of Count Lievitson, with, however, the understanding, that on days of action it was to be more at liberty than that corps, and subjected only to the direction of Captain Bogue. Conformably with this arrangement, at the commencement of the action on the morning of the 18th, Captain Bogue addressed himself to General Winzingerode, commanding the advance of the crown prince, expressing his desire to see the enemy, with permission to engage. The general, struck with the gallantly and spirit of the address, granted, as guard, a squadron of dragoons, and requested Captain Bogue to follow his own plans and judgment.

"Captain Bogue lost no time in approaching to the attack of the village of Pounsdorf, then in the possession of live enemy's battalions; upon whom he opened, in advance of the whole, a most destructive fire. This was returned by musketry, and for some time a very hot combat ensued; when the enemy, unable to withstand the well-directed fire of Captain Bogue's brigade, fell into confusion, and began to retreat. Captain Bogue, seizing this moment, charged at the head of the squadron of cavalry; and the enemy, terrified at his approach, turned round, and taking off their caps, gave three huzzas; and every man, to the number of between two and three thousand, surrendered to the Rocket Brigade, not, I believe, exceeding 200 men.

"The intelligence of this success being communicated to the crown prince, he sent his thanks to Captain Bogue for such eminent services, requesting at the same time that he would continue his exertions; and the brigade proceeded, in consequence, to the attack of (I believe) the village of Sommerfeldt, still further in advance. Sir C. Steward accompanied the brigade, and I was of the party. The situation taken up on the flank of the village was exposed to a most heavy fire, both of cannon-balls and grape-shot from the enemy's line, and from the riflemen in the village. A ball from the latter soon deprived us of the exertions of poor Bogue; it entered below the eye, and, passing through the head, caused instantaneous death.

"You will see, I am sure, how impossible it is for me to say anything that can do justice to such actions. I had long been happy in the acquaintance and friendship of Captain Bogue; and no one, I am sure, more sincerely than I do, regrets the loss of a friend and a man whom I was most proud to have it in my power to call a brother-soldier. It remains for me to tell you, that the body was found a few hours afterwards; and decently interred the next morning, at the town of Jaucha, about two miles from Leipsig, all the brigade attending, with the deepest regret, the melancholy ceremony.

"With regard to the horses and effects of Captain Bogue, I hope you will have the frankness to make me, without ceremony, the instrument, on my return, for putting into execution any arrangements you may desire.

"I trust the sufferings of Mrs. Bogue are not so severe as you feared they would be. May I request to have my respects presented to her, and believe me, etc, etc.,

"John James."

No. 3

All that was intended to be said in this number of the Appendix, has been long ago anticipated.—See Chapter 14

No. 4

Lieutenant-Colonel Ponsonby, of the 12th Light Dragoons, gives the following account of himself on being wounded. He says:—

"In the *mêlée* (thick of the fight) I was almost instantly disabled in both my arms, losing first my sword, and then my rein; and, followed by a few of my men, who were presently cut down, no quarter being asked or given, I was carried along by my horse, till, receiving a blow from a sabre, I fell senseless on my face to the ground. Recovering, I raised myself a little to look around, being at that time in a condition to get up and run away, when a lancer passing by, cried out, '*Tu n'est pas mort, coquin!*' and struck his lance through my back. My head dropped, the blood gushed into my mouth, a difficulty of breathing came on, and I thought all was over. Not long after, a skirmisher stopped to plunder me, threatening my life: I directed him to a small side-pocket, in which he found three dollars, all I had; but he continued to threaten, tearing open my waistcoat, and leaving me in a very uneasy posture.

"But he was no sooner gone, than an officer bringing up some troops, and happening to halt where I lay, stooped down, and addressing me, said, he feared I was badly wounded. I answered that I was, and expressed a wish to be moved to the rear. He said, it was against orders to remove even their own men; but that if they gained the day, (and he understood that the Duke of Wellington was killed, and that six of our battalions had surrendered,) every attention in his power should be shown me. I complained of thirst, and he held his brandy bottle to my lips, directing one of his soldiers to lay me straight on my side, and place a knapsack under my head; they then passed on into action, soon perhaps to want, though not to receive, the same assistance; and I shall never know to whose generosity I was indebted, as I believe, for my life.

"By and by, another skirmisher came up, a fine young man, full of ardour, loading and firing; he knelt down and fired over me many times, conversing with me very gaily all the while; at last he ran off, saying:'*Vous serez bien aise d'apprendre que nous allons nous retirer. Bonjour mon ami!*' ('You will be pleased to learn that we are going to fall back. Good day, my friend!')

"It was dusk, when two squadrons of Prussian cavalry crossed the valley in full trot, lifting me from the ground, and tumbling me about cruelly.

"The battle was now over, and the groans of the wounded all around me became more and more audible. I thought the night would never end. About this time, I found a soldier lying across my legs, and his weight, his convulsive motions, his noises, and the air issuing through a wound in his side, distressed me greatly; the last circumstance most of all, as I had a wound of the same nature myself. It was not a dark night, and the Prussians were wandering about to plunder:

many of them stopped to look at me as they passed; at last one of them stopped to examine me; I told him that I was a British officer, and had been already plundered. He did not however desist, and pulled me about roughly.

"An hour before midnight, I saw a man in an English uniform coming towards me; he was, I suspected, on the same errand. I spoke instantly, telling him who I was. He belonged to the 40th, and had missed his regiment. (This was most probably the same man of the 40th whom I came across, when the 52nd were passing over the killed and wounded of the Imperial Guard.) He released me from the dying soldier, took up a sword, and stood over me as sentinel. Day broke, and at six o'clock in the morning a messenger was sent to Hervé; a cart came for me, and I was conveyed to the; village of Waterloo, and laid in the bed, as I afterwards understood, from which Gordon had but just before been carried out. I had received seven wounds; a surgeon slept in my room; and I was saved by excessive bleeding."

No. 5.

Lieutenant Hill's French letter.

"*De Lichfield en Staffordshire,*
"*Le 8me Janvier, 1820.*

"*Ne vous inquietez pas mon ami du sort de la musique, elle est arrivée heureusement il y a quelques jours, et on ne cesse de vous en louer. Les trompettes n'en ont pas encore joué. Mais ces amateurs qui ont eu l'occasion d'assister à l'essai de quelques-uns des Pièces les ont trouvées infiniment jolies. Le Colonel Rowan vient à l'instant de passer chez moi pour me prier de vous faire part, qu'il écrivit le jour même de l'arrivée de votre present pour vous en rendre graces. Enfin tout le monde est d'accord que vous meritez autant de congé que vous voudrez demander, et nous ne regrettons plus votre absence que pour la perte que nous y faisons de votre societé.*

"*Nous nous attendons de passer l'hiver en cette ville, ce qui parait satisfaire aux voeux de tout le monde. Les amitiés que l'on y fait au regiment n'ont plus de bornes. Les compagnies Young et Yorke sont à Derby. Celles de Diggle et de Kenny à Nottingham. Mais ces dernières s'attendent à tout moment de se retourner à Derby. C'est avec plaisir que j'apprends, que vous vous portez mieux depuis qui vous êtes de retour en Angleterre. Il ne vous manquait peut-être que le rost boeuf et tous les comforts que l'on trouve dans notre isle unique. Le soupe maigre et le pain noir de l'Allemagne ne conviennent nullement au temperament Anglais. Allons donc! buvez et mangez; réjouissez vous et portez vous bien, par force. Voila les remèdes qui valent bien toute la médecine du* monde.

"*Ne suis-je pas bien hardi, d'oser m'entretenir avec vous dans une langue dont je ne connais à peine les premiers rudimens, et dans laquelle vous avez sans doutes autant de facilité que dans la votre?*

Tres dévouément à vous

R. K. Hill.

"*Je trouverai toujours le plus grand plaisir à recevoir de vos nouvelles.*"

1815: List of 52nd Waterloo Officers and Their Services

The following 52nd officers served at Waterloo. They are almost all taken from the Appendix to the *52nd Record,* in which the names of those were omitted, whose services could not be ascertained:—

Lieut.-Colonel Sir John Colborne, K.C.B., Colonel, afterwards Lord Seaton. Major Charles Rowan, Lieut.-Colonel, wounded. Captains—P. Campbell, Major; W. Chalmers, Major W. Rowan, Major, w.; J. F. Love, Major, w.; C. Earl of March, (Staff); C. Diggle, w.; J. Shedden; J. McNair; E. Langton; J. Cross; C. Yorke (Staff). Lieutenants—C. Dawson, w.; M. Anderson, w.; C. Kenny; G. H. Love; W. Ripley; J. C. Barrett; W. H. Clerke; G. Hall; W. R. Nixon; G. Gawler; G. Whichcote; Hon. W. Ogilvy; E. R. Northey; Hon. W. Browne; E. Scoones; G. Campbell, w.; W. Austin; J. Snodgrass; J. S. Cargill; W. Hunter; W. C. Yonge; T. Cottingham, w.; C. Holman; G. Moore; E. Mitchell; C. Shawe, J. Hart; G. E. Scott; H. T. Oakes; J. R. Griffith; J. Burnett; R. Steward; G. Robson; F. W. Love. Ensigns—J. Jackson; T. Massie; W. Nettles, killed; J. Macnab; J. Montague; J. F. May; E. Monins; W. Leeke. Paymaster—J. Clarke, Lieut. and Adjutant—Winterbottom, w. (Quarter-Master—B. Sweeten. Surgeon—J. B. Gibson. Assistant-Surgeons—P. Jones; W. Macartney.)

Lieutenant-Colonel Sir Charles Rowan, K.C.B., entered the 52nd in 1798, and served with the regiment in Sicily, Denmark, Portugal, and Spain. He was for some time Assistant-Adjutant-General to the Light Division, and as such distinguished himself at the action of Almeida. He was present at the sieges of Ciudad Rodrigo and Badajos, and at the Battle of Salamanca, besides numerous intervening affairs, for which he received the war-medal with clasps. He also served in the Battle of Waterloo, where he was severely wounded. On his retirement from active service, Sir Charles Rowan undertook the organisation and management of the new Metropolitan Police, which task he executed in a manner reflecting the highest credit on his ability.

Lieut.-General Sir William Chalmers, K.C.H. and C.B., served in Sicily in 1806, and 1807, in Portugal and Spain in 1808, and 1809. In the Walcheren expedition; at Cadiz in 1810, and 1811; and in all the succeeding Peninsular campaigns, including the Battles of Barossa, Salamanca, Vittoria, the Pyrenees, Nivelle, and various minor actions and most of the sieges. He commanded a wing of the 52nd at the Battle of Waterloo, and has received the war-medal with eight clasps.

General Sir William Rowan, G.C.B., entered the 52nd in 1803. Served in Sicily in 1806; in Sweden in 1808; at Flushing in 1809; in Portugal in 1811, including the action of Sabugal; in the Peninsular and France in 1813, and 1814, including the Battles of Vittoria, and the Pyrenees, the attack of Vera, the Battles of the Nivelle, the Nive, Orthes, and Toulouse, and the intermediate affairs. He has received for these services the Peninsular war medal with six clasps. He served also in the campaign and Battle of Waterloo, and on the capture of Paris was appointed Commandant of the first Arrondissement of that city. Sir William has subsequently held the high appointment of Commander of the forces in Canada.

(*Sir William Rowan is now, in 1866, Colonel of his old regiment, the 52nd.*)

Lieut.-General Sir J. Frederick Love, K.C.B., entered the 52nd in 1801, and served in the expedition to Sweden under Sir John Moore, and afterwards in Portugal and Spain, including the retreat to and Battle of Corunna, and the various intervening affairs, he served afterwards in the Peninsula, and was present at the storming of Ciudad Rodrigo, and in all the battles and affairs of the Light Division till 1812. He served in the campaign of Holland under Lord Lynedoch, and was engaged in the affairs during the advance and unsuccessful attack on New Orleans, where he was wounded.

★★★★★★

Sir J. F. Love told the author that, after the attack on New Orleans, he slept in the same room with the dead bodies of the two gallant English generals, Pakenham and Gibbs, who were killed there.

★★★★★★

He also served in the campaign of Waterloo, where he received four severe wounds when the 52nd charged the French Imperial Guards. Sir Frederick has received the war-medal with four clasps for

Corunna, Busaco, Fuentes d'Onor, and Ciudad Rodrigo.

Colonel Charles, Duke of Richmond, K.G., entered the 52nd in 1813, having previously, while on the staff of Lord Wellington, placed himself in the ranks of the regiment with the stormers of Ciudad Rodrigo. His Grace was present at all the affairs and battles and sieges in which the Duke of Wellington's army was engaged from 1810, till 1814, including Busaco, Fuentes d'Onor, Ciudad Rodrigo, Badajoz, Salamanca, Vittoria, the Pyrenees, the first assault of St. Sebastian, the action at Vera, and the Battle of Orthes, where he voluntarily left the Staff to take command of his company of the 52nd, and was severely wounded in the chest by a musket-ball, which was never extracted.

His Grace subsequently served in the Battles of Quatre Bras and Waterloo as *aide-de-camp* to the Prince of Orange, and after the prince was wounded, he served as *aide-de-camp* to the Duke of Wellington. His Grace has received the Peninsular war-medal with eight clasps, and is now, in 1860, in command of and constantly with his regiment, the Royal Sussex (Light Infantry) Militia. It was owing to the repeated efforts of the late Duke of Richmond that the war-medal and clasps were accorded to those who had served in the general actions of the Peninsula.

Major-General Charles Diggle, K.H. served with the 52nd in Sicily in 1806, and 1807, and also in the expedition to Sweden under Sir John Moore. He was present during the retreat, and in the Battle of Corunna, and in the action of the Coa (Almeida), the Battle of Busaco, and the various affairs when the wing fell back on Torres Vedras. He served in the campaign of 1813, and 1814, in Holland, and also at Waterloo, where he was severely wounded. He has received the war-medal with two clasps.

Captain and Brevet-Major John Shedden entered the 52nd in 1804, and served with the regiment in the Peninsula and at Waterloo.

(*Major Shedden died at Hull in 1821.*)

Lieut.-Colonel James M'Nair entered the 52nd in 1804. Served in the expedition to Sweden in 1808, and afterwards in Portugal and Spain, and was present during the retreat to, and Battle of Corunna. He afterwards served in the Peninsula with the 52nd in most of the battles and affairs until the assault of Badajos, where he volunteered for the storming party, and was severely wounded. He was promoted to the command of the 73rd regiment. He commanded No. 9 company of the 52nd at Waterloo.

Captain Edward Langton served with the 52nd in the Peninsula, and was present at the Battles of Corunna, Fuentes d'Onor, Ciudad

Rodrigo, and Salamanca, for which he has received the war-medal with four clasps. He was also present with the 52nd at the Battle of Waterloo.

Lieut.-Colonel John Cross served with the 52nd in the Peninsula, and was present at Waterloo. He was afterwards selected for the command of the 68th Light Infantry.

General Sir Charles Yorke, G.C.B., entered the 52nd in 1807, and was present at the Battles of Vimiero, Fuentes d'Onor, Salamanca, Vittoria, the Pyrenees, the Nivelle, (where he was wounded,) the Nive, and Orthes, (where he was again wounded,) besides several smaller affairs during the same period. He served at the sieges of Ciudad Rodrigo and Badajos, at the latter of which he was wounded. He also served at Waterloo, on the Staff. He subsequently served in the Caffre campaigns of 1850, to 1853, as second in command to Sir George Cathcart, and was recently military secretary to the Commander-in-Chief at the Horse Guards. Sir Charles Yorke has received the war-medal with ten clasps.

Lieutenant Charles Dawson served in the Peninsula and at Waterloo, where he commanded a company and was shot through the lungs. He died about a year afterwards. The name of his gallant brother, Captain Henry Dawson, of the 52nd, who distinguished himself at Almeida, and was killed in 1812, in defending the position on the Huebra, was often mentioned, in after times, amongst the officers of the regiment.

There is no account of Lieutenant M. Anderson's services in the 52nd record; but he was an old Peninsula officer, and at Waterloo he commanded No. 5 company, the left-front company of the 52nd when in their four-deep line, which extended and moved down the British position, and fired into, and first stopped the advance of the French Imperial Guard. He lost a leg on this occasion.

Captain Charles Kenny served in the 52nd in the Peninsula and at Waterloo.

Captain G. H. Love died at Cape Breton in 1830. He entered the regiment as ensign in 1810, and served with credit during all the Peninsular campaigns till the Battle of Orthes, when he was wounded in the face. He also served with the 52nd in the Battle of Waterloo, and was much endeared to his comrades by his amiable manners, as well as respected for his services.

Lieut.-Colonel Sir William Henry Clerke, Bart., served with the 52nd in the Peninsula, and was present at the Battles of the Nivelle, Nive, Orthes, and Toulouse, and the intervening combats. He was also present at the Battle of Waterloo. He has received the war-medal with four clasps.

Lieut.-Colonel George Hall served in the Peninsula in 1811, and 1812, and again from October 1813, to the end of the war in 1814, and was present at the Battles of Fuentes d'Onor, the sieges of Ciudad Rodrigo and Badajos, (where he was severely wounded,) the Battles of the Nive, Orthes, and Toulouse. He was also present at the Battle of Waterloo. He afterwards commanded the 72nd Highlanders.

Lieutenant William Richmond Nixon, entered the 52nd in 1810, and served with the regiment at the Battles of Fuentes d'Onor and Orthes, and at the siege of Badajos, where he greatly distinguished himself and was severely wounded at the storming of Fort Picurina. He also served at Waterloo, and was assistant adjutant there. He received the Peninsular war-medal with three clasps.

Colonel George Gawler was essentially a 52nd officer. He served in this regiment only, and was a type of that steady, cool, and gallant set of company-officers, whose attention to regimental duty and experience in the field so materially helped to place the 52nd amid the most distinguished in the service of Britain. Entering the 52nd Light Infantry in November, 1811, Colonel Gawler served to the end of the Peninsula war in 1814, and was present at the storming of Badajos, (when he led the ladder party of the 52nd stormers,) at the Battles of Vittoria, Vera, the Nivelle, the Nive, Orthes, and Toulouse, besides various minor affairs. At Waterloo he commanded the right company of the 52nd after his captain (Diggle) was placed *hors de combat*. He was wounded below the right knee at Badajos, and in the neck at San Munos, and has received the war-medal with seven clasps. Colonel Gawler was Governor of South Australia for several years.

Major-General George Whichcote served with the 52nd in the Peninsula and at Waterloo.

Captain the Hon. William Ogilvy joined the 52nd in May, 1811, and was engaged in all the actions in which the regiment took part, from Badajos to the end of the war. He also served at Waterloo. He received the medal for Waterloo, and the Peninsula medal with seven clasps, for Badajos, Salamanca, Vittoria, Nivelle, Nive, Orthes, and Toulouse.

Captain Edward Richard Northey entered the 52nd in 1811, and served with the first battalion in every action in which it was engaged from 1812, commencing with the retreat from Madrid, and at Vittoria was slightly wounded. For these services Captain Northey received the Peninsula war-medal with six clasps. He also served in the campaign and Battle of Waterloo.

The Hon. William Browne served in the 52nd in the Peninsula and at Waterloo.

Major Edward Scoones served in the 52nd during the retreat from Burgos in 1812; he was also present with the regiment in the Pyrenees and at the Battle of Toulouse. Major Scoones subsequently served in the campaign and Battle of Waterloo. He was afterwards a major in the 81st Regiment.

Lieutenant Campbell was very severely wounded when advancing with the 52nd skirmishers on the French Imperial Guard.

Major William Austen served in the Peninsula in 1811, and 1812, in the campaign of Holland in 1814, and in the Battle of Waterloo. He has received the war-medal with one clasp for the siege and storm of Ciudad Rodrigo.

Lieutenant William Crawley Yonge's services are mentioned in chapter 12.

Lieutenant Thomas Cottingham served with the 52nd in the Peninsula campaigns of 1812, 1813, and 1814, and was present, as a volunteer at the storming of Badajos, at the Battles of Salamanca, Vittoria, the Pyrenees, Nivelle, Nive, Orthes, and Toulouse, and also at Waterloo. He has received the war-medal with eight clasps.

Captain Charles Holman served in the Peninsula from 1811, and was present at the Battle of Salamanca, the siege of Burgos, the Battles of the Pyrenees, the Nivelle, the Nive, Orthes, and Toulouse, and the intervening actions. He was also present at the Battle of Waterloo, and has received the war-medal with six clasps. He had three musket-balls through the blade of his sword at Waterloo.

Lieutenant G. E. Scott served at Waterloo. He was the author of a prize poem on the Battle of Waterloo.

Lieutenant J. P. Griffith entered the 52nd in 1813, served in the campaign of Holland in 1813, and 1814, and also in the campaign and Battle of Waterloo, after which he acted as adjutant in the absence (from wounds) of Lieutenant Winterbottom.

Major-General Eaton Monius entered the 52nd in 1814, and served in the campaign of 1815, and was present at the Battle of Waterloo, and the subsequent advance on and occupation of Paris.

ALSO FROM LEONAUR
AVAILABLE IN SOFTCOVER OR HARDCOVER WITH DUST JACKET

THE 9TH—THE KING'S (LIVERPOOL REGIMENT) IN THE GREAT WAR 1914 - 1918 *by Enos H. G. Roberts*—Mersey to mud—war and Liverpool men.

THE GAMBARDIER *by Mark Severn*—The experiences of a battery of Heavy artillery on the Western Front during the First World War.

FROM MESSINES TO THIRD YPRES *by Thomas Floyd*—A personal account of the First World War on the Western front by a 2/5th Lancashire Fusilier.

THE IRISH GUARDS IN THE GREAT WAR - VOLUME 1 *by Rudyard Kipling*—Edited and Compiled from Their Diaries and Papers—The First Battalion.

THE IRISH GUARDS IN THE GREAT WAR - VOLUME 1 *by Rudyard Kipling*—Edited and Compiled from Their Diaries and Papers—The Second Battalion.

ARMOURED CARS IN EDEN *by K. Roosevelt*—An American President's son serving in Rolls Royce armoured cars with the British in Mesopatamia & with the American Artillery in France during the First World War.

CHASSEUR OF 1914 *by Marcel Dupont*—Experiences of the twilight of the French Light Cavalry by a young officer during the early battles of the great war in Europe.

TROOP HORSE & TRENCH *by R.A. Lloyd*—The experiences of a British Lifeguardsman of the household cavalry fighting on the western front during the First World War 1914-18.

THE EAST AFRICAN MOUNTED RIFLES *by C.J. Wilson*—Experiences of the campaign in the East African bush during the First World War.

THE LONG PATROL *by George Berrie*—A Novel of Light Horsemen from Gallipoli to the Palestine campaign of the First World War.

THE FIGHTING CAMELIERS *by Frank Reid*—The exploits of the Imperial Camel Corps in the desert and Palestine campaigns of the First World War.

STEEL CHARIOTS IN THE DESERT *by S. C. Rolls*—The first world war experiences of a Rolls Royce armoured car driver with the Duke of Westminster in Libya and in Arabia with T.E. Lawrence.

WITH THE IMPERIAL CAMEL CORPS IN THE GREAT WAR *by Geoffrey Inchbald*—The story of a serving officer with the British 2nd battalion against the Senussi and during the Palestine campaign.

AVAILABLE ONLINE AT **www.leonaur.com**
AND FROM ALL GOOD BOOK STORES

www.ingramcontent.com/pod-product-compliance
Lightning Source LLC
Chambersburg PA
CBHW030217170426
43201CB00006B/121